Ireland and Britain, 1798–1922

An Anthology of Sources

Ireland and Britain, 1798–1922

An Anthology of Sources

Edited, with an Introduction, by

Dennis Dworkin

Hackett Publishing Company, Inc.
Indianapolis/Cambridge

16 15 14 13 12   1 2 3 4 5 6 7

For further information, please address
        Hackett Publishing Company, Inc.
        P.O. Box 44937
        Indianapolis, Indiana 46244-0937

        www.hackettpublishing.com

Cover design by Abigail Coyle
Interior design and composition by Mary Vasquez
Map by William Nelson
Printed at Edwards Brothers, Inc.

Library of Congress Cataloging-in-Publication Data

Ireland and Britain, 1798–1922 : an anthology of sources / edited, with an introduction, by
Dennis Dworkin.
    p. cm.
  Includes bibliographical references and index.
  ISBN 978-1-60384-741-4 (pbk.) — ISBN 978-1-60384-742-1 (cloth)
  1. Ireland—History—19th century—Sources. 2. Ireland—Politics and government—
19th century—Sources. 3. Ireland—Relations—Great Britain—Sources. 4. Great
Britain—Relations—Ireland—Sources. 5. Ireland—History—20th century—Sources. 6.
Ireland—Politics and government—20th century—Sources. I. Dworkin, Dennis L., 1951–
    DA950.I635 2012
    941.5081—dc23

                                                                        2011041654

CONTENTS

ACKNOWLEDGMENTS

Ireland and Britain, 1798–1922: An Anthology of Sources has developed from a passionate interest in understanding the "Irish question" and from teaching courses on the modern Anglo-Irish relationship at the University of Nevada, Reno (UNR). Above all, I want to thank the students who have taken that course and inspired me as a teacher. Others have been important to the writing of this book as well. I am grateful to colleagues, friends, and students who have generously listened to me develop my ideas and have provided invaluable support. They include Jamie Blea, Stacy Burton, Neal Ferguson, Alison Harvey, Michael Koontz, Jessica Maddox, Sandra More, Caroline Musselman, Hugh Shapiro, and Robert Whitefield. I would also like to thank Martha Hildreth for helping me translate French phrases in Chapter 2 and Deborah Achtenberg for providing the Greek translation in Chapter 3. Elizabeth Raymond has read and commented on all the book's introductions. She has provided helpful comments and constructive suggestions on achieving clarity in my prose. At an earlier stage, Michelle Tusan of the History Department at the University of Nevada, Las Vegas, gave me some much needed feedback on the book's general introduction. Thanks also to Kaarin Mann for helping me ensure that the primary sources were accurately reproduced and to Thomas Maxon for checking the accuracy of footnotes. I am grateful to Kimberly Esse who has worked on all dimensions of this manuscript and whose close attention to detail and style has made it a better book.

I conceived of *Ireland and Britain* while I was a visiting fellow at the Eisenberg Institute for Historical Studies at the University of Michigan. The writing of the book has been partially funded by the John and Marie Noble Endowment for Historical Research and the UNR College of Liberal Arts Scholarly and Creative Activities Grant Program. Rick Todhunter of Hackett Publishing has generously encouraged and supported this project. Mary Vasquez, the project editor at Hackett, has steered this book through the production process with professionalism and dedication. The final version of the book has benefited from the comments and observations of the anonymous readers. Richard English of the University of St. Andrews has been supportive of this project at all stages. I have greatly profited from his reading of the first draft. Finally, I want to thank my partner, Amelia Currier, who has had to live with me while I have been absorbed by the Anglo-Irish relationship and has done her best to keep me centered.

INTRODUCTION

The modern world is comprised of nation states. Australia and China, France and Kenya, Russia and Saudi Arabia are just a few of the nearly two hundred that currently exist. In theory, the state[1] reflects the interests of a group of people who share a common national identity. In practice, the state often governs heterogeneous populations that engage in different religions, favor different languages, and consist of different races and ethnicities. There are also cases where a group of people who live in a bounded geographic area and claim a common national identity end up living in different states because of the way borders have been drawn. Sometimes different ethnic, racial, and religious groups in a given state can live together relatively harmoniously or at least accept each other. In the United States, multiculturalism is etched into the texture of American life, although the path to achieving this has neither been smooth, short, nor complete. At the other end of the spectrum, there are states and areas within states where ethnic, racial, and religious differences have given rise to cycles of hatred and violence that make reconciliation between groups or a resolution of their competing claims difficult or impossible to achieve. Afghanistan, Bosnia, Chechnya, Israel/Palestine, Kashmir, and Kosovo are examples that come to mind.

Ireland, the subject of this book, is among the oldest of such cases. Its conflicts originate with the colonization of Ireland by English and Scottish Protestants in the seventeenth century. Catholicism was marginalized in England, in contrast to Ireland where it remained the religion of the majority. The result was an enduring Catholic-Protestant divide that, although it has changed over time, still exists today and entails more than a clash of religious views. Marianne Elliot (2009) has recently portrayed Catholics and Protestants in Ireland as having antagonistic identities defined and sustained through cultural difference. The stereotypes that Catholics and Protestants have constructed of each other are crucial to each group's own self-definition. From a slightly different angle, we might think of the political dynamics of modern Ireland as resulting from the historical interaction between three distinct ethno-religious groups: Roman Catholics with Gaelic or Irish roots; Presbyterians originally from Scotland and mostly living in the northeastern province of Ulster; and the Anglo-Irish who, as their name suggests, are originally from England and belong to the Anglican Church, in Ireland known as the Church of Ireland. In his classic book *Culture and Anarchy in Ireland, 1890–1939* (1979), F. S. L. Lyons argued that political anarchy was attributable to the inability of these groups to envision Ireland as an inescapably multicultural space. He suggested that Ireland's turmoil was "an anarchy in the mind and in the heart, an anarchy which forbade not just unity of territories,

---

1. There exists an extensive literature on the state. While it is common in today's world for transnational entities (such as the European Union) to supersede the authority of their member states, for our purposes the state may be thought of as an administrative, judicial, legislative, and military apparatus in a geographically bounded territory. The state is usually sovereign; that is, it has supreme authority over its territory.

but also 'unity of being', an anarchy that sprang from the collision within a small and intimate island of seemingly irreconcilable cultures, unable to live together or to live apart, caught inextricably in the web of their tragic history" (176).

Central to this dynamic has been England and later Britain's[2] long political dominance of Ireland, which resulted in the formation of the United Kingdom (UK), a legislative union between the two islands created by acts of the British and Irish Parliaments in 1800. (While all of Ireland was part of the UK until 1922, today only six Irish counties, all of them in Ulster, remain part of it.) In the period covered by this book—from the 1790s to the 1920s—Protestants predominantly aligned themselves with the British state and were known as Unionists. In contrast, Catholics were predominantly nationalists. They tended either to oppose the Union outright, embracing full separation and an independent state, or they sought to revise the Union's framework and supported legislative autonomy, better known as Home Rule. The Irish philosopher Richard Kearney has viewed the clash between nationalists and Unionists as two competing nationalist blocs, one British, the other Irish (Dworkin 2007). From this point of view, Unionism was a disguised form of nationalism. In Kearney's (1997, 9) words, it had "been one of the most ingenious ploys of British (or more particularly English) nationalism: to pretend that it *doesn't exist*, that the irrational and unreasonable claimants to sovereignty, territory, power, and nationhood are always *others*." Yet generalizations linking Catholics and nationalism on the one hand and Protestants and Unionism (or British nationalism) on the other have their limits. There were nationalists who believed Ireland's aspirations were best realized within the context of the Union. Indeed, the founder of the Home Rule movement in the 1870s, the Irish Protestant Isaac Butt (1813–79), was committed to this position. At the same time, important nationalist political leaders and writers—from the parliamentary leader Charles Stewart Parnell and the poet and dramatist William Butler Yeats to the militant activist Constance Markievicz—were Anglo-Irish Protestants who had Irish identities and were committed to Irish political self-determination.

British perspectives on Ireland were also diverse. Although there were few supporters of Irish independence in Britain, many recognized that for the Union to survive intact it needed to be rethought and renegotiated. Conservatives overwhelmingly considered the Union to be sacrosanct and regarded it as pivotal to the unity

---

2. England and Britain are distinct terms yet have been used interchangeably owing to England's historically dominant position in the British Isles. Britain refers to the three nations— England, Scotland, and Wales—that make up the largest of the islands and were constituted as a sovereign state in 1707 with the creation of Great Britain. Thus, before that time it is misleading to refer to a British government, just as afterward it is inaccurate to talk of an English one (although doing the latter has been fairly common due to England's political and cultural dominance). I have sought to use these terms as accurately as possible. For example, if I am discussing the actions of the English government continued by the British one that succeeded it, I have indicated this. In addition, the term *British government* is also inaccurate following the legislative union between Britain and Ireland that created the United Kingdom (UK) in 1801. Since this latter term is almost never used—either then or now—when discussing the government or politics of the British Isles in the nineteenth century, I have continued to use the more conventional term *British government.*

of the British Empire. Sir Randolph Churchill, for one, compared the Home Rule movement to the American South's challenge to another union—the United States (no. 35).[3] Liberals were more open to renegotiation but were deeply divided over the appropriate political form that the Anglo-Irish relationship should take. Eventually they passed the Home Rule Bill in 1912, scheduled to become law in September 1914, but they were unable to deliver on it. Britain's entry into World War I in August pushed Irish issues to the backburner.

The Irish question would not be a question, then, if it were not for Ireland's historically quarrelsome relationship with its larger, wealthier, and more powerful neighbor across the Irish sea: England, which was Britain's economic, political, cultural, and linguistic center. The Anglo-Irish relationship has been multidimensional, but for much of its history it has by no means been an equal one. It is rooted, as previously noted, in English and British conquest and colonization. Usually, we associate the British Empire at its apex with either control over India and parts of East Asia, the Middle East, and Africa, or the oversight of self-governing dominions such as Australia, Canada, and New Zealand. Ireland fits into neither of these two constellations. It was England and later Britain's oldest and nearest colony, the distance between Ulster in the northeast of Ireland and the west of Scotland being as little as twelve miles. Ireland was the only colony to have parliamentary representation. As a result of the Act of Union, it received one hundred Members of Parliament (MPs) in the House of Commons at Westminster in London.

Indeed, Ireland was simultaneously a colony and part of the colonizing process. On the one hand, even when it entered into a union with Britain, Ireland continued to be accorded a subservient status. A lord lieutenant or viceroy appointed by the British government administered it, suggesting a political relationship to London more reminiscent of India's than Scotland's.[4] On the other hand, Irish people played important roles in extending and maintaining the British Empire across the globe. As Kevin Kenny (2004, 16) stated it: "As well as belonging to a colony at the heart of the Empire, Irish people helped conquer, govern, and evangelize imperial possessions overseas." Thus, it is not that Ireland was an atypical colony: it is that we need to recast our understanding of the British Empire to accommodate it. Ireland had a *distinctive* rather than an *atypical* relationship to the English and later the British Empire, but it is still useful to think of the connection as imperial and/or colonial depending on time and place.

There are a variety of reasons for English and British incursions into Ireland. The obvious fact of the proximity between the two islands is at the top or near the top of any list. English and British governments feared that Ireland could be used as a stepping-stone for invasion. Such fears were certainly not unfounded. Between the early seventeenth century and the second quarter of the twentieth, Irish rebellions found Spanish, French, and German support. In the name of what we could now call

---

3. Designates the number of the primary source in this book to which reference is being made.

4. The office of viceroy of India was created in 1858. But in contrast to Ireland, the Indian viceroy was a governor-general, an office created in 1773, rather than a lord lieutenant.

national security, English and British governments made it a priority to keep Ireland safe militarily and politically. As Thomas Bartlett (2004, 61) stated it: "But even if Ireland had been barren rock, its proximity to both continental Europe and to England meant that it constituted in English eyes an all-too-convenient base for foreign enemies and a likely haven for domestic rebels and malcontents." Military invasion, direct and indirect forms of political control, and colonization became vehicles for achieving what from the English and British perspective was security and stability. It is in this context that Ireland's union with Britain should be understood. It was a response to multiple French attempts between 1796 and 1798 to invade Ireland, undertaken with the support of Irish revolutionaries. While Prime Minister William Pitt (no. 4) imagined that the new political entity might represent a union of hearts, it ultimately rested on the belief that more direct forms of control over Ireland would reduce the threat of foreign invasion.

What were the origins of England's conquest of Ireland? What were the important stages of conquest and control? What were the internal relationships within Ireland that resulted? The narrative provided here is not meant to be in any way comprehensive. That is certainly beyond the scope of this brief introduction. Rather my goal is to provide the background, the basic terms, and the necessary frames of reference that will begin to allow readers to delve into the Irish question.

Roughly speaking, there were two phases of conquest. The first began in the twelfth century and resulted from a plea by Dermot MacMurrough (c. 1110–71), the deposed king of Leinster, to Henry II (1133–89), king of England, to help win back Dermot's kingdom. In what may be the first—but certainly not the last—irony in the long Anglo-Irish relationship, the invaders who came to Ireland on Dermot's behalf were not English. They were descendants of the Normans from France, the offspring of those who conquered England the previous century, most famously at the Battle of Hastings in 1066. Henry himself, the first king of England to come to Ireland, was born in Normandy, spoke French, and spent most of his life on the European continent. England was only one part of an empire that included several French provinces. Henry had for some time been interested in expanding his reach into Ireland, and Adrian IV (c. 1100–59), the first and only English pope, had given his blessings to an invasion in 1155. Henry's eventual decision to make the journey resulted from his concern with the growing power of Richard de Clare (c. 1130–76), nicknamed Strongbow, one of Henry's own nobles. Strongbow had made a political pact with Dermot, married his daughter, and became king of Leinster when his father-in-law died. Henry had originally supported this alliance, but came to see it as a potential threat to his own power, and he went to Ireland to assert his authority over Strongbow and the Anglo-Norman nobility. Gaelic lords reached out to Henry, whom they regarded as a counterbalance to growing Anglo-Norman power in Ireland.

Henry and his descendants achieved only a partial conquest, controlling as much as two-thirds of the country by the end of the thirteenth century. Ireland now consisted of two distinct cultures that nonetheless influenced each other. As Christine Kinealy (2004, 56) stated it: "Although some Gaels became Anglicised and some Normans Hibernicised, they were still separate. Ireland therefore remained divided—a divide that was geographically demarcated and reflected in language, culture, religion, and politics." English control of Irish territory varied, but a constant was dominance over the Pale—the area roughly comprising the counties of Louth, Meath, Dublin, and Kildare, its center being the city of Dublin. It was here that English institutions and political structures took root. Dublin Castle was built in the thirteenth century and became the administrative nerve center of English power. It was governed by a crown appointment that went by different names at different times—"justiciar," "king's lieutenant," and "lord deputy"—until "lord lieutenant" in the second half of the seventeenth century was settled upon. An Irish parliament consisting of nobles loyal to the king began to meet in 1264. In what proved to prefigure later developments, Poynings' Law (1494) established the Crown's authority over the Irish legislature. It could only meet with the king's permission, and it could only pass laws already approved by the king and his council. The original intention of Poynings' Law was to reign in the power of the lord deputy. In practice it placed limits on the actions of the Irish Parliament and facilitated royal control of it.

However important these early incursions may be, the political conflicts treated in this book have their origins not in the medieval but in the early modern period, between the sixteenth and the eighteenth centuries. In the second stage of the colonizing process, new English and Scottish interests, attitudes, perspectives, and ambitions transformed the Anglo-Irish relationship. It was during these two centuries that England and later Britain went from being a peripheral to a major European power. There are many elements that went into this transformation. A full explanation would take into account England's and Scotland's path to Protestantism; expanding finance capital and trade; the rise of the gentry and the middle classes; the inception of agrarian capitalism; struggles over sovereignty between king and Parliament; the first stage of overseas imperial ambition; and most importantly, the growth of English power in the British Isles, which led to the legislative union with Scotland in 1707, creating Great Britain. Against this background, a new breed of colonizers remade Ireland in the seventeenth century. They were more determined, more resolute, and more ideological than their predecessors. Committed Protestants—either Anglicans from England or Presbyterians from Scotland—they aspired to make Ireland Protestant and British. This aspiration was directed at the native Irish, whom they regarded much as English colonists in America viewed Native Americans. It was also aimed at their forerunners, the *old* English, who had lived in Ireland for centuries. For the most part, the old English remained resolutely Catholic, and many absorbed Irish values and culture over the course of centuries, while still identifying deeply with their English roots. For the *new* English colonists, the old English were barely discernible from the natives. Despite their predecessors' proclaimed loyalty to the Crown, the new English viewed them as a political threat to the making of Protestant Ireland.

The new wave of colonization produced a massive shift in landownership. In 1641, Catholics owned 59 percent of the land; in 1688, the percentage had fallen to 22. In 1703, the percentage of landownership by Catholics had deteriorated further: they owned only 14 percent. In the middle of the eighteenth century, the Catholic percentage of land ownership had disintegrated to a mere 5 percent (Kinealy 2004, 102, 121). The mechanism for this shift was plantation and warfare. The subduing of Ireland had already begun under the Tudor dynasty,[5] which in the sixteenth century had brought the entire island under English control for the first time. But the creation of Protestant communities in Ireland, though begun in the 1500s, did not really take off until the next century. Their growth was accelerated by the defeat of Hugh O'Neill,[6] who, despite having benefited from royal patronage, led a rebellion—with Spanish support—to resist English intrusions in predominantly Gaelic Ulster and ultimately in Ireland as a whole. Following his defeat in 1603, and despite being granted generous terms, O'Neill and a group of Gaelic chiefs who were his supporters chose European exile rather than being clipped of their political wings. As a consequence of what is known as the Flight of the Earls in 1607, there was a vacuum in political leadership in Ulster that made possible an ambitious experiment in colonization and resettlement. The native Irish were displaced and confined to their own areas. Protestant settlements were created by confiscating the land of those who had been defeated and fled. This land was in turn rented out cheaply in parcels of one to two thousand acres to *undertakers*, the stipulation being that they would seek out Protestant tenants willing to create permanent settlements or *plantations*. English and Scottish settlers remade Ulster. They *planted* their own traditions, religions, and values. They created towns and villages, schools and churches, markets and industry. In contrast to the pastoral way of life of the native Irish, they engaged in arable farming. In the words of Aidan Clarke (2001, 154): "A whole new society was created, one which was not only entirely alien to the native traditions of the area, but also entirely different in character from every other part of Ireland. It was not just the Protestantism of the planters that made Ulster distinctive, but their whole way of life."

The scale of the Ulster plantation was not to be repeated in the rest of Ireland, and even in Ulster, where English and Scottish settlers became a majority of the population, Anglicization was not as total as its planners envisioned. What ensued through the course of the seventeenth century was a monumental political struggle. On one side were the new English and the Scottish Presbyterians, and on the other the old English and the native Irish—although it must be stressed that these alliances were unstable and permeable. They were prone to shifting, internal disputes, and fragmentation. The common interests within each of these two blocs were thrown into sharper relief, however, as Irish politics became intertwined with the political convulsions that swept through England and Scotland in the middle of the seventeenth

5. Originally from Wales, the Tudors ruled over England and Ireland between 1485 and 1603. The monarchs were Henry VII (1457–1509), Henry VIII (1491–1547), Edward VI (1537–53), Mary I (1516–58), and Elizabeth I (1533–1603).

6. Hugh O'Neill (c. 1550–1616), 2nd Earl of Tyrone. From an Ulster Gaelic family yet owing his title of earl to royal patronage, O'Neill is the key figure in the Nine Years' War (1594–1603), which came close to ending English dominance in Ireland. The disastrous engagement at Kinsale in 1601, however, ended in total defeat and ultimately paved the way for the Anglicization of Ulster. Despite his flight to the European continent in 1607 (the Flight of the Earls), O'Neill remained in touch with Irish politics. Rumors of his imminent return continued until his death.

century. The English Civil War, pitting Parliament against King Charles I,[7] who was defeated and executed in 1649, produced political instability not only in England but also in Ireland. It exposed the vulnerability of English and Scottish settlement and the pent-up hostilities of Catholics toward Protestants. Catholic uprisings in Ulster in 1641 resulted in the massacre of as many as four thousand Protestants and ignited sectarian violence that spread throughout the island. The Irish Catholic Confederation, founded in 1642 by a coalition of old English and native Irish interests, supported the contradictory principles of an independent Ireland and the sanctity of the English Crown. Loyalty to Catholicism and hostility toward Protestants united the coalition. In response to these Catholic challenges, Oliver Cromwell (1599–1658), on behalf of the English Parliament, launched an invasion of Ireland in 1649–50 to cleanse it of monarchism and Catholicism. His military campaign was brief yet ruthless and thorough. In Wexford alone two thousand people were massacred. In addition, Cromwell regarded the invasion as a means of gaining revenues and paying off his soldiers at the expense of Catholic landowners, whether they opposed him or not. Catholics who participated in the rebellion lost their estates, while those who did not were forced to give up their property and relocate to the western part of the country where the land was of poorer quality.

Cromwell's invasion was a devastating blow to Catholic Ireland. The knockout punch was delivered in the course of another political conflict of English origin that subsequently spread to Ireland—the Glorious Revolution. It arose out of the contentious relationship between King James II (1633–1701) and Parliament more than twenty years after the monarchy had been restored in 1660. A convert to Catholicism, James was bent on turning back the clock and making Catholicism more conspicuous in English life. In 1687, he disseminated a Declaration of Indulgence that suspended religious tests for holders of public office. Thus, where religious tests had meant that only Anglicans could hold public office, the Declaration of Indulgence made it possible for Catholics to be eligible as well. James brought Catholics into the government and the military. Like his father, Charles I, he regarded Parliament as a nuisance and consulted it as little as possible. As long as James did not have a son, his opponents were willing to simply ride out the storm. They looked forward to the succession of his daughter Mary[8]—a committed Protestant and the wife of the Protes-

7. Charles I (1600–1649), king of England, Scotland, and Ireland. When he came to the throne in 1625, Charles believed that he was divinely ordained and resented Parliament's attempt to curb the royal prerogative. For much of the 1630s, he sought to rule without consulting Parliament. This conflict (among others) ultimately led to the English Civil War (1642–49), in which the parliamentary army defeated his troops. As a result of the dignity that he showed during his imprisonment, trial, and in the days prior to his execution, Charles helped repair the image of the Crown. Following the restoration of the monarchy in 1660, the Church of England made him into a saint.

8. Mary II (1662–94), queen of England, Scotland, and Ireland. She was the eldest daughter of James II by his first marriage, one of eight children. When six of them died, she became the heir to the throne. Despite her father's conversion to Catholicism in 1668–69, she was brought up as a Protestant, and her marriage to William of Orange was intended to solidify her Protestant

tant William of Orange (1650–1702). When James' second wife, the Catholic Mary of Modena,[9] gave birth to a son, James Francis Edward,[10] the opposition became alarmed. There was now a real possibility that England might return to the Catholic fold. Consequently, a contingent of parliamentary leaders and magnates began negotiating with William. In addition to being a Protestant and married to James' daughter, he was a grandson of Charles I. James was both Williams' father-in-law and his uncle. William had for some time viewed England as a potential ally in his quest to halt the expansion of Catholic France, which under Louis XIV[11] had become the single most powerful state in Europe. The invitation to seize the English throne came at the same time as France was invading the Palatinate (now part of Germany). Snatching the opportunity, William came to England with twenty thousand troops. He prevailed without a struggle. James threw the royal seal into the Thames and fled to France. As a sign of its appreciation, the English Parliament declared William and Mary joint monarchs.

The Glorious Revolution was celebrated in England as the triumph of parliamentary sovereignty, as a great Protestant victory, and as a milestone in the advancement of individual rights and liberties. For Ireland, these events proved to be no less momentous. Under James II, ethnic and religious tensions in Ireland had been mounting. Catholics saw his reign as an opportunity to reclaim some of their lost power and authority. They once again were allowed to join the army, becoming a majority after having been purged from it almost completely. They were given key appointments in central and local government. Richard Talbot,[12] the Earl of Tyrconnell, became

---

credentials. She became queen in 1688 following the Glorious Revolution, although she was anguished that it resulted from deposing her father. She ruled jointly with her husband.

9. Mary of Modena (1658–1718), queen consort of England, Scotland, and Ireland. She was born a princess in the Italian duchy of Modena and was a devout Catholic. She married James when he was still Duke of York in 1671 and became queen when he succeeded to the throne in 1685. When she gave birth to her son James Francis Edward Stuart, it was widely but falsely believed that he was a changeling who had been brought into the birth chamber in a warming pan in order to ensure that the succession would be Catholic.

10. James Francis Edward Stuart (1688–1766), Prince of Wales. As the only son of James II, upon his birth he became first in line to succeed his father to the throne. But his father was deposed and the English Parliament made it illegal for a Catholic to become king. Unwilling to convert, James was stripped of his English titles and subsequently, with the support of Louis XIV, attempted an unsuccessful invasion of Scotland in 1708. He is known in English political culture as the Old Pretender.

11. Louis XIV (1638–1715), king of France and Navarre. Known as the Sun King, his seventy-two year reign is unprecedented in European history. He believed in the divine right of kings and absolute monarchy, and he played a prominent role in laying the foundation for the centralized state in France. For much of his reign France was the major power on the European continent, and he led his country through three major European wars. The war that the Glorious Revolution became entangled in is known variously but most commonly as the Nine Years' War or the War of the League of Augsburg.

12. Richard Talbot (1630–91), 1st Earl of Tyrconnell. Born in County Limerick, he was a Catholic and a royalist who supported Charles I during the English Civil War and was arrested

the first Catholic lord lieutenant in over a hundred years. Although he had not made specific commitments, the drift of James' policies could be interpreted as leading to overturning the Cromwellian land settlement. Protestant landowners, alarmed at the current trends, began to flee Ireland by the thousands. Settlers in Ulster, not for the last time, armed themselves in anticipation of a confrontation. While the demise of James was certainly a setback to Catholic recovery and a welcome development for besieged Protestants, many of the latter were ambivalent about the overthrow of a legitimate monarch. An already incendiary situation was further inflamed when James, who in the words of J. G. Simms (1976, 485) had worked himself into a state of "dazed apathy," was prevailed upon by Louis XIV to reclaim his kingdom, using Ireland as a base.

While the war between their supporters lasted for two years, the military confrontation between the two kings themselves—known as the War of Two Kings—was brief and decisive. James' defeat at the Battle of the Boyne in July 1690, perhaps the most famous military engagement in Irish history, marked the end of his bid for the English Crown. His precipitous escape to France greatly damaged his image and gave rise to harsh memories among his Irish supporters. Protestant morale was further boosted by the Jacobite[13] siege of Derry in which the Protestant townspeople held out for 105 days until relief came. For *Orange* Protestants, both the Battle of the Boyne and the siege of Derry represented the triumph of Protestant liberty over Catholic tyranny and dogmatism. They annually commemorate these events in Northern Ireland to this day. Defeated Catholics, and later Irish nationalists, also viewed these events symbolically. For them, the Jacobite cause represented a heroic but tragic defense of Irish nationhood and freedom. It was implicitly given its due in the Easter Proclamation of 1916 (no. 50), the Irish equivalent of the Declaration of Independence.

The reality was much less straightforward. On the one side were the supporters of James: the native Irish and old English landed classes supported by the military might of Louis XIV's France. The Jacobite cause was supported by French, German, and Belgian troops. On the other side were the allies of William, the Dutch king of England: the new English and Scottish Presbyterians backed by an army of English, Dutch, German, and Danish soldiers. Their cause was backed by the papacy, which feared the growth of French power. The confrontation undoubtedly had a national component, although both sides had supporters whose ancestors were English. Most importantly, the War of the Two Kings was part of a battle for the control of Europe, a struggle for control of the English state, and a contest between Protestant and Catholic landed elites in Ireland. In sum, if the war between James and William was a confrontation between England and Ireland, it was also a lot of other things.

---

for plotting against Oliver Cromwell's Protectorate in 1655. As lord deputy (1687–88), he reshaped the Irish army and administration from being substantially Protestant to mostly Catholic, and he sought to convince James to overturn the Cromwellian land settlement. He fought for James during the War of the Two Kings to be discussed shortly.

13. The term is derived from the Latin for James and originally meant a supporter of James II but was generalized to refer to one who supported the restoration of the Stuart kings.

Unionist mural commemorating William of Orange's 1690 victory at the Battle of the Boyne. Belfast, Northern Ireland. Image courtesy of Hannah Merron.

The seventeenth century then saw the decisive subjugation of Catholic Ireland, the result of three devastating defeats: the Flight of the Earls, the Cromwellian conquest, and the War of the Two Kings. These setbacks made possible the unchallenged domination of what in Irish political culture is known as the *Protestant ascendancy:* a ruling class of landowning, Irish Protestants from English backgrounds who were adherents of the Church of Ireland. It is estimated that in 1776, when Protestants owned 95 percent of the land, they consisted of about five thousand landowners. The ascendancy was simultaneously triumphant and self-assured, but also anxious and insecure. It believed in the superiority of its values, culture, and religion, especially when it compared itself to the native Irish. The ascendancy's insecurity can be attributed to the fact that it comprised a small Protestant island in a much larger Catholic sea whose waves were far from tranquil. The ascendancy also resented its subservience to the English and later the British state, but it was dependent on those states' military support.

The ascendancy sought to protect its dominant position and ensure political stability by passing a series of laws between the middle of the 1690s and the 1720s (often with begrudging English and British approval) whose intention was to stamp out any hint of opposition, either religious or political. Known as the penal or anti-popery laws, they were part and parcel of the European politics of the time. In France,

Spain, and the Holy Roman Empire, analogous legislation had been enacted against Protestants and Jews. What made Ireland unique was that this overtly discriminatory legislation was being perpetrated upon the majority of its people. Catholics are estimated to have been between two-thirds and three-quarters of the population.

The penal laws were predominantly aimed at landed Catholics and to a lesser extent Protestant Dissenters. The legislation against Catholics was twofold. First, there were attempts to stamp out or at least to limit the practice of Catholicism. Bishops and regular clergy were banished from Ireland; parish priests were forced to register with the government; and no new priests were allowed to be ordained. Second, there was a series of laws aimed at ensuring that the Catholic landowning class would no longer be a political and military threat. Catholics were banned from leasing land for more than thirty-one years, and they were forbidden to purchase property owned by Protestants. When a Catholic landowner died, he was forced to divide his property equally among his sons. The only circumstance under which a son could inherit the land was if he were to become a Protestant convert. Moreover, Catholics were not allowed to become lawyers, join the army or navy, have a university education, or vote for or sit in the Irish Parliament. They could neither carry a pistol nor a gun nor own a valuable horse.

Legislation aimed at Dissenters, primarily Presbyterians in Ulster, was less punitive but still egregious. Presbyterians were most often tenant farmers or merchants and seldom part of the gentry. They lived predominantly in Ulster, where they may have been more than one-half of the Protestant population. Although they had supported William in the war against James, continued to be loyal subjects, and had supported legislation curtailing the rights of Catholics, the ascendancy perceived Presbyterians as a threat to its power. It was envious of Presbyterians' "considerable influence" in Ireland, owing to their "close-knit ecclesiastical church organization" and "their commercial wealth" (Beckett 1981, 159). Dissenters could own land, but they (like Catholics) were compelled to pay tithes (taxes that supported the Church of Ireland), although their clergy received annual state payments or *regium donum* in recognition of their loyalty. Dissenters could vote and hold parliamentary office (if they met the property qualifications), but they neither could serve on town councils nor be officers in the army or militias. Their marriages did not have legal standing unless Church of Ireland clergy performed the ceremonies.

It is, of course, one thing to pass laws, another to enforce them. The penal laws were intermittently and inconsistently implemented. Eliminating the practice of Catholicism itself was in fact impossible, given the scale of the necessary effort and the meager resources that actually existed to achieve it. From an early point, Catholic religious communities continued to exist, masses went on, and churches were built. Priests were trained in Irish seminaries from the 1750s. Historians have noted that rather than Catholicism languishing, as was the intention, the opposite in fact took place. There was an intensified bond between priests and their parishioners, a bond that over time facilitated the connection between Catholicism and Irish nationalism.

While the Protestant Dissenters of Ulster did not face the same obstacles as Catholics, the constraints placed upon them similarly provided the grounds for discontent with, and in some case opposition to, the regime. Their exclusion from government and the military did not end until 1780. In today's world, Ulster Presbyterians are known for their staunch support of the union with Britain. However, during the eighteenth century, many of them left for the American colonies, where they found greater religious tolerance and where they often enthusiastically supported the American Revolution. An important segment of Presbyterians who remained in Ireland were inspired by the French revolutionary events of 1789 and helped found the Society of United Irishmen in 1791. That group demanded a democratic and independent Ireland and forged an alliance with the French revolutionary regime.

The efforts to create a monopoly in Protestant landownership were more successful, given the tiny percentage of Catholics who owned land by the end of the eighteenth century. Even here a more complex picture emerges. The remnants of the Catholic gentry endured, especially in the western part of the country. Catholics might hold on to their land by converting in much the same way that Western European Jews who coveted social mobility did in the nineteenth century. Moreover, the penal laws did not exclude Catholics from engaging in industry and trade. Indeed, as the eighteenth century unfolded, one of its most important developments was the rise of the Catholic middle class in towns, many of whom made their money as merchants. With the remnants of the old Gaelic landed classes, and the support of the Church, the Catholic middle class articulated a new politics based on acceptance of ascendancy landholdings and power and overt expressions of loyalty to the Crown. Catholics counted on the fact that gestures of support for the status quo would lead to the restoration of their rights, which in turn would strengthen their ability to shape political outcomes. The Catholic Committee, founded in 1760, gave this politics a concrete form.

The new Catholic politics found a receptive audience in the British government, which came to view the penal laws as obsolete and a threat to political stability. It likewise came to see the Catholic Church as a force that contributed to maintaining the status quo. By the early 1760s, the British government advocated that the penal laws begin to be rolled back, in part because it saw Catholics as potential recruits for the British army. Ascendancy politicians saw such concessions as the beginning of a slippery slope that would lead to their downfall. They linked Catholic middle-class demands with sporadic bouts of agrarian violence in the 1760s and early 1770s by secret societies, notably the Whiteboys in Munster. These groups practiced forms of agrarian protest common in societies where small farmers, cottagers, and laborers had no voice within the political system. Ireland in the eighteenth century experienced a marked increase of wealth owing to the expansion of manufacturing, tillage, and trade. However, peasants did not share in this greater wealth. Indeed, their position may have deteriorated (Beckett 1981, 244–45). Contemporary observers were often shocked by the degree of Irish poverty. Similar forms of agrarian protest to those found in Ireland were found in Britain during the eighteenth century. Yet in Ireland the fact that the great majority of landowners were Anglo-Irish Protestants—and their tenants Catholics—complicated what in Britain could be construed as class conflict. Excluded from legal channels, Irish secret societies used violence to overturn what they conceived as injustices: unemployment, exorbitant rents, and tithes were frequent targets.

Agrarian unrest gave rise to alarm within the establishment, which portrayed the Whiteboys as fomenting *popish* or Catholic plots and being French agents. As a result, the Irish Parliament was able to forestall legislation for Catholic relief and, indeed, forced through a coercion bill in 1766, aimed at stamping out the Whiteboys. Maureen Wall (2001, 187) describes this legislation as an "admission that Ireland was in a state of smothered war." The act alienated the peasantry further and enhanced the credibility of agrarian secret societies. Despite being condemned by the Catholic clergy, secret societies persisted, and in times of distress were often regarded by the rural poor as more beneficial to the defense of their interests than groups that worked through legal channels. So influential were these groups that nearly seventy years later, the great constitutional nationalist politician Daniel O'Connell could still be heard condemning the Whiteboys and other secret agrarian societies. Writing in *The Times*, he stated that any man who supported them "is not only a criminal in the sight of an all-judging God, but is a practical enemy of the rights and liberties of Ireland" (O'Connell 1833).

Ascendancy intransigence was no match for the determination of the British government in a national emergency. The process of repealing the penal laws began in the midst of Britain's struggle with American colonists in the 1770s and was all but completed in the years that saw its confrontation with revolutionary France two decades later. The first Catholic Relief Act was passed in 1778 during the American Revolutionary War, following France's decision to enter the conflict on the side of the American colonists. The act was an initial step in removing restrictions on Catholic land ownership. As a consequence of the French Revolution, which led to war between Britain and France in 1793, Prime Minister William Pitt pressured the Irish Parliament to overturn the remainder of the penal laws. He hoped that by restoring their rights, Irish Catholics would be immune from French revolutionary politics and ideas. By 1793, Catholics could buy and sell land and vote if they met the property qualification. But Catholics continued to pay tithes to the Church of Ireland and could still not be MPs. The existence of these two remaining constraints helped define Anglo-Irish politics for decades to come.

An important dimension of eighteenth-century Ireland was the British army stationed there. It is estimated that there were fifteen thousand English troops in Ireland in the early eighteenth century. In 1800, following the uprising of the United Irishmen and the invasion of Ireland by revolutionary France, British troops had expanded to sixty thousand (Foster 1988, 244). R. F. Foster captured the degree to which the military was integral to eighteenth-century Ireland. In his words, "army barracks remained an essential part of the way Irish towns were 'landscaped' along with the market square and the row of estate cottages" (Foster 1992, 142). Despite the fact that ascendancy power depended on British military power, from the late seventeenth century a segment of ascendancy politicians and writers contended that the English and later the British state was running slipshod over their rights and privileges. They were enraged by the English Parliament's 1697 effort to ban the export of Irish wool. They deeply resented the Declaratory Act of 1719, which reaffirmed the British Parliament's right to legislate for Ireland and the British House of Lords' right to act as a final court of appeal in Irish cases. They took umbrage when the English ironmaster William Wood (1671–1730), under a royal patent, was authorized to mint Irish coinage in 1722.

These resentments were given a political form in the eighteenth century. A pioneering voice in the emerging patriot movement was the philosopher and political writer William Molyneux (1656–98), who in *The Case of Ireland's Being Bound by Acts of Parliament in England, Stated* (1698) argued that it was "against reason and the common rights of all mankind" for laws originating in England to be binding on Ireland (quoted in Lydon 1998, 229). For Molyneux, being taxed without consent was unnatural and tantamount to robbery. The most famous of the ascendancy critics was undoubtedly the celebrated poet and satirist Jonathan Swift (1667–1745). He viewed English interference with Irish trade as the root cause of endemic Irish poverty. Like Molyneux, to whom he was indebted, he defended the right of the Irish Parliament to enact its own legislation. Swift's own identity was ambivalent. Historians have viewed him as either an Englishman in Ireland or an Irishman who demanded the same rights as an Englishman. Most importantly, Swift took the path-breaking step of addressing "the whole people of Ireland" in the fourth of his *Drapier's Letters* (1724). However, just as American colonists' demands for the recognition of their rights excluded those of African slaves, so Swift's championship of Irish rights was limited to those of Protestants. Writing in 1726, he observed that in England "all persons in *Ireland* are called and treated as *Irishmen*, although their fathers and grandfathers were born in *England*; and their predecessors having been conquerors of *Ireland*. . . . [Yet] they ought to be on as good a foot as any subjects of *Britain* . . ." (Swift 1991, 894).

Swift articulated an Anglo-Irish identity and a patriot politics that advocated self-governance for Protestant Ireland. This viewpoint only fully materialized under the pressure of yet another event originating outside of Ireland, in this case the American Revolution. From the onset there was empathy in Ireland for the rebelling American colonists, who were viewed by patriots as making analogous demands. American colonists recognized the bond between them as well. Benjamin Franklin, on a visit to Dublin in 1771, talked of future collaborations whereby Ireland and the American colonies would achieve "a more equitable treatment" (quoted in Beckett 1981, 206). In addition, Ulster Presbyterians had friends and family who had immigrated to America in the fifty or sixty years prior to the American revolt, and thus their compassion for the plight of the rebellious colonists went beyond empathizing with their political demands. There was, however, a difference between the position espoused by Irish patriots and their American counterparts: the patriots demanded a restoration of rights to a parliament that they claimed already had these rights by tradition and heritage.

Britain's war against the American colonists soon involved Ireland. France and Spain supported the colonists, and a French invasion of Ireland was greatly feared. Britain needed the flexibility to be able to send soldiers stationed in Ireland to North America. It is in this context that Protestant civilian militias or Volunteers stepped up to defend the country. At its height in the early 1780s, the Volunteer movement consisted of as many as sixty thousand Protestants, Anglicans and Presbyterians, and a small contingent of Catholics. The Volunteers were organized along military lines:

they were divided into regiments, wore uniforms, and were armed. Their public demonstrations soon became a focal point for resentments against British economic and political restrictions placed on Ireland, and provided occasions to challenge the status quo. In addition, historians have recently viewed their protests in gendered terms, whereby the Volunteers' manliness "validated their role in broader political affairs and even suggested the need for reform of the political system itself" (Higgins 2010, 19).

Reformers in the Irish Parliament used the threat of armed violence by the Volunteers to give added weight to their demands, a harbinger of later periods where politicians formed alliances with paramilitary groups. For both a contingent of the Volunteers and the reformers in Parliament, contempt for British interference in Irish affairs was coupled with reaching out to Catholics, a gesture suggesting that opposition to British dominance in Ireland could be framed in terms of a common Irish identity transcending the religious divide. At the Volunteer convention held at Dungannon in February 1782, a declaration stated support for the relaxation of the penal laws. The declaration was the work of men who thought of themselves as part of a universal brotherhood, as Christians like their Catholic neighbors, and as Protestants (Kinealy 2004, 135). Henry Grattan,[14] the most eloquent voice of the patriot politicians, envisioned an Ireland in which Catholics and Protestants joined together in a single "great national sacrament" (quoted in Boyce 1995, 114), although his vision of Catholic rights was framed in terms of a Protestant ascendancy.

After being defeated at the hands of the American colonists, the British government, faced with its own political turmoil, gave in to the demands of the reformers. In 1782, it granted legislative autonomy to the Irish Parliament and accepted the Irish House of Lords as the final court of appeal in Irish cases. This was a victory for the patriot movement, which viewed such actions as a harbinger of national rebirth. With characteristic hyperbole, Grattan declared: "I found Ireland on her knees, I watched over her with an eternal solicitude; I have traced her progress from injuries to arms, and from arms to liberty. Spirit of Swift! Spirit of Molyneux! Your genius has prevailed! Ireland is now a nation" (quoted in Boyce 1995, 113). The changes, however, proved to be not nearly as momentous upon closer examination. The king could veto but not rewrite legislation. The lord lieutenant remained a crown appointment and was thus not accountable to the Irish Parliament. Dublin Castle was still able to exert significant control over the legislative agenda by dispensing patronage. Most problematically, the refashioned legislature remained a Protestant parliament for a Protestant people.

At this point we reach the 1790s, the period when Chapter 1 begins. My goal in writing this book is to bring to life the Anglo-Irish relationship and communal relationships within Ireland through a selection of original sources—texts produced by historical actors rather than historians. My hope is that readers will thereby develop a greater appreciation for the complexity of the events, the multiple twists and turns

14. Henry Grattan (1746–1820), Irish politician and MP in both the Irish and later British Parliaments. He was a conservative nationalist and among the most eloquent advocates of legislative autonomy. Because of his association with the reform of the Irish legislature in 1782, the Irish Parliament developed the nickname "Grattan's parliament" in tribute to him.

of the debates and controversies, and the creative and passionate but also at times doctrinaire and unbending views of the historical actors. When first exploring the Anglo-Irish relationship, many of us, including myself, tend to form an immediate empathy with the historical plight of Catholics and identify with Irish nationalist aspirations. Correlatively, we often view England and Britain as ruthlessly imperialistic and Protestants in Ireland as an oppressive ruling class. It is difficult, for instance, to contemplate the Great Irish Famine of the 1840s—in which over two million people either died or emigrated—without being moved by the suffering of the Catholic peasants who were predominantly its victims or condemning Irish Protestant landlords and the British government who often seemed to stand by and let it happen. However, if such sentiments have a historical basis, they are best viewed as a starting rather than an ending point. They easily become judgments on the past based on the values and experience of the present. Unless the actions of nationalists and Unionists, Protestants and Catholics, the British and the Irish are viewed in their historical context, we end up reducing a multilayered and multifaceted phenomenon into a morality tale. Thus, I hope that readers both sympathize with Irish nationalist aims and critically scrutinize them and that they bring the same blend of empathy and critique to understanding the worldview of Protestant Ireland and British political culture.

The book consists of fifty-six original texts or primary sources organized into four chapters. The sources represent numerous genres, from newspaper articles and speeches to plays, poetry, and short stories. Some sources have been chosen because an Irish history reader is unimaginable without them. Others, such as the relationship between feminism and nationalism, reflect the changing ground of historiographical discussions. Still others have been selected because, while often cited by historians, they either have never been reprinted or have been long unavailable. A central feature of this reader is its emphasis on the cultural dimension of Irish politics. Chapters 1, 3, and 4 form a roughly chronological narrative of major events, but Chapter 2 explores the cultural dimension of Irish nationalism in a time period that is virtually the same as the other three chapters combined. Its central focus is the numerous and varied attempts to implicitly and explicitly define "Irishness" and the political implications of these efforts. Not only did such efforts have an impact on the course of Irish politics, but they also may be viewed as part of a broader history of nationalist discourse.

In the process of producing this collection, I have made numerous choices along the way. As often as has seemed prudent, texts have been reproduced in their entirety. If they have been edited, it is either because they are simply too long, too repetitive, or parts of them are irrelevant to this book's themes. Given the closeness between British and American spelling, the original spellings found in texts have been retained. When a definition of a word is not apparent, its meaning has been clarified with a footnote. Every effort has been made to give birth and death years for individuals mentioned in the book. The birth and death years of the writers of the primary sources are given in the introductions to those texts. All others can be found either where the name first appears or in an explanatory footnote. The use of abbreviations has been avoided, but some are so commonly used that they have been adopted: IRA for the Irish Republican Army; IRB for the Irish Republican Brotherhood; MP for Member of Parliament; and UK for the United Kingdom.

To help the reader navigate through these texts, each chapter begins with an introduction that weaves together the sources in a historical narrative and suggests, when appropriate, their relationship to each other. These introductions are supplemented by headnotes for the individual texts. The headnotes consist of brief biographies, historical contextualization of the sources, and an analytical framework for initial exploration. To assist the reader further, explanatory footnotes and a glossary at the end of the book explain references—numerous names, places, events, terms, and quotes from literature—that the intended audience for these texts would have known but today's readers might not. The Glossary consists of references that appear more than once and thus will not be found in the footnotes. There are also maps, a Chronology of Main Events, and a bibliography that consists of both works cited in the introductions and footnotes and texts that might form the basis for further reading.

This book focuses on Ireland under the Union. It begins in the 1790s, a decade in which Ireland was destabilized by the impact of the French Revolution. It ends in 1922 following the Anglo-Irish War (a confrontation between Irish militants and Irish and British authorities in 1919–21), protracted and intricate negotiations between the two sides, and the signing of a peace treaty in 1921. As a consequence of the treaty, Ireland was partitioned into the twenty-six-county, autonomous Irish Free State (modeled after nations with dominion status such as Canada and Australia) and the six-county Northern Ireland, which remained part of the UK. Bitter disputes over the peace treaty plunged the Free State into a devastating civil war (1922–23) that left an indelible imprint on its political culture. Over time, however, the twenty-six counties achieved what had eluded the Irish negotiators in the Anglo-Irish Treaty— an independent democratic republic. It was accomplished through stages. The 1937 constitution declared Ireland to be a "sovereign, independent democratic state," and the Irish Free State was renamed Éire. But Ireland remained within the British Commonwealth, and hence the British government could ignore what was clearly a radical departure from what had been agreed upon in the Anglo-Irish Treaty. In 1949, Commonwealth ties were finally severed, and Éire was renamed the Republic of Ireland. A major step in overcoming cultural insularity and achieving sustained economic growth resulted from Ireland joining the European Community (now the European Union) in 1973. While a late-twentieth-century economic boom has been supplanted by a financial crisis and economic stagnation, Ireland has substantially changed since the early 1920s. It is more secular, more urban, and less reliant on agriculture. The extent to which its conflicts with Britain have been overcome is manifest in the enthusiastic crowds that greeted Queen Elizabeth II during her 2011 visit to Ireland. She is the first British monarch to have visited Ireland since George V in 1911.

As a result of the Anglo-Irish Treaty, the Catholic minority in Northern Ireland— more than a third of the population—was cut off from its brethren in the Free State and was the object of systematic economic and political discrimination at the hands of the Protestant establishment. Northern Protestants saw Catholics as potentially disloyal, a threat to political stability, and a menace to their way of life. Like the Protestant ascendancy in the eighteenth century, their actions seemed to stem from a blend of pride and insecurity. What happened in Northern Ireland has significant parallels with the American south during the era of segregation. In addition, friction between Protestant and Catholic workers also had American parallels. A divide analogous to racial divisions separating black and white working-class people in the United States existed among the urban working class in Northern Ireland and was an impediment to expressing class grievances.

The situation in Northern Ireland exploded in the late 1960s when Catholic reformers and nationalists, inspired by the American civil rights movement, lodged peaceful protests. It was like lighting a match in a barn full of dry hay. The result was the return of communal violence, the resurfacing of nationalist and Unionist paramilitaries, the dissolution of the Northern Irish legislature, and direct rule by the British government. As a consequence of the events of the late 1960s and early 1970s, Northern Ireland experienced a civil war lasting for more than a generation and responsible for more than 3,500 deaths. With the signing of the Good Friday Agreement in 1998, meaningful steps were agreed upon to resolve the conflict. The agreement was possible because it simultaneously addressed the three dimensions of the struggle—British and Irish, North and South (Republic of Ireland and Northern Ireland), and Protestant and Catholic (in Northern Ireland). The scope of the agreement might well provide other places torn by ethnic, national, and religious divisions with key insights into how to achieve peace and reconciliation after a period of sustained political violence. This book does not cover events in Northern Ireland since the 1960s, but it offers a historical genealogy that helps explain them.

Map of Ireland, showing political divisions and important towns and cities.

CHAPTER ONE

Making and Unmaking the Union

In his classic account of Anglo-Irish relations, Oliver MacDonagh (2003, xix) described the union of Britain and Ireland in 1801—to form the United Kingdom (UK)—as "the most important single factor in shaping Ireland as a nation in the modern world." Created in response to the 1798 rebellion of the Society of United Irishmen, whose attempt to create an independent Ireland was undertaken in alliance with revolutionary France, the Union sought to secure Ireland from invasion and to bring Britain and Ireland closer together. It abolished the Irish Parliament and gave Ireland representation in the British House of Commons and House of Lords. But it stopped short of granting Ireland the same status as Scotland, for under the Union, Ireland was still administered by a lord lieutenant. The Union also failed to grant Catholics equal status with Protestants: the former were unable to become members of Parliament. This chapter's focus is on the making of the union between Britain and Ireland and the Union's initial political phase in the first half of the nineteenth century. The original sources comprising the chapter are roughly divided into two groups. The first group explores the legacy of the French Revolution and the 1798 rebellion for the making of the Union in particular and Ireland in general. The second group investigates Catholic emancipation in the 1820s, the Irish nationalist movement to repeal the Union in the 1830s and 1840s, and the Great Irish Famine in the 1840s.

By the eve of the French Revolution, the British government had granted limited autonomy to the all-Protestant Irish Parliament, a major victory for the liberal patriot movement. But what did this mean for Irish Catholics, who were still laboring under the remnants of the penal laws? Hardliners continued to believe that expanding those rights spelled the beginning of the end for Protestant ruling-class dominance. But there was a growing sentiment among liberal reformers that Irish Catholics, particularly the expanding middle class, had accepted the status quo and that Ireland's future stability and health depended on their being granted full rights.

The debate on Catholic rights was complicated by the French revolutionary explosion in 1789: its bywords—liberty, equality, and fraternity—challenged not only the assumptions of Ireland's political regime but the rule of Europe's hereditary aristocracies and monarchies more generally. The waters were muddied further when Britain declared war on France in 1793, raising the potential of a French invasion of Ireland supported by dissonant Irish men and women. Within Anglo-Irish politics, Edmund Burke, best known for his widely influential critique of the French Revolution, argued that Ireland's British connection was indispensable but that continued discrimination against Catholics was likely to drive an essentially loyal and conservative group to support an alliance with revolutionary France (no. 2). In this he was supported by Prime Minister William Pitt, who, though not wanting to alienate the Protestant ruling class nonetheless encouraged them to abolish the remaining penal laws, appointed the liberal Lord William Wentworth-Fitzwilliam (1748–1833) as lord lieutenant in 1794, and endowed St. Patrick's College in Maynooth to train Catholic priests in 1795. Pitt and his liberal allies were only partially successful. Fitzwilliam was forced to resign in less than three months. The Irish Parliament abolished all the remaining penal laws except for emancipation: a male Catholic could vote if he met the property qualifications, but he could not be a Member of Parliament (MP). Whether the glass was now half full or half empty was a matter of perspective.

The liberal, middle-class, United Irishmen believed that it was half empty. Founded by Presbyterians in Belfast (and a little later in Dublin) in 1791, they extended the tradition of Protestant dissent, which in Ireland was reinforced by the subservience of Dissenters to the Anglo-Irish ruling class and the Church of Ireland. They created a movement based on popular sovereignty and established what was arguably the first Irish nationalist movement. The United Irishmen were initially willing to work within the parliamentary framework, but they drifted toward insurrectionary politics, accelerated by government attempts to suppress them in 1793. From 1794 they advocated an independent Irish republic modeled after France's, and though as children of the Enlightenment they found Catholicism dogmatic and reactionary, they nonetheless reached out to disgruntled Catholics. Theobald Wolfe Tone, the most famous among them, described their goal as abolishing "the memory of all past dissensions" and substituting "the common name of Irishman in place of the denominations of Protestant, Catholic, and Dissenter" (no. 1). To achieve this goal, the United Irishmen made common cause with the Catholic Defenders, a secret society originating in Ulster but spreading to the southeast. The Defenders were less committed to abstract notions of republicanism and more interested in traditional ones of agrarian justice. They were inspired by the example of revolutionary France, but, perhaps more importantly, their politics was viscerally anti-Protestant.

The United Irishmen also embarked on an alliance with revolutionary France. Tone, who left for America rather than face imprisonment in 1795, subsequently traveled to France, seeking to convince the French revolutionary government to launch an invasion of Ireland in conjunction with an Irish uprising. A French attempt in 1796 to land at Bantry Bay was scuttled because of severe weather. But a small force of approximately a thousand soldiers under General Jean Humbert's[1] command landed in Killala, County Mayo, in northwest Ireland, in August 1798. By then, Irish insurgent forces in Ulster and Leinster had been brutally put down (perhaps as many as thirty thousand dead), and the French invading force, following initial success, surrendered at Ballinamuck in September. Marching through the Irish countryside, the French troops detected little republican or nationalist support. But they did find recruits among the peasants, who believed, according to J. C. Beckett (1981, 265), that the French had come "as champions of the pope and the Virgin Mary." Following their surrender, the French soldiers were imprisoned and then allowed to go home. Many of the Irish peasants who had supported them were summarily executed.

---

1. Jean Joseph Amable Humbert (1755–1823), a French soldier, participant in the French Revolution, and general of the French invasion force that landed in Ireland in August 1798.

The legacy of this 1790s political unrest was at least threefold. First, it entailed the formation of a tradition committed to an independent Irish republic based on physical force. In this context the failed insurrection of Robert Emmet in 1803 (no. 5) was the United Irishmen's final gesture. However, these rebellions left behind collective memories that, though more mythic than real, endured and inspired future generations of nationalists. A second important dimension was that enmity surfaced, producing violence and bloodshed and further hardening already existing divisions. Here, the most important legacy of this communal confrontation was the birth of the Orange Society (later renamed the Orange Order) following a sectarian confrontation with the Defenders in 1795 known as the Battle of the Diamond. The Orange Order militantly defended Protestant interests, embodied in its idealization of King William III (1650–1702), whose victory at the Battle of the Boyne in 1690 represented (for them) the triumph of Protestant liberty over Catholic tyranny. Their commemoration of William's victory in July 12 marches continues to this day. The group's 1796 march in Armagh, Ulster, resulted in seven thousand Catholic homes being burned and the forced expulsion of Catholics from the area. But Catholics were by no means free of sectarianism, as evidenced by the 1798 United Irishmen and Defender rebellion in Wexford. Following the news of government reprisals against rebels in Ulster, their rebellion took the form of an anti-Protestant crusade. On June 5 more than a hundred Protestants were burned in a barn at Scullabogue, while on June 20 rebels in Wexford town systematically executed seventy Protestants.

The third—and arguably the most important—legacy of 1798 was the Union. The idea of a legislative union predated 1798, but the rebellion gave it a new impetus, as Prime Minister William Pitt now believed that Ireland was an ongoing security risk. Perhaps not foremost in Pitt's mind—but not to be dismissed—was the hope that a united kingdom might finally allay the long-term bitter Anglo-Irish conflict and create an entity greater than the sum of its parts. Pitt stated this himself (no. 4). He envisioned a time when "a man cannot speak as a true Englishman, unless he speaks as a true Irishman, nor as a true Irishman, unless he speaks as a true Englishman." In the conclusion to *The Wild Irish Girl* (1806), the novelist Sydney Owenson expressed similar sentiments (no. 6).

The Union got off to a rocky start. Ironically, given their subsequent devotion to Unionism, it was Irish Protestants, rather than Catholics, who resolutely opposed the new framework. They imagined that their hard-won autonomy and dominance was being swept away. It was only as a result of the greatest arm-twisting, greased by bribery and promises of patronage, that Robert Stewart,[2] Viscount Castlereagh, the Irish chief secretary, engineered passage of the bill in the Irish Parliament. Under the

2. Robert Stewart (1769–1822), Viscount Castlereagh. From an Irish Protestant background, he was originally a reformer but subsequently opposed the association of the United Irishmen with revolutionary France and as a county magistrate was active in the group's suppression. In Irish politics he is best known as the leading figure in pushing the Act of Union through the Irish Parliament. More generally, he is perhaps best known for his critical role in establishing the foundation for nineteenth-century European international politics at the Congress of Vienna (1815).

Union, Ireland received 100 MPs out of the 658 in the House of Commons. Given that its population was approximately 33 percent of the UK, Ireland was underrepresented; in the decades following the Great Famine, when its total of the population fell to 20 percent, the opposite was the case. Yet despite the rhetoric of integration, Ireland was still administered by a lord lieutenant. This reinforced the idea that Ireland's status was more like a colony than a partner. In addition, King George III (1738–1820) blocked Pitt's legislative effort to achieve Catholic emancipation. He saw it as incompatible with his coronation oath to uphold the established Church of England. Pitt resigned.

During the Union's first thirty years, Catholic emancipation dominated the political agenda. It was the rallying cry of Daniel O'Connell, whose Catholic Association, founded in 1823, helped produce the first modern mass political campaign in Ireland (and Europe), based on peasants' monthly subscription of a penny and huge political rallies. Despite liberal Protestant support, its strength was the Catholic majority and the Catholic Church. O'Connell's determination to take his seat following his parliamentary victory in the 1828 Clare county by-election[3] (no. 7) found support among liberal reformers in England who regarded Catholic emancipation as part of a larger project of parliamentary reform. They advocated expanding the electorate and creating legislative districts that mirrored the growth and shifts in population. Facing a possible uprising in Ireland and dissent in England, the Tory prime minister, Arthur Wellesley, the Duke of Wellington (1769–1852), capitulated rather than risk a confrontation. Legislation in 1829 altered the oath of allegiance, making it possible for a Catholic, but not a Jew, to be an MP. Nationalist Ireland's appreciation might have been greater for this shift in policy if emancipation had been granted when the Union was formed. The British establishment's begrudging surrender in 1829 tended to produce resentment rather than gratitude. What, in fact, O'Connell and his allies learned from the experience was that extra-parliamentary pressure, coupled with the veiled threat of violence, could lead to British surrender to Irish demands. That the price of emancipation was the suppression of the Catholic Association and the limiting of the electorate by the imposition of a higher property qualification added salt to the wound.

O'Connell's second great campaign was the repeal of the Union. He had opposed the Union from the beginning and was skeptical that emancipation would transform Anglo-Irish relations. Yet he also used the Union as a bargaining chip: he would support it if the British government gave justice to Ireland. The most conspicuous instance of his willingness to work within the system was the Lichfield House Compact, hammered out with the Whig government in 1835. In exchange for his support, the Whigs passed tithe reform, passed Irish municipal government reform, and established the rudiments of an Irish national education system. They likewise passed Irish poor law reform based on English precedents that ignored the vast differences of the economic structures between the two nations. At what point did working with the Whigs become counterproductive?

---

3. A *by-election* is a special election that is held to fill a vacant seat in the House of Commons.

If working with the Whigs was problematic, a pact with the Tories—the party of the establishment and the champions of the monarchy and the Anglican Church—was out of the question. Indeed, it was when the Tories under the leadership of Robert Peel (1788–1850) were elected in 1841 that O'Connell revved up the repeal movement and subsequently declared 1843 "the year of repeal." The movement revived the organizational apparatus that had proved successful in the 1820s—inexpensive subscriptions, liberal Protestant support, mass or monster meetings, and support from the Catholic Church. It could no longer count on the support of British reformers who despite their backing for Catholic emancipation were mostly diehard Unionists. The drive for repeal was invigorated by a younger generation of intellectuals, who formed a group known as Young Ireland. It was made up of Protestants and Catholics, and its newspaper, *The Nation*, first published in 1842, renewed Wolfe Tone's call for an Ireland that transcended the religious divide. O'Connell would eventually break with Young Ireland over the group's willingness to entertain violence as a means of achieving political goals. But in 1843 their combined forces attracted mass support, culminating in a series of monster meetings with crowds in the hundreds of thousands. O'Connell's speech at Mullaghmast (no. 9) gives some inkling of the spell that he could cast over a crowd.

O'Connell's populist triumph proved short-lived. When Peel's government banned the October 8 monster meeting at Clontarf, near Dublin, he called it off rather than resort to violence, for he was opposed in principle to using violence to achieve political goals. Furthermore, he and other leaders of the repeal movement were arrested and convicted on charges of conspiracy. Between conviction and sentencing, O'Connell entered the House of Commons to a standing ovation from the Whig opposition, a reminder that British political opinion should never be construed as homogeneous. The repeal movement did not exactly die following Clontarf, but it was never the same either. Most important, it was beginning to be overshadowed by the Irish Famine, which first surfaced in 1845 and ravaged the countryside for approximately five years. Describing the Easter Rising of 1916, the poet W. B. Yeats memorably proclaimed: "All changed, changed utterly" (no. 53). He could have said the same about the Great Famine.

Crop failures and food shortages were not new to Ireland. There were several famines or near-famines in the eighteenth century, and as recently as 1842 there had been partial potato-crop failures. Observers were alarmed by the magnitude of Irish poverty, the rise in the population, and overdependence on the potato crop. Ireland's population was 8.5 million people in 1845, about half of England's. The size of the former's economy was a fraction of the latter's. The cause of the Famine was a fungal disease, *Phytophthora infestans*, better known as the potato blight. Ireland was not the only place that felt its effects. However, owing to the structure of its agrarian economy and the length of the Famine's duration, its impact was unprecedented. As many as a million people may have died either from starvation or disease; a further 1.5 million emigrated between 1845 and 1855, including two to three hundred thousand emigrants from Ireland to Britain between 1845 and 1855. All told, the population fell by 25 percent in only six years. The west was most affected; the southeast the least. All regions decreased in population.

Yet the facts do not speak for themselves. There was a clash of opinions regarding what the Famine revealed about the state of Ireland. On the one hand, there is the view found in *The Times* (the paper of the British establishment), which, while not blaming the Irish per se, finds in their national character a lack of drive and industry that compounds the results (no. 10). On the other hand, there is the perspective of John Mitchel, the Young Ireland radical (no. 11). His view that God created the blight but that the British government was responsible for the Famine became etched into the consciousness of Irish nationalists and significant components of the wider population.

There can be no doubt that the Whig government of Lord John Russell,[4] in power from 1846, was ideologically committed to the magic of the market and often seemed more concerned with sustaining the laws of political economy than saving lives. Furthermore, the government's policies were informed by the Protestant providentialism of the British public. In the words of historian Peter Gray: "The belief that the blight was a providential visitation, sent to bring Ireland into a higher state of social and moral organization through a necessary measure of pain, shaped contemporary attitudes and subsequent apologetics" (1999, 337). In addition, there were those in the government who regarded the Famine as an opportunity to reshape Ireland's agrarian economy, either by encouraging the sale of inefficient estates or fostering emigration.

Yet this did not mean that the Russell government, or Peel's before it, did nothing to relieve distress or that its efforts did not save lives, even if its actions seemed at times to lack sympathy for the starving or to be misconceived. Government intervention included buying up American grain and feeding the hungry, employing people in public works, and creating soup kitchens. It also involved reshaping poor law administration: expanding workhouse occupancy and introducing outdoor relief.[5] However, since poor law administration was paid out of local tax revenues, Irish landowners bore the heaviest burden. This was an expression of the British establishment's enduring belief that Irish landowners had shirked their responsibilities as a ruling class. There were undoubtedly landowners who acted cruelly toward their tenants and in some cases saw evictions and emigration as an opportunity for consolidating their holdings and leasing them in larger chunks. But this is not the whole story. Not only were there landlords who acted responsibly toward their tenants, but some also faced financial ruin as a result of their tenants' failure to pay their rent. The shift of famine relief from the British to the Irish taxpayer—even though in practice the government ended up making loans to cover some of the increased expense—raised a critical question. If Ireland was an integral part of the UK, why did the government come to see the Famine as an Irish problem?

4. John Russell (1792–1878), 1st Earl Russell, Whig politician who was prime minister on two separate occasions: 1846–52 and 1865–66. In British politics he is known as an advocate of parliamentary reform, playing an important role in passing the Great Reform Act (1832). In the Irish context he is known as the prime minister whose government was guided by laissez-faire principles during the Great Famine, although in practice it also engaged in acts of intervention to alleviate hunger and distress.

5. Poverty relief that did not require a recipient to reside in an institution such as a workhouse.

Emigration: a permanent feature of Irish life (1856).

Given the Famine's importance to Ireland's history, subsequent analysts, many of them historians, have viewed it from an array of perspectives, in part reflecting Ireland's contentious politics. It has been seen as everything from an inevitable Malthusian calamity,[6] rooted in an imbalance between population and food, to a conspiracy hatched by the British authorities, and several theories in between. Among recent interpreters, the historian Christine Kinealy has argued that the Famine must ultimately be seen as a judgment on the Union: "Clearly, the Act of Union neither conferred economic advantages on Ireland nor safeguarded her population at a time of crisis" (2002, 220). For the economic historian Cormac Ó Gráda, it was neither inevitable nor a conspiracy but an ecological disaster whose devastating results were compounded by bad timing: "Taking fuller account of developments both in the domestic economy and further afield, in the end the Irish were desperately unlucky" (1989, 68).

However the Famine is understood, its long-term impact is beyond dispute. In addition to Ireland's decline in population and increase in emigration, those who remained experienced a rising standard of living, in large part because of diminished population pressures and a shift towards more profitable large-scale farming. One quarter of all farms disappeared, and the average size of a holding increased between 1845 and 1851. More specifically, there was a shift in agrarian structure from tillage to pasture: from the economy of the potato—worked by a large population of cottiers, or poor rural laborers, living on small holdings—to one increasingly driven by medium and large farmers raising livestock. Not only were farmers becoming more prominent, but their values and outlook were becoming more important as well. They were a receptive audience for an emerging Catholic devotional revolution, which sought to supplant the remnants of paganism and halfhearted forms of Catholic worship with an evangelical revival. Signs of the devotional revolution surfaced prior to the Famine, but, as Emmet Larkin argued in a pioneering essay, it helped facilitate the process (1972, 648).

6. *Malthusian* refers to the influential ideas of Thomas Malthus (1766–1834), who argued that the quantity of food increased at a slower rate than the growth of the population. If population increased unchecked, starvation was inevitable.

Another noticeable change was a marked decline in the speaking of the Irish language, as the part of the population most affected by the Famine, through either death or emigration, were often Irish speakers. The implications of this trend for Irish cultural nationalism will be discussed in Chapter 2. Finally, there was undoubtedly an intensification of Anglophobia owing to widespread perceptions that the British government was, in the words of the moderate Young Irelander Charles Gavan Duffy, responsible for "a fearful murder committed to the mass of the people" (quoted in Donnelly 2001, 207). This collective memory was important to both people in Ireland and Irish emigrants who took their bitter feelings toward Britain to the United States, Canada, and Australia, among other places, and passed it on to their descendants. The consequences of all of these changes for the Anglo-Irish relationship were profound.

1. Theobald Wolfe Tone, Selections from *Life of Theobald Wolfe Tone* (1797) (published 1826)

Wolfe Tone (1763–98) is the father of Irish republicanism, an inspiration to militant nationalists who have struggled to create an independent and united Ireland. He was born in Dublin into a Protestant family. His father was a coach maker, and his mother was born Catholic but converted to Protestantism. He was educated at Trinity College, Dublin, where he pursued legal studies, becoming a barrister in 1789 after attending the Inns of Court in London. Yet the legal profession bored Tone. He was more drawn to life as a soldier, which he described as possessing "a romantic spirit of adventure," and he gravitated toward the reform movement taking shape in Belfast, helping found the Society of United Irishmen in 1791.

Tone, like the United Irishmen, originally supported constitutional reform—including granting the electoral franchise to Catholics—and he believed that Ireland might still benefit from the British connection. Yet he (and the United Irishmen more generally) became skeptical that the British government and the Protestant ascendancy would accept such change, and he increasingly gravitated to the politics of separation. Indeed, writing in his journal in 1796, Tone stated that he hated the very name of England. In the selection from his autobiography reprinted here, The Life of Theobald Wolfe Tone, *he reveals his hopes for a united and independent Ireland as well as his awareness that sectarian divisions stand in the way of achieving it. It was written while Tone was in France, where he tirelessly sought to convince the revolutionary regime to launch an invasion of Ireland in conjunction with an Irish uprising against British rule led and organized by the United Irishmen. Tone was captured in October 1798 as a participant during the third attempted French invasion of Ireland during the 1790s. He was wearing a French adjutant-general's uniform at the time. At his trial Tone requested that he be executed as a soldier by a firing squad. When the tribunal convicted him of treason and ordered that he be hung, he took his life in his cell rather than face a public hanging, an act that enhanced his later status as a martyr to the cause of nationalist Ireland.*

Wolfe Tone: the father of Irish republicanism. (Image courtesy of the Mary Evans Picture Library.)

The French revolution had now been above a twelvemonth in its progress; at its commencement, as the first emotions are generally honest, every one was in its favour; but, after some time, the probable consequences to monarchy and aristocracy began to be forseen, and the partisans of both to retrench considerably in their admiration; at length, Mr. Burke's famous invective appeared;[7] and this in due season produced Paine's reply, which he called 'Rights of Man'.[8] This controversy, and the gigantic event which gave rise to it, changed in an instant the politics of Ireland. Two years before, the nation was in lethargy. The puny efforts of the Whig Club,[9] miserable and defective as their system was, were the only appearance of any thing like exertion, and

7. Edmund Burke, *Reflections on the French Revolution* (1790).
8. Thomas Paine, *Rights of Man* (1791).
9. Founded in Dublin in 1789 (and Belfast the next year), the Whig Club advocated moderate reform: less English influence on the governance of Ireland and an executive more responsible to the Irish Parliament, while leaving the power of the ruling class unchallenged.

he was looked on as extravagant who thought of a parliamentary reform, against which, by the by, all parties equally set their face. I have already mentioned that, in those days of apathy and depression, I made an unsuccessful blow at the supremacy of England by my pamphlet on the expected rupture with Spain;[10] and I have also fairly mentioned that I found nobody who ventured to second my attempt, or paid the least attention to the doctrine I endeavoured to disseminate. By the rapid succession of events, and, above all, the explosion which had taken place in France and blown into the elements a despotism rooted for fourteen centuries, had thoroughly aroused all Europe, and the eyes of every man, in every quarter, were turned anxiously on the French National Assembly.[11] In England, Burke had the triumph completely to decide the public; fascinated by an eloquent publication, which flattered so many of their prejudices, and animated by their unconquerable hatred of France, which no change of circumstances could alter, the whole English nation, it may be said, retracted from their first decision in favour of the glorious and successful efforts of the French people; they sickened at the prospect of the approaching liberty and happiness of that mighty nation; they calculated, as merchants, the probable effects which the energy of regenerated France might have on their commerce; they rejoiced when they saw the combination of despots formed to restore the ancient system, and perhaps to dismember the monarchy; and they waited with impatience for an occasion which, happily for mankind, they soon found, when they might, with some appearance of decency, engage in person in the infamous contest.

But matters were very different in Ireland, an oppressed, insulted, and plundered nation. As we well knew, experimentally, what it was to be enslaved, we sympathized most sincerely with the French people, and watched their progress to freedom with the utmost anxiety; we had not, like England, a prejudice rooted in our very nature against France. As the revolution advanced, and as events expanded themselves, the public spirit of Ireland rose with a rapid acceleration. The fears and animosities of the aristocracy rose in the same, or a still higher proportion. In a little time the French revolution became the test of every man's political creed, and the nation was fairly divided into two great parties, the Aristocrats and the Democrats (epithets borrowed from France), who have ever since been measuring each other's strength and carrying on a kind of smothered war, which the course of events, it is highly probable, may soon call into energy and action.

It is needless, I believe, to say that I was a democrat from the very commencement, and, as all the retainers of government, including the sages and judges of the law,

10. *Spanish War!: An Enquiry How Far Ireland Is Bound, of Right, to Embark in the Impending Contest on the Side of Great-Britain? Addressed to the Members of Both Houses of Parliament* (1790). In 1790, Britain and Spain were on the verge of war, a result of conflicting claims in the Pacific Northwest. Tone advocated that Irish politicians view the conflict from an independent perspective rather than automatically follow Britain's lead.

11. On June 17, 1789, the representatives of the Third Estate (the medieval designation for the vast majority of the French people) declared themselves a national assembly of the *people* rather than of the *estates*—a defining moment in the first stage of the French Revolution. The National Assembly met between June 17 and July 9, 1789; the National Constituent Assembly supplanted it.

were, of course, on the other side, this gave the coup de grace[12] to any expectations, if any such I had, of my succeeding at the bar, for I soon became pretty notorious; but, in fact, I had for some time renounced all hope, and, I may say, all desire, of succeeding in a profession which I always disliked, and which the political prostitution of its members (through otherwise men of high honour and of great personal worth) had taught me sincerely to despise. I therefore seldom went near the four courts,[13] nor did I adopt any one of the means, and, least of all, the study of the law, which are successfully employed by those young men whose object it is to rise in their profession.

As I came, about this period, rather more forward than I had hitherto done, it is necessary for understanding my history to take a rapid survey of the state of parties in Ireland, that is to say, of the members of the established religion, the Dissenters and the Catholics.[14]

The first party, whom, for distinction's sake, I call the Protestants, though not above the tenth of the population, were in possession of the whole of the government, and of five-sixths of the landed property of the nation; they were, and had been for above a century, in the quiet enjoyment of the church, the law, the revenue, the army, the navy, the magistracy, the corporations, in a word, of the whole patronage of Ireland. With properties whose title was founded in massacre and plunder, and being, as it were, but a colony of foreign usurpers in the land, they saw no security for their persons and estates but in a close connection with England, who profited of their fears, and, as the price of her protection, exacted the implicit surrender of the commerce and liberties of Ireland. Different events, particularly the revolution in America, had enabled and emboldened the other two parties, of whom I am about to speak, to hurry the Protestants into measures highly disagreeable to England and beneficial to their country; but in which, from accidental circumstances, they durst not refuse to concur. The spirit of the corps, however, remained unchanged, as they have manifested on every occasion since which chance has offered. This party, therefore, so powerful by their property and influence, were implicitly devoted to England, which they esteemed necessary for the security of their existence; they adopted, in consequence, the sentiments and the language of the British cabinet; they dreaded and abhorred the principles of the French revolution, and were, in one word, an aristocracy, in the fullest and most odious extent of the term.

The Dissenters, who formed the second party, were at least twice as numerous as the first. Like them, they were a colony of foreigners in their origin, but, being most engaged in trade and manufactures, with few overgrown landed proprietors among them, they did not, like them, feel that a slavish dependence on England was essential to their very existence. Strong in their numbers and their courage, they felt that they were able to defend themselves, and they soon ceased to consider themselves as any other than Irishmen. It was the Dissenters who composed the flower of the famous

---

12. A deathblow (French).

13. The building containing the four principal courts of Ireland.

14. Tone uses the term *established religion* for the Anglican Church, known in Ireland as the Church of Ireland. He uses *Dissenters* to mean those who dissented from the established church, notably Presbyterians from Ulster.

volunteer army of 1782, which extorted from the English minister the restoration
of what is affected to be called the constitution of Ireland; it was they who first
promoted and continued the demand of a parliamentary reform, in which, however,
they were baffled by the superior address and chicanery of the aristocracy; and it was
they, finally, who were the first to stand forward, in the most decided and unqualified
manner, in support of the principles of the French revolution.

The Catholics, who composed the third party, were above two-thirds of the nation,
and formed, perhaps, a still greater proportion. They embraced the entire peasantry
of three provinces,[15] they constituted a considerable portion of the mercantile interest,
but, from the tyranny of the penal laws enacted at different periods against them, they
possessed but a very small proportion of the landed property, perhaps not a fiftieth
part of the whole. It is not my intention here to give a detail of that execrable and
infamous code, framed with the art and the malice of demons, to plunder and degrade
and brutalize the Catholics. Suffice it to say that there was no injustice, no disgrace,
no disqualification, moral, political or religious, civil or military, that was not heaped
upon them; it is with difficulty that I restrain myself from entering into the abomi-
nable detail; but it is the less necessary, as it is to be found in so many publications of
the day. This horrible system, pursued for above a century with unrelenting acrimony
and perseverance, had wrought its full effect, and had, in fact, reduced the great body
of the Catholic peasantry of Ireland to a situation, morally and physically speaking,
below that of the beasts of the field. The spirit of their few remaining gentry was
broken, and their minds degraded; and it was only in the class of their merchants and
traders, and a few members of the medical profession, who had smuggled an education in despite of the penal code, that any thing like political sensation existed. Such
was pretty nearly the situation of the three great parties at the commencement of the
French revolution, and certainly a much more gloomy prospect could not well present
itself to the eyes of any friend to liberty and his country. But, as the luminary of truth
and freedom in France advanced rapidly to its meridian splendour, the public mind in
Ireland was proportionably illuminated; and to the honour of the Dissenters of Belfast
be it said, they were the first to reduce to practice their newly received principles, and
to show, by being just, that there were deserving to be free.

The dominion of England in Ireland had been begun and continued in the disunion of the great sects which divided the latter country. In effectuating this disunion, the Protestant party were the willing instruments, as they saw clearly that if
ever the Dissenters and Catholics were to discover their true interests and, forgetting
their former ruinous dissentions, were to unite cordially and make common cause,
the downfall of English supremacy and, of course, of their own unjust monopoly,
would be the necessary and immediate consequence. They therefore laboured continually, and for a long time successfully, to keep the other two sects asunder, and
the English government had even the address to persuade the Catholics that the
non-execution of the penal laws, which were, in fact, too atrocious to be enforced in
their full rigor, was owing to their clemency; that the Protestants and Dissenters, but
especially the latter, were the enemies, and themselves, in effect, the protectors of the

15. Catholics were a majority in Leinster, Munster, and Connacht, but not Ulster.

Catholic people. Under this arrangement, the machine of government moved forward on carpet ground, but the time was at length come when this system of iniquity was to tumble in the dust, and the day of truth and reason to commence. . . .

The Catholics, on their part, were rapidly advancing in political spirit and information. Every month, every day, as the revolution in France went prosperously forward, added to their courage and their force, and the hour seemed at last arrived when, after a dreary oppression of above one hundred years, they were once more to appear on the political theatre of their country. They saw the brilliant prospect of success, which events in France opened to their view, and they determined to avail themselves with promptitude of that opportunity, which never returns to those who omit it. For this, the active members of the General Committee[16] resolved to set on foot an immediate application to parliament, praying for a repeal of the penal laws. The first difficulty they had to surmount arose in their own body; their peers, their gentry (as they affected to call themselves), and their prelates, either seduced or intimidated by government, gave the measure all possible opposition; and at length, after a long contest in which both parties strained every nerve and produced the whole of their strength, the question was decided in the Committee, by a majority of at least six to one, in favour of the intended application. The triumph of the young democracy was complete; but, though the aristocracy were defeated, they were not yet entirely broken down. By the instigation of government they had the meanness to secede from the General Committee, to disavow their acts, and even to publish in the papers that they did not wish to embarrass the government by advancing their claims of emancipation. It is difficult to conceive such a degree of political degradation; but what will not the tyranny of an execrable system produce in time? Sixty-eight gentlemen, individually of high spirit, were found who, publicly and in a body, deserted their party and their own just claims, and even sanctioned this pitiful desertion by the authority of their signatures. Such an effect had the operation of the penal laws in the minds of the Catholics of Ireland, as proud a race as any in all Europe! . . .

. . . The Catholic question was, at this period, beginning to attract the public notice; and the Belfast volunteers, on some public occasion, I know not precisely what, wished to come forward with a declaration in its favour. For this purpose Russell,[17] who by this time was entirely in their confidence, wrote to me to draw up and transmit to him such a declaration as I thought proper, which I accordingly did. A meeting of the corps was held in consequence, but an opposition unexpectedly arising to that part of the declarations which alluded directly to the Catholic claims, that passage

16. Founded in 1760, the General Committee of the Catholics of Ireland, or Catholic Committee, represented the upper ranks of Catholics who were seeking to reconcile themselves to the reality of the Protestant ascendancy while advancing their rights. Moderate objectives, such as challenging the power of the Protestant guilds, were succeeded by a more assertive declaration of political rights.

17. Thomas Russell (1767–1803), revolutionary and founding member of the United Irishmen. He was imprisoned between 1796 and 1802 and released on the understanding that he would live abroad. While in Paris, he met Robert Emmet, and they planned an unsuccessful rising in 1803, for which he was executed in October of that year.

was, for the sake of unanimity, withdrawn for the present, and the declaration then passed unanimously. Russell wrote me an account of all this, and it immediately set me on thinking more seriously than I had yet done upon the state of Ireland. I soon formed my theory, and on that theory I have unvaryingly acted ever since.

To subvert the tyranny of our execrable government, to break the connection with England, the never-failing source of all our political evils, and to assert the independence of my country—these were my objects. To unite the whole people of Ireland, to abolish the memory of all past dissensions, and to substitute the common name of Irishman in place of the denominations of Protestant, Catholic, and Dissenter—these were my means. To effectuate these great objects, I reviewed the three great sects. The Protestants I despaired of from the outset, for obvious reasons. Already in possession, by an unjust monopoly, of the whole power and patronage of the country, it was not to be supposed they would ever concur in measures, the certain tendency of which must be to lessen their influence as a party, how much soever the nation might gain. To the Catholics I thought it unnecessary to address myself, because, that, as no change could make their political situation worse, I reckoned upon their support to a certainty; besides, they had already begun to manifest a strong sense of their wrongs and oppressions; and, finally, I well knew that, however it might be disguised or suppressed, there existed in the breast of every Irish Catholic an inextirpable abhorrence of the English name and power. There remained only the Dissenters, whom I knew to be patriotic and enlightened; however, the recent events at Belfast had showed me that all prejudice was not yet entirely removed from their minds. I sat down accordingly, and wrote a pamphlet, addressed to the Dissenters, and which I entitled 'An Argument on behalf of the Catholics of Ireland',[18] the object of which was to convince them that they and the Catholics had but one common interest, and one common enemy; that the depression and slavery of Ireland was produced and perpetuated by the divisions existing between them, and that, consequently, to assert the independence of their country and their own individual liberties, it was necessary to forget all former feuds, to consolidate the entire strength of the whole nation, and to form for the future but one people. . . .

2. Edmund Burke, "A LETTER on the Affairs of Ireland, written in the year 1797" (1797)

Edmund Burke (1729–97) is best known today for his influence on modern conservative thought, most famously expressed in his Reflections on the French Revolution *(1790). He opposed the abstract principles and natural-rights theory underpinning the Revolution, and he argued for political reform in France founded on tradition, hierarchy, and evolutionary, organic change. Yet Burke is, in fact, a more complex intellectual and political figure than champions and detractors have often portrayed him. Described by Seamus Deane as "the most remarkable political philosopher of eighteenth-century Ireland" (1991, 807), he was sympathetic to the grievances of American colonists,*

---

18. *An Argument on Behalf of the Catholics of Ireland* (1791).

arguing that they retain the rights that their forebears had in Britain. He was critical of the corruption among British officials in the East India Company, advocating that independent commissioners supplant patronage in the governance of India. He was a critic of the Protestant ascendancy in Ireland, maintaining that the continued oppression of Catholics threatened the country's political stability.

Burke was born in Dublin. He was brought up as an Anglican, but both his mother and his wife were Catholic. His father was a Protestant, although he may have converted from Catholicism. A graduate of Trinity College, Dublin, Burke was known for his philosophical writings. A Philosophical Enquiry into the Origin of Our Ideas of the Sublime and Beautiful *(1757) was highly influential on discussions about aesthetics. However, it is as a politician and a political theorist that Burke became most important, first being elected to Parliament in 1765, a position that he held for most of the next thirty years.*

The text published here is a letter Burke wrote in the last year of his life, although whom it was written to has never been determined. It was chosen by Matthew Arnold, the Victorian poet and cultural critic, for a volume of Burke's writings on Ireland, Letters, Speeches and Tracts on Irish Affairs *(1881). Published at the height of the Land War, a tumultuous moment in Anglo-Irish relations, Arnold recognized the significance and value of Burke's "liberal" position: Burke was critical of the Protestant ascendancy; he championed the rights of Catholics; yet he supported the British connection, which he thought mutually beneficial to Britain and Ireland. Burke's views on Ireland were interwoven with his condemnation of the Jacobinism of the French Revolution. He regarded the Protestant ascendancy in Ireland as an illegitimate aristocracy without genuine roots in the country. In oppressing Catholics, it was driving them to support a revolution along French lines—a revolution that had ironically suppressed Catholicism. For Burke, Irish Catholics, if allowed to share in the fruits of the British constitution, would be loyal subjects and allies in the struggle against revolutionary France. Their Catholicism would act as a support for the landed civilization that he so much admired. The Protestant ascendancy, like the French revolutionaries, was the real usurper.*

Dear Sir,

In the reduced state of body, and in the dejected state of mind, in which I find myself at this very advanced period of my life, it is a great consolation to me to know that a cause I ever had so very near my heart is taken up by a man of your activity and talents.

It is very true that your late friend, my ever dear and honoured son,[19] was in the highest degree solicitous about the final event of a business which he also had pursued for a long time with infinite zeal and no small degree of success. It was not above half-an-hour before he left me for ever that he spoke with considerable earnestness on this

19. Richard Burke (1758–94), son of Edmund Burke, barrister and a member of the British Parliament. Like his father, he was an advocate of Catholic emancipation, and he became English agent of the Catholic Committee in 1791. Richard Burke was known for having neither ability nor tact, but, as Paul Bew (2007, 20) has argued, he "flailed mercilessly and bravely against a government which remained inert in the face of a major and pressing political problem."

very subject. If I had needed any incentives to do my best for freeing the body of my country from the grievances under which they labour, this alone would certainly call forth all my endeavours.

The person[20] who succeeded to the Government of Ireland about the time of that afflicting event had been all along of my sentiments and yours upon this subject; and far from needing to be stimulated by me, that incomparable person and those in whom he strictly confided even went before me in their resolution to pursue the great end of Government, the satisfaction and concord of the people, with whose welfare they were charged. I cannot bear to think on the causes by which this great plan of policy, so manifestly beneficial to both kingdoms, has been defeated. . . .

There is no hope for the body of the people of Ireland, as long as those who are in power with you shall make it the great object of their policy to propagate an opinion on this side of the water, that the mass of their countrymen are not be trusted by their Government; and that the only hold which England has upon Ireland consists in preserving a certain very small number of gentlemen in full possession of a monopoly of that kingdom. This system has disgusted many others besides Catholics and Dissenters. . . .

As every one knows, that a great part of the constitution of the Irish House of Commons was formed about the year 1614, expressly for bringing that House into a state of dependence; and that the new representative was that time seated and installed by force and violence; nothing can be more impolitic than for those who wish the House to stand on its present basis (as for one, I most sincerely do), to make it appear to have kept too much the principle of its first institution, and to continue to be as little a virtual, as it is an actual representative of the Commons. It is the *degeneracy* of such an institution, *so vicious in its principle*, that is to be wished for. If men have the real benefit of a *sympathetic* representation, none but those who are heated and intoxicated with theory will look for any other. This sort of representation, my dear sir, must wholly depend, not on the force with which it is upheld, but upon the *prudence* of those who have influence upon it. Indeed, without some such prudence in the use of authority, I do not know, at least in the present time, how any power can long continue.

If it be true that both parties are carrying things to extremities in different ways, the object which you and I have in common, that is to say, the union and concord of our country, *on the basis of the actual representation,* without risking those evils which any change in the form of our Legislature must inevitably bring on, can never be obtained. On the part of the Catholics (that is to say, of the body of the people of the kingdom) it is a terrible alternative, either to submit to the yoke of declared and insulting enemies; or to seek a remedy in plunging themselves into the horrors and crimes of that Jacobinism, which unfortunately is not disagreeable to the principles and inclinations of, I am afraid, the majority of what we call the Protestants of Ireland. The Protestant part of that kingdom is represented by the Government itself to be, by whole counties, in nothing less than open rebellion. I am sure that it is everywhere teeming with dangerous conspiracy.

I believe it will be found that though the principles of the Catholics, and the incessant endeavours of their clergy, have kept them from being generally infected with

20. William Wentworth-Fitzwilliam.

the systems of this time, yet, whenever their situation brings them nearer into contact with the Jacobin Protestants, they are more or less infected with their doctrines.

It is a matter for melancholy reflection; but I am fully convinced that many persons in Ireland would be glad that the Catholics should become more and more infected with the Jacobin madness, in order to furnish new arguments for fortifying them in their monopoly. On any other ground it is impossible to account for the late language of your men in power. If statesmen (let me suppose for argument), upon the most solid political principles, conceive themselves obliged to resist the wishes of the far more numerous, and, as things stand, not the worst part of the community, one would think they would naturally put their refusal as much as possible upon temporary grounds; and that they would act towards them in the most conciliatory manner, and would talk to them in the most gentle and soothing language; for refusal in itself is not a very gracious thing, and, unfortunately, men are very quickly irritated out of their principles. Nothing is more discouraging to the loyalty of any description of men than to represent to them that their humiliation and subjection make a principal part in the fundamental and invariable policy, which regards the conjunction of these two kingdoms. This is not the way to give them a warm interest in that conjunction.

My poor opinion is, that the closest connection between Great Britain and Ireland is essential to the wellbeing, I had almost said to the very being of the two kingdoms. For that purpose I humbly conceive, that the whole of the superior, and what I should call *imperial* politics ought to have its residence here; and that Ireland, locally, civilly, and commercially independent, ought politically to look up to Great Britain in all matters of peace or of war; in all those points to be guided by her: and, in a word, with her to live and die. At bottom, Ireland has no other choice—I mean no other rational choice.

I think, indeed, that Great Britain would be ruined by the separation of Ireland; but as there are degrees even in ruin, it would fall the most heavily on Ireland. By such a separation Ireland would be the most completely undone country in the world, the most wretched, the most distracted, and, in the end, the most desolate part of the habitable globe. Little do many people in Ireland consider how much of its prosperity has been owing to, and still depends upon, its intimate connection with this kingdom. But, more sensible of this great truth than perhaps any other man, I have never conceived, or can conceive, that the connection is strengthened by making the major part of the inhabitants of your country believe that their ease, and their satisfaction, and their equalisation with the rest of their fellow-subjects of Ireland, are things adverse to the principles of that connection; or that their subjection to a small monopolising junto, composed of one of the smallest of their own internal factions, is the very condition upon which the harmony of the two kingdoms essentially depends. . . .

As to a participation on the part of the Catholics in the privileges and capacities which are withheld, without meaning wholly to depreciate their importance, if I had the honour of being an Irish Catholic I should be content to expect satisfaction upon that subject with patience, until the minds of my adversaries, few but powerful, were come to a proper temper; because if the Catholics did enjoy without fraud, chicane, or partiality, some fair portion of those advantages which the law, even as now the law is, leaves open to them; and if the rod were not shaken over them at every turn, their present condition would be tolerable—as compared with their former condition it would be happy. But the most favourable laws can do very little towards the happiness of a people when the disposition of the ruling power is adverse to them. Men do not live upon blotted paper. The favourable or the hostile mind of the ruling power is of far more importance to mankind, for good or evil, than the black letter of any statute. Late Acts of Parliament,[21] whilst they fixed at least a temporary bar to the hopes and progress of the larger description of the nation, opened to them certain subordinate objects of equality; but it is impossible that the people should imagine that any fair measure of advantage is intended to them, when they hear the laws by which they were admitted to this limited qualification publicly reprobated as excessive and inconsiderate. They must think that there is a hankering after the old penal and persecuting code. . . .

All this is very unfortunate. I have the honour of an old acquaintance, and entertain, in common with you, a very high esteem for the few English persons who are concerned in the Government of Ireland; but I am not ignorant of the relation these transitory ministers bear to the more settled Irish part of your Administration. It is a delicate topic, upon which I wish to say but little; though my reflections upon it are many and serious. There is a great cry against English influence. I am quite sure that it is Irish influence that dreads the English habits.

Great disorders have long prevailed in Ireland. It is not long since that the Catholics were the suffering party from those disorders. I am sure they were not protected as the case required. Their sufferings became a matter of discussion in Parliament. It produced the most infuriated declamation against them that I have ever read.[22] An inquiry was moved into the facts. The declamation was at least tolerated, if not approved. The inquiry was absolutely rejected. In that case what is left for those who are abandoned by Government but to join with the persons who are capable of injuring them or protecting them, as they oppose or concur in their designs? This will produce a very fatal kind of union amongst the people, but it is a union which an unequal administration of justice tends necessarily to produce.

If anything could astonish one at this time, it is the war that the rulers in Ireland think it proper to carry on against the person whom they call the pope, and against all his adherents, whenever they think they have the power of manifesting their hostility. Without in the least derogating from the talents of your theological politicians, or from the military abilities of your commanders (who act on the same principles) in Ireland, and without derogating from the zeal of either, it appears to me that the Protestant Directory of Paris,[23] as statesmen, and the Protestant hero, [Napoleon] Bonaparte, as a general, have done more to destroy the said pope and all his adherents, in all their capacities, than the junto in Ireland have ever been able to effect. You must submit

---

21. Burke is perhaps referring to relief acts that repealed the penal laws, with the exception of the right to sit in Parliament, the most recent having been in 1793.

22. According to R. B. McDowell (1991), Burke is referring to debates surrounding the Indemnity Bill of 1796, a bill that absolved magistrates who in seeking to preserve the peace had gone beyond the limits of the law.

23. The French revolutionary government (1795–99).

your *fasces*[24] to theirs, and at best be contented to follow with songs of gratulation, or invectives, according to your humour, the triumphal car of those great conquerors. Had that true Protestant *Hoche*,[25] with an army not infected with the slightest tincture of Popery,[26] made good his landing in Ireland, he would have saved you from a great deal of the trouble which is taken to keep under a description of your fellow-citizens, obnoxious to you from their religion. It would not have a month's existence, supposing his success. This is the alliance which, under the appearance of hostility, we act as if we wished to promote. All is well, provided we are safe from Popery. . . .

. . . Let every man be as pious as he pleases, and in the way that he pleases; but it is agreeable neither to piety nor to policy to give exclusively all manner of civil privileges and advantages to a *negative* religion,—such is the Protestant without a certain creed—and at the same time to deny those privileges to men whom we know to agree to an iota in every one *positive* doctrine, which all of us who profess the religion authoritatively taught in England hold ourselves, according to our faculties, bound to believe. The Catholics of Ireland (as I have said) have the whole of our *positive* religion; our difference is only a negation of certain tenets of theirs. If we strip ourselves of *that* part of Catholicism we abjure Christianity. If we drive them from that holding, without engaging them in some other positive religion (which you know by our qualifying laws we do not), what do we better than to hold out to them terrors on the one side, and bounties on the other, in favour of that which, for anything we know to the contrary, may be pure Atheism?

You are well aware that when a man renounces the Roman religion there is no civil inconvenience or incapacity whatsoever which shall hinder him from joining any new or old sect of Dissenters, or of forming a sect of his own invention upon the most antichristian principles. Let Mr. Thomas Paine[27] obtain a pardon (as on change of Ministry he may), there is nothing to hinder him from setting up a church of his own in the very midst of you. He is a natural-born British subject. His French citizenship does not disqualify him, at least upon a peace. This Protestant Apostle is as much above all suspicion of Popery as the greatest and most zealous of your Sanhedrim[28] in Ireland can possibly be. On purchasing a qualification (which his friends of the Directory are not so poor as to be unable to effect) he may sit in Parliament; and there is no doubt that there is not one of your tests against Popery that he will not take as fairly and as much *ex animo*[29] as the best of your zealous statesmen. I push this point

---

24. A symbol of power and authority (Latin).

25. Lazare Hoche (1768–97), general in the French Revolutionary Army, who in 1796 led a naval invasion of Ireland in support of an uprising by the United Irishmen. Bad weather made it impossible for the French fleet to land.

26. A derogatory term describing the views of a Roman Catholic.

27. Thomas Paine (1737–1809), revolutionary writer and political activist who supported and took part in the American and French revolutions. His *Rights of Man* was a wide-ranging critique of Burke's *Reflections on the Revolution in France*. He was elected to the French National Convention in 1792.

28. The supreme court of ancient Israel.

29. From the heart (Latin).

no farther, and only adduce this example (a pretty strong one, and fully in point) to show what I take to be the madness and folly of driving men, under the existing circumstances, from any *positive* religion whatever into the irreligion of the times and its sure concomitant principles of anarchy.

When religion is brought into a question of civil and political arrangement, it must be considered more politically than theologically, at least by us, who are nothing more than mere laymen. In that light the case of the Catholics of Ireland is peculiarly hard, whether they be laity or clergy. If any of them take part, like the gentleman you mention, with some of the most accredited Protestants of the country, in projects, which cannot be more abhorrent to your nature and disposition than they are to mine; in that case, however few these Catholic factions, who are united with factious Protestants, may be—(and very few they are now, whatever shortly they may become)—on their account the whole body is considered as of suspected fidelity to the Crown, and as wholly undeserving of its favour. But if, on the contrary, in those districts of the kingdom where their numbers are the greatest, where they make, in a manner, the whole body of the people (as, out of cities, in three-fourths of the kingdom they do), these Catholics show every mark of loyalty and zeal in support of the Government, which at best looks on them with an evil eye; then their very loyalty is turned against their claims. They are represented as a contented and happy people; and that it is unnecessary to do anything more in their favour. Thus the factious disposition of a few among the Catholics, and the loyalty of the whole mass, are equally assigned as reasons for not putting them on a *par* with those Protestants, who are asserted by the Government itself, which frowns upon Papists, to be in a state of nothing short of actual rebellion, and in a strong disposition to make common cause with the worst foreign enemy that these countries have ever had to deal with. What in the end can come of all this?

As to the Irish Catholic Clergy, their condition is likewise most critical: if they endeavour by their influence to keep a dissatisfied laity in quiet, they are in danger of losing the little credit they possess, by being considered as the instruments of a Government adverse to the civil interests of their flock. If they let things take their course, they will be represented as colluding with sedition, or at least tacitly encouraging it. If they remonstrate against persecution, they propagate rebellion. Whilst Government publicly avows hostility to that people, as a part of a regular system, there is no road they can take, which does not lead to their ruin.

If nothing can be done on your side of the water, I promise you that nothing will be done here. Whether in reality or only in appearance, I cannot positively determine; but you will be left to yourselves by the ruling powers here. It is thus ostensibly and aboveboard; and in part, I believe, the disposition is real. As to the people at large in this country, I am sure they have no disposition to intermeddle in your affairs. They mean you no ill whatever; and they are too ignorant of the state of your affairs to be able to do you any good. Whatever opinion they have on your subject is very faint and indistinct; and if there is anything like a formed notion, even that amounts to no more than a sort of humming, that remains on their ears, of the burthen of the old song about Popery. Poor souls, they are to be pitied, who think of nothing but dangers long passed by; and but little of the perils that actually surround them. . . .

I have the honour to be, etc.

3. De Latocnaye, Selections from *A Frenchman's Walk through Ireland, 1796–97* (1797)

Jacques Louis de Bourgenet, Chevalier de Latocnaye (1767–1823), was a French royalist officer from an aristocratic background in Brittany. Forced to leave revolutionary France, de Latocnaye immigrated to Britain in 1792, not knowing any English. He subsequently traveled throughout the British Isles, publishing two books on his experiences, A Walk through Great Britain *(1797) and* A Frenchman's Walk through Ireland. *Based on travels mostly done on foot, de Latocnaye's book on Ireland captures the mood of the country in the midst of political turmoil. Yet it suggests an outsider's and an aristocratic royalist's perspective.*

. . . This country[30] is entirely occupied in the manufacture of linen, but the late troubles have made trade to languish. The mills, however, are still going, and it is hoped that a year of peace will restore order and prosperity. Military law was rigorously enforced here on the inhabitants; they were not permitted to have lights in their houses after nine o'clock, and any person found in the streets after that hour was in danger of being arrested. A fair was held during the time I stayed in this little town, and it passed over quite peacefully; the soldiers promenaded through the marketplace and obliged women who wore anything green, ribbon or otherwise, to take it off.[31] Had one-fourth of the precaution taken here been observed in France, there would certainly have been no Revolution. I was much struck here by the thought of the different results which different characters in government may produce. It is remarkable how in France a weak government and foolish ministers have led a people entirely Royalist to slay a King they loved, and whose good qualities they respected, and to destroy a flourishing monarchy for whose prosperity they had been enthusiastic; while here, surrounded by enemies, a vigorous government in Ireland has been able to repress, and hold in the path of duty, a people discontented and seduced by the success of the French innovations.

The boldness of the United Irishmen increased each day as long as the Government did not interfere; many who had joined them had done so out of fear, and there were with them a number of weak, undecided people ready to range themselves on the winning side, and so immediately on the Government's determination to act vigorously, it was only necessary to let the soldiers appear upon the scene, and the difficulties disappeared.

The poor peasant on this occasion, as in so many others, was the dupe of rogues, who put him in the front, and were very careful themselves to stay behind the curtain. The troops went through the country, burning the houses of those who were suspected of having taken the 'Union oath', or of having arms, and on many occasions they acted with great severity.

---

30. By country, de Latocnaye does not mean Ireland; he means the region in which he is traveling: Ulster, one of the four provinces of Ireland.
31. The green ribbon was the distinction adopted by the United Irishmen. [Author's note.]

On the way to Armagh I passed through a superb country; there is a charming valley, and well-wooded, near Tandragee. Between this town and Armagh I met a company of Orangemen, as they are called, wearing orange cockades, and some of them having ties of the same colour. The peasantry seemed very much afraid of them. I went into one or two cabins to rest myself, and was offered, certainly, hospitality in the ordinary way, but it did not seem to be with the same air as before, and at last, near the town, a good woman said to me, 'You seem to have come from far, my dear Sir, I hope that your umbrella or the string of it will not bring you into trouble'. I laughed at the good woman's fears, but, on reflection, I felt that since she had re-marked that my umbrella was greenish, and the cord of a bright green, soldiers might make the same observation, and that in any case it would be very disagreeable to have any trouble over such a silly thing, and I cut the green cord off my umbrella. . . .

Newry is situated among high mountains, and nevertheless enjoys all the advan-tages of the plain. The sea is only at three or four miles distance, and vessels reach the town easily by the river mouth and the canal, which is continued from here to Lough Neagh. There is here a very considerable trade in linen, but the late troubles have reduced it.

The divisions here have very little connection with those of Armagh; they were more like those of Belfast, being entirely political. Some time before my arrival, the military had used severe measures, and once, unfortunately, on false information and inconsiderately. On this occasion eighteen men were killed. Some story-tellers came to the town saying that a troop of the United Irishmen were encamped in a little wood, that they had committed various depredations, and had attacked the militia. On this information the troops took horse, and going to the place indicated, sacked several houses and shot a few unfortunates, who fled before them. The gathering in the wood turned out to be merely a number of people who from fear had there sought shelter. They were neither armed nor provisioned, but before this was discov-ered eighteen were shot.

The cavalry regiment then at Newry was Welsh, a newly raised troop. When they came to Ireland they came with all the English prejudices, expecting to find the Irish to be half-savages, in complete insurrection. In consequence, they disembarked with the idea that they were in an enemy's country, and at the commencement of their stay made themselves much to be feared by the inhabitants. With all that, it is to be admitted that the terror which they inspired was perhaps in many cases salutary, and I have no doubt that the inhabitants of Newry for a long time will remember the ancient *Bretons*.[32] . . .

I crossed the narrow chain of mountains near Newry, and perceived with sorrow that the inhabitants had there suffered much more than their neighbours. I saw many houses which had been burned in order to force the owner to give up his arms. The peasant conducted himself in a peculiar way on these occasions. First of all he would deny that he had any; then he would be threatened with the burning of his house and unshrinkingly he would stand by to see the act performed; but when it was really

32. Both the Bretons from northwestern France and the Welsh spoke Celtic languages. Here, the Welsh are portrayed as having been an offshoot of the Bretons.

burned his courage would abandon him, and it has happened more than once that he has gone quietly to unearth from the ruin a gun, which he would hand over to the magistrates. One would think it would have paid him much better to have found it before the fire.

It cannot but be true, however, that many innocent people have suffered through false information supplied by rascally enemies; these destructions of the property of the innocent are very regrettable, but it is absolutely impossible that there should not be some such cases in such time. It seemed to me that the peasant made the difficulty about giving up arms simply because he feared to lose their intrinsic value. If they had offered to pay him even half the cost, there would have been no trouble.

4. William Pitt, Selections from *Speech of the Right Honourable William Pitt in the House of Commons, Thursday, January 31, 1799* (1799)

For some observers, the 1798 rebellion represented the end of a phase rather than the beginning: it was an event that was unlikely to be repeated and, in any case, had never seriously threatened the established order. The British prime minister, William Pitt the Younger (1759–1806), thought otherwise, as is demonstrated in his 1799 speech to the House of Commons. Following Edmund Burke, Pitt regarded Catholic emancipation as pivotal to Ireland's political stability. He also believed that as long as Ireland was autonomous, it risked a French invasion. Convinced that the status quo was simultaneously incapable of political reform or producing national security, he introduced a bill for a legislative union, which after prolonged debate and the dispensing of bribery and patronage passed both the British and Irish Parliaments in 1800. To attain the support of those antagonistic to emancipation, Pitt excluded it from the bill. He simultaneously promised Roman Catholics that the British Parliament of the new United Kingdom would enact it. However, George III opposed emancipation, as he believed it violated his coronation oath, which bound him to maintain "the true profession of the gospel and the Protestant reformed religion established by law." Thus, while the Union came into being, Catholic emancipation was not part of it. Pitt resigned in protest in February 1801.

. . . This Country is at this time engaged in the most important, and momentous conflict that ever occurred in the History of the World; a conflict in which Great Britain is distinguished for having made the only manly successful stand against the common enemies of civilized society. We see the point in which that Enemy think us the most assailable. Are we not then bound in policy and prudence, to strengthen that vulnerable point, involved as we are in a contest of Liberty against Despotism, of Property against Plunder and Rapine, of Religion and Order against Impiety and Anarchy? There was a time when this would have been termed declamation; but, unfortunately, long and bitter experience has taught us to feel that it is only the feeble and imperfect representation of those calamities (the result of French Principles and French Arms) which are attested by the wounds of a bleeding world.

Is there a man who does not admit the importance of a measure which, at such a crisis, may augment the strength of the Empire, and thereby ensure its safety? Would not that benefit to Ireland be of itself so solid, so inestimable, that, in comparison with it, all Commercial Interests, and the preservation of local habits and manners, would be trifling, even if they were endangered by the present measure; which they undoubtedly are not? The people of Ireland are proud, I believe, of being associated with us in the great contest in which we are engaged, and must feel the advantage of augmenting the general force of the Empire. That the present measure is calculated to produce that effect, is a proposition which I think cannot be disputed. There is not in any Court of Europe a Statesman so ill informed as not to know, that the general power of the Empire would be increased to a very great extent indeed, by such a consolidation of the strength of the two kingdoms. . . .

But it is not merely in this general view, that I think the Question ought to be considered.—We ought to look to it with a view peculiarly to the permanent Interest and security of Ireland. When that Country was threatened with the double danger of hostile attacks by Enemies without, and of Treason within,[33] from what quarter did she derive the means of her deliverance? from the Naval Force of Great Britain, from the voluntary exertions of her Military of every description, not called for by Law, and from her pecuniary resources, added to the loyalty and energy of the Inhabitants of Ireland itself; of which it is impossible to speak with too much praise, and which shews[34] how well they deserve to be called the Brethren of Britons. Their own courage might, perhaps have ultimately succeeded, in repelling the dangers by which they were threatened, but it would have been after a long contest, and after having waded through seas of blood. Are we sure that the same ready and effectual assistance which we have happily afforded, on the present occasion, will be always equally within our power? Great Britain has always felt a common interest in the safety of Ireland; but that common interest was never so obvious and urgent as when the Common Enemy made her attack upon Great Britain, through the medium of Ireland, and when their attack upon Ireland went to deprive her of her Connection with Great Britain, and to substitute in stead, the new Government of the French Republic. When that danger threatened Ireland, the purse of Great Britain was open for the wants of Ireland, as for the necessities of England.

I do not, Sir, state these circumstances, as upbraiding Ireland for the benefits we have conferred; far from it; but I state them with pleasure, as shewing[35] the friendship and good will with which this Country has acted towards her. But if struggles of this sort may and must return again, if the worst dangers are those which are yet to come, dangers which may be greater from being more disguised—if those situations may arise when the same means of relief are not in our power, what is the remedy that reason and policy point out? It is to identity them with us—it is to make them part of the same Community, by giving them a full share of those accumulated blessings which are diffused throughout Great Britain; it is, in a word, by giving them a full participation of the Wealth, the Powers and the Glory of the British Empire. If then this Measure

33. Pitt is referring to the combined threat of the French invasion of Ireland and the uprising of the United Irishmen.

34. Shews.

35. Showing.

comes recommended not only by the obvious defects of the system which now exists, but that it has also the pre-eminent recommendation of increasing the general power of the Empire, and of guarding against future danger from the Common Enemy, we are next to consider it as to its effects upon the internal condition of Ireland. . . .

. . . Until the Kingdoms are united, any attempt to make regulations here for the internal state of Ireland must certainly be a violation of her Independence. But feeling as I do, for their interests and their welfare, I cannot be inattentive to the events that are passing before me; I must therefore repeat, that whoever looks at the circumstances to which I have alluded—whoever considers that the Enemy have shewn by their conduct, that they considered Ireland as the weakest and most vulnerable part of the Empire; whoever reflects upon those dreadful and inexcusable cruelties instigated by the Enemies of both Countries, and upon those lamentable severities by which the exertions for the defence of Ireland were unhappily, but unavoidably, attended, and the necessity of which is itself one great aggravation of the Crimes and Treasons which led to them, must feel that, as it now stands composed, in the hostile division of its Sects, in the animosities existing between ancient Settlers and original Inhabitants, in the ignorance and want of Civilization, which marks that Country more than almost any other Country in Europe, in the unfortunate prevalence of Jacobin Principles, arising from these causes, and augmenting their malignity, and which have produced that distressed state which we now deplore; every one, I say, who reflects upon these circumstances, must agree with me in thinking, that there is no cure but in the formation of a General Imperial Legislature, free alike from terror and from resentment, removed from the danger and agitation, and uninflamed by the prejudices and passions of that distracted Country.

I know that it is impossible, if we wish to consider this subject properly, to consider it in any other point of view than as it affects the Empire in general. I know that the interests of the two Countries must be taken together, and that a man cannot speak as a true Englishman, unless he speaks as a true Irishman, nor as a true Irishman, unless he speaks as a true Englishman: But if it was possible to separate them, and I could consider myself as addressing you, not as interested for the Empire at large, but for Ireland alone, I should say, that it would be indispensably necessary, for the sake of that Country, to compose its present distractions, by the adoption of another system: I should say, that the establishment of an Imperial Legislature was the only means of healing its wounds and of restoring it to tranquility. I must here take the liberty of alluding to some topics which were touched upon during the discussion of the former night.

Among the great and known defects of Ireland, one of the most prominent features is, its want of industry and a capital; how are those wants to be supplied, but by blending more closely with Ireland, the industry and the capital of this Country. But, above all, in the great leading distinctions between the People of Ireland, I mean their religious distinctions, what is their situation? The Protestant feels that the claims of the Catholics threaten the existence of the Protestant ascendancy; while, on the other hand, the great body of Catholics feel the establishment of the National Church,[36] and their exclusion from the exercise of certain rights and privileges, a grievance. Between the two, it

36. The Church of Ireland.

becomes a matter of difficulty in the minds of many persons, whether it would be better to listen only to the fears of the former, or to grant the claims of the latter.

I am well aware that the subject of religious distinction is a dangerous and delicate topic, especially when applied to a country such as Ireland; the situation of which is different in this respect from that of every other. Where the established religion of the State is the same as the general religion of the Empire, and where the property of the Country is in the hands of a comparatively small number of persons professing that established religion, while the religion of a great majority of the people is different, it is not easy to say, on general principles, what system of Church Establishments in such a Country would be free from difficulty and inconvenience. By many I know it will be contended, that the religion professed by a majority of the people, would at least be entitled to an equality of Privileges. I have heard such an argument urged in this House; but those who apply it without qualification to the case of Ireland, forget surely the principles on which English Interest and English Connection has been established in that Country, and on which its present Legislature is formed. No man can say, that, in the present state of things, and while Ireland remains a separate kingdom, full concessions could be made to the Catholics, without endangering the State, and shaking the Constitution of Ireland to its centre.

On the other hand, without anticipating the discussion, or the propriety of agitating the question, or saying how soon or how late it may be fit to discuss it; two propositions are indisputable: First, When the conduct of the Catholics shall be such as to make it safe for the Government to admit them to the participation of the privileges granted to those of the Established Religion, and when the temper of the times shall be favourable to such a measure. When these events take place, it is obvious that such a question may be agitated in an United, Imperial Parliament, with much greater safety, than it could be in a separate Legislature. In the second place, I think it certain that, even for whatever period it may be thought necessary, after the Union, to withhold from the Catholics the enjoyment of those advantages, many of the objections which at present arise out of their situation would be removed, if the Protestant legislature were no longer separate and local, but general and Imperial; and the Catholics themselves would at once feel a mitigation of the most goading and irritating of their present causes of complaint.

How far, in addition to this great and leading consideration, it may also be wise and practicable to accompany the measure by some mode of relieving the lower orders from the pressure of Tithes, which in many instances operate at present as a great practical evil, or to make under proper Regulations, and without breaking in on the security of the present Protestant Establishment an effectual and adequate provision for the Catholic Clergy, it is not now necessary to discuss. It is sufficient to say, that these and all other subordinate points connected with the same subject, are more likely to be permanently and satisfactorily settled by an United Legislature, than by any local arrangements. On these grounds I contend, that with a view to providing an effectual remedy for the distractions which have unhappily prevailed in Ireland, with a view of removing those causes which have endangered, and still endanger its security, the measure which I am now proposing promises to be more effectual than any other which can be devised, and on these grounds alone, if there existed no other, I should feel it my duty to submit it to the House. . . .

5. Robert Emmet, "Speech from the Dock" (1803)

While the 1798 rebellion represented the most famous historical episode involving the United Irishmen, the group's last significant effort to overthrow the existing order was in 1803, led by Robert Emmet (1778–1803). From a well-connected Irish Protestant family that was active in the Irish patriot movement, Emmet attended Trinity College, Dublin. He was a leading debater in the College Historical Society and secretary of the clandestine United Irish Committee before being expelled from the university for his subversive activities. Like Wolfe Tone before him, Emmet traveled to France to seek military aid to help support a rebellion. He returned in 1802 with an ill-formed plan. He and his associates would seize Dublin Castle and other key sites in the capital, which would spark a rebellion that would spread to the entire country. The rebellion took place on July 23, 1803. French aid never materialized; too many of the counted-on militants never showed up; some of those who did were drunk; and the attack on Dublin Castle was quickly abandoned. However, about three hundred men took control of two streets for a couple of hours, and around fifty people died, including Lord Chief Justice Kilwarden, who was killed along with his nephew by militants with pikes. The uprising was never a serious threat, but the government, having been caught off-guard, reacted strongly, executing Emmet along with twenty-one others.

Emmet achieved in death what he had failed to achieve in life: his eloquent and inspiring speech from the dock, following his conviction in September 1803, led to a prominent place in the pantheon of fallen Irish nationalist heroes. The existing text was created from accounts of witnesses, and it is plausible that it was embellished in the process. However, the precise words are less important than the impact it had on subsequent perceptions of Emmet. In 1896, the separatist paper Shan Van Vocht *described him as "the most beloved of our patriot-martyrs" (quoted in English 2006, 121).*

I am asked what I have to say why sentence of death should not be pronounced on me, according to law. I have nothing to say that can alter your pre-determination, nor that it will become me to say, with any view to the mitigation of that sentence which you are to pronounce and I must abide by. But I have that to say which interests me more than life and which you have laboured to destroy. I have much to say why my reputation should be rescued from the load of false accusation and calumny which has been cast upon it. I do not imagine that, seated where you are, your minds can be so free from prejudice as to receive the least impression from what I am going to utter. I have no hope that I can anchor my character in the breast of a court constituted and trammeled as this is.

I only wish, and that is the utmost that I can expect, that your lordships may suffer it to float down your memories untainted by the foul breath of prejudice, until it finds some more hospitable harbour to shelter it from the storms by which it is buffeted. Were I only to suffer death, after being adjudged guilty by your tribunal, I should bow in silence, and meet the fate that awaits me without a murmur; but the sentence of the law which delivers my body to the executioner will, through the ministry of the law, labour in its own vindication, to consign my character to obloquy; for there must be guilt somewhere, whether in the sentence of the court or in the catastrophe—time must determine. A man in my situation has not only to encounter the difficulties of fortune, and the force of power over minds which it has corrupted or subjugated, but the difficulties of established prejudice. The man dies, but his memory lives. That mine may not perish, that it may live in the respect of my countrymen, I seize upon this opportunity to vindicate myself from some of the charges alleged against me. When my spirit shall be wafted to a more friendly port, when my shade shall have joined the bands of those martyred heroes who have shed their blood on the scaffold and in the field in defense of their country and of virtue, this is my hope: I wish that my memory and my name may animate those who survive me, while I look down with complacency on the destruction of that perfidious government which upholds its domination by blasphemy of the Most High; which displays its power over man as over the beasts of the forest; which sets man upon his brother, and lifts his hand in the Name of God, against the throat of his fellow who believes or doubts a little more or a little less than the government standard, a government which is steeled to barbarity by the cries of the orphans and the tears of the widows it has made.

Here Lord Norbury[37] *interrupted Emmet, saying that 'the mean and wicked enthusiasts who felt as he did, were not equal to the accomplishment of their wild designs'.*

I appeal to the immaculate God, I swear by the Throne of Heaven, before which I must shortly appear, by the blood of the murdered patriots who have gone before me, that my conduct has been, through all this peril, and through all my purposes, governed only by the conviction which I have uttered, and by no other view than that of the emancipation of my country from the super-inhuman oppression under which she has so long and too patiently travailed; and I confidently hope that, wild and chimerical as it may appear, there is still union and strength in Ireland to accomplish this noblest of enterprises. Of this I speak with confidence, with intimate knowledge, and with the consolation that appertains to that confidence. Think not, my lords, I say this for the petty gratification of giving you a transitory uneasiness. A man who never yet raised his voice to assert a lie will not hazard his character with posterity by asserting a falsehood on a subject so important to his country, and on an occasion like this. Yes, my lords, a man who does not wish to have his epitaph written until his country is liberated, will not leave a weapon in the power of envy, or a pretense to impeach the probity which he means to preserve, even in the grave to which tyranny consigns him.

Here he was again interrupted by Norbury.

Again I say that what I have spoken was not intended for your lordship, whose situation I commiserate rather than envy—my expressions were for my countrymen. If there is a true Irishman present, let my last words cheer him in the hour of his affliction.

Here he was again interrupted. Lord Norbury said he did not sit there to hear treason.

---

37. John Toler (1745–1831), 1st Earl of Norbury, chief justice of the Irish Common Pleas (1800–27). He was a fierce defender of the Protestant ascendancy, and his appointment as chief justice was controversial, as his knowledge of the law was scanty. Because of his callous treatment toward defendants in his courts who faced the death sentence, he was known as the "hanging judge." The judge at Emmet's trial, he is remembered for his abuse of Emmet during the proceedings.

I have always understood it to be the duty of a judge, when a prisoner has been convicted, to pronounce the sentence of the law. I have also understood that judges sometimes think it their duty to hear with patience, and to speak with humanity; to exhort the victim of the laws, and to offer, with tender benignity, their opinions of the motives by which he was actuated in the crime of which he was adjudged guilty. That a judge has thought it his duty so to have done, I have no doubt; but where is the boasted freedom of your institutions, where is the vaunted impartiality, clemency and mildness of your courts of justice if an unfortunate prisoner, whom your policy and not justice is about to deliver into the hands of the executioner, is not suffered to explain his motives sincerely and truly, and to vindicate the principles by which he was actuated? My lord, it may be a part of the system of angry justice to bow a man's mind by humiliation to the purposed ignominy of the scaffold; but worse to me than the purposed shame of the scaffold's terrors would be the shame of such foul and unfounded imputations as have been laid against me in this court. You, my lord, are a judge; I am the supposed culprit. I am a man; you are a man also. By a revolution of power we might exchange places? Though we never could change characters. If I stand at the bar of this court and dare not vindicate my character, what a farce is your justice! If I stand at this bar and dare not vindicate my character, how dare you calumniate it? Does the sentence of death, which your unhallowed policy inflicts on my body, condemn my tongue to silence and my reputation to reproach? Your executioner may abridge the period of my existence; but while I exist I shall not forebear to vindicate my character and motives from your aspersion; and as a man to whom fame is dearer than life, I will make the last use of that life in doing justice to that reputation which is to live after me, and which is the only legacy I can leave to those I honour and love and for whom I am proud to perish. As men, my lords, we must appear on the great day at one common tribunal; and it will then remain for the Searcher of all hearts to show a collective universe, who was engaged in the most virtuous actions or swayed by the purest motives, my country's oppressor, or—

Here he was interrupted and told to listen to the sentence of the court.

My lords, will a dying man be denied the legal privilege of exculpating himself in the eyes of the community from an undeserved reproach, thrown upon him during his trial, by charging him with ambition and attempting to cast away for paltry consideration the liberties of his country? Why did your lordships insult me? Or rather, why insult justice, in demanding of me why sentence of death should not be pronounced against me? I know my lords, that form prescribes that you should ask the question, the form also presents the right of answering. This, no doubt, may be dispensed with, and so might the whole ceremony of the trial, since sentence was already pronounced at the Castle[38] before the jury was impaneled. Your lordships are but the priests of the oracle, and I insist on the whole of the forms.

I am charged with being an emissary of France. An emissary of France! And for what end? It is alleged that I wished to sell the independence of my country. And for what end? Was this the object of my ambition? And is this the mode by which a

38. Dublin Castle.

tribunal of justice reconciles contradiction? No, I am no emissary; and my ambition was to hold a place among the deliverers of my country, not in power nor in profit, but in the glory of the achievement. Sell my country's independence to France! And for what? Was it a change of masters? No, but for my ambition. O, my country, was it a personal ambition that could influence me? Had it been the soul of my actions, could I not by my education and fortune, by the rank and consideration of my family, have placed myself amongst the proudest of your oppressors. My country was my idol. To it I sacrificed every selfish, every endearing sentiment, and for it I now offer up myself, O God! No, my lords; I acted as an Irishman, determined on delivering my country from the yoke of a foreign and unrelenting tyranny and the more galling yoke of a domestic faction, which is its joint partner and perpetrator in the patricide,[39] from the ignominy existing with an exterior of splendour and a conscious depravity. It was the wish of my heart to extricate my country from this doubly riveted despotism; I wished to place her independence beyond the reach of any power on earth. I wished to exalt her to that proud station in the world. Connection with France was, indeed, intended, but only as far as mutual interest would sanction or require. Were the French to assume any authority inconsistent with the purest independence, it would be the signal for their destruction. We sought their aid and we sought it as we had assurance we should obtain it as auxiliaries in war and allies in peace. Were the French to come as invaders or enemies uninvited by the wishes of the people, I should oppose them to the utmost of my strength. Yes, my countrymen, I should advise you to meet them upon the beach with a sword in one hand and a torch in the other. I would meet them with all the destructive fury of war. I would animate my countrymen to immolate them in their boats, before they had contaminated the soil of my country. If they succeeded in landing, and if forced to retire before superior discipline, I would dispute every inch of the ground, burn every blade of grass, and the last entrenchment of liberty should be my grave. What I could not do myself, if I should fall, I should leave as a last charge to my countrymen to accomplish; because I should feel conscious that life, any more than death, is unprofitable when a foreign nation holds my country in subjection. But it was not as an enemy that the soldiers of France were to land. I looked, indeed, for the assistance of France; but I wished to prove to France and to the world that Irish men deserved to be assisted; that they were indignant at slavery, and ready to assert the independence and liberty of their country. I wished to procure for my country the guarantee which Washington procured for America; to procure an aid which, by its example would be as important as its valour disciplined, gallant, pregnant with science and experience, that of a people who would perceive the good and polish the rough points of our character. They would come to us as strangers and leave us as friends, after sharing in our perils and elevating our destiny. These were my objects; not to receive new task-masters, but to expel old tyrants. It was for these ends I sought aid from France; because France, even as an enemy, could not be more implacable than the enemy already in the bosom of my country.

Here he was interrupted by the court.

39. The murder of one's father. Here Emmet is suggesting that the Protestant ascendancy is guilty of the murder of its own nationality or past.

I have been charged with that importance in the emancipation of my country as to be considered the keystone of the combination of Irishmen; or, as your lordships expressed it, 'the life and blood of the conspiracy'. You do me honour over much; you have given to the subaltern all the credit of a superior. There are men engaged in this conspiracy who are not only superior to me, but even to your own conceptions of yourself, my lord; men before the splendour of whose genius and virtues I should bow with respectful deference and who would think themselves disgraced by shaking your blood-stained hand.

Here he was interrupted.

What! my lord, shall you tell me on the passage to the scaffold, which that tyranny (of which you are only the intermediary executioner) has erected for my murder, that I am accountable for all the blood that has been shed and will be shed in this struggle of the oppressed against the oppressor; shall thou tell me this, and must I be so very a slave as not to repel it? I do not fear to approach the Omnipotent Judge to answer for the conduct of my whole life; and am I to be appalled and falsified by a mere remnant of mortality here? By you, too, although if it were possible to collect all the innocent blood that you have shed in your unhallowed ministry in one great reservoir, your lordship might swim in it.

Here the judge interrupted.

Let no man dare, when I am dead, to charge me with dishonour; let no man taint my memory by believing that I could have engaged in any cause but that of my country's liberty and independence; or that I could have become the pliant minion of power in the oppression of my country. The Proclamation of the Provisional Government[40] speaks for our views; no inference can be tortured from it to countenance barbarity or debasement at home, or subjection, humiliation or treachery from abroad. I would not have submitted to a foreign oppressor, for the same reason that I would resist the foreign and domestic oppressor. In the dignity of freedom I would have fought upon the threshold of my country, and its enemy would enter only by passing over the lifeless corpse. And am I who lived but for my country, and have subjected myself to the dangers of the jealous and watchful oppressor, and the bondage of the grave, only to give my countrymen their rights and my country her independence, am I to be loaded with calumny and not suffered to resent it? No; God forbid!

Here Norbury told the prisoner that his sentiments and language disgraced his family and education, but more particularly his father, Dr. Robert Emmet,[41] who was a man that would, if alive, discountenance such opinions. To which Emmet replied:

If the spirit of the illustrious dead participate in the concerns and cares of those who were dear to them in this transitory life, O, ever dear and venerated shade of my departed father, look down with scrutiny upon the conduct of your suffering son

---

40. A proclamation issued by Emmet and his supporters on July 23, 1803, establishing a provisional government for an Irish republic.

41. Dr. Robert Emmet (1729–1802), born in Tipperary, practiced medicine in Cork, was appointed state physician for Ireland in 1770, and was governor of Swift's Hospital for the Insane. Dr. Emmet is known to have supported the grievances of American colonists against Britain and to have advocated reform of the Irish Parliament.

and see if I have even for a moment, deviated from those principles of morality and patriotism which it was your care to instill into my youthful mind, and for which I am now about to offer up my life! My lords, you are impatient for the sacrifice. The blood which you seek is not congealed by the artificial terrors which surround your victim; it circulates warm and unruffled through the channels which God created for noble purpose, but which you are now bent to destroy for purposes so grievous that they cry to heaven. Be yet patient! I have but a few more words to say. I am going to go to my cold and silent grave. My lamp of life is nearly extinguished. My race is run. The grave opens to receive me and I sink into its bosom. I have but one request to ask at my departure from this world. It is the charity of its silence. Let no man write my epitaph; for as no man who knows my motives dare now vindicate them, let not prejudice or ignorance asperse them. Let them and me rest in obscurity and peace; and my tomb remain uninscribed and my memory in oblivion until other times other men can do justice to my character. When my country takes her place among the nations of the earth, then, and not till then let my epitaph be written. I have done.

6. Sydney Owenson (Lady Morgan), Selections from *The Wild Irish Girl: A National Tale* (1806)

Sydney Owenson (c. 1776–1859), also known as Lady Morgan, was a novelist, poet, travel writer, and journalist. Her mother was an English Protestant and her father was an Irish Catholic actor, who brought up Sydney and her sister following their mother's death in 1793. Owenson is best known for her novel The Wild Irish Girl. *The novel's plot line is too complex to summarize in a brief space, but its focus is the courtship and marriage of Glorvina, an Irish princess, and Horatio, the son of an English absentee landlord, the Earl of M____. At the beginning of the novel, Horatio views the Irish in disparaging, stereotypical terms. As a result of his courtship of Glorvina—and his getting to know both her father, the Prince of Inismore, and the Catholic priest Father John— Horatio comes to appreciate the richness and complexity of Irish history and culture and to bemoan England's ignorance of Ireland and its responsibility for Irish oppression. The novel catapulted Owenson to literary stardom, a role that she nurtured: she would dress up as Glorvina at social gatherings and play the Irish harp.*

The Wild Irish Girl was patriotic and nationalistic, but it did not preach political independence. It was written in the immediate years following the Act of Union. The marriage of Glorvina and Horatio is a metaphor for the restoration of Irish dignity within an English/British political framework. The novel's conclusion consists of a letter written to Horatio by his father, who unlike the stereotypical English absentee landlord, had great compassion for Ireland's plight. He implores Horatio to use his power, influence, and position to achieve harmony between the two nations.

. . . Take then to thy bosom *her* whom heaven seems to have chosen as the intimate associate of thy soul, and whom national and hereditary prejudice would in vain withhold from thee.—In this the dearest, most sacred, and most lasting of all human ties, let the name of Inismore and M____ be inseparably blended, and the distinctions of English and Irish, of protestant and catholic, for ever buried. And, while you look forward with hope to this family alliance being prophetically typical of a national unity of interests and affections between those who may be factiously severe, but who are naturally allied, lend your *own individual efforts* towards the consummation of an event so devoutly to be wished by every liberal mind, by every benevolent heart.

During my life, I would have you consider those estates as your's which I possess in this country; and at my death such as are not entailed. But this consideration is to be indulged conditionally, on your spending eight months out of every twelve on that spot from whence the very nutrition of your existence is to be derived; and in the bosom of those from whose labour and exertion your independence and prosperity are to flow. Act not with the vulgar policy of vulgar greatness, by endeavouring to exact respect through the medium of self-wrapt reserve, proudly shut up in its own self-invested grandeur; nor think it can derogate from the dignity of the *English landholder* openly to appear in the midst of his Irish peasantry, with an eye beaming complacency, and a countenance smiling confidence, and inspiring what it expresses. Shew them you do not distrust them, and they will not betray you; give them reason to believe you feel an interest in their welfare, and they will endeavour to promote your's even at the risk of their lives; for the life of an Irishman weighs but light in the scale of consideration with his feelings; it is immolated without murmur to the affections of his heart; it is sacrificed without a sigh to the suggestions of his honour.

Remember that you are not placed by despotism over a band of slaves, creatures of the soil, and as such to be considered; but by Providence, over a certain portion of men, who, in common with the rest of their nation, are the descendants of a brave, a free, and an enlightened people. Be more anxious to remove *causes*, than to punish *effects*; for trust me that is only to

"Scotch the snake—not kill it,"[42]

to confine error, and to awaken vengeance.

Be cautious how you condemn; be more cautious how you deride, but be ever watchful to moderate that ardent impetuosity, which flows from the natural tone of the national character, which is the inseparable accompaniment of quick and acute feelings, which is the invariable concomitant of constitutional sensibility; and remember that the same ardour of disposition, the same vehemence of soul, which inflames their errors beyond the line of moderate failing, nurtures their better qualities beyond the growth of moderate excellence.

Within the influence then of your own bounded circle pursue those means of promoting the welfare of the individuals consigned to your care and protection, which lies within the scope of all those in whose hands the destinies of their less fortunate brethren are placed. Cherish by kindness into renovating life those national virtues, which, though so often blighted in the full luxuriance of their vigorous blow by the fatality of circumstances, have still been ever found vital at the root, which only want the nutritive beam of encouragement, the genial glow of confiding affection, and the refreshing

---

42. Shakespeare, *Macbeth* III. ii. 13. *Scotch* here suggests to injure in order to make harmless.

dew of tender commiseration, to restore them to their pristine bloom and vigour: place the standard of support within their sphere; and like the tender vine, which has been suffered by neglect to waste its treasures on the sterile earth, you will behold them naturally turning and gratefully twining round the fostering stem, which rescues them from a cheerless and groveling destiny; and when by justly and adequately rewarding the laborious exertions of that life devoted to your service, the source of their poverty shall be dried up, and the miseries that flowed from it shall be forgotten: when the warm hand of benevolence shall have wiped away the cold dew of despondency from their brow; when reiterated acts of tenderness and humanity shall have thawed the ice which chills the native flow of their ardent feelings; and when the light of instruction shall have dispelled the gloom of ignorance and prejudice from their neglected minds, and their lightened hearts shall again throb with the cheery pulse of national exility:— then, *and not till then,* will you behold the day-star of national virtue rising brightly over the horizon of their happy existence; while the felicity, which has awakened to the touch of reason and humanity, shall return back to, and increase the source from which it originally flowed: as the elements, which in gradual progress brighten into flame, terminate in a liquid light, which, reverberating in sympathy to its former kindred, genially warms and gratefully cheers the whole order of universal nature.

7–9. Daniel O'Connell on Catholic Emancipation and Repeal

Daniel O'Connell (1775–1847) is the most important Irish politician of the first half of the nineteenth century. Within Irish political culture, he is known as the Liberator. O'Connell was from County Kerry, and his family, though Catholic, were landowners. He studied to become a lawyer in France. He finished his law studies in London, fleeing the intensifying violence and radicalism of the French Revolution. His experience of the revolutionary environment, in tandem with the failure of the 1798 rebellion, led him to reject violence as a means of achieving justice for Ireland. Indeed, O'Connell was an admirer of the British constitutional tradition. However, he believed that Ireland had failed to benefit from it.

He surfaced on the national stage in 1800 as a principled opponent of the Union. His opposition was implicitly and explicitly the foundation of the two great political campaigns that he led: Catholic emancipation and repeal of the Union. When O'Connell began to organize for emancipation in 1805, the emerging Catholic middle class dominated the movement: it had only superficial support from the peasantry, the largest component of the Catholic population. O'Connell transformed emancipation into a mass movement in 1823, when he helped found the Catholic Association, based on a penny-per-month subscription—the Catholic rent, *as it came to be known. O'Connell's bold shift in political strategy enlarged the scope of Irish nationalist politics. Moreover, it was unprecedented in Europe and became a model for mass organization.*

Daniel O'Connell: *The Champion of Liberty* (1847).

The emancipation movement, as the repeal movement that succeeded it, redefined not only the scope but also the nature of nationalist and Catholic aspiration. At the center of O'Connell's vision was the belief that Catholics embodied the Irish nation and that Protestants, though welcome, must acquiesce to the emerging realities. His movement, always difficult to keep together, was comprised of the Catholic peasants and middle class, the Catholic clergy, and liberal Protestants who shared Wolfe Tone's vision of a common Irish identity that transcended the religious divide. On the one hand, O'Connell proclaimed that "the Catholic church is a national church and if people rally with me they will have a nation for that church" (quoted in Boyce 1995, 146). On the other hand, and in another context, he toasted William III: "The assistance of Protestants generates so much good feeling and such a national community of sentiment that I deem it more valuable than even emancipation itself" (quoted in Boyce 1995,143). Furthermore, as an ardent constitutionalist, O'Connell continually struggled to marginalize proponents of violence, both the nationalist tradition that surfaced in 1798 and the agrarian violence of peasant groups such as the Ribbonmen and the Whiteboys. It is possible, in part, to view O'Connell's monster meetings of the 1840s, in which thousands upon thousands participated, as efforts to harness outrage and potential violence into peaceful and constitutional channels.

The three selections that follow are drawn from O'Connell's two great political campaigns. The first, a letter that appeared in the Dublin Register *(reproduced in* The Times*), was written after O'Connell's momentous election to Parliament in 1828. It is addressed to those who had elected him, but it is written for a wider audience, calling upon the "countenance and assistance of gentlemen who are acquainted with, and who can speak the sentiments of all parts of Ireland" (no. 7). The second and third primary sources are from the repeal campaign of the 1840s. O'Connell's letter to Paul Cullen (no. 8), a conservative, highly influential Catholic clergyman who became an archbishop and a cardinal, expresses O'Connell's views on the communal divide. The occasion of his 1843 speech at Mullaghmast (no. 9) was one of the monster meetings that harnessed the political energies of nationalist Ireland and was seen by the British government as a threat to its authority. O'Connell promised that the Irish Parliament would be loyal to Queen Victoria, but he also threatened unilateral action, a council of three hundred "bogtrotters" that would set in motion what was Ireland's by right. The term* bogtrotters *had been originally used by* The Times *to mock O'Connell's advocacy of possible unilateral action. He skillfully converted the insult into yet another instance of English condescension towards the Irish. (The idea of a council prefigured Sinn Féin's strategy implemented in 1918.) Only eight days following the Mullaghmast speech, the government banned the meeting to be held at Clontarf and arrested O'Connell, even though he canceled it rather than provoke a confrontation.*

7. Daniel O'Connell, "Mr. O'Connell's Letter to the Freeholders[43] of the County of Clare," *The Times* [London], February 2, 1829 (originally published in the *Dublin Morning Register*)

Merrion Square, Jan. 28

Esteemed and beloved Friends, I had intended to assert, on the first day of the now approaching session, your right and mine, that I, as your chosen representative, should sit and vote in Parliament. . . .

---

43. A person with permanent and absolute claims to land or property and who is free to dispose of it at will. At the time of the Clare election, freeholders with property worth forty shillings were eligible to vote. To convey a rough sense of what this meant in concrete terms, in 1831, the population of Ireland is estimated to have been 7,767,401. Of those, about 75,960 were eligible to vote. In 1833 approximately one in five adult males could vote in England and Wales. In Ireland, one adult male out of twenty was eligible (Fleming and O'Day 2005, 312, 489).

I intend to leave Dublin on the 5th of February, or, at the latest, on the 6th. I shall not reach London until after the discussion on the King's speech shall have closed.[44]

It is my fixed intention to repair to the House of Commons so soon after my arrival in London as will allow me sufficient time to make those preliminary arrangements, in point of formal detail, as shall prevent me from being entrapped by mere matter of form, and as shall bring the question of my right to sit and vote in a deliberate manner before the House of Commons.

I contend for it, that the house has no power or authority to decide that question in the negative. The question that arises is a question of law; and there are abundant means to try that question without the house usurping an authority which, I say, and can prove, is not intrusted to it by the common law, or any statute whatsoever. If the Minister intends to have the question fairly tried; he will not oppose the sending it to the proper tribunal. But does he mean to meet it fairly? His conduct will soon answer in the manner you all anticipate.

I deem it of great importance that the gentlemen you have named to attend with me in London should be there before the 12th of February. In my sober and deliberate judgment, it is of vital importance to have a numerous assemblage of Irish noblemen and gentlemen in London on this occasion. The more numerous the better: not for the purpose of intimidation or violence; that would be as absurd as it would be criminal, so absurd, that I deem it unnecessary to refute the paltry calumny which has attributed that motive to us.

In making this great experiment, I shall want the countenance and assistance of gentlemen who are acquainted with, and who can speak the sentiments of all parts of Ireland. I shall want those who have a right to command the services of the Irish members of Parliament on this momentous question. I shall want that combination of moral force and intellect which will give weight and dignity to the struggle, and enable me to convert even a defeat into the sure grounds of future triumph, and into a more comprehensive and even national advantage.

Men of Clare, the English made many treaties with us Irish: they never kept one of them, they violated all. I go, authorized by you, to try whether the British Parliament will observe the treaty of the Union. I will make the experiment respectfully, but firmly, decorously, but with unalterable pertinacity.

> I am, beloved countrymen,
> Your faithful and devoted servant,
> DANIEL O'CONNELL.

44. George IV (1762–1830) opened the parliamentary session on February 5, 1829, by giving a speech outlining the government's legislative agenda, which included asking Parliament to consider Catholic emancipation.

8. Daniel O'Connell to Rev. Dr. Paul Cullen, Rector of the Irish College, Rome, May 9, 1842

Liverpool, May 9, 1842

Rev. and most respected Sir,

. . . British!!! I am not British. You are not British. When the British north and south fell away and dissipated amongst the profligate and the renegades of Protestantism and of every species of infidelity, the inheritance of the Lord amidst the land, the Irish Nation and the Irish Church were the victims of and not the participators in these crimes. But why should I indulge in dreamy recollections of the past. It is better [to] consider the present, to reflect on the times in which we live and to seek to discover whether the church of Ireland is not abundantly sufficient to carry on all its relations with the Holy See[45] without the intervention or intermeddling of any British clergyman however dignified. I do not wish to have the relations of Ireland with the Holy See relaxed or diminished. On the contrary, my anxious desire is that nothing should arise to injure those relations which I most cordially wish to see strengthened and increased and confirmed for all ages. No man can be more attached to the centre of unity than I am. No man can be more entirely convinced that the stability of the faith depends on the submission to and union with the Holy See. It is because I fear least anything should occur, least any intervention between the Irish Church and his Holiness should be obtruded which might have a tendency to disgust any persons or to weaken in any way the respectful and most affectionate attachment which Ireland proudly boasts of and zealously entertains towards Christ's Vicar on earth.

You perhaps will smile at the alarms I strongly feel though I do not adequately express on this subject. I blink myself at these alarms because Ireland has a shield in the prudent zeal of her episcopacy to protect her from any intervention which *could* possibly injure the deposit of faith committed to their care. Ours are faithful shepherds who would as their sainted predecessors—many of them did—die for their flocks. . . .

I would obtrude on you some of the heads of that memorial to use if you pleased to do so discreetly but not to transpire to the general public through the press or otherwise. Here are some of these heads:

1st. That the Catholics of Ireland were no parties to the Union. They were at that time excluded from all participation in legislation, unjustly so deprived and in violation of the Treaty of Limerick.[46] Their right to domestic legislation therefore remains untouched.

2d. The Protestants in Ireland are not so much religionists as politicians. They are political protestants, that is, Protestants by reason of their participation in political

---

45. Refers to the government of the Catholic Church with the papacy at its head.

46. The 1691 treaty ending the invasion of Ireland by William III and his allies. It guaranteed property and religious rights to the defeated Catholics but was supplanted by the much harsher penal laws.

power, by reason in fact of political power being almost entirely confided in them to the exclusion of all but very few Catholics.

3d. If the Union were repealed and the exclusive system abolished, the great mass of the Protestant community would with little delay melt into the overwhelming majority of the Irish nation. Protestantism would not survive the Repeal ten years. Nothing but persecution would keep it alive and the Irish Catholics are too wise and too good to persecute.

4th. The Union was carried in order to prevent or at all events to postpone the Emancipation of the Catholic people of Ireland. It had that effect for twenty-nine years.

5th. The Repeal of the Union would free the Catholic people of Ireland from the burden of supporting the useless Protestant Church. The tithe-rent charge alone produces near half a million sterling per annum. The Repeal of the Union would disengage this mass of property and enable the people to support their own church.

6th. The Repeal of the Union would at once disengage the Church lands from the hands to which they have been unjustly transferred by means of the so-called Reformation. . . .

9. Daniel O'Connell, "Speech at Mullaghmast" (October 1, 1843)

I ACCEPT with the greatest alacrity the high honor you have done me in calling me to the chair of this majestic meeting. I feel more honored than I ever did in my life, with one single exception, and that related to, if possible, an equally majestic meeting at Tara.[47] But I must say that if a comparison were instituted between them, it would take a more discriminating eye than mine to discover any difference between them. There are the same incalculable numbers; there is the same firmness; there is the same determination; there is the same exhibition of love to old Ireland; there is the same resolution not to violate the peace; not to be guilty of the slightest outrage; not to give the enemy power by committing a crime, but peacefully and manfully to stand together in the open day, to protest before man and in the presence of God against the iniquity of continuing the Union.

At Tara I protested against the Union—I repeat the protest at Mullaghmast. I declare solemnly my thorough conviction as a constitutional lawyer, that the Union is totally void in point of principle and of constitutional force. I tell you that no portion of the empire had the power to traffic on the rights and liberties of the Irish people. The Irish people nominated them to make laws, and not legislatures. They were appointed to act under the Constitution, and not annihilate it. Their delegation from the people was confined within the limits of the Constitution, and the moment the Irish Parliament went beyond those limits and destroyed the Constitution, that moment it annihilated its own power, but could not annihilate the immortal spirit of liberty which belongs, as a rightful inheritance, to the people of Ireland. Take it, then, from me that the Union is void.

47. It is estimated that 750,000 people gathered on the Hill of Tara on August 15, 1843, to listen to O'Connell speak.

I admit there is the force of a law, because it has been supported by the police-man's truncheon,[48] by the soldier's bayonet, and by the horseman's sword; because it is supported by the courts of law and those who have power to adjudicate in them; but I say solemnly, it is not supported by constitutional right. The Union, therefore, in my thorough conviction, is totally void, and I avail myself of this opportunity to announce to several hundreds of thousands of my fellow subjects that the Union is an unconstitutional law and that it is not fated to last long—its hour is approach-ing. America offered us her sympathy and support. We refused the support, but we accepted the sympathy; and while we accepted the sympathy of the Americans, we stood upon the firm ground of the right of every human being to liberty; and I, in the name of the Irish nation, declare that no support obtained from America should be purchased by the price of abandoning principle for one moment, and that principle is that every human being is entitled to freedom.

My friends, I want nothing for the Irish but their country, and I think the Irish are competent to obtain their own country for themselves. I like to have the sympathy of every good man everywhere, but I want not armed support or physical strength from any country. . . .

. . . I have physical support enough about me to achieve any change; but you know well that it is not my plan—I will not risk the safety of one of you. I could not afford the loss of one of you—I will protect you all, and it is better for you all to be merry and alive, to enjoy the repeal of the Union; but there is not a man of you there that would not, if we were attacked unjustly and illegally, be ready to stand in the open field by my side. Let every man that concurs in that sentiment lift up his hand. . . .

O my friends, I will keep you clear of all treachery—there shall be no bargain, no compromise with England—we shall take nothing but repeal, and a Parliament in College Green.[49] You will never, by my advice, confide in any false hopes they hold out to you; never confide in anything coming from them, or cease from your struggle, no matter what promise may be held to you, until you hear me say I am satisfied; and I will tell you where I will say that—near the statue of King William [III], in College Green. No; we came here to express our determination to die to a man, if necessary, in the cause of old Ireland. We came to take advice of each other, and, above all, I believe you came here to take my advice. I can tell you, I have the game in my hand—I have the triumph secure—I have the repeal certain, if you but obey my advice.

I will go slow—you must allow me to do so—but you will go sure. No man shall find himself imprisoned or persecuted who follows my advice. I have led you thus far in safety; I have swelled the multitude of repealers until they are identified with the entire population, or nearly the entire population, of the land, for seven-eighths of the Irish people are now enrolling themselves repealers. I do not want more power; I have power enough; and all I ask of you is to allow me to use it. I will go on quietly and slowly, but I will go on firmly, and with a certainty of success. I am now arrang-ing a plan for the formation of the Irish House of Commons.

48. A club.
49. The site of the Irish Parliament prior to the union with Britain.

It is a theory, but it is a theory that may be realized in three weeks. The repeal arbitrators are beginning to act; the people are submitting their differences to men chosen by themselves. You will see by the newspapers that Doctor Gray[50] and my son,[51] and other gentlemen, have already held a petty session[52] of their own, where justice will be administered free of all expense to the people. The people shall have chosen magistrates of their own in the room of the magistrates who have been removed. The people shall submit their differences to them, and shall have strict justice administered to them that shall not cost them a single farthing. I shall go on with that plan until we have all the disputes settled and decided by justices appointed by the people themselves.

I wish to live long enough to have perfect justice administered to Ireland, and liberty proclaimed throughout the land. It will take me some time to prepare my plan for the formation of the new Irish House of Commons—that plan which we will yet submit to her majesty for her approval when she gets rid of her present paltry administration and has one that I can support. But I must finish that job before I go forth, and one of my reasons for calling you together is to state my intentions to you. Before I arrange my plan, the Conciliation Hall[53] will be finished, and it will be worth any man's while to go from Mullaghmast to Dublin to see it.

When we have it arranged I will call together three hundred, as the *Times* called them, "bogtrotters," but better men never stepped on pavement. But I will have the three hundred, and no thanks to them. Wales is up at present, almost in a state of insurrection. The people there have found that the landlords' power is too great, and has been used tyrannically, and I believe you agree with them tolerably well in that. They insist on the sacredness of the right of the tenants to security of possession, and with the equity of tenure which I would establish we will do the landlords full justice, but we will do the people justice also. We will recollect that the land is the landlord's, and let him have the benefit of it, but we will also recollect that the labor belongs to the tenant, and the tenant must have the value of his labor, not transitory and by the day, but permanently and by the year.

Yes, my friends, for this purpose I must get some time. I worked the present repeal year tolerably well. I believe no one in January last would believe that we could have such a meeting within the year as the Tara demonstration. You may be sure of this— and I say it in the presence of Him who will judge me—that I never will wilfully deceive you. I have but one wish under heaven, and that is for the liberty and prosperity of Ireland. I am for leaving England to the English, Scotland to the Scotch; but we must have Ireland for the Irish. I will not be content until I see not a single man in

50. Sir John Gray (1816–75), Irish physician and surgeon, owner of the nationalist newspaper the *Freemen's Journal*, journalist and politician, and a supporter of O'Connell's repeal movement.

51. John O'Connell (1810–58), the third of Daniel O'Connell's four sons, MP, and a leading figure in the repeal movement.

52. Regular courts presided over by justices of the peace. At petty sessions, trials were held for minor criminal offenses.

53. Built as a headquarters for the repeal movement. It opened in 1843.

any office, from the lowest constable to the lord chancellor, but Irishmen. This is our land, and we must have it. We will be obedient to the queen, joined to England by the golden link of the Crown, but we must have our own Parliament, our own bench, our own magistrates. . . .

Yes, my friends, the Union was begot in iniquity—it was perpetuated in fraud and cruelty. It was no compact, no bargain, but it was an act of the most decided tyranny and corruption that was ever yet perpetrated. . . .

Yes, among the nations of the earth, Ireland stands number one in the physical strength of her sons and in the beauty and purity of her daughters. Ireland, land of my forefathers, how my mind expands, and my spirit walks abroad in something of majesty, when I contemplate the high qualities, inestimable virtues, and true purity and piety and religious fidelity of the inhabitants of your green fields and productive mountains. Oh, what a scene surrounds us! It is not only the countless thousands of brave and active and peaceable and religious men that are here assembled, but Nature herself has written her character with the finest beauty in the verdant plains that surround us.

Let any man run around the horizon with his eye, and tell me if created nature ever produced anything so green and so lovely, so undulating, so teeming with production. The richest harvests that any land can produce are those reaped in Ireland; and then here are the sweetest meadows, the greenest fields, the loftiest mountains, the purest streams, the noblest rivers, the most capacious harbors—and her water power is equal to turn the machinery of the whole world. O my friends, it is a country worth fighting for—it is a country worth dying for; but, above all, it is a country worth being tranquil, determined, submissive, and docile for; disciplined as you are in obedience to those who are breaking the way, and trampling down the barriers between you and your constitutional liberty, I will see every man of you having a vote, and every man protected by the ballot from the agent or landlord. I will see labor protected, and every title to possession recognized, when you are industrious and honest. I will see prosperity again throughout your land—the busy hum of the shuttle and the tinkling of the smithy shall be heard again. We shall see the nailer[54] employed even until the middle of the night, and the carpenter covering himself with his chips. I will see prosperity in all its gradations spreading through a happy, contented, religious land. I will hear the hymn of a happy people go forth at sunrise to God in praise of His mercies—and I will see the evening sun set down among the uplifted hands of a religious and free population. Every blessing that man can bestow and religion can confer upon the faithful heart shall spread throughout the land. Stand by me—join with me—I will say be obedient to me, and Ireland shall be free.

10 and 11. Perspectives on the Irish Famine

The Famine transformed Ireland, and the Irish collective memory of it altered Anglo-Irish relations. The potato blight had struck elsewhere but without the same devastating effects. Numerous efforts surfaced to explain why the Famine had been so catastrophic,

---

54. A person who drives in nails.

and remedies were espoused to restore Ireland to health. The editorial from The Times
(no. 10) and the conclusion to John Mitchel's (1815–75) The Last Conquest of Ireland (Perhaps) *(no. 11) comprise contrasting diagnoses and prescriptions.*

The Times, *the newspaper of the British establishment, conceived of the Famine
from the perspective of classical liberalism and political economy, what today we would
call political conservatism. The editorial suggested that the Irish national character was
an obstacle to the workings of the free market and the production of wealth. It blamed
Irish workers, for, in its view, they preferred government handouts to hard work. But
it also singled out landlords who did not invest in their properties nor feel the kind of
responsibility for their tenants that was found in England.*

*For the radical nationalist John Mitchel, the Irish Famine was the work of the Brit-
ish government, who for centuries had exploited and oppressed Ireland. Mitchel had been
part of the Young Ireland movement and later wrote for the radical* United Irishman.
*He was subsequently convicted of treason and went to the United States after escaping
from Van Diemen's Land, or Tasmania, now part of Australia. In* The Last Conquest
of Ireland (Perhaps), *he accused Britain of not only being responsible for the Famine
but also using it for its own advantages.*

10. Editorial, *The Times*, September 22, 1846

The worst symptoms of the Irish famine, as we had to observe yesterday, have begun
to show themselves in the way of popular gatherings and processions, which at present are only turbulent, but may soon become outrageous. The twin powers of Fear
and Rumour have lent their hands to the colouring of a picture already sufficiently
sombre. The people have made up their minds to report the worst and believe the
worst. Human agency is now denounced as instrumental in adding to the calamity
inflicted by Heaven. It is no longer submission to Providence, but a murmur against
the Government. The potatoes were blighted by a decree from on high, but labour
is defrauded by the machinations of earthly power. Such are the first aspirations of
discontent, inflamed by rumour, and diffused by fear. Such are the thanks that a
Government gets for attempting to palliate great afflictions and satisfy corresponding
demands by an inevitable but a ruinous beneficence.

The alarm of the populace in the provincial towns has arisen in some cases from
the fact of the wages paid by Government being below the average standard of wages
in the vicinity; in others, from the report that it is the intention to reduce them below that standard. This is the secret of the murmur. But how much does it disclose!
How much does it indicate! It is the old thing; the old grievance is at the bottom; the
old malady is breaking out. It is the national character, the national thoughtlessness,
the national indolence. It is that which demands the attention of Governments, of
patriots, and philanthropists, not a whit less than the potato disease. The Government provided work for a people who love it not. It made this the absolute condition
of relief. Doing so, it only did that which every Executive is bound to do in similar
circumstances. But, in laying out its plan, it was obliged to square the execution of
it by the habits of the people. It knew that the latter would at all times rather be idle

than toil; would live on a small gratuity rather than large or regular earnings; and would trust to the beneficence of a Cabinet rather than to the sweat of their brows, or the steady work of their hands. It saw distinctly the prospect of more than half a nation becoming complacently dependent upon specious alms. There was but one way to avoid a calamity compared with which the potato blight is a trivial thing. This was to enjoin that work, slovenly and sluggishly performed—as Government work was sure to be—should procure subsistence for the peasant, but nothing more. The Government was required to ward off starvation, not to pamper indolence; to stimulate others to give employment, not to outbid them, or drive them from the labour-market. It therefore threw itself between the poor man and his gaunt foe; but it would not interfere between him and his best friend—the man who would employ him. It diminished the competition which the labourer had to fear; it increased that which none but a foolish proprietor could dislike. It provided literally bread for the famished, but it held out more than bread to the active and industrious. The squire and the farmer found that, in order to get labourers at all, they must appeal not only to the indigence, but the acquisitiveness of the poor. The contest thus arose between 8d. or 10d. a-day of the Executive and the 1s. or 1s. 2d. of the landholder.[55] In England or Scotland—in any country but Ireland—the issue would have been clear from the beginning. All hands would have tendered their services to the squire or the farmer. The Government contractor would have been left to treat with the refuse of the population. Private works would have enlisted youth, health, vigour, activity, and zeal. The public works would have devolved on age, infirmity, or indolence. But, in the end, the nation—the empire—would have gained. On the spur of a temporary emergency permanent improvements would have been effected, and normal habits established. The emulation of the peasant would have conspired with the ambition or the avarice of the landlord to redeem the soil of Ireland from the curse of perpetual neglect, and the condition of Irishmen from the shame of hereditary squalor. That which taught men first of all to work, would have taught Irishmen to work well, steadily, and continuously. Hunger would have been (as elsewhere) the herald of comfort, Necessity the parent of luxuries. The disappearance of the potato, instead of being a curse, might have been hailed as a boon; and the Celtic tiller, eating better food and cultivating a nobler crop, might have learned to wonder how he could ever have existed on so poor and innutritious a root.

But what would happen in other countries never does happen In Ireland. There the process as well as the motive of every action is inverted. Instead of increased exertion and renewed industry, passive submission and despondent indolence awaited a famine epoch. Even the annual migration of labour was suspended in many instances. The English corn-fields lacked their wonted reapers. The Celtic features and the Celtic dialect were missed from our northern and eastern harvest. The quays of Liverpool and Bristol were unusually scant of those strongly-marked lineaments and that peculiar garb which distinguish the native Irishman from every other denizen of Europe. England was rife of varied employment and a multiform speculation. Every hand

---

55. As there were twelve pennies (d.) in one shilling (s.), the landowners were paying more than the government.

that could be turned to account was pressed into service. Our own peasantry were, in many counties, insufficient to meet the demands of multi-form occupation. Still the Irishman—he who, in other and less happy seasons, has filched more than his share from the competition of his English fellow-labourer—he who was erst reviled as a pernicious rival, but who then would have been hailed an useful and kindly help-mate—he kept aloof. Here and there you might hear the western brogue, but, almost universally, the harvest wooed in vain the sickle of the sister isle. Why was this? Why was it that the prospect—the certainty of a great calamity, did not animate to great exertions? Alas! the Irish peasant had tasted of famine and found that it was good. He saw the cloud looming in the distance, and he hailed its approach. To him it teemed with goodly manna and salient waters. He wrapped himself up in the ragged mantle of inert expectancy, and said that he trusted to Providence. But the deity of his faith was the Government—the manna of his hopes was a Parliamentary grant. He called his submission a religious obedience, and he believed it to be so. But it was the obedience of a religion which, by a small but material change, reversed the primaeval decree. It was a religion that holds "Man shall *not* labour by the 'sweat of his brow'."[56]

All this was natural, and might have been expected from the original character and antecedent conditions of the Irish people. It was the same rooted and innate disposition which thwarts, and baffles, and depresses them whithersoever they turn their steps. On the banks of the Liffey or the Liver, the Thames or the St. Lawrence, the Murray or the Mississippi, it's the same thing. It is this that prevents them from working when they can idle; from growing rich when they work; from saving when they receive money. It seems a law of their being—a hard, a pitiable, a saddening law; but one hitherto unaltered, and—we hope only to external appearance—unalterable. But why is it that in Manchester, or Leeds, or Stockport,[57] when he works and is well paid, the Irishman never thrives? The Englishman and the Scotchman from small beginnings struggle into comfort, respectability, competence; nay, sometimes, even into wealth and station. The Scotch or English spinner, in no few cases, has become a manufacturer and a capitalist; the Irish hardly in any. Thrown amongst mechanics of the two nations,—receiving the same wages as they do,—stimulated by the same competition,—with the same prospect, and the same encouragement,—displaying, too, at times, an equal, if not a greater energy,—still, he rarely attains the same position, or improves his condition in the same degree. He remains, if not poor, at least uncomfortable. His family inherit[s] the squalid slovenliness which their father imported. His quarter—as may be seen in Liverpool, Bristol, Manchester, Oldham, or Drury Lane[58]—is always the most forlorn and cheerless in the district.

All these things are facts beyond doubt and denial. We repeat them not for reproach or contumely, but to show that there are ingredients in the Irish character

---

56. This is a play on words. In Genesis 3:19, God punishes Adam and says to him: "By the sweat of your brow you will eat your food until you return to the ground, since from it you were taken; for dust you are and to dust you will return."

57. Industrial cities in England.

58. Bristol, Manchester, and Oldham are cities in England. Drury Lane is a street in the Covent Garden area of London and was at the time one of the city's worst slums.

which must be modified and corrected before either individuals or Governments can hope to raise the general condition of the people. It is absurd to prescribe political innovations for the remedy of their sufferings or the alleviation of their wants. Extended suffrage and municipal reform for a peasantry who have for six centuries consented to alternate between starvation on a potato and the doles of national charity! You might as well give them *bonbons*[59] and ratafias.[60] Nothing effectual can be achieved until the habits of the people are changed. And this change cannot be effected unless the landholders and squireens[61] exert themselves. Had the smaller gentry resident in Ireland done their duty to their tenants and dependents—for the best landlords are its absentees—had they set the example of attention to their properties and improvement of their estates, the Irish would long ago have repudiated the potato. Neglected by others, they neglected themselves. Hence the universal prostration of self-complacent poverty and unrepining discomfort.

We have a great faith in the virtues of good food. Without attributing the splendid qualities of the British Lion wholly to the agency of beef steaks, we may pronounce that a people that has been reared on solid edibles will struggle long and hard against the degradation of a poorer sustenance. The stomach is more than the mind a creature of habit. Accustom it to leeks or potatoes, it is indifferent to a generous diet. Once habituate it to substantial solids, it rebels against leguminous impostures. The consequence is obvious. *Le ventre gouverne le monde.*[62] He who is in danger of being starved by idleness will make one more struggle to earn his bread, his beef and his porter. On a question of this kind all agree. The philosopher and the gastronomist—Socrates, Adeimantus, and Athenaeus[63]—the framers of the Republic and the coterie of Deipnosophists[64]—concur in ascribing virtues, not only physical, but moral and intellectual, to the excellence of man's food, and its variety. The study of justice and the proficiency in political science are represented by Plato as correlative with, and almost dependent on, a supply of the finest grain and the most wholesome meats.

For our own parts, we regard the potato blight as a blessing. When the Celts once cease to be potatophagi,[65] they must become carnivorous. With the taste of meats will grow the appetite for them; with the appetite, the readiness to earn them. With this

59. A candy or sweet.

60. A kind of liqueur, an almond-based drink similar to a cordial, or a biscuit with an almond flavor.

61. Small landowners.

62. The stomach governs the world (French).

63. Socrates (c. 469–399 BCE) is a classical Greek philosopher; Adeimantus (c. 429–c. 382 BCE) is Plato's (427–347 BCE) older brother and a participant in Plato's *Republic*; and Athenaeus is a Greek rhetorician and grammarian who was active at the end of the second and the beginning of the third centuries CE.

64. A reference to *Deipnosophistae,* or *Philosophers at Dinner,* written by Atheanaus in the early third century CE. Its subject matter is a banquet at a scholar's house in which, among other things, food and wine are the subjects of discussion.

65. Potato eating.

will come steadiness, regularity, and perseverance; unless, indeed, the growth of these qualities be impeded by the blindness of Irish patriotism, the short-sighted indifference of petty landlords, or the random recklessness of Government benevolence. The first two may retard the improvement of Ireland; the last, continued in a spirit of thoughtless concession, must impoverish both England and Ireland. But nothing will strike so deadly a blow, not only at the dignity of Irish character, but also the elements of Irish prosperity, as a confederacy of rich proprietors to dun the national Treasury, and to eke out from our resources that employment for the poor which they are themselves bound to provide, by every sense of duty, to a land from which they derive their incomes. It is too bad that the Irish landlord should come to ask charity of the English and Scotch mechanic, in a year in which the export of produce to England has been beyond all precedent extensive and productive. But it seems that those who forget all duties forget all shame. The Irish rent must be paid twice over.

11. John Mitchel, *The Last Conquest of Ireland (Perhaps)* (1876)

. . . This very dismal and humiliating narrative draws to a close. It is the story of an ancient nation stricken down by a war more ruthless and sanguinary than any seven years' war, or thirty years' war, that Europe ever saw.[66] No sack of Mageburg, or ravage of the Palatinate,[67] ever approached in horror and desolation to the slaughters done in Ireland by mere official red tape and stationery, and the principles of political economy. A few statistics may fitly conclude this dreary subject.

The Census of Ireland, in 1841, gave a population of 8,175,125. At the usual rate of increase, there must have been, in 1846, when the famine commenced, at least eight and a half millions; at the same rate of increase, there ought to have been, in 1851 (according to the estimate of the Census Commissioners), 9,018,799. But in that year, after five seasons of artificial famine, there were found alive only 6,552,385—a deficit of about two million and a half. Now, what became of those two million and a half?

The "government" Census Commissioners, and compilers of returns of all sorts, whose principal duty it has been, since that fatal time, to conceal the amount of the havoc, attempt to account for nearly the whole deficiency by emigration. In Thom's Official Almanac,[68] I find set down on one side the actual decrease from 1841 to 1851 (that is, without taking into account the increase by births in that period), 1,623,154. Against this, they place their own estimate of the emigration during those same ten years, which they put down at 1,589,133. But, in the first place, the decrease did not *begin* till 1846—there had been till then a rapid increase in the population: the government returns, then, not only ignore the increase, but set the emigration of *ten*

66. The Thirty Years' War (1618–48) and the Seven Years' War (1756–63) were major European conflicts.

67. Magdeburg, a German town, and the Palatinate, a historical territory of the Holy Roman Empire in southwestern Germany, were both ravaged during the Thirty Years' War.

68. The preeminent almanac in Ireland, first published in 1843 and still being produced.

years against the depopulation of *five*. This will not do: we must reduce their emigrants by one-half, say to six hundred thousand—and add to the depopulation the estimated increase *up* to 1846, say half a million. This will give upwards of two millions whose disappearance is to be accounted for—and six hundred thousand emigrants in the other column. Balance unaccounted for, *a million and a half.*

This is without computing those who were born in the five famine years, whom we may leave to be balanced by the deaths from *natural* causes in the same period.

Now, that million and a half of men, women, and children, were carefully, prudently, and peacefully *slain* by the English government. They died of hunger in the midst of abundance, which their own hands created; and it is quite immaterial to distinguish those who perish in the agonies of famine itself from those who died of typhus fever, which in Ireland is always caused by famine.

Further, I have called it an artificial famine: that is to say, it was a famine which desolated a rich and fertile island, that produced every year abundance and superabundance to sustain all her people and many more. The English, indeed, call that famine a "dispensation of Providence;" and ascribe it entirely to the blight of the potatoes. But potatoes failed in like manner all over Europe; yet there was no famine save in Ireland. The British account of the matter, then, is first, a fraud—second, a blasphemy. The Almighty, indeed, sent the potato blight, but the English created the famine.

And lastly, I have shown, in the course of this narrative, that the depopulation of the country was not only encouraged by artificial means . . . but that extreme care and diligence were used to prevent relief coming to the doomed island from abroad; and that the benevolent contributions of Americans and other foreigners were turned aside from their destined objects—not, let us say, in order that none should be saved alive, but that no interference should be made with the principles of political economy. . . .

The subjection of Ireland is now probably assured until some external shock shall break up that monstrous commercial firm, the British Empire; which, indeed, is a bankrupt firm, and trading on false credit, and embezzling the goods of others, or robbing on the highway, from Pole to Pole; but its doors are not yet shut; its cup of abomination is not yet running over. If any American has read this narrative, however, he will never wonder hereafter when he hears an Irishman in America fervently curse the British Empire. So long as this hatred and horror shall last—so long as our island refuses to become, like Scotland, a contented province of her enemy, Ireland is not finally subdued. The passionate aspiration for Irish nationhood will outlive the British Empire.

CHAPTER TWO

National Identity

The United Irishmen launched the first Irish nationalist movement. They derived their principles from the European Enlightenment as manifested in the American and French revolutions. For Wolfe Tone, the people of Ireland were sovereign and as such had the right to create their own political system free of British interference. Tone imagined an Ireland transcending religious conflicts. He equated Irishness with the citizens of Ireland. His nationalist perspective exemplifies what contemporary scholars describe as civic nationalism.

As the nineteenth century unfolded, however, new ideas regarding nationalism, the nation, and national identity coalesced. Originating within German romanticism, the new nationalism conceived of the nation as a unique entity with a distinctive history, destiny, and culture. A people were often bound together, from this point of view, by a common language. Yet depending on the circumstances, other shared characteristics might unite them as well—race, religion, ethnicity, and descent, among others. In Ireland, as throughout Europe, cultural nationalism put down roots. Cultural nationalists regarded the foundation of the Irish nation as Gaelic culture and the Irish language. Sometimes this perspective stressed the pagan roots of Irishness, effacing differences between Protestants and Catholics. It also took the form of linking the Gaelic past with the Catholic majority. Both perspectives tended to minimize the historical impact of either the Anglo-Irish or Ulster Presbyterians on Irish culture.

Within cultural nationalism, intellectuals in the widest sense—poets, novelists, journalists, teachers, clergymen, and politicians—played an indispensible role. For the paradox of cultural nationalism was this: although it thought of the nation as an extended family, the nation's size and the physical distance between people made it impossible for individuals to have the kind of knowledge of each other that characterizes familial relations. The nation was thus, as the anthropologist Benedict Anderson (1983) stated, an *imagined community*. It was intellectuals who imagined and conveyed what the community shared via the emergent system of mass communications. In the nineteenth century this process took place through a rapidly expanding print capitalism—the expanding market of newspapers, magazines, journals, and books. Given its dependence on popular sovereignty and mass communications, nationalism has been viewed by an important contingent of contemporary theorists as a modern rather than an ancient phenomenon, even if it drew its content from a much older—sometimes embellished or invented—cultural repertoire. In Ireland, cultural nationalist intellectuals played an important role in articulating national identity by making the past meaningful. Sometimes this involved recovering it, and sometimes this involved producing it. However, their efforts took place in a modern context. They went back to the future.

The texts in this chapter comprise various efforts—implicit and explicit—at defining Irishness inside and outside of Irish cultural nationalism. They are the work of writers who defined, recovered, and constructed Irishness and explored its implications for cultural and political life. Most of the texts are clustered around two important moments of intense cultural energy: the Young Ireland movement of the 1840s, and the Gaelic cultural and literary revival that began to take shape in the 1890s. This chapter differs from the others in this book, as it is not nearly as tied to a chronology of political events. Moreover, because the cultural politics of Irish nationalism was often interfused with political nationalist initiatives—the repeal and Home Rule movement to name two—readings from other chapters are relevant here as well and will accordingly be cited.

The language of Irish cultural nationalism emerged in the early nineteenth century. It was powerfully expressed in Sydney Owenson's *The Wild Irish Girl* (no. 6), which represented Irishness as passionate, lyrical, imaginative, and generous, while Englishness was represented as stodgy, narrow-minded, and unimaginative. It is present in the poetry of Thomas Moore (nos. 12 and 13). His effort to liberate the "Dear Harp" of his country, relegated to "The cold chain of silence" (no. 12), resonated deeply with both the Irish and English public. However, it was the Young Ireland movement of the 1840s, drawing on romantic philosophy and literature, which initiated the first influential cultural nationalist project.

Young Irelanders were both Protestant and Catholic and continued the tradition of inclusiveness found in the United Irishmen. Yet the *young* in Young Ireland was not there for nothing: it was meant to capture the contrast between the *young* generation of Thomas Davis and Charles Gavan Duffy and the *old* one of Daniel O'Connell, who, rather than being a romantic, was a Benthamite utilitarian.[1] One way in which Young Irelanders differed from O'Connell was in their interest in the Irish language, which they feared might disappear from daily use, a result of rapidly encroaching Anglicization. Language was a major preoccupation of cultural nationalists: in romantic terms, it was the soul of the nation. For Davis (no. 15), the ancient Irish language and the Gaelic culture in which it was embedded defined Irishness. He contrasted its spiritual vitality with the superficial and materialistic civilization being imported from Britain. He derived his critique of contemporary Britain from the British themselves. It was adapted from the "condition of England" debate of the 1830s and 1840s in which numerous, often conservative critics—notably the Scottish writer Thomas Carlyle (1795–1881)—contrasted the tawdry materialism of industrial life with the organic society of the past. Davis' portrayal of Ireland as a "people, pious, hospitable, and brave, faithful observers of family ties, cultivators of learning, music, and poetry" (no. 15) was—like Sydney Owenson's—an inversion of negative Irish stereotypes found in Britain. By grounding Irishness in Gaelic culture and history, he produced an identity transcending Catholicism and Protestantism, hence making it possible for Protestants like himself to be part of the imagined community. In addition, for Young Ireland, the Gaelic past was something that could no

---

1. Refers to the ideas of the English philosopher and social reformer Jeremy Bentham (1748–1832). His utilitarian philosophy, based on the principle of the greatest happiness of the greatest number and on the attempt to quantify happiness in terms of pleasure, was the basis for reform of the legal system.

longer be taken for granted as being central to Irish life. The movement was a crusade to save the Irish people from becoming Anglicized *West Britons*. As Duffy argued in his unsigned article for *The Nation* (no. 14), one of the group's central tasks was to communicate the advantages of nationality to the Irish people, to remind them "National feelings, National habits, and National government, are indispensable to individual prosperity."

Yet this image of Ireland as a Gaelic nation would not have resonated with all audiences. Ulster loyalists, who saw themselves as British, would have scoffed at it. It would only have been partially accepted by those parts of the Catholic community who regarded Ireland's Gaelic and Catholic past as part of a seamless whole. They conceived of Ireland as a Catholic nation. Writing in the aftermath of the Church of Ireland's disestablishment some thirty years later, the Catholic priest Thomas N. Burke argued that Irish identity was Catholic, and he prophesized Catholicism's inevitable triumph over Protestantism (no. 18). O'Connell himself was also capable in specific contexts of expressing views that would have made many of his Protestant allies shudder. In his letter to Paul Cullen (no. 8), who at the time was rector of the Irish College in Rome, O'Connell forecast that "the great mass of the Protestant community would with little delay melt into the overwhelming majority of the Irish nation" within ten years of the Union's repeal.

Many of the Anglo-Irish and English would probably also have contested Young Ireland's view of Irish nationality. The English Victorian poet and critic Matthew Arnold, for instance, portrayed the Irish or Celts as imaginative, sensual, and feminine (no. 17). England's Celtic inheritance potentially modified its Saxon pragmatism, stodginess, and narrow-mindedness. Ireland, being wholly Celtic, might be capable of poetry but not self-government. Arnold's politics differed from that of Irish cultural nationalists, but both assumed a world of distinct national types or essences whose characteristics shaped the parameters of the nation's social, cultural, and political life.

Originating in the late nineteenth century, the literary and cultural revival developed themes begun by Young Ireland. The revival became a critical component of Irish political culture in the twentieth century, its influence being felt, for instance, in the Easter Rising of 1916 and the cultural politics of the Irish Free State. In a famous observation, W. B. Yeats suggested that the revival represented a response to the death of the parliamentary nationalist leader Charles Stewart Parnell in 1891: it signified a cultural and sometimes spiritual alternative to the failed parliamentary movement (cited in Jackson 1999, 169). Historians have pointed out that there were revivalist initiatives prior to Parnell's fall, and initiatives that came afterward might also arguably be linked to rising expectations resulting from the second Home Rule Bill (1893). Nonetheless, the belief that parliamentary politics was not enough and, indeed, that Irish nationalist politicians had become part of the status quo, seems to have been a powerful motivating force for providing alternatives. James Joyce's short story "Ivy Day in the Committee Room" (no. 22) powerfully contrasts the unfulfilled promise embodied in the figure of Parnell with the sleaze and corruption in a local Dublin election: all that was left of the nationalist spirit was the mouthing of pieties.

The revival was manifested in multiple ways, produced and consumed by people from a wide array of backgrounds and politics. What they shared was a commitment to salvaging and restoring the Gaelic past to what they saw as its rightful place in Irish culture. One such realm was sports. The Gaelic Athletic Association (GAA), founded in 1884, privileged Irish rather than English sports. It promoted hurling and Gaelic football, an example of the revival's shaping of popular culture. Moreover, the links established between the GAA and the Irish Republican Brotherhood (IRB) proved to be an important breeding ground for nationalist militants. The revival is perhaps best known for its achievements in literature, theater, journalism, and promotion of the Irish language. It was the work of an enormously talented group of writers. Many of the writers were Anglo-Irish: Lady Isabella (Augusta) Gregory (1852–1932), Douglas Hyde, George Russell (also known as Æ), John Millington (J. M.) Synge (1871–1909), and W. B. Yeats, among others. Some, including David Patrick (D. P.) Moran (1869–1936) and Pádraic Pearse,[2] were from Catholic backgrounds. Joyce, although a critic of revivalism, was nonetheless a nationalist at heart and must count as part of this renaissance of the literary imagination.

What it meant to be Gaelic or what the Gaelic past meant for politics and the Irish future were ferociously debated. Revivalism could be compatible with Unionism or physical-force nationalism. In the hands of a writer such as D. P. Moran, who argued for an "Irish Ireland," it was the basis for the advocacy of Catholic hegemony. It is perhaps possible to divide the writers of the revival into two by no means separable categories: those writers regarding English as an appropriate vehicle to express Irishness, and those believing that national aspiration could only be realized by the recovery and spread of the Irish language. Among those for whom Irish sensibility could be communicated in English, Yeats is the towering figure. He was committed to creating a national literature and theater—frequently by mining ancient myth and folktales—yet he argued that such practices must have artistic and aesthetic integrity. He was a founder of the Irish Literary Society of London (1891) and the National Literary Society (1892). But Yeats' crowning achievement in cultural politics might be the Irish Literary Theatre (1898) and its successor the Irish National Theatre Society (1903), the forerunner to the Abbey Theatre (1904).

Yeats sought to create a national theater that took popular traditions and mythology as their subject matter but did not pander to their audience. He imagined a nationalist theater that did not disintegrate into propaganda but was intellectually and aesthetically challenging. Given Yeats' multifaceted cultural agenda, the plays that he helped bring to the stage were often controversial, none more so than J. M. Synge's *The Playboy in the Western World* (1907). Synge's efforts to render the peasantry authentically, warts and all, proved offensive to an audience used to thinking of peasants in heroic and idealistic terms. Yeats' own play *Cathleen Ni Houlihan* (no. 21), though it did not produce riots, provided challenges of its own. Set in 1798, on the eve of the French invasion of Ireland, the play blended Gaelic imagery and Fenian and United Irishmen politics. It represented a rejection not only of British rule and Anglicization but also of modernization itself. Indeed, it seems that for Yeats, as for Davis, Anglicization and modernization were virtually interchangeable.

2. Pearse's first name appears in various forms in addition to Pádraic, notably, Padraig, Pádraig, and Patrick.

The second aspect of the revival—the Irish language movement—was undertaken in the context of the rapid decline in Irish speaking. It had already been a concern of Young Ireland. By the time of the revival, the use of Irish in everyday life was in free-fall. In 1845 perhaps 50 percent of the population spoke the Irish language. Following the Famine in 1851, 23 percent did. In 1891 the number of Irish speakers had fallen to 14.5 percent (Jackson 1999, 177). Here the key figure was Douglas Hyde. His essay "The Necessity for De-Anglicising Ireland" (no. 19), originally a talk given to the Irish Literary Society, was a call to arms to save the Irish language from extinction. Hyde's impassioned plea was, in fact, a critique of the politics of O'Connell and his successors. He was not opposed to constitutional nationalism, but saw it as representing the surface rather than the heart of the nationalist cause. Above all, he viewed Irishness, embodied in Gaelic culture and the Irish language, as a spiritual essence that had been allowed to atrophy. Like Davis and Yeats, Hyde regarded Gaelic culture as transcending the Catholic-Protestant divide and as an alternative to Anglicization, middle-class Philistinism, and modernization. It was intellectuals (like himself) and peasants who still spoke Irish that provided the basis for renewal. Like Davis and Yeats, Hyde also had no place for Ulster in his representation of Ireland. Gaelic Ireland had absorbed Danes, Normans, the old English, and the Anglo-Irish; but Ulster Presbyterians had been more recalcitrant. Hyde implied that they would eventually submit as well, a viewpoint that was not all that different than Thomas Burke's (no. 18).

Hyde's call for the renewal and spread of the Irish language in literature and everyday life, and his belief that Ireland's future must be based on the Gaelic culture of the past, was the foundation of one of the most important products of the revival—the Gaelic League. Founded in 1893, with Hyde as its first president, the League brought together activists of many political stripes, nationalist and Unionist alike, for the purpose of promoting the Irish language in private and public life. It helped to create, for instance, a lectureship in Irish at University College, Cork, and was instrumental in making Irish a required subject at the new National University of Ireland established in 1908. Significantly, unlike other nationalist organizations, women were allowed to be Gaelic League members. Maud Gonne MacBride's autobiography (no. 23) clearly conveys the obstacles faced by women who wanted to participate in the male-dominated nationalist movement and the determination that it took to overcome them. In contrast, Mary Butler, a Gaelic League activist, acknowledged that male dominance existed within nationalist circles but envisioned a political role for women in the domestic rather than the public sphere; she advocated that women learn Irish and teach it to their children (no. 20).

In the end, the Gaelic League's attempt to transform Ireland culturally, while remaining aloof from party politics, proved impossible to sustain. Pádraic Pearse's "The Coming Revolution" (no. 46) paid tribute to the League's achievement but argued that it represented a stepping-stone toward revolution rather than being an end in itself. In his words: "The deed of the generation that has now reached middle life was the Gaelic League: the beginning of the Irish Revolution. Let our generation not shirk *its* deed, which is to accomplish the revolution." In his essay, Pearse represented his own development as a nationalist: from being a Gaelic League activist to being a political revolutionary who in the end would die for republican principles. He was the leader in the Easter Rising of 1916 and subsequently executed by British authorities. His transformation was emblematic of some but not all of his generation.

12 and 13. Thomas Moore, *Irish Melodies* (1808–34)

Thomas Moore (1779–1852) was among the most widely read and admired writers of his day. In his lifetime his name was spoken of in the same breath as writers such as Lord Byron (1788–1824) and Sir Walter Scott (1771–1832). He was born in Dublin, the son of a Catholic grocer, who instilled in him an admiration for the Volunteers of 1782. He was one of the first Catholics to attend Trinity College, Dublin, where he became close friends with Robert Emmet, whom he later dedicated poems to and made a subject of his poetry. Moore was not an active participant in the United Irishmen, but his nationalist feeling was closer to its spirit than the Catholic nationalism that achieved prominence in the nineteenth century. He spent much of his life in England, and he married a sixteen-year-old English Protestant actress, Elizabeth Dyke (1796–1885), in 1811. He spent his last days in Wiltshire in the English countryside.

Moore's original literary success in England resulted from his Odes of Anacreon *(1800). But* Irish Melodies *(1808–34)—consisting of more than a hundred poems, published over a nearly forty-year span, in ten numbers, seven of which were set to music by Sir John Stevenson (1761–1833)—is the basis of his fame. The poems are romantic, sentimental, and melancholy. They draw on Irish history and legend. Many of them are explicitly political. "Dear Harp of My Country" (no. 12) and "Erin, oh Erin" (no. 13) are among the best known of the collection and exude melancholic hope and longing for national freedom. As a result of their wide distribution and popularity, they, as well as others of Moore's poems, played an important role in articulating and spreading Irish national aspiration, arguably more so than the published work of many of the best-known political writers.*

12. Thomas Moore, "Dear Harp[3] of My Country"

> Dear Harp of my Country! in darkness I found thee,
>   The cold chain of silence had hung o'er thee long,
> When proudly, my own Island Harp, I unbound thee,
>   And gave all thy chords to light, freedom, and song!
>
> The warm lay of love and the light note of gladness
>   Have waken'd thy fondest, thy liveliest thrill;
> But, so oft has thou echo'd the deep sigh of sadness,
>   That ev'n in thy mirth it will steal from thee still.

3. Symbol for Ireland.

Dear Harp of my Country! farewell to thy numbers,
    This sweet wreath of song is the last we shall twine![4]
Go, sleep with the sunshine of Fame on thy slumbers,
    Till touch'd by some hand less unworthy than mine;
If the pulse of the patriot, soldier, or lover,
    Have throbb'd at our lay, 'tis thy glory alone;
I was *but* as the wind, passing heedlessly over,
    And all the wild sweetness I wak'd was thy own.

13. Thomas Moore, "Erin, oh Erin"

Like the bright lamp, that shone in Kildare's holy fane,[5]
    And burn'd thro' long ages of darkness and storm,
Is the heart that sorrows have frown'd on in vain,
    Whose spirit outlives them, unfading and warm.
Erin, oh Erin, thus bright thro' the tears
Of a long night of bondage, thy spirit appears.

The nations have fallen, and thou still art young,
    Thy sun is but rising, when others are set;
And tho' slavery's cloud o'er thy morning hath hung
    The full noon of freedom shall beam round thee yet.
Erin, of Erin, tho' long in the shade,
Thy star will shine out when the proudest shall fade.

Unchill'd by the rain, and unwak'd by the wind,
    The lily lies sleeping thro' winter's cold hour,
Till Spring's light touch her fetter unbind,
    And daylight and liberty bless the young flower.
Thus Erin, oh Erin, *thy* winter is past,
And the hope that liv'd thro' it shall blossom at last.

14. Editorial, Unsigned Article from *The Nation* (1842)

Young Ireland's cultural nationalism spread as a consequence of its newspaper, The
Nation, *first published in October 1842. The Nation was inexpensive, published
weekly, and produced in a tabloid format. It sold ten thousand copies per week, and its*

4. Twist together.
5. A holy temple or church. Here the reference is to St. Bridgid (also Brigid) of Kildare (c.
451–525), one of Ireland's twelve patron saints, associated with perpetual sacred flames.
Gerald of Wales (c.1146–c.1223) relates that at her shrine the nuns kept a fire going that
burned continuously for centuries.

readership was as many as a quarter million. The newspaper was suppressed in 1848 for its revolutionary politics, but it was allowed to publish the following year. It would never again have the same influence.

The great majority of The Nation*'s articles were anonymous. The essay reprinted here is attributed to the newspaper's first editor, Charles Gavan Duffy (1816–1903), a journalist from a middle-class Catholic family in County Monaghan. Duffy supported Young Ireland's break with Daniel O'Connell's repeal movement in 1847. He subsequently supported an armed rising in 1848 and was imprisoned as a result. Duffy was MP for New Ross (1852–55), but he became disillusioned with Irish politics and immigrated to Australia, where he had a distinguished political career: he was prime minister (1871–72) and speaker of the Assembly (1876–80), and he was knighted in 1873. In retirement, Duffy wrote widely read autobiographical and historical accounts of the 1840s and 1850s in Ireland.*

Duffy's essay can be regarded as The Nation*'s manifesto, a call to arms for a new kind of Irish nationalist movement. His contention that the newspaper will "foster nationality" and that the people must be taught national identity's "intrinsic advantage" raises questions regarding the relationship between national identity and nationalism. It is usually assumed that a common national identity gives rise to a nationalist movement that gives it a political voice. It is also conceivable, as the theorist of nationalism Ernest Gellner (1983) has argued, that the nationalist movement plays a critical role in articulating the meaning of national identity.*

'*To create and to foster public opinion in Ireland—to make it racy of the soil. — Chief Baron Woulfe*'.[6]

DUBLIN, SATURDAY, OCTOBER 15, 1842

With all the nicknames that serve to delude and divide us—with all their Orangemen and Ribbonmen, Torymen and Whigmen, Ultras and Moderados,[7] and Heaven knows what rubbish besides, there are, in truth, but two parties in Ireland: those who suffer from her National degradation, and those who profit by it. To a country like ours, all other distinctions are unimportant. This is the first article of our political creed; and as we desire to be known for what we are, we make it our earliest task to announce that the object of the writers of this journal is to organise the greater and better part of those parties, and to strive, with all our soul and with all our strength, for the diffusion and establishment of its principles. This will be the beginning, middle, and end of our labours.

6. Arthur Wolfe (1739–1803), 1st Viscount Kilwarden, Lord Chief Justice of the King's Bench of Ireland from 1798 until his death. During the rising led by Robert Emmet, Wolfe was dragged from his carriage and murdered.

7. *Orangemen* and *Ribbonmen* were militant groups, the former defending Protestant interests and the latter Catholic. The *Tories* and *Whigs* were the two major political parties in England, the Tories being the more conservative of the two. *Moderados* and *Ultras* were more general terms signifying extremists and moderates, respectively.

And we come to the task with a strong conviction that there never was a moment more favorable for such a purpose than the present. The old parties are broken, or breaking up, both in England and Ireland—Whiggery,[8] which never had a soul, has now no body;[9] and the simplest partisan, or the most selfish expectant—who is generally a creature quite as unreasonable cannot ask us to fix the hopes of our country on the fortunes of a party so weak and fallen. Far less can we expect anything from Toryism, which could only serve us by ceasing to *be* Toryism;[10] even in its new and modified form it means the identical reverse of all we require to make the masses in this country happier and better. But this shifting of parties—this loosening of belief in old distinctions and dogmas, has prepared men's minds for new and greater efforts. Out of the contempt for mere party politics will naturally grow a desire to throw aside small and temporary remedies—to refuse to listen any longer to those who would plaster a cut finger, or burn an old wart and call this doctoring the body politic—and to combine for great and permanent changes. The point of honor which restrained multitudes from abandoning Whiggery, while their service could sustain it in its old accustomed place, can operate no more. The idiot hope, that Toryism might for once produce something good, has been pretty well disappointed; and, after an unexampled lull in politics, the popular party are ready, and willing, and anxious once again to be up and doing.

On this new spirit our hope for Ireland depends—and it will be our frequent duty hereafter to impress our views in detail on our readers, and to indicate all the ways and means of their accomplishment. We believe we will have the advice and co-operation of many of the wisest and best of our countrymen; and as our pages will be always open to fair discussion, we hope to reflect the popular mind, and gather the popular suffrage, within our columns upon this and all other questions of national politics.

But let us guard ourselves, from the very beginning, against being understood, when we speak of politics, to mean the thing which the phrase expresses in the vulgar tongue of journalism. By politics we mean the science of government, and all the facts and circumstances with which it must naturally deal. . . .

For this National party in Ireland we believe it indispensable to its usefulness to claim, now and always, the right to stand at the head of all combined movements of Reformers in this country. They have too long forgotten or mistaken their true position. Is it not a lamentable absurdity—a blunder almost too ludicrous for an English commander in Afghanistan[11]—to have the officers of an army less resolute and courageous than the soldiers? NAPOLEON [BONAPARTE], we believe, did not choose the

8. A contemptuous reference to the Whigs.

9. The Whigs were defeated in the 1841 parliamentary elections.

10. As the defenders of the established order, the Tories were generally unsympathetic to Irish national aspiration.

11. In what became known as the first Anglo-Afghan War, a force of British and Indian soldiers took control of Kabul in 1837. They were forced to withdraw in 1842 (just months prior to the publication of this editorial). Of the sixteen thousand men who departed, only one lived.

Generals who led his legions to victory from the most timid and hesitating of the aristocracy, but from bold and sagacious men, whether in the ranks or on the staff. Those who go farthest ought naturally to lead the way. 'Come with us as far as we go together,' say the Moderate or Non-National party. 'Certainly,' we are prepared on all occasions to reply; 'but as we go farthest, just permit us, for convenience sake, to go foremost.' This is the tone which naturally belongs to a National party, and wanting which they must always want the dignity and solidity necessary to accomplish great effects.

But the first duty of men who desire to foster Nationality, is to teach the People not only the elevating influence but the intrinsic advantage of the principle and the thing. You cannot kindle a fire with damp faggots; and every man in the country who has not an interest in the existing system ought to be shown, as clearly as an abstract truth can be demonstrated, that National feelings, National habits, and National government, are indispensable to individual prosperity. This will be our task; and we venture to think we will perform it indifferently well.

But no National feeling can co-exist with the mean and mendicant spirit[12] which esteems everything English as greater and better than if it belonged to our own country, and which looks at all the rest of the world through the spectacles of Anglican prejudice. There is no doubt at all that the chief source of the contempt with which we are treated by England is our own sycophancy. We abandon our self-respect, and we are treated with contempt; nothing can be more natural—nothing, in fact, can be more just. But we must open our eyes and look our domineering neighbour in the face—we must inspect him, and endeavour to discover what kind of a fellow he is. Not that we ought to do him injustice—not that we ought to run into opposite extremes—not, above all, that we ought to take universal England to be fairly represented by the disagreeable person who sometimes condescends to visit *H*ireland—a fat man, with his head in the clouds and his brains in his belly, looking the incarnation of self-importance, and saying, as plainly as plum-pudding countenance can speak—'I am a Great Briton.' JOHN BULL[13] is as much a better fellow than this animal, as he is worse than what our shameful sycophancy would make him. We must learn to think sensibly and candidly about him; and we do not doubt that THE NATION will tend materially to this end.

We may be told that we expect to effect too much through the means of a newspaper, but nobody who knows this country thoroughly will say this. A newspaper is the only conductor to the mind of Ireland. Periodicals or books make no considerable impression because they have no considerable circulation. Speeches are more effective; but we include them among the materials of journalism. [DANIEL] O'CONNELL the orator, is as much the food of the Press as O'CONNELL the writer. And it is undeniable that the journals, with all their means and appliances, were, and are, and are to be for many a day, the stimulating power in Ireland. Their work may not be apparent, but it is not the less sure; its slow and silent operation acts on the masses as the wind, which we do not see, moves the dust, which we do see—and in both cases the invisible giant is sometimes forgotten.

12. One who is miserly and dependent on handouts.
13. Personification of England.

But, in addition to all that journalism has been, we shall add a new element to its strength. Men who have hitherto only written books, will now take this shorter and surer road to the popular mind. Already the ablest writers in the country are banded together to do this work; but we shall, besides, rally round us the young intellect of the country. Many a student, pent among books, has his mind full of benevolent and useful thoughts for his country, which the habits of a student's life would prevent him for ever from pouring out in the hot arena of politics. Such men will find a fitting vehicle in THE NATION; and our kindred love of letters will often induce them to turn with us from the study of mankind in books, to the service of mankind in politics. Such a legion will be more formidable than 'a thousand men all clad in steel'; each of them may fairly represent the multitude whom his intellect can set in motion; and the weapons which they will lay to the root of corruption will not be less keen or trenchant because they may cover them with the flowers of literature.

15 and 16. Thomas Davis

Thomas Davis (1814–45) was a founder of The Nation, *a leader of the Young Ireland movement, and a writer of poetry and prose. He was arguably the most admired and influential voice of his generation. Davis was from Mallow, County Cork; from a Protestant background (the son of an English army surgeon and Irish Protestant mother); and, like many activists in the nationalist movement, educated at Trinity College, Dublin. He joined the Repeal Association in 1841 and was an ally of Daniel O'Connell. However, the relationship between the two men was fraught with tension: they disagreed about education and political strategy. Most important, as an Irish Protestant, Davis was troubled by O'Connell's equation of the Irish nation with Catholics. Like Wolfe Tone before him, Davis sought to move beyond the Catholic-Protestant divide, imagining the Irish nation as the people of Ireland. At the same time, Davis was under the sway of German romanticism, which conceived of nationality in cultural terms. He located Irish nationhood in the national soul—its history, literature, antiquities, and, above all, its language. Paradoxically, Davis' conception of the repeal movement was inclusive, but his notion of Ireland's identity minimized the historical role of Ireland's diverse populations.*

Two dimensions of Davis' writing are featured here. The scholarly essay "Old Ireland" (no. 15), originally published in The Nation, *suggests Davis' debt to romantic criticism, particularly the Scottish writer Thomas Carlyle. Davis contrasts the imposition of England's materialistic and mechanistic culture with Ireland's threatened yet enduring ancient civilization. His advocacy of promoting Irish consciousness through a secular education set him apart from O'Connell and the Catholic Church. Never considered by literary critics to be an important poet, Davis nonetheless was a popular one, especially known for those of his poems that were set to music. "A Nation Once Again" (no. 16) was not only popular in its own day. In a 2002 BBC World Service global poll (unscientific), the version of the song performed by the Wolfe Tones, a renowned Irish folk band, was voted the world's most popular song.*

15. Thomas Davis, "Old Ireland," *The Nation* (August 10, 1844)

There was once civilization in Ireland. We never were very eminent to be sure for
manufactures in metal, our houses were simple, our very palaces rude, our furniture
scanty, our saffron shirts not often changed, and our foreign trade small. Yet was
Ireland civilized. Strange thing! says one whose ideas of civilization are identical with
carpets and cut glass, fine masonry, and the steam-engine; yet 'tis true. For there was
a time when learning was endowed by the rich and honoured by the poor, and taught
all over our country. Not only did thousands of natives frequent our schools and col-
leges, but men of every rank came here from the Continent to study under the professors and system of Ireland, and we need not go beyond the testimonies of English
antiquaries, from Bede to Camden,[14] that these schools were regarded as the first in
Europe. Ireland was equally remarkable for piety. In the Pagan times it was regarded as
a sanctuary of the Magian or Druid creed.[15] From the fifth century it became equally
illustrious in Christendom. Without going into the disputed question of whether the
Irish church was or was not independent of Rome, it is certain that Italy did not send
out more apostles from the fifth to the ninth centuries than Ireland, and we find their
names and achievement remembered through the Continent.

Of the two names which Hallam[16] thinks worth rescuing from the darkness of the
dark ages one is the Irish metaphysician, John Erigena.[17] In a recent communication
to the [Repeal] "Association," we had Bavarians acknowledging the Irish St. Kilian[18]
as the apostle of their country.

Yet what beyond a catalogue of names and a few marked events, do even the
educated Irish know of the heroic Pagans or the holy Christians of old Ireland. These
men have left libraries of biography, religion, philosophy, natural history, topography,

14. Bede (672/673–735), also known as St. Bede or the Venerable Bede, an Anglo-Saxon
scholar, historian, and theologian. William Camden (1551–1623), English antiquarian and
historian, compiled *Britannia*, a topographical account in Latin of the British Isles from ancient times.

15. *Magian* denotes a follower of Zoroaster, the Ancient Iranian prophet and poet, but more
generally it suggests the ability to interpret the meaning of the stars and to manipulate outcomes based on that interpretation. A *Druid* is a priestly and learned man in ancient Celtic
culture. It is believed that Druids were responsible for maintaining the oral tradition.

16. Henry Hallam (1777–1859), English historian, best known for *The View of the State of
Europe during the Middle Ages* (1818), *Constitutional History of England from the Accession of
Henry VII to the Death of George III* (1827), and *Introduction to the Literature of Europe in the
Fifteenth, Sixteenth, and Seventeenth Centuries* (1838–39).

17. Johannes Scotus Erigena (also Eriugena) (c. 815–77), Irish theologian, philosopher, and
poet. He translated and made commentaries upon the work of Pseudo-Dionysius, an anonymous theologian and philosopher of the late fifth and early sixth centuries.

18. Saint Kilian (Irish: Cilian) (late seventh century), an Irish bishop and missionary who, as
a result of his missionary work in Franconia (which includes what is now the northern part of
Bavaria), became known as its apostle.

history, and romance. They *cannot all be worthless;* yet, except the few volumes given us by the Archæological Society,[19] which of their works have any of us read?

It is also certain that we possessed written laws with extensive and minute comments and reported decisions. These Brehon laws[20] have been foully misrepresented by Sir John Davies.[21] Their tenures were the Gavelkind[22] once prevalent over most of the world. The land belonged to the clan, and, on the death of a clansman his share was reapportioned according to the number and wants of his family. The system of erics or fines for offences has existed amongst every people from the Hebrews downwards, nor can any one knowing the multitude of crimes now punishable by fines or damages, think the people of this [British] empire justified in calling the ancient Irish barbarous, because they extended the system. There is in these laws, so far as they are known, minuteness and equity; and, what is a better test of their goodness, we learn from Sir John Davies himself, and from the still abler Baron Finglass,[23] that the people reverenced, obeyed, and clung to these laws, though to decide by or obey them was a high crime by England's code. Moreover, the Norman and Saxon settlers[24] hastened to adopt these Irish laws, and used them more resolutely, if possible, than the Irish themselves.

Orderliness and hospitality were peculiarly cultivated. Public caravanserais[25] were built for travellers in every district, and we have what would almost be legal evidence of the grant of vast tracts of land for the supply of provisions for these houses of hospitality. The private hospitality of the chiefs was equally marked, nor was it quite rude. Ceremony was united with great freedom of intercourse; age, and learning, and rank, and virtue were respected, and these men whose cookery was probably as coarse as that of Homer's heroes,[26] had around their board harpers and bards who sang

19. Irish Archaeological Society, founded in 1840, its aim being to publish scholarly material on Irish antiquities.

20. Ancient Irish laws, the name being derived from *Brehon*, the administrator of the law.

21. Sir John Davies (1569–1626), English court poet, and solicitor-general and attorney general of Ireland (1603–19). His *A Discovery of the True Causes Why Ireland Was Never Entirely Subdued* (1612) argued that it was only under James I that English common law had successfully penetrated Ireland.

22. A system of land tenure, prevalent in Anglo-Saxon times, in which the sons of an estate owner inherited the land equally upon his death. After the Normans invaded England in the eleventh century, it was largely supplanted by primogeniture, where the estate goes to the eldest son.

23. Patrick Finglass, chief baron of the exchequer, later chief justice of the King's Bench, both during the reign of Henry VIII. He is the author of *A Breviate of the Getting of Ireland and the Decay of the Same*, written around 1529, which contains a valuable historical account of Ireland.

24. Colonists from England and Wales who first came to Ireland as part of the Anglo-Norman invasion in the twelfth century.

25. Also caravanserai, caravansarai, or caravansary. Roadside inns for travelers found along eastern trade routes. Here Davis is using the word in a more general sense.

26. Homer, ancient Greek poet, author of the epic poems the *Iliad* and the *Odyssey*, which are known for, among many things, their portrayals of heroes such as Achilles and Odysseus.

poetry as gallant and fiery, though not so grand as the Homeric ballad singers, and flung off a music which Greece never rivalled.

Shall a people, pious, hospitable, and brave, faithful observers of family ties, cultivators of learning, music, and poetry, be called less than civilized, because mechanical arts were rude, and "comfort" despised by them?

Scattered through the country in MS.,[27] are hundreds of books wherein the law and achievements, the genealogies and possessions, the creeds, and manners and poetry of these our predecessors in Ireland are set down. Their music lives in the traditional airs of every valley.

Yet *mechanical civilization*, more cruel than time, is trying to exterminate them, and, therefore, it becomes us all who do not wish to lose the heritage of centuries, nor to feel ourselves living among nameless ruins, when we might have an ancestral home—it becomes all who love learning, poetry, or music, or are curious of human progress, to aid in or originate a series of efforts to save all that remains of the past.

It becomes them to lose no opportunity of instilling into the minds of their neighbours, whether they be corporators or peasants, that it is a brutal, mean, and sacrilegious thing, to turn a castle, a church, a tomb, or a mound, into a quarry or a gravel pit, or to break the least morsel of sculpture, or to take any old coin or ornament they may find to a jeweller, so long as there is an Irish Academy[28] in Dublin to pay for it or accept it.

Before the year is out we hope to see A SOCIETY FOR THE PRESERVATION OF IRISH MUSIC[29] established in Dublin, under the joint patronage of the leading men of all politics, with branches in the provincial towns for the collection and diffusion of Irish airs.

An effort—a great and decided one—must be made to have the Irish Academy so endowed out of the revenues of Ireland, that it may be A NATIONAL SCHOOL OF IRISH HISTORY AND LITERATURE AND A MUSEUM OF IRISH ANTIQUITIES, on the largest scale. In fact, the Academy should be a secular Irish College with professors of our old language, literature, history, antiquities, and topography; with suitable schools, lecture-rooms and museums.

16. Thomas Davis, "A Nation Once Again" (1845)

When boyhood's fire was in my blood
I read of ancient freemen,
For Greece and Rome who bravely stood,
THREE HUNDRED MEN and THREE MEN.
And then I prayed I yet might see

27. Manuscript (abbreviation).

28. The Royal Irish Academy, founded in 1785, promoted and discussed science, literature, and antiquities and facilitated discussion and debate among scholars from varied backgrounds.

29. The Society for the Preservation and Publication of the Melodies of Ireland was founded in 1851.

Our fetters rent in twain,
And Ireland, long a province, be
A NATION ONCE AGAIN.

II.

And from that time, through wildest woe,
That hope has shone, a far light;
Nor could love's brightest summer glow,
Outshine that solemn starlight;
It seemed to watch above my head
In forum, field, and fane,
It's angel voice sang round my bed,
"A NATION ONCE AGAIN"

III.

It whispered too, that "freedom's ark
And service high and holy,
Would be profan'd by feelings dark
And passions vain or lowly;
For freedom comes from God's right hand,
And needs a godly train;
And righteous men must make our land
A NATION ONCE AGAIN"

IV.

So, as I grew from boy to man
I bent me to that bidding—
My spirit of each selfish plan
And cruel passion ridding;
For, thus I hoped some day to aid—
Oh! can such hope be vain?—
When my dear country shall be made
A NATION ONCE AGAIN.

17. Matthew Arnold, Selections from *On the Study of Celtic Literature* (1867)

Matthew Arnold (1822–88) is among the most important English Victorian poets and cultural critics. As a critic, Arnold is best known for Culture and Anarchy *(1869), in which he portrayed Britain as torn by class antagonism and suffering from middle-class materialism. He argued that culture, defined as the best that has been thought and written, transcended class interests. It should provide the basis for the state and its governing class, whose selection should be based on critical intelligence irrespective of origins. Arnold also gave considerable attention to the Irish question. He empathized with the*

grievances of Catholic Ireland and thought of the Protestants there as exemplifying the
English narrow-mindedness and acquisitiveness that he despised. Yet Arnold believed
that Ireland could be given a fair and equitable government without Home Rule, which
he regarded as a dangerous experiment.

Arnold's most influential writings on the Anglo-Irish relationship began as a series of
four lectures at Oxford University, subsequently published in Cornhill Magazine *and*
reprinted as On the Study of Celtic Literature *(1867). Arnold's arguments drew notably*
on the French scholar Ernest Renan (1823–92), who, using arguments from philology,
ethnology, and anthropology, located national character and national difference in lan-
guage. Arnold contrasted the national characters of the (English) Saxon and the (Irish)
Celt, the former expressing deliberateness and practicality, the latter emotion, creativity,
and flightiness. He argued that the English character produced philistinism, that is, nar-
row and materialistic values, when founded on its Saxon origins alone. However, as the
English experience was also founded on a Celtic past, the English could achieve a more vi-
brant, creative, and balanced disposition. The Irish, in contrast, had no Saxon component
in their character, and thus, while creative and imaginative, needed English guidance
and supervision. He regarded the Irish language as the remnant of a defeated people, and,
while he believed that the language should be studied in universities, he believed that Eng-
lish should be the language of daily life in Ireland. In the following excerpt, Arnold defines
the Celtic personality, contrasting it with the disposition of the Saxon and the Greek.

. . . [N]ow let us come to the beautiful and amorous Gaedhil.[30] Or rather, let us find a
definition which may suit both branches of the Celtic family, the Cymri as well as the
Gael.[31] It is clear that special circumstances may have developed some one side in the
national character of Cymri or Gael, Welshman or Irishman, so that the observer's
notice shall be readily caught by this side, and yet it may be impossible to adopt it as
characteristic of the Celtic nature generally. For instance, in his beautiful essay on the
poetry of the Celtic races, M. Renan,[32] with his eyes fixed on the Bretons[33] and the
Welsh, is struck with the timidity, the shyness, the delicacy of the Celtic nature, its
preference for a retired life, its embarrassment at having to deal with the great world.
He talks of the *douce petite race naturellement chrétienne,*[34] his *race fière et timide,*[35]
à l'extérieur gauche et embarrassée.[36] But it is evident that this description, however
well it may do for the Cymri, will never do for the Gael, never do for the typical
Irishman of Donnybrook fair.[37] Again, M. Renan's *infinie délicatesse de sentiment qui*

---

30. A person of Gaelic descent.

31. Arnold distinguishes between two types of Celts, the Cymri being the Welsh and the Gael
the Irish.

32. Ernest Renan, "Poetry of the Celtic Races" (1854).

33. People of the province of Brittany in northwestern France.

34. Small, gentle race that is inherently Christian (French).

35. Proud and timid race (French).

36. With a crude yet restrained manner (French).

37. A fair held in Donnybrook, south Dublin, that was known for its rowdiness.

caractérise la race Celtique,[38] how little that accords with the popular conception of an Irishman who wants to borrow money! *Sentiment* is, however, the word which marks where the Celtic races really touch and are one; sentimental, if the Celtic nature is to be characterised by a single term, is the best term to take. An organisation quick to feel impressions, and feeling them very strongly; a lively personality therefore, keenly sensitive to joy and to sorrow; this is the main point. If the downs of life too much outnumber the ups, this temperament, just because it is so quickly and nearly conscious of all impressions, may no doubt be seen [as] shy and wounded; it may be seen in wistful regret, it may be seen in passionate, penetrating melancholy; but its essence is to aspire ardently after life, light, and emotion, to be expansive, adventurous, and gay. Our word *gay,* it is said, is itself Celtic. It is not from *gaudium,* but from the Celtic *gair,* to laugh; and the impressionable Celt, soon up and soon down, is the more down because it is so his nature to be up—to be sociable, hospitable, eloquent, admired, figuring away brilliantly. He loves bright colours, he easily becomes audacious, overcrowing, full of fanfaronade.[39] The German, say the physiologists, has the larger volume of intestines (and who that has ever seen a German at a table-d'hôte[40] will not readily believe this?), the Frenchman has the more developed organs of respiration. That is just the expansive, eager Celtic nature; the head in the air, snuffing and snorting; *a proud look and a high stomach,* as the Psalmist says,[41] but without any such settled savage temper as the Psalmist seems to impute by those words. For good and for bad, the Celtic genius is more airy and unsubstantial, goes less near the ground, than the German. The Celt is often called sensual; but it is not so much the vulgar satisfactions of sense that attract him as emotion and excitement; he is truly, as I began by saying, sentimental.

Sentimental,—*always ready to react against the despotism of fact,* that is the description a great friend of the Celt gives of him;[42] and it is not a bad description of the sentimental temperament; it lets us into the secret of its dangers and of its habitual want of success. Balance, measure, and patience, these are the eternal conditions, even supposing the happiest temperament to start with, of high success; and balance, measure, and patience are just what the Celt has never had. Even in the world of spiritual creation, he has never, in spite of his admirable gifts of quick perception and warm emotion, succeeded perfectly, because he never has had steadiness, patience, sanity enough to comply with the conditions under which alone can expression be perfectly given to the finest perceptions and emotions. The Greek has the same perceptive, emotional temperament as the Celt; but he adds to this temperament the sense of *measure;* hence his admirable success in the plastic arts, in which the Celtic genius, with its chafing against the despotism of fact, its perpetual straining after mere emotion, has accomplished nothing. In the comparatively petty art of ornamentation, in

---

38. A profound tenderness of feeling within the Celtic race (French).

39. Bragging or bravado.

40. A fixed-price menu made up of multiple courses.

41. "Whoso hath also a proud look and a high stomach: I will not suffer him" (Psalms 101:7).

42. "Monsieur Henri Martin, whose chapters on the Celts, in his *Histoire de France,* are full of information and interest." [Note from 1899 edition.]

rings, brooches, crosiers,[43] relic-cases, and so on, he has done just enough to show his delicacy of taste, his happy temperament; but the grand difficulties of painting and sculpture, the prolonged dealings of spirit with matter, he has never had patience for. Take the more spiritual arts of music and poetry. All that emotion alone can do in music the Celt has done; the very soul of emotion breathes in the Scotch and Irish airs; but with all this power of musical feeling, what has the Celt, so eager for emotion that he has not patience for science, effected in music, to be compared with what the less emotional German, steadily developing his musical feeling with the science of a Sebastian Bach[44] or a Beethoven,[45] has effected? In poetry, again,—poetry which the Celt has so passionately, so nobly loved; poetry where emotion counts for so much, but where reason, too, reason, measure, sanity, also count for so much,—the Celt has shown genius, indeed, splendid genius; but even here his faults have clung to him, and hindered him from producing great works, such as other nations with a genius for poetry,—the Greeks, say, or the Italians,—have produced. The Celt has not produced great poetical works, he has only produced poetry with an air of greatness investing it all, and sometimes giving, moreover, to short pieces, or to passages, lines, and snatches of long pieces, singular beauty and power. And yet he loved poetry so much that he grudged no pains to it; but the true art, the *architectonicé*[46] which shapes great works, such as the *Agamemnon*[47] or the *Divine Comedy*,[48] comes only after a steady, deep-searching survey, a firm conception of the facts of human life, which the Celt has not patience for. So he runs off into technic,[49] where he employs the utmost elaboration, and attains astonishing skill; but in the contents of his poetry you have only so much interpretation of the world as the first dash of a quick, strong perception, and then sentiment, infinite sentiment, can bring you. Here, too, his want of sanity and steadfastness has kept the Celt back from the highest success.

If his rebellion against fact has thus lamed the Celt even in spiritual work, how much more must it have lamed him in the world of business and politics! The skilful and resolute appliance of means to ends which is needed both to make progress in material civilisation, and also to form powerful states, is just what the Celt has least turn for. He is sensual, as I have said, or at least sensuous; loves bright colours, company, and pleasure; and here he is like the Greek and Latin races; but compare the talent the Greek and Latin (or Latinised) races have shown for gratifying their senses, for procuring an outward life, rich, luxurious, splendid, with the Celt's failure to reach any material civilisation sound and satisfying, and not out at elbows, poor, slovenly, and half-barbarous. The sensuousness of the Greek made Sybaris and

43. A staff with a cross at the end.

44. Johann Sebastian Bach (1685–1750), German Baroque composer.

45. Ludwig van Beethoven (1770–1827), German composer who straddles the Classical and the Romantic eras.

46. A unified structure suggestive of an architectural design.

47. A play by the Greek playwright Aeschylus written around 458 BCE.

48. An epic poem written by the Italian writer Dante Alighieri between 1308 and 1321.

49. The theory or principles of an art form.

Corinth,[50] the sensuousness of the Latin made Rome and Baiæ,[51] the sensuousness of the Latinised Frenchman makes Paris; the sensuousness of the Celt proper has made Ireland. Even in his ideal heroic times, his gay and sensuous nature cannot carry him, in the appliances of his favourite life of sociability and pleasure, beyond the gross and creeping Saxon whom he despises; the regent Breas,[52] we are told in the *Battle of Moytura of the Fomorians*,[53] became unpopular because "the knives of his people were not greased at his table, nor did their breath smell of ale at the banquet." In its grossness and barbarousness is not that Saxon, as Saxon as it can be? [J]ust what the Latinised Norman, sensuous and sociable like the Celt, but with the talent to make this bent of his serve to a practical embellishment of his mode of living, found so disgusting in the Saxon.

And as in material civilisation he has been ineffectual, so has the Celt been ineffectual in politics. This colossal, impetuous, adventurous wanderer, the Titan[54] of the early world, who in primitive times fills so large a place on earth's scene, dwindles and dwindles as history goes on, and at last is shrunk to what we now see him. For ages and ages the world has been constantly slipping, ever more and more, out of the Celt's grasp. "They went forth to the war," Ossian says most truly, "*but they always fell.*"

And yet, if one sets about constituting an ideal genius, what a great deal of the Celt does one find oneself drawn to put into it! Of an ideal genius one does not want the elements, any of them, to be in a state of weakness; on the contrary, one wants all of them to be in the highest state of power; but with a law of measure, of harmony, presiding over the whole. So the sensibility of the Celt, if everything else were not sacrificed to it, is a beautiful and admirable force. For sensibility, the power of quick and strong perception and emotion, is one of the very prime constituents of genius, perhaps its most positive constituent; it is to the soul what good senses are to the body, the grand natural condition of successful activity. Sensibility gives genius its materials; one cannot have too much of it, if one can but keep its master and not be its slave. Do not let us wish that the Celt had had less sensibility, but that he had been more master of it. Even as it is, if his sensibility has been a source of weakness to him, it has been a source of power too, and a source of happiness. Some people have found in the Celtic nature and its sensibility the main root out of which chivalry and romance and the glorification of a feminine ideal spring; this is a great question, with which I cannot deal here. Let me notice in passing, however, that there is, in truth, a Celtic air about the extravagance of chivalry, its reaction against the

50. Cities built by the Greeks in Italy and Greece.

51. Cities in Italy built by the Romans.

52. A solar deity and at one point the ruler of the Tuatha Dé Danann, who according to medieval tradition ruled Ireland prior to the arrival of the sons of Mil, mythological predecessors of dynasties that presided over Ireland during the historical period.

53. A text from Irish mythology. "Moytura" is the anglicization of *Mag Tuired* or "The Plain of Towers." It narrates the conquest of Ireland by the Tuatha Dé Danann, their subsequent oppression by the Fomorians, and their battle to liberate themselves.

54. In Greek mythology, deities who ruled during the Golden Age before being overthrown by the Olympians.

despotism of fact, its straining human nature further than it will stand. But putting all this question of chivalry and its origin on one side, no doubt the sensibility of the Celtic nature, its nervous exaltation, have something feminine in them, and the Celt is thus peculiarly disposed to feel the spell of the feminine idiosyncrasy; he has an affinity to it; he is not far from its secret. Again, his sensibility gives him a peculiarly near and intimate feeling of nature and the life of nature; here, too, he seems in a special way attracted by the secret before him, the secret of natural beauty and natural magic, and to be close to it, to half-divine it. In the productions of the Celtic genius, nothing, perhaps, is so interesting as the evidences of this power: I shall have occasion to give specimens of them by and by. The same sensibility made the Celts full of reverence and enthusiasm for genius, learning, and the things of the mind; *to be a bard, freed a man*,—that is a characteristic stroke of this generous and ennobling ardour of theirs, which no race has ever shown more strongly. Even the extravagance and exaggeration of the sentimental Celtic nature has often something romantic and attractive about it, something which has a sort of smack of misdirected good. The Celt, undisciplinable, anarchical, and turbulent by nature, but out of affection and admiration giving himself body and soul to some leader, that is not a promising political temperament, it is just the opposite of the Anglo-Saxon temperament, disciplinable and steadily obedient within certain limits, but retaining an inalienable part of freedom and self-dependence; but it is a temperament for which one has a kind of sympathy notwithstanding. And very often, for the gay defiant reaction against fact of the lively Celtic nature one has more than sympathy; one feels, in spite of the extravagance, in spite of good sense disapproving, magnetised and exhilarated by it. The Gauls had a rule inflicting a fine on every warrior who, when he appeared on parade, was found to stick out too much in front,—to be corpulent, in short. Such a rule is surely the maddest article of war ever framed, and to people to whom nature has assigned a large volume of intestines, must appear, no doubt, horrible; but yet has it not an audacious, sparkling, immaterial manner with it, which lifts one out of routine, and sets one's spirits in a glow?

18. Thomas N. Burke, Selections from "The History of Ireland, as Told in Her Ruins," *Lectures on Faith and Fatherland* (1874)

Thomas Burke (1830–83) was born in Galway. The son of a baker, he was educated in Italy. A Dominican priest and preacher, he is best known for his tour of the United States, which lasted eighteen months and included over four hundred lectures, including a gathering of nearly fifty thousand people in Boston, which according to one source was the largest audience ever gathered in the United States up to that point. Known for his fiery and powerful rhetoric, Burke sought during his American tour to refute the ideas of James Anthony Froude (1818–94), who in his own American lecture tour defended British rule in Ireland, including Oliver Cromwell's invasion of Ireland in the seventeenth century. According to Burke's admirers, he was so successful in dismantling Froude's argument that Froude ended his trip earlier than planned, returning to England disappointed in his inability to gain sympathy for his views.

The excerpt from Burke's writings reprinted here explicitly joins nationalism and Catholicism. It was published five years following the disestablishment of the Church of Ireland, which redefined the relationship between religion and the state. For Burke, disestablishment signified a shift in the relationship between Irish men and women, one that would lead to Catholicism's inevitable triumph. It was rhetoric like this that reconfirmed Protestants' worst fears.

. . . And now, my friends, it is for me simply to draw one conclusion, and to have done. Is there a man amongst us here tonight who is ashamed of his race or his native land, if that man have the high honour to be an Irishman? Is there a man living that can point to a more glorious and a purer source whence he draws the blood in his veins, than the man who can point to the bravery of his Irish forefathers, or the immaculate purity of his Irish mother? We glory in them, and we glory in the faith for which our ancestors have died. We glory in the love of country that never—never, for an instant—admitted that Ireland was a mere province—that Ireland was merely a "West Britain." Never, in our darkest hour, was that idea adapted to the Irish mind, or adopted by the will of the Irish people. And, therefore, I say, if we glory in that faith—if we glory in the history of their national conduct and of their national love, oh, my friends and fellow-countrymen—I say it, as well as a priest as an Irishman— let us emulate their example; let us learn to be generous to those who differ from us, and let us learn to be charitable, even to those who would fain injure us. We can thus conquer them. We can thus assure to the future of Ireland the blessings that have been denied to her past—the blessing of religious equality, the blessing of religious liberty, the blessing of religious unity, which, one day or other, will spring up in Ireland again. I have often heard words of bitterness, aye, and of insult, addressed to myself in the north of Ireland, coming from Orange lips; but I have always said to myself, He is an Irishman; though he is an Orangeman, he is an Irishman. If he lives long enough, he will learn to love the priest that represents Ireland's old faith; but, if he die in his Orange dispositions, his son or his grandson will yet shake hands with and bless the priest, when he and I are both in our graves. And why do I say this? Because nothing bad, nothing uncharitable, nothing harsh or venomous ever yet lasted long upon the green soil of Ireland. If you throw a poisonous snake into the grass of Ireland, he will be sweetened, so as to lose his poison, or else he will die. Even the English people, when they landed, were not two hundred and fifty years in the land, until they were part of it; the very Normans who invaded us became "more Irish than the Irish themselves." They became so fond of the country that they were thoroughly imbued with its spirit. And so, any evil that we have in Ireland, is only a temporary and a passing evil, if we are only faithful to our traditions, and to the history of our country. To-day, there is religious disunion; but, thanks be to God, I have lived to see religious disabilities destroyed. And, if I were now in the position of addressing Irish Orangemen, I would say, "Men of Erin, three cheers for the Church disestablishment!" And if they should ask me, "Why?" I would answer, "It was right and proper to disestablish the Church, because the 'Established Church' was put in between you and me, and we ought to love each other, for we are both Irish!" Every class in Ireland will be drawn closer to the other by this disestablishment; and the honest Protestant man will begin to know a little more of his Catholic brother, and to admire him; and the Catholic will begin to know a little more of the Orangeman, and, perhaps, to say, "After all, he is not half so bad as he appears." And believe me, my friends, that, breathing the air of Ireland, which is Catholic, eating the bread made out of the wheat which grows out on Irish soil—they get so infused with Catholic blood, that as soon as the Orangeman begins to have the slightest regard or love for his Catholic fellow-countrymen, he is on the highway to become a Catholic—for a Catholic he will be, some time or other. As a man said to me very emphatically once: "They will all be Catholics one day, surely, sir, if they only stay long enough in the country!" I say, my friends, that the past is the best guarantee for the future. . . .

19. Douglas Hyde, "The Necessity for De-Anglicising Ireland" (1892), *The Revival of Irish Literature* (published 1894)

In the crusade to reassert an Irish identity—perceived as under threat from rapidly spreading Anglicization—Douglas Hyde (1860–1949) is among the most influential voices. The son of an Anglican clergyman, Hyde was a brilliant linguist who learned Irish from the local people of Roscommon where he spent his childhood years. He was a graduate of Trinity College, Dublin; a professor of modern Irish at University College, Dublin (1909–32); briefly a senator of the Irish Free State in 1925; and the first president of the successor to the Irish Free State, Éire (1938–45). Hyde is perhaps best known as a leading light in the Irish cultural revival, most importantly, as one of the founders of the Gaelic League in 1893 and as the group's first president. He also wrote poetry in Irish based on the oral tradition and manuscript sources. He collaborated with W. B. Yeats and Lady Gregory on theatrical productions, including the first Irish-language play performed in the theater. In addition, Hyde was the author of the highly influential Literary History of Ireland *(1899).*

"The Necessity for De-Anglicising Ireland" is among Hyde's most influential pieces of writing. Originally given as the inaugural address to the Irish National Literary Society, it is an impassioned plea for Irish cultural nationalism and an attack on parliamentary Home Rulers, who, Hyde believed, had purchased their "external" political prominence at the cost of an "inner" sense of Irish national identity. Like Thomas Davis (another Protestant) before him, Hyde located what was distinctive about Irishness in the Gaelic culture of the ancient past. However, in contrast to Davis, he was more adamant about the connection between the Irish language and cultural renewal and more explicit regarding the destructive influence of English culture on Ireland. Hyde's militant effort on behalf of the Irish language suggests that Protestants could be just as fervent in the revivalist cause of an Irish Ireland as Catholics. An unforeseen consequence, as D. George Boyce (1995, 240) has observed, was that Protestants such as Hyde may have been responsible for making it more difficult for their coreligionists to feel as if they could participate in an Irish nationalist future.

When we speak of "The Necessity for De-Anglicising the Irish Nation," we mean it, not as a protest against imitating what is *best* in the English people, for that would be absurd, but rather to show the folly of neglecting what is Irish, and hastening to adopt, pell-mell, and indiscriminately, everything that is English, simply because it *is* English.

This is a question which most Irishmen will naturally look at from a National point of view, but it is one which ought also to claim the sympathies of every intelligent Unionist, and which, as I know, does claim the sympathy of many.

If we take a bird's-eye view of our island to-day, and compare it with what it used to be, we must be struck by the extraordinary fact that the nation which was once, as every one admits, one of the most classically learned and cultured nations in Europe, is now one of the least so; how one of the most reading and literary peoples has become one of the *least* studious and most *un*-literary, and how the present art products of one of the quickest, most sensitive, and most artistic races on earth are now only distinguished for their hideousness.

I shall endeavour to show that this failure of the Irish people in recent times has been largely brought about by the race diverging during this century from the right path, and ceasing to be Irish without becoming English. I shall attempt to show that with the bulk of the people this change took place quite recently, much more recently than most people imagine, and is, in fact, still going on. I should also like to call attention to the illogical position of men who drop their own language to speak English, of men who translate their euphonious[55] Irish names into English monosyllables, of men who read English books, and know nothing about Gaelic literature, nevertheless protesting as a matter of sentiment that they hate the country which at every hand's turn they rush to imitate.

I wish to show you that in Anglicising ourselves wholesale we have thrown away with a light heart the best claim which we have upon the world's recognition of us as a separate nationality. What did Mazzini[56] say? What is Goldwin Smith[57] never tired of declaiming? What do the *Spectator* and *Saturday Review* harp on?[58] That we ought to be content as an integral part of the United Kingdom because we have lost the notes of nationality, our language and customs.

It has always been very curious to me how Irish sentiment sticks in this half-way house—how it continues to apparently hate the English, and at the same time continues to imitate them; how it continues to clamour for recognition as a distinct nationality, and at the same time throws away with both hands what would make it so. If Irishmen only went a little farther they would become good Englishmen in sentiment also. But—illogical as it appears—here seems not the slightest sign or probability of

---

55. Pleasant or agreeable to the ear.

56. Giuseppe Mazzini (1805–72), Italian nationalist, philosopher, politician, and leading figure in the movement for Italian unification.

57. Goldwin Smith (1823–1910), British-Canadian journalist and historian who lived substantial parts of his life in the United States. He was sympathetic to Irish grievances against Britain and supported disestablishment of the Church of Ireland but was opposed to Home Rule.

58. *The Spectator* is a conservative British magazine first published in 1828. The *Saturday Review* (1855–1938) was a moderately conservative British newspaper that covered politics, literature, science, and the arts.

their taking that step. It is the curious certainty that come what may Irishmen will continue to resist English rule, even though it should be for their good, which prevents many of our nation from becoming Unionists upon the spot. It is a fact, and we must face it as a fact, that although they adopt English habits and copy England in every way, the great bulk of Irishmen and Irishwomen over the whole world are known to be filled with a dull, ever-abiding animosity against her, and—right or wrong—to grieve when she prospers, and joy when she is hurt. Such movements as Young Irelandism, Fenianism, Land Leagueism, and Parliamentary obstruction[59] seem always to gain their sympathy and support. It is just because there appears no earthly chance of their becoming good members of the Empire that I urge that they should not remain in the anomalous position they are in, but since they absolutely refuse to become the one thing, that they become the other; cultivate what they have rejected, and build up an Irish nation on Irish lines.

But you ask, why should we wish to make Ireland more Celtic than it is—why should we de-Anglicise it at all?

I answer because the Irish race is at present in a most anomalous position, imitating England and yet apparently hating it. How can it produce anything good in literature, art, or institutions as long as it is actuated by motives so contradictory? Besides, I believe it is our Gaelic past which, though the Irish race does not recognise it just at present, is really at the bottom of the Irish heart, and prevents us becoming citizens of the Empire, as, I think, can be easily proved.

To say that Ireland has not prospered under English rule is simply a truism; all the world admits it, England does not deny it. But the English retort is ready. You have not prospered, they say, because you would not settle down contentedly, like the Scotch, and form part of the Empire. "Twenty years of good, resolute, grandfatherly government," said a well-known Englishman,[60] will solve the Irish question. He possibly made the period too short, but let us suppose this. Let us suppose for a moment—which is impossible—that there were to arise a series of [Oliver] Cromwells in England for the space of one hundred years, able administrators of the Empire, careful rulers of Ireland, developing to the utmost our national resources, whilst they unremittingly stamped out every spark of national feeling, making Ireland a land of wealth and factories, whilst they extinguished every thought and every idea that was Irish, and left us, at last, after a hundred years of good government, fat, wealthy, and populous, but with all our characteristics gone, with every external that at present differentiates us from the English lost or dropped; all our Irish names of places and people turned into English names; the Irish language completely extinct; the O's and the Macs dropped; our Irish intonation changed, as far as possible by English schoolmasters into something English; our history no longer remembered or taught;

59. Beginning in 1874, Joseph Biggar (1828–90) and later Charles Stewart Parnell gave interminably long speeches so as to obstruct the proceedings of the British Parliament. The goal was to force Parliament to consider Irish issues.

60. The source of this quote is Robert Gascoyne-Cecil, 3rd Marquess (also Marquis) of Salisbury (1830–1903), at the time the leader of the British Conservative Party. In 1886, he said of British governance in Ireland, "Apply that recipe honestly, consistently and resolutely for 20 years."

the names of our rebels and martyrs blotted out; our battlefields and traditions forgotten; the fact that we were not of Saxon origin dropped out of sight and memory, and let me now put the question—How many Irishmen are there who would purchase material prosperity at such a price? It is exactly such a question as this and the answer to it that shows the difference between the English and Irish race. Nine Englishmen out of ten would jump to make the exchange, and I as firmly believe that nine Irishmen out of ten would indignantly refuse it.

And yet this awful idea of complete Anglicisation, which I have here put before you in all its crudity, is, and has been, making silent inroads upon us for nearly a century. Its inroads have been silent, because, had the Gaelic race perceived what was being done, or had they been once warned of what was taking place in their own midst, they would, I think, never have allowed it. When the picture of complete Anglicisation is drawn for them in all its nakedness Irish sentimentality becomes suddenly a power and refuses to surrender its birthright.

What lies at the back of the sentiments of nationality with which the Irish millions seem so strongly leavened, what can prompt them to applaud such sentiments as:

"They say the British empire owes much to Irish hands,
That Irish valour fixed her flag o'er many conquered lands;
And ask if Erin takes no pride in these her gallant sons,
Her Wolseleys[61] and her Lawrences,[62] her Wolfes[63] and Wellingtons.[64]

Ah! these were of the Empire—we yield them to her fame,
And ne'er in Erin's orisons[65] are heard their alien name;
But those for whom her heart beats high and benedictions swell,
They died upon the scaffold and they pined within the cell."

Of course it is a very composite feeling which prompts them; but I believe that what is largely behind it is the half unconscious feeling that the race which at one time held possession of more than half Europe, which established itself in Greece, and burned infant Rome, is now—almost extirpated and absorbed elsewhere—making its last stand for independence in this island of Ireland;[66] and do what they may the race of to-day cannot wholly divest itself from the mantle of its own past.

61. Garnet Joseph Wolseley (1833–1913), 1st Viscount, a British field marshal born in Ireland, known for his role in modernizing the British army.

62. Brothers who had an Irish grandfather and served in India: John Laird Mair Lawrence (1811–79), British viceroy and governor-general of India; Sir Henry Montgomery Lawrence (1806–57), brigadier general and chief commissioner of Oudh; and Sir George St. Patrick Lawrence (1804–84), a general.

63. James Wolfe (1727–59), commander in the British army, captured Quebec from France in 1759, meeting death in the process. He had Irish ancestors on his father's side.

64. Arthur Wellesley, 1st Duke of Wellington.

65. Prayers.

66. Here Hyde sees Ireland as the last manifestation of the ancient Celts who inhabited Europe in the centuries before Roman dominance. The Celtic Gauls, who lived in what is now Belgium and France, burned Rome to the ground in 390 BCE.

Through early Irish literature, for instance, can we best form some conception of what that race really was, which, after overthrowing and trampling on the primitive peoples of half Europe, was itself forced in turn to yield its speech, manners, and independence to the victorious eagles of Rome. We alone of the nations of Western Europe escaped the claws of those birds of prey; we alone developed ourselves naturally upon our own lines outside of and free from all Roman influence; we alone were thus able to produce an early art and literature, *our* antiquities can best throw light upon the pre-Romanised inhabitants of half Europe, and—we are our father's sons.

There is really no exaggeration in all this, although Irishmen are sometimes prone to overstating as well as to forgetting. Westwood[67] himself declares that, were it not for Irishmen, these islands would possess no primitive works of art worth the mentioning; Jubainville[68] asserts that early Irish literature is that which best throws light upon the manners and customs of his own ancestors the Gauls; and Zimmer,[69] who has done so much for Celtic philology, has declared that only a spurious criticism can make an attempt to doubt about the historical character of the chief persons of our two epic cycles, that of Cuchullain and of Finn.[70] It is useless elaborating this point; and Dr. Sigerson[71] has already shown in his opening lecture the debt of gratitude which in many respects Europe owes to ancient Ireland. The dim consciousness of this is one of those things which are at the back of Irish national sentiment, and our business, whether we be Unionists or Nationalists, should be to make this dim consciousness an active and potent feeling, and thus increase our sense of self-respect and of honour.

What we must endeavour to never forget is this, that the Ireland of to-day is the descendant of the Ireland of the seventh century, then the school of Europe and the torch of learning. It is true that Northmen[72] made some minor settlements in it in the ninth and tenth centuries, it is true that the Normans made extensive settlements during the succeeding centuries, but none of those broke the continuity of the social life of the island. Dane and Norman drawn to the kindly Irish breast issued forth in a generation or two fully Irishised, and more Hibernian[73] than the Hibernians themselves, and even after the Cromwellian plantation[74] the children of numbers of

67. John Obadiah Westwood (1805–93), English entomologist and archaeologist.

68. Marie Henri d'Arbois de Jubainville (1827–1910), French historian and philologist, known for his expertise on the ancient Celts.

69. Heinrich Zimmer (1851–1910), German linguist and philologist with a specialty in both Celtic and South Asian languages and cultures.

70. Irish mythological heroes.

71. George Sigerson (1836–1925), Irish translator and physician. He was Dublin's first neurologist. In 1892 he gave the first address of the Irish Literary Society with a lecture on Irish literature.

72. The Vikings of Scandinavia, who first made raids on Ireland in 795 CE. Their involvement in Ireland lasted almost four hundred years. Over time, they became farmers and traders.

73. Hibernia is the Latin name for Ireland.

74. The colonization of Ireland begun under the Tudors and the Stuarts was based on or-

the English soldiers who settled in the south and midlands, were, after forty years' residence, and after marrying Irish wives, turned into good Irishmen, and unable to speak a word of English, while several Gaelic poets of the last century have, like Father English, the most unmistakably English names. In two points only was the continuity of the Irishism of Ireland damaged. First, in the north-east of Ulster, where the Gaelic race was expelled and the land planted with aliens, whom our dear mother Erin, assimilative as she is, has hitherto found it difficult to absorb, and in the ownership of the land, eight-ninths of which belongs to people many of whom always lived, or live, abroad, and not half of whom Ireland can be said to have assimilated.

During all this time the continuation of Erin's national life centred, according to our way of looking at it, not so much in the Cromwellian or Williamite landholders[75] who sat in College Green,[76] and governed the country, as in the mass of the people whom Dean Swift[77] considered might be entirely neglected, and looked upon as hewers of wood and drawers of water; the men who, nevertheless, constituted the real working population, and who were living on in the hopes of better days; the men who have since made America, and have within the last ten years proved what an important factor they may be in wrecking or in building the British Empire. These are the men of whom our merchants, artisans, and farmers mostly consist, and in whose hands is to-day the making or marring of an Irish nation. But, alas, *quantum mutatus ab illo!*[78] What the battleaxe of the Dane, the sword of the Norman, the wile of the Saxon were unable to perform, we have accomplished ourselves. We have at last broken the continuity of Irish life, and just at the moment when the Celtic race is presumably about to largely recover possession of its own country,[79] it finds itself deprived and stript of its Celtic characteristics, cut off from the past, yet scarcely in touch with the present. It has lost since the beginning of this century almost all that connected it with the era of Cuchullain and of Ossian, that connected it with the Christianisers of Europe, that connected it with Brian Boru and the heroes

---

ganized settlements or plantations. This process was intensified as a consequence of Oliver Cromwell's invasion of Ireland in 1649. His invasion resulted in the confiscation of the land of his opponents. It was given to soldiers in his army to produce communities with British and Protestant identities.

75. Landholders who owned land resulting from the conquests of Oliver Cromwell in 1649–52 and William III in 1690–91.

76. The site of the Irish Parliament in Dublin until 1800, when Ireland joined the Union and sent its representatives to the British Parliament in 1801.

77. Jonathan Swift (1667–1745), Anglo-Irish satirist, poet, essayist, political writer, and dean of St. Patrick's Cathedral (affiliated with the Church of Ireland) in Dublin.

78. How changed we are from what we were! (Latin). The reference is from Virgil's *Aeneid*, II, 274.

79. Hyde is referring to the Home Rule movement. Because a contingent of British Liberals supported Home Rule in principle, for the first time it seemed like it might come to pass.

of Clontarf,[80] with the O'Neills[81] and O'Donnells,[82] with Rory O'More,[83] with the Wild Geese,[84] and even to some extent with the men of '98.[85] It has lost all that they had—language, traditions, music, genius, and ideas. Just when we should be starting to build up anew the Irish race and the Gaelic nation—as within our own recollection Greece has been built up anew[86]—we find ourselves despoiled of the bricks of nationality. The old bricks that lasted eighteen hundred years are destroyed; we must now set to, to bake new ones, if we can, on other ground and of other clay. Imagine for a moment the restoration of a German-speaking Greece.

The bulk of the Irish race really lived in the closest contact with the traditions of the past and the national life of nearly eighteen hundred years, until the beginning of this century. Not only so, but during the whole of the dark Penal times[87] they produced amongst themselves a most vigorous literary development. Their schoolmasters and wealthy farmers, unwearied scribes, produced innumerable manuscripts in beautiful writing, each letter separated from another as in Greek, transcripts both of the ancient literature of their sires and of the more modern literature produced by themselves. Until the beginning of the present century there was no county, no barony, and, I may almost say, no townland which did not boast of an Irish poet, the people's representative of those ancient bards who died out with the extirpation of the great Milesian families.[88] The literary activity of even the eighteenth century among the Gaels was very great, not in the South alone, but also in Ulster—the number of poets it produced was something astonishing. It did not, however, produce many works in Gaelic prose, but it propagated translations of many pieces from the French, Latin, Spanish, and English. Every well-to-do farmer could read and write Irish, and many of them could understand even archaic Irish. I have myself heard persons reciting the poems of Donogha More O'Daly, Abbot of Boyle,[89] in Roscommon, who

80. Brian Boru (c. 941–1014), an Irish king slain fighting the Danes at the battle of Clontarf in 1014.

81. Ulster family responsible for several high kings of Ireland during the medieval period.

82. Powerful Irish clan of ancient origins.

83. Rory O'More (c. 1620–55), an Irish rebel who led the rebellion against English rule in 1641.

84. The Wild Geese were part of the army that fought for James II and subsequently left for France in the aftermath of the victory of William III. More generally, the term is used to describe Irish soldiers who served in European armies on the Continent.

85. The rebellion of 1798.

86. Greek nationalists fought a war for independence against the Ottoman Empire (1821–29) and became an independent state in 1832. Hyde's implication is that the movement for political independence was accompanied by a cultural revival of the ancient Greek language and culture.

87. Hyde is referring here to the eighteenth century when Catholics and to a much lesser extent Protestant Dissenters, notably Presbyterians, suffered various degrees of limits on their rights as a result of the penal laws.

88. Milesians are legendary ancestors of the Irish people.

89. Donogha More O'Daly (d. 1244), abbot of Boyle, the author of about thirty known poems, nearly all of them religious in their subject matter.

died sixty years before Chaucer[90] was born. To this very day the people have a word for archaic Irish, which is much the same as though Chaucer's poems were handed down amongst the English peasantry, but required a special training to understand. This training, however, nearly every one of fair education during the Penal times possessed, nor did they begin to lose their Irish training and knowledge until after the establishment of Maynooth[91] and the rise of [Daniel] O'Connell. These two events made an end of the Gaelicism of the Gaelic race, although a great number of poets and scribes existed even down to the forties and fifties of the present century, and a few may linger on yet in remote localities. But it may be said, roughly speaking, that the ancient Gaelic civilisation died with O'Connell, largely, I am afraid, owing to his example and his neglect of inculcating the necessity of keeping alive racial customs, language, and traditions, in which with the one notable exception of our scholarly idealist, Smith O'Brien,[92] he has been followed until a year ago by almost every leader of the Irish race.

Thomas Davis and his brilliant band of Young Irelanders came just at the dividing of the line, and tried to give to Ireland a new literature in English to replace the literature which was just being discarded. It succeeded and it did not succeed. It was a most brilliant effort, but the old bark had been too recently stripped off the Irish tree, and the trunk could not take as it might have done to a fresh one. It was a new departure, and at first produced a violent effect. Yet in the long run it failed to properly leaven our peasantry who might, perhaps, have been reached upon other lines. I say they *might* have been reached upon other lines because it is quite certain that even well on into the beginning of this century, Irish poor scholars and schoolmasters used to gain the greatest favour and applause by reading out manuscripts in the people's houses at night, some of which manuscripts had an antiquity of a couple of hundred years or more behind them, and which, when they got illegible from age, were always recopied. The Irish peasantry at that time were all to some extent cultured men, and many of the better off ones were scholars and poets. What have we now left of all that? Scarcely a trace. Many of them read newspapers indeed, but who reads, much less recites, an epic poem, or chants an elegiac or even a hymn?

Wherever Irish throughout Ireland continued to be spoken, there the ancient MSS.[93] continued to be read, there the epics of Cuchullain, Conor MacNessa, Déirdre, Finn, Oscar, and Ossian[94] continued to be told, and there poetry and music held sway. Some people may think I am exaggerating in asserting that such a state of things existed down to the present century, but it is no exaggeration. I have myself spoken

---

90. Geoffrey Chaucer (c. 1343–1400), an English poet, most famous for the *Canterbury Tales*.

91. St. Patrick's College, Maynooth, a Catholic seminary in County Kildare established in 1795 with the support of the British government.

92. William Smith O'Brien (1803–64), Irish nationalist, participant in the Young Ireland movement, and leader in the 1848 rebellion.

93. Manuscripts (abbreviation).

94. Characters from the literature of Irish mythology.

with men from Cavan and Tyrone[95] who spoke excellent Irish. Carleton's[96] stories bear witness to the prevalence of the Irish language and traditions in Ulster when he began to write. My friend Mr. Lloyd[97] has found numbers in Antrim[98] who spoke good Irish. And, as for Leinster,[99] my friend Mr. Cleaver[100] informed me that when he lived in Wicklow[101] a man came by from the County Carlow in search of work who could not speak a word of English. Old labourers from Connacht, who used to go to reap the harvest in England and take shipping at Drogheda,[102] told me that at that time, fifty years ago, Irish was spoken by every one round that town. I have met an old man in Wicklow, not twenty miles from Dublin, whose parents always repeated the Rosary[103] in Irish. My friend Father O'Growny, who has done and is doing so much for the Irish language and literature at Maynooth, tells me that there, within twenty miles of Dublin, are three old people who still speak Irish. O'Curry[104] found people within seven miles of Dublin city who had never heard English in their youth at all, except from the car-drivers of the great town. I gave an old man in the street who begged from me, a penny, only a few days ago, saying, "*Sin pighin agad,*"[105] and when he answered in Irish I asked him where he was from, and he said from *Newna* (*n'Eamhain*), i.e., Navan.[106] . . . In fact, I may venture to say, that, up to the beginning of the present century, neither man, woman, nor child of the Gaelic race, either of high blood or low blood, existed in Ireland who did not either speak Irish or understand it. But within the last ninety years we have, with an unparalleled frivolity, deliberately thrown away our birthright and Anglicised ourselves. None of the children of those people of whom I have spoken know Irish, and the race will from henceforth be changed; for as Monsieur Jubainville says of the influence of Rome upon Gaul, England "has definitely conquered us, she has even imposed upon us her language, that is to say, the form of our thoughts during every instant of our existence." It is curious that those who most fear West Britainism have so eagerly consented to im-

95. Irish counties.

96. William Carleton (1794–1869), Irish novelist and writer of short stories, known for his realistic representations of Irish rural life.

97. Possibly Joseph Henry Lloyd (Seosamh Laoide) (1865–1939), folklorist and editor of the *Gaelic Journal*, member and joint treasurer of the Gaelic League.

98. County in Ulster.

99. Southeastern province of Ireland.

100. Quite possibly Euseby Digby (Eusebh D. Mac Cliabhair) (1826–94), Church of England clergyman and promoter of the Irish language. Hyde dedicated his book *Leabar Sgéuaigheachta* (1889) to him.

101. A county—and also the name of the county town—in Leinster.

102. Town in County Louth, north of Dublin.

103. Roman Catholic prayers to the Virgin Mary.

104. Eugene O'Curry (Eoghan Ó Comhraí) (1796–1862), scholar of ancient Irish history and culture, earned his living translating and copying ancient manuscripts.

105. There's a penny for you (Irish).

106. Town in County Meath.

posing upon the Irish race what, according to Jubainville, who in common with all the great scholars of the continent, seems to regret it very much, is "the form of our thoughts during every instant of our existence."

So much for the greatest stroke of all in our Anglicisation, the loss of our language. I have often heard people thank God that if the English gave us nothing else they gave us at least their language. In this way they put a bold face upon the matter, and pretend that the Irish language is not worth knowing, and has no literature. But the Irish language *is* worth knowing, or why would the greatest philologists of Germany, France, and Italy be emulously studying it, and it *does* possess a literature, or why would a German savant have made the calculation that the books written in Irish between the eleventh and seventeenth centuries, and still extant, would fill a thousand octavo volumes.[107]

I have no hesitation at all in saying that every Irish-feeling Irishman, who hates the reproach of West-Britonism, should set himself to encourage the efforts which are being made to keep alive our once great national tongue. The losing of it is our greatest blow, and the sorest stroke that the rapid Anglicisation of Ireland has inflicted upon us. In order to de-Anglicise ourselves we must at once arrest the decay of the language. We must bring pressure upon our politicians not to snuff it out by their tacit discouragement merely because they do not happen themselves to understand it. We must arouse some spark of patriotic inspiration among the peasantry who still use the language, and put an end to the shameful state of feeling—a thousand-tongued reproach to our leaders and statesmen—which makes young men and women blush and hang their heads when overhead speaking their own language. . . .

20. Mary E. L. Butler, "Irishwomen and the Home Language," *All Ireland Review* (1900–1901)

In the late nineteenth century, Irish women were beginning to enter the public sphere. Although they were excluded from voting for members of Parliament, by 1890 they could vote in local government elections and hold municipal offices. As part of this shift toward a less male-dominated society, the Gaelic League, unlike other nationalist organizations, accepted both male and female members. In 1906 women were elected to seven of the forty-five seats on the organization's executive board (Biletz 2002, 60).

Mary Butler (1874–1920) was prominent among the women who were Gaelic League activists. From a pro-Unionist gentry family of both Catholics and Protestants, Butler was raised in a home that had an un-Irish atmosphere. She was a cousin of Edward Carson (1854–1935), the Unionist leader, and she was educated at Alexandria College, Dublin, which mostly consisted of young Protestant women and whose curriculum excluded Irish history. Butler's conversion to nationalism resulted from a chance encounter with the writings of Young Ireland, and like many blossoming cultural nationalists, she immersed herself in the culture of the western part of the country, visiting the Aran Islands on several occasions. Butler was not a feminist, but she believed that

---

107. A book folded to form eight leaves or sixteen pages.

women had a critical role to play in the nationalist movement. In her essay "Irishwomen and the Home Language," she argued that women might only play a marginal role in Irish politics, but, as wives and mothers, they could shape the consciousness of the emerging generation by making their homes Irish.

As an Irishwoman, I appeal to Irishwomen on a subject of vital importance to the country to which we have the honour to belong.

It has been allotted to us to live in a history-making epoch, when though the political atmosphere is murky, a light is breaking through the heavy clouds, a light shining with no will-o'-the-wisp gleam, but with a clear and steady glow. Guided by this "solemn starlight" we who so long groped hither and thither, are at length treading with sure, swift steps, the right road—the road of which the goal is the realisation of a true national ideal.

It is possible that this pamphlet may fall into the hands of some to whom Gaelic League doctrines are unfamiliar, though these doctrines have been prop[a]gated so widely and vigorously for a considerable time, and there is little excuse for any thinking person remaining in ignorance of them. It would, however, be impossible to discuss the motives and aims of the language movement at length in these pages. Anyone who is unacquainted with the scope of the movement, should, before reading what follows, first refer to former publications of the Gaelic League, in which the case is clearly set forth, and the inseparable connection between language and nationality convincingly demonstrated. I take it for granted then, that readers are convinced of the truth:—"A nation's soul is its language," and proceed to deal exclusively with one aspect of the question, namely, the part which Irishwomen may play in the revival movement at present proceeding in Ireland.

The country is passing through a crisis. It is engaged in a life and death struggle for the preservation of that which it has come, at the eleventh hour, to recognise as essential to the continuance of its separate and distinct existence. Whether this struggle end in dismal failure or in triumphant success, depends entirely on the people who are waging the war. "If I ought, I can"; the proposition laid down by Kant[108] is one that cannot be disproved when we fight for an ideal, however it may be as regards material matters. "The soul is stronger than statutes"; penal laws succeeded in robbing the Irish people of their property, but they could not rob them of their religion. A spiritual possession can only be taken from us by our own free will, and the language is a spiritual possession. To their bitter shame and grief the Irish people stood passively by while the language, that priceless heritage, was "slipping into the grave." But what they lost they may regain by exercise of will power. No government, no "Educational" Board, no dolts or bigots of an alien ascendancy party, can thwart their purpose. The people, as they have been recently told, have the power in this case absolutely in their own hands.

What then remains to be said when this view has been forcibly and convincingly put before the public? One thing remains to be said. This power is in the hands of the

108. Immanuel Kant (1724–1804), German philosopher, whose contributions to the theory of knowledge and ethics are among the most influential in the history of modern philosophy.

whole people of Ireland, it is true, but it is in an especial manner in the hands of the women of Ireland. Why? Because this language movement is not an academic one. It is a living one. What is wanted to make the language living in the land; to do this it is necessary to make it the home language; and to make it the home language it is necessary to enlist the co-operation of woman—the home maker. Home makers of Ireland, make Irish the home language. You, and you alone, can do it. This is the issue to be placed before our countrywomen. The heavy responsibility rests with them of deciding the fate of the language, and with it the fate of the nation, the existence of which is inextricably bound up with it. How are they going to acquit themselves of this responsibility?

This movement in which Irishwomen are now earnestly asked to join, is frequently described as "the language war," and rightly so. It is a war to the death between Irish ideals and British sordid soullessness.

Now the women of our race are dignified and decorous; they shrink from mingling in a melee, and retiring into the inner courtyard, they leave the scene of strife in the outer world to the sterner sex. They may, therefore, think that in this language war they have no place, but they are mistaken, for it is warfare of an especial kind, warfare which can best be waged not by shrieking viragoes of aggressive amazons, but by gentle, low-voiced women who teach little children their first prayers, and, seated at the hearth-side, make these around them realise the difference between a home and a dwelling. To most Irish people it is extremely distasteful to see a woman mount a platform and hold forth in public. We are the most conservative people in the world, and the deeply-rooted conviction regarding the desirability of women acting a retiring part is not likely to be eradicated. Let it then be thoroughly understood that when Irishwomen are invited to take part in the language movement they are not required to plunge into the vortex of public life. No, the work which they best can do is work to be done at home. Their mission is to make the homes of Ireland Irish. If the homes are Irish the whole country will be Irish. The spark struck on the hearthstone will fire the soul of the nation.

All friends of the movement are agreed that to make Irish the home language is of the most vital importance, but perhaps all do not realise how entirely it depends on women to bring this end to pass. It would be as futile to seek to make Irish the language of the law courts without the consent of both judge and jury, as to endeavour to make it the language of the home without obtaining the consent and co-operation of the women. Woman reigns as an autocrat in the kingdom of her home. Her sway is absolute. She rules and serves simultaneously in the home circle. Not only does she attend to the organisation of the practical details, and the supplying of material wants, but the spiritual side of home life is starved or satisfied according as her nature is noble or ignoble. She decides how the house is to be furnished, and interests herself in the outfit of the household, her voice being usually the one to decide whether the goods invested in are of Irish or foreign manufacture. She suggests what songs should be sung, what books read, what topics discussed, what language spoken. It is she in fine[109] who gives the tone to the establishment, whether that tone be native or

---

109. In the end (Latin).

foreign, uplifting or lowering. Every member of the household comes under her influence; relatives, servants, visitors, but above and beyond all, the children. "Give me the first seven years of a child's life and I care not who has the rest," said a great French educationalist. Up to this age children are entirely under the control of women, who mould their ideas according to their liking. The characters of the future citizens of the country are built up in the chimney corner, where a woman tells stories in the twilight to wide-eyed listeners. What are these stories about? Patriotic people should make it their business to ascertain the answer to this question. Are they stories of the boyhood of Cuchulainn, or is "With Kitchener to Khartoum"[110] the text taken?

The man in the house goes abroad every day for business or pleasure, the woman stays at home as a rule. What is she doing at home all day long? Many things; but one thing incessantly. Let it be written in capital letters—TALKING. When the man of the house goes out in the morning he leaves her talking, and when he comes home in the evening he finds her still talking to those about her. It must be recognised, therefore, that what this indefatigable talker talks about, and through what medium she conveys her ideas, is important. She is bound to talk about something in some way or other. It is necessary to ensure that she is talking about the right things in the right way. Verily, a language movement is of all movements one in which the woman is bound to take part.

Some of those who have the interest of the movement at heart, recognise that the attitude adopted towards it by the women of the country may well be regarded as the determining factor in the situation. Here is the recently expressed opinion of a prominent authority on the subject. "If all the women of Ireland spoke Irish it would not matter about the rest." Again the Rev. Dr. Henebry[111] says, "When the women of a country become denationalised, the very hearthstone, the foundation of all true nationality, is uprooted, and over-turned." These emphatically expressed opinions are widely held, but if there is one thing more than another for which our countrymen are remarkable, it is inconsistency. We, their countrywomen, know them pretty well, and understand them if anyone does, and we are therefore not surprised to find most of them making no attempt to carry their theories into practice, and to bring their home life into harmony with their platform utterances. Resolutions are passed with acclamation on nationalising of education, and the maker of an eloquent speech who takes as his text "My hope is in the youth of the country," sends his young people to some institution where they will get "a superior English education," while those who dilate on the "hearthstone" aspect of nationality, do not press their own womenfolk into the service. They are too much taken up discoursing about other people's hearthstones to pay any attention to their own. Now, there is an old saying, "It is manners to wait until you are asked," and perhaps Irishwomen are piqued at not being urged more persistently to take part in the movement, and have stood by on this account. But action, or rather inaction, of this kind would show a pretty spirit unworthy of

110. Horatio Herbert Kitchener (1850–1916) was a major general in the British army when, with a combined British and Egyptian force, he defeated Sudanese troops at the Battle of Omdurman (1898) near Khartoum.

111. Richard Henebry (1863–1916), priest and scholar of Irish culture, especially music.

them. This is not an occasion on which people should wait for an invitation. The nation is in danger; the question of the preservation of its very soul is at stake, and it behoves all who have sprung from this sacred soil to rally and make one unwavering stand, so that the last conquest of Ireland, the conquest of her soul, may never be completed. Every section of the community has been to blame in the past for the decline of the language; clergy and laity, gentle and simple, men and women. It is unjust to single out any single class for exclusive blame. Instead of indulging in mutual recrimination—most profitless and discreditable of our pursuits—let us each and all try to do our part in retrieving as far as possible the all but irreparable harm which has been done. So, instead of wasting time discussing whether it has been fault of the men or the fault of the women that up to this the latter have taken so inconsiderable a part in the movement, let every Irishwoman worthy of the name throw herself whole-heartedly into it from this day forth. Let it be no longer noticeable that for every ten men who join the Gaelic League scarcely one woman does. Let a sharp line of demarcation be no longer drawn by patriotic people between their public work and their private lives. If nationality is to have any reality, if it is to imply a living force and not an empty formula, it must permeate every department of life, must have its origin in the home, and spread thence to church and school, to Press, platform, and market-place. Women can do this for nationality. They can steep their surroundings in an Irish atmosphere. Their love of country, if it takes possession of them at all, will not be, "of their lives a thing apart," it will be their "whole existence," and will be communicated by them to those who come under their sphere of influence. How boundless that sphere of influence is, none who know the esteem in which woman is held in this country require to be told. His Eminence Cardinal Logue,[112] recently declared, speaking at a public gathering:—"The influence of woman is the grandest and most beautiful left to us in our fallen nature." The Irishman who would not endorse this sentiment would not be a characteristic one, for, whatever failings our countrymen may have, lack of chivalry and reverence for woman is not one of them. Denationalisation and demoralisation have unfortunately made deep inroads in these latter days, and the integrity of the national character has been seriously sapped, but there are few Irishmen grown so-unIrish as to lose their veneration for woman. May the time never come to pass when this Irish ideal will be lowered. The fact, however, must not be lost sight of, that if Irishwomen are regarded with such esteem it is because they deserve it.

This illimitable influence which woman wields in Ireland on account of the high esteem in which she is held, must be turned to account for her country's good. Rightly or wrongly she has acquired the reputation of being less national than her male compatriots. However that may be it is time for her to give more practical proof than she has hitherto given on whatever patriotism she may be endowed with.

112. Michael Logue (1840–1924), archbishop of Armagh and Primate of All Ireland (a title of honor designating ceremonial precedence) (1887–1924) and a cardinal in the Roman Catholic Church (1893–1924).

William Butler Yeats, the year the Abbey Theatre opened (1904).
(Image originally appeared in *The Tatler.*)

21. William Butler Yeats, *Cathleen Ni Houlihan* (1902)

*William Butler Yeats (1865–1939) casts a long shadow on Ireland's political and cultur-
al history. Often considered by critics to be one of the very best poets writing in English
in the twentieth century, Yeats is arguably Ireland's greatest poet and certainly its greatest
Anglo-Irish poet. In addition to being a poet, Yeats was a playwright, critic, and essayist.
He was a nationalist, mystic, occultist, and modernist. He was both a senator of the Irish
Free State (1922–28) and the recipient of the Nobel Prize for Literature (1923). As he
aged, Yeats became a more pronounced critic of democracy. He equated it with tawdry
materialism, and as a consequence, he became attracted to right-wing authoritarianism,
including flirtations with fascism in the 1930s. In his later years, Yeats idealized the
Anglo-Irish past.*

*Son of the artist John Butler Yeats (1839–1922), W. B. Yeats was born and attended
school in Dublin and grew up in County Sligo, in Ireland, and in London. As a young
man, he was part of the literary and political circle that congregated around the Fenian*

veteran John O'Leary (1830–1907). It was here that in 1889 Yeats met Maud Gonne, who was politically more militant than he was but shared his enthusiasm for Irish culture and his fascination with the occult. Gonne became a close friend, the unrequited love of his life, and a muse for his poetry. In the 1890s, Yeats surfaced as a major figure in the Irish literary revival, and with Lady Gregory, George Moore (1852–1933), and Edward Martyn (1859–1923) founded the Irish Literary Theatre of Dublin in 1899, subsequently renamed the Abbey Theatre in 1904. The Irish Literary Theatre aspired to produce a school of Celtic and Irish dramatic literature. Conceived in this spirit, Cathleen Ni Houlihan *was attributed to Yeats but written with Gregory. It was first performed in the National Literary Theatre with Gonne in the title role. It is set in Killala, County Mayo, in 1798, where revolutionary French troops fought their first battle on Irish soil. The play is militantly nationalist. Cathleen, a symbol of Irish national liberation, casts a spell on the spirit of the soon-to-be-married Michael, and by implication, young Irish men everywhere. Later in his life, Yeats may well have developed some regrets on the impact that the play had on a generation of Irish men and women. In the poem "The Man and the Echo" (1933), he wrote:*

> All that I have said and done,
> Now that I am old and ill,
> Turns into a question till
> I lie awake night after night
> And never get the answers right.
> Did that play of mine send out
> Certain men the English shot?

PETER GILLANE.
MICHAEL GILLANE, his Son, going to be married.
PATRICK GILLANE, a lad of twelve, Michael's Brother.
BRIDGET GILLANE, Peter's Wife.
DELIA CAHEL, engaged to Michael.
THE POOR OLD WOMAN.
Neighbours.

SCENE: *Interior of a cottage close to Killala, in* 1798, BRIDGET *is standing at a table undoing a parcel.* PETER *is sitting at one side of the fire,* PATRICK *at the other.*
Peter. What is that sound I hear?
Patrick. I don't hear anything. [*He listens.*] I hear it now. It's like cheering. [*He goes to the window and looks out.*] I wonder what they are cheering about. I don't see anybody.
Peter. It might be a hurling match.[113]
Patrick. There's no hurling to-day. It must be down in the town the cheering is.
Bridget. I suppose the boys must be having some sport of their own. Come over here, Peter, and look at Michael's wedding-clothes.
Peter. [*Shifts his chair to table.*] Those are grand clothes, indeed.

---

113. An Irish outdoor game of ancient origins. It is played with sticks called *hurleys* and a ball called a *sliotar.* For Irish nationalists, it was a component of national identity.

Bridget. You hadn't clothes like that when you married me, and no coat to put on of a Sunday any more than any other day.

Peter. That is true, indeed. We never thought a son of our own would be wearing a suit of that sort for his wedding, or have so good a place to bring a wife to.

Patrick. [*Who is still at the window.*] There's an old woman coming down the road. I don't know, is it here she's coming?

Bridget. It will be a neighbour coming to hear about Michael's wedding. Can you see who it is?

Patrick. I think it is a stranger, but she's not coming to the house. She's turned into the gap that goes down where Murteen and his sons are shearing sheep. [*He turns towards* BRIDGET.] Do you remember what Winny of the Cross Roads was saying the other night about the strange woman that goes through the country whatever time there's war or trouble coming?

Bridget. Don't be bothering us about Winny's talk, but go and open the door for your brother. I hear him coming up the path.

Peter. I hope he has brought Delia's fortune[114] with him safe, for fear her people might go back on the bargain and I after making it. Trouble enough I had making it.

[PATRICK *opens the door and* MICHAEL *comes in.*]

Bridget. What kept you, Michael? We were looking out for you this long time.

Michael. I went round by the priest's house to bid him be ready to marry us tomorrow.

Bridget. Did he say anything?

Michael. He said it was a very nice match, and that he was never better pleased to marry any two in his parish than myself and Delia Cahel.

Peter. Have you got the fortune, Michael?

Michael. Here it is.

[*He puts bag on table and goes over and leans against chimney-jamb.* BRIDGET, *who has been all this time examining the clothes, pulling the seams and trying the lining of the pockets, etc., puts the clothes on the dresser.*]

Peter. [*Getting up and taking the bag in his hand and turning out the money.*] Yes, I made the bargain well for you, Michael. Old John Cahel would sooner have kept a share of this a while longer. "Let me keep the half of it till the first boy is born," says he. "You will not," says I. "Whether there is or is not a boy, the whole hundred pounds must be in Michael's hands before he brings your daughter in the house." The wife spoke to him then, and he gave in at the end.

Bridget. You seem well pleased to be handling the money, Peter.

Peter. Indeed, I wish I had had the luck to get a hundred pounds, or twenty pounds itself, with the wife I married.

Bridget. Well, if I didn't bring much I didn't get much. What had you the day I married you but a flock of hens and you feeding them, and a few lambs and you driving them to the market at Ballina.[115] [*She is vexed and bangs a jug on the dresser.*] If I brought no fortune I worked it out in my bones, laying down the baby, Michael that

114. Yeats is referring to the dowry given by Delia's family.
115. Town in County Mayo.

is standing there now, an a stook of straw, while I dug the potatoes, and never asking big dresses or anything but to be working.

Peter. That is true, indeed. [*He pats her arm.*]

Bridget. Leave me alone now till I ready the house for the woman that is to come into it.

Peter. You are the best woman in Ireland, but money is good, too. [*He begins handling the money again and sits down.*] I never thought to see so much money within my four walls. We can do great things now we have it. We can take the ten acres of land we have a chance of since Jamsie Dempsey died, and stock it. We will go to the fair of Ballina to buy stock. Did Delia ask any of the money for her own use, Michael?

Michael. She did not, indeed. She did not seem to take much notice of it, or to look at it at all.

Bridget. That's no wonder. Why would she look at it when she had yourself to look at, a fine, strong young man, it is proud she must be to get you; a good steady boy that will make use of the money, and not be running through it or spending it on drink like another.

Peter. It's likely Michael himself was not thinking much of the fortune either, but of what sort the girl was to look at.

Michael. [*Coming over towards the table.*] Well, you would like a nice comely girl to be beside you, and to go walking with you. The fortune only lasts for a while, but the woman will be there always.

Patrick. [*Turning round from the window.*] They are cheering again down in the town. May be they are landing horses from Enniscrone.[116] They do be cheering when the horses take the water well.

Michael. There are no horses in it. Where would they be going and no fair at hand? Go down to the town, Patrick, and see what is going on.

Patrick. [*Opens the door to go out, but stops for a moment on the threshold.*] Will Delia remember, do you think, to bring the greyhound pup she promised me when she would be coming to the house?

Michael. She will surely.

[PATRICK *goes out leaving the door open.*

Peter. It will be Patrick's turn next to be looking for a fortune, but he won't find it so easy to get it and he with no place of his own.

Bridget. I do be thinking sometimes, now things are going so well with us, and the Cahels such a good back to us in the district, and Delia's own uncle a priest, we might be put in the way of making Patrick a priest some day, and he so good at his books.[117]

Peter. Time enough, time enough, you have always your head full of plans, Bridget.

Bridget. We will be well able to give him learning, and not to send him tramping the country like a poor scholar that lives on charity.

116. Town in County Sligo.

117. As the eldest son inherited the family farm, younger sons were less marriageable and the family viewed the priesthood as a viable alternative.

Michael. They're not done cheering yet.

[*He goes over to the door and stands there for a moment putting up his hand to shade his eyes.*

Bridget. Do you see anything?

Michael. I see an old woman coming up the path.

Bridget. Who is it, I wonder. It must be the strange woman Patrick saw a while ago.

Michael. I don't think it's one of the neighbours anyway, but she has her cloak over her face.

Bridget. It might be some poor woman heard we were making ready for the wedding and came to look for her share.

Peter. I may as well put the money out of sight. There is no use leaving it out for every stranger to look at.

[*He goes over to a large box in the corner, opens it and puts the bag in and fumbles at the lock.*

Michael. There she is, father! [*An* Old Woman *passes the window slowly, she looks at* MICHAEL *as she passes.*] I'd sooner a stranger not to come to the house the night before my wedding.

Bridget. Open the door, Michael; don't keep the poor woman waiting.

[The OLD WOMAN comes in. MICHAEL stands aside to make way for her.

Old Woman. God save all here!

Peter. God save you kindly!

Old Woman. You have good shelter here.

Peter. You are welcome to whatever shelter we have.

Bridget. Sit down by the fire and welcome.

Old Woman. [*Warming her hands.*] There is a hard wind outside.

[MICHAEL *watches her curiously from the door.* PETER *comes over to the table.*

Peter. Have you travelled far to-day?

Old Woman. I have travelled far, very far, there are few have travelled so far as myself, and there's many a one that doesn't make me welcome. There was one that had strong sons I thought were friends of mine, but they were shearing their sheep, and they wouldn't listen to me.

Peter. It's a pity indeed for any person to have no place of their own.

Old Woman. That's true for you indeed, and it's long I'm on the roads since I first went wandering.

Bridget. It is a wonder you are not worn out with so much wandering.

Old Woman. Sometimes my feet are tired and my hands are quiet, but there is no quiet in my heart. When the people see me quiet, they think old age has come on me and that all the stir has gone out of me. But when the trouble is on me I must be talking to my friends.

Bridget. What was it put you wandering?

Old Woman. Too many strangers in the house.

Bridget. Indeed you look as if you'd had your share of trouble.

Old Woman. I have had trouble indeed.

Bridget. What was it put the trouble on you?

Old Woman. My land that was taken from me.

Peter. Was it much land they took from you?

Old Woman. My four beautiful green fields.[118]

Peter. [*Aside to* BRIDGET.] Do you think could she be the widow Casey that was put out of her holding at Kilglass[119] a while ago?

Bridget. She is not. I saw the widow Casey one time at the market in Ballina, a stout fresh woman.

Peter. [*To* OLD WOMAN.] Did you hear a noise of cheering, and you coming up the hill?

Old Woman. I thought I heard the noise I used to hear when my friends came to visit me.

[*She begins singing half to herself.*

I will go cry with the woman,
For yellow-haired Donough is dead,
With a hempen rope for a neckcloth,
And a white cloth on his head,—[120]

Michael. [*Coming from the door.*] What is that you are singing ma'am?

Old Woman. Singing I am about a man I knew one time, yellow-haired Donough that was hanged in Galway.

[*She goes on singing, much louder.*

I am come to cry with you, woman,
My hair is unwound and unbound;
I remember him ploughing his field,
Turning up the red side of the ground,

And building his barn on the hill
With the good mortared stone;
O! we'd have pulled down the gallows
Had it happened in Enniscrone!

Michael. What was it brought him to his death?

Old Woman. He died for love of me: many a man has died for love of me.

Peter. [*Aside to* BRIDGET.] Her trouble has put her wits astray.

Michael. It is long since that song was made? Is it long since he got his death?

Old Woman. Not long, not long. But there were others that died for love of me a long time ago.

Michael. Were they neighbours of your own ma'am?

118. A metaphor for the four provinces of Ireland.

119. A village in County Sligo.

120. According to Yeats, this song was inspired by an old Gaelic folk song, possibly "Fair-haired Donagh," which had been published by Lady Gregory in an article in 1902.

Old Woman. Come here beside me and I'll tell you about them. [MICHAEL *sits down beside her at the hearth.*] There was a red man of the O'Donnells from the north, and a man of the O'Sullivans from the south, and there was one Brian that lost his life at Clontarf by the sea,[121] and there were a great many in the west, some that died hundreds of years ago, and there are some that will die to-morrow.

Michael. Is it in the west that men will die to-morrow?

Old Woman. Come nearer, nearer to me.

Bridget. Is she right, do you think? Or is she a woman from the north.[122]

Peter. She doesn't know well what she's talking about, with the want and the trouble she has gone through.

Bridget. The poor thing, we should treat her well.

Peter. Give her a drink of milk and a bit of the oaten cake.

Bridget. Maybe we should give her something along with that, to bring her on her way. A few pence, or a shilling itself, and we with so much money in the house.

Peter. Indeed I'd not begrudge it to her if we had it to spare, but if we go running through what we have, we'll soon have to break the hundred pounds, and that would be a pity.

Bridget. Shame on you, Peter. Give her the shilling and your blessing with it, or our own luck will go from us.

[PETER *goes to the box and takes out a shilling.*

Bridget. [*To the* OLD WOMAN.] Will you have drink of milk?

Old Woman. It is not food or drink that I want.

Peter. [*Offering the shilling.*] Here is something for you.

Old Woman. That is not what I want. It is not silver I want.

Peter. What is it you would be asking for?

Old Woman. If anyone would give me help he must give me himself, he must give me all.

[PETER *goes over to the table staring at the shilling in his hand in a bewildered way, and stands whispering to* BRIDGET.

Michael. Have you no man of your own, ma'am?

Old Woman. I have not. With all the lovers that brought me their love, I never set out the bed for any.

Michael. Are you lonely going the roads, ma'am?

Old Woman. I have my thoughts and I have my hopes.

Michael. What hopes have you to hold to?

Old Woman. The hope of getting my beautiful fields back again; the hope of putting the strangers out of my house.

Michael. What way will you do that, ma'am?

Old Woman. I have good friends that will help me. They are gathering to help me

---

121. "Red" Hugh O'Donnell (1571–1602) and Donal O'Sullivan Beare (1561–1613) died fighting the English forces in Ireland. Brian Bórú, the high king of Ireland, died at the Battle of Clontarf (1014) battling forces assembled by the king of Leinster, including the Dublin Norse.

122. From Ulster. It is also a colloquial expression for a woman with spiritual powers.

now. I am not afraid. If they are put down to-day they will get the upper hand to-morrow. [*She gets up.*] I must be going to meet my friends. They are coming to help me and I must be there to welcome them. I must call the neighbours together to welcome them.

Michael. I will go with you.

Bridget. It is not her friends you have to go and welcome, Michael; it is the girl coming into the house you have to welcome. You have plenty to do, it is food and drink you have to bring to the house. The woman that is coming home is not coming with empty hands; you would have an empty house before her. [*To the* OLD WOMAN.] Maybe you don't know, ma'am, that my son is going be married to-morrow.

Old Woman. It is not a man going to his marriage that I look to for help.

Peter. [*To* BRIDGET.] Who is she, do you think, at all?

Bridget. You did not tell us your name yet, ma'am.

Old Woman. Some call me the Poor Old Woman, and there are some that call me Cathleen, the daughter of Houlihan.

Peter. I think I knew someone of that name once. Who was it, I wonder? It must have been someone I knew when I was a boy. No, no, I remember, I heard it in a song.

Old Woman. [*Who is standing in the doorway.*] They are wondering that there were songs made for me; there have been many songs made for me. I heard one on the wind this morning. [*She sings.*

> Do not make a great keening[123]
> When the graves have been dug to-morrow.
> Do not call the white-scarfed riders
> To the burying that shall be to-morrow.
> Do not spread food to call strangers
> To the wakes that shall be to-morrow;
> Do not give money for prayers
> For the dead that shall die to-morrow . . .

they will have no need of prayers, they will have no need of prayers.

Michael. I do not know what that song means, but tell me something I can do for you.

Peter. Come over to me, Michael.

Michael. Hush, father, listen to her.

Old Woman. It is a hard service they take that help me. Many that are red-cheeked now will be pale-cheeked; many that have been free to walk the hills and the bogs and the rushes, will be sent to walk hard streets in far countries; many a good plan will be broken; many that have gathered money will not stay to spend it; many a child will be born and there will be no father at its christening to give it a name. They that had red cheeks will have pale cheeks for my sake; and for all that, they will think they are well paid.

[*She goes out, her voice is heard outside singing.*

---

123. A loud and wailing lament for the dead traditionally found in Irish burials.

They shall be remembered for ever,
They shall be alive for ever,
They shall be speaking for ever,
The people shall hear them for ever.

Bridget. [*To* PETER.] Look at him, Peter; he has the look of a man that has got the touch.[124] [*Raising her voice.*] Look here, Michael, at the wedding-clothes. Such grand clothes as these are. You have a right to fit them on now, it would be a pity to-morrow if they did not fit. The boys would be laughing at you. Take them, Michael, and go into the room and fit them on. [*She puts them on his arm.*

Michael. What wedding are you talking of? What clothes will I be wearing to-morrow?

Bridget. These are the clothes you are going to wear when you marry Delia Cahel to-morrow.

Michael. I had forgotten that.

[*He looks at the clothes and turns towards the inner room, but stops at the sound of cheering outside.*

Peter. There is the shouting come to our own door. What is it has happened?

[Neighbours *come crowding in,* PATRICK *and* DELIA *with them.*

Patrick. There are ships in the Bay; the French are landing at Killala!

[PETER *takes his pipe from his mouth and his hat off, and stands up. The clothes slip from* MICHAEL'S *arm.*

Delia. Michael! [*He takes no notice.*] Michael! [*He turns towards her.*] Why do you look at me like a stranger?

[*She drops his arm.* BRIDGET *goes over towards her.*

Patrick. The boys are all hurrying down the hillsides to join the French.

Delia. Michael won't be going to join the French.

Bridget. [*To* PETER.] Tell him not to go, Peter.

Peter. It's no use. He doesn't hear a word we're saying.

Bridget. Try and coax him over to the fire.

Delia. Michael, Michael! You won't leave me! You won't join the French, and we going to be married!

[*She puts her arms about him, he turns towards her as if about to yield.*

OLD WOMAN'S *voice outside.*

They shall be speaking for ever,
The people shall hear them for ever.

[MICHAEL *breaks away from* DELIA *and goes towards* Neighbours *at the door.*

Michael. Come, we have no time to lose; we must follow her.

---

124. "Got the touch" is an expression for having been put under a spell.

[MICHAEL *and the* Neighbours *go out.*

Peter. [*To* PATRICK, *laying a hand on his arm.*] Did you see an old woman going down the path?

Patrick. I did not, but I saw a young girl, and she had the walk of a queen.

22. James Joyce, "Ivy Day in the Committee Room," *Dubliners* (1914)

Like W. B. Yeats, James Joyce (1882–1941) is best known for his towering influence on twentieth-century literature, notably the short story and the novel. Joyce was a cosmopolitan who, like Gabriel Conway in the short story "The Dead" in Dubliners *(1914), sought to escape the narrowness of Irish life through identification with continental Europe. Joyce had nationalist sympathies, but he was not an Irish cultural nationalist in the Gaelic League mold. He was an opponent of British colonial rule, was an advocate of Irish self-determination, and had sympathies for Fenian politics. In contrast to nationalists who championed Irish Ireland, he was critical of the Roman Catholic Church, which he regarded as being just as imperialistic and oppressive as the British Empire. In 1907, Joyce (1991, 10) wrote that he did "not see what good it does to fulminate against the English tyranny while the Roman tyranny occupies the palace of the soul."*

Joyce was a Dubliner from a Catholic middle-class family that experienced increasing adversity as a result of his father's alcoholism. He attended Clongowes Wood College and Belvedere College (both of which were run by Jesuits). He completed his education at University College, Dublin. With his longtime partner (and later wife in 1931), Nora Barnacle (1884–1951), Joyce left behind what he regarded as the intellectual and political stasis of Dublin for the greater freedom of the European Continent. He originally lived in Trieste, Italy, later in Paris, France, and finally in Zurich, Switzerland. Joyce never returned to Dublin after a visit in 1912, but it was the continual focus of his literary imagination, first in Dubliners, *the collection of short stories completed in 1905 in which "Ivy Day in the Committee Room" appears.*

The story takes place on October 6, 1902, the eleventh anniversary of the death of the nationalist leader Charles Stewart Parnell, the "uncrowned king of Ireland." The "committee room" in the title evokes Committee Room 15 in the British House of Commons, where a majority of the Irish Parliamentary Party repudiated Parnell in 1890. Like all of Joyce's literary output, the story is multilayered. Politically, it explores the degeneration of Irish nationalism following the collapse of the Home Rule movement, the specific context being the Dublin municipal elections of 1902. The major issue was the approaching visit of King Edward VII (1841–1910), who, like Parnell, engaged in extramarital relationships but sat on the English throne rather than being dethroned, and who was to be officially welcomed during his trip to Dublin in 1903. While the "The People's Protection Committee," a forerunner of the militant nationalist party Sinn Féin, opposed the idea of a welcoming address, others, including the candidate in the story, Mr. Tierney, advocated accommodation. More generally, the story involves the collapse and potential regeneration of nationalist ideals through recurring attention to the committee room's fireplace. The fire is kept going only with the greatest attention and arguably represents the funeral pyre of Irish nationalism. Yet like the phoenix, which by legend dies in self-made flames and surfaces again from its own ashes, nationalism might still be renewed.

Old Jack raked the cinders together with a piece of cardboard and spread them judiciously over the whitening dome of coals. When the dome was thinly covered his face lapsed into darkness but, as he set himself to fan the fire again, his crouching shadow ascended the opposite wall and his face slowly re-emerged into light. It was an old man's face, very bony and hairy. The moist blue eyes blinked at the fire and the moist mouth fell open at times, munching once or twice mechanically when it closed. When the cinders had caught he laid the piece of cardboard against the wall, sighed and said:

—That's better now, Mr O'Connor.

Mr O'Connor, a grey-haired young man, whose face was disfigured by many blotches and pimples, had just brought the tobacco for a cigarette into a shapely cylinder but when spoken to he undid his handiwork meditatively. Then he began to roll the tobacco again meditatively and after a moment's thought decided to lick the paper.

—Did Mr Tierney say when he'd be back? he asked in a husky falsetto.

—He didn't say.

Mr O'Connor put his cigarette into his mouth and began to search his pockets. He took out a pack of thin pasteboard cards.

—I'll get you a match, said the old man.

—Never mind, this'll do, said Mr O'Connor.

He selected one of the cards and read what was printed on it:

MUNICIPAL ELECTIONS
ROYAL EXCHANGE WARD[125]

Mr Richard J. Tierney, P. L. G.,[126] respectfully solicits the favour of your vote and influence at the coming election in the Royal Exchange Ward.

Mr O'Connor had been engaged by Mr Tierney's agent to canvass one part of the ward but, as the weather was inclement and his boots let in the wet, he spent a great part of the day sitting by the fire in the Committee Room in Wicklow Street[127] with Jack, the old caretaker. They had been sitting thus since the short day had grown dark. It was the sixth of October, dismal and cold out of doors.

Mr O'Connor tore a strip off the card and, lighting it, lit his cigarette. As he did so the flame lit up a leaf of dark glossy ivy in the lapel of his coat. The old man watched him attentively and then, taking up the piece of cardboard again, began to fan the fire slowly while his companion smoked.

—Ah, yes, he said, continuing, it's hard to know what way to bring up children.

125. One of twenty wards in Dublin where the municipal election for the city council was taking place.

126. Poor Law Guardian. It refers to an official who distributes public funding to the poor.

127. Street in central Dublin. It is also the name of the county where Parnell was born.

Now who'd think he'd turn out like that! I sent him to the Christian Brothers[128] and I done what I could for him, and there he goes boosing[129] about. I tried to make him someway decent.

He replaced the cardboard wearily.

—Only I'm an old man now I'd change his tune for him. I'd take the stick to his back and beat him while I could stand over him—as I done many a time before. The mother, you know, she cocks him up with this and that. . . .

—That's what ruins children, said Mr O'Connor.

—To be sure it is, said the old man. And little thanks you get for it, only impudence. He takes th'upper hand of me whenever he sees I've a sup taken. What's the world coming to when sons speaks that way to their father?

—What age is he? said Mr O'Connor.

—Nineteen, said the old man.

—Why don't you put him to something?

—Sure, amn't I never done at the drunken bowsy[130] ever since he left school? *I won't keep you,* I says. *You must get a job for yourself.* But, sure, it's worse whenever he gets a job; he drinks it all.

Mr O'Connor shook his head in sympathy, and the old man fell silent, gazing into the fire. Someone opened the door of the room and called out:

—Hello! Is this a Freemasons' meeting?[131]

—Who's that? said the old man.

—What are you doing in the dark? asked a voice.

—Is that you, Hynes? asked Mr O'Connor.

—Yes. What are you doing in the dark? said Mr Hynes, advancing into the light of the fire.

He was a tall slender young man with a light brown moustache. Imminent little drops of rain hung at the brim of his hat and the collar of his jacket-coat was turned up.

—Well, Mat, he said to Mr O'Connor, how goes it?

Mr O'Connor shook his head. The old man left the hearth and, after stumbling about the room returned with two candlesticks which he thrust one after the other into the fire and carried to the table. A denuded room came into view and the fire lost all its cheerful colour. The walls of the room were bare except for a copy of an election address. In the middle of the room was a small table on which papers were heaped.

Mr Hynes leaned against the mantelpiece and asked:

—Has he paid you yet?[132]

128. A male Catholic teaching order whose first school was founded in Wexford (1802). It is known for providing the poor with a primary school education, for its harsh forms of discipline, and for its support of Irish nationalism.

129. *Boose* is slang for "alcohol." *Boosing* is slang for drinking alcohol excessively.

130. A lout or a ruffian.

131. A secret organization associated with Protestantism and anticlericalism. Freemason meetings were thought of as being shrouded in mystery.

132. Electioneering in this story is for monetary gain.

—Not yet, said Mr O'Connor. I hope to God he'll not leave us in the lurch to-night.
Mr Hynes laughed.

—O, he'll pay you. Never fear, he said.

—I hope he'll look smart about it if he means business, said Mr O'Connor.

—What do you think, Jack? said Mr Hynes satirically to the old man.

The old man returned to his seat by the fire, saying:

—It isn't but he has it, anyway. Not like the other tinker.[133]

—What other tinker? said Mr Hynes.

—Colgan, said the old man scornfully.

—It is because Colgan's a working-man you say that? What's the difference be-tween a good honest bricklayer and a publican—eh? Hasn't the working-man as good a right to be in the Corporation as anyone else—ay, and a better right than those shoneens[134] that are always hat in hand before any fellow with a handle to his name? Isn't that so, Mat? said Mr Hynes, addressing Mr O'Connor.

—I think you're right, said Mr O'Connor.

—One man is a plain honest man with no hunker-sliding[135] about him. He goes in to represent the labour classes. This fellow you're working for only wants to get some job or other.

—Of course, the working-classes should be represented, said the old man.

—The working-man, said Mr Hynes, gets all kicks and no halfpence. But it's labour produces everything. The working-man is not looking for fat jobs for his sons and nephews and cousins. The working-man is not going to drag the honour of Dublin in the mud to please a German monarch.[136]

—How's that? said the old man.

—Don't you know they want to present an address of welcome to Edward Rex[137] if he comes here next year? What do we want kowtowing to a foreign king?

—Our man won't vote for the address, said Mr O'Connor. He goes in on the Nationalist ticket.

—Won't he? said Mr Hynes. Wait till you see whether he will or not. I know him. Is it Tricky Dicky Tierney?

—By God! perhaps you're right, Joe, said Mr O'Connor. Anyway, I wish he'd turn up with the spondulics.[138]

---

133. Originally meaning a nomadic craftsmen, *tinker* is used here as a pejorative term, evok-ing a group of traveling people in Ireland regarded as disreputable.

134. A pejorative term referring to those who benefit from collaborating with and imitating the British.

135. Suggestive of laziness or groveling.

136. This is a pejorative reference to the king of England, Edward VII, who came to the throne in 1901. His mother, Victoria, was descended from the German Hanoverians and had married the German-born Prince Albert. In addition, the Dublin Corporation had voted not to officially greet Edward on his visit to Ireland in 1903. The official greeting took place outside the city limits.

137. King (Latin).

138. Money.

The three men fell silent. The old man began to rake more cinders together. Mr Hynes took off his hat, shook it and then turned down the collar of his coat, displaying, as he did so, an ivy leaf in the lapel.

—If this man was alive, he said, pointing to the leaf, we'd have no talk of an address of welcome.

—That's true, said Mr O'Connor.

—Musha,[139] God be with them times! said the old man. There was some life in it then.

The room was silent again. Then a bustling little man with a snuffling nose and very cold ears pushed in the door. He walked over quickly to the fire, rubbing his hands as if he intended to produce a spark from them.

—No money, boys, he said.

—Sit down here, Mr Henchy, said the old man, offering him his chair.

—O, don't stir, Jack, don't stir, said Mr Henchy.

He nodded curtly to Mr Hynes and sat down on the chair which the old man vacated.

—Did you serve[140] Aungier Street? he asked Mr O'Connor.

—Yes, said Mr O'Connor, beginning to search his pockets for memoranda.

—Did you call on Grimes?

—I did.

—Well? How does he stand?

—He wouldn't promise. He said: *I won't tell anyone what way I'm going to vote.* But I think he'll be all right.

—Why so?

—He asked me who the nominators were; and I told him. I mentioned Father Burke's name. I think it'll be all right.

—Mr Henchy began to snuffle and to rub his hands over the fire at a terrific speed. Then he said:

—For the love of God, Jack, bring us a bit of coal. There must be some left.

The old man went out of the room.

—It's no go, said Mr Henchy, shaking his head. I asked the little shoeboy,[141] but he said: *O, now, Mr Henchy, when I see the work going on properly I won't forget you, you may be sure.* Mean little tinker! 'Usha,[142] how could he be anything else?

—What did I tell you, Mat? said Mr Hynes. Tricky Dicky Tierney.

—O, he's as tricky as they make 'em, said Mr Henchy. He hasn't got those little pigs' eyes for nothing. Blast his soul! Couldn't he pay up like a man instead of: *O, now, Mr Henchy, I must speak to Mr Fanning. . . . I've spent a lot of money?* Mean little shoeboy of hell! I suppose he forgets the time his little old father kept the hand-me-down shop in Mary's Lane.[143]

139. Derived from Irish, meaning "indeed" or "oh well."

140. Canvas.

141. One who is always looking up at his client, that is, a flatterer.

142. Shortened version of *Musha* meaning "indeed" or "oh well."

143. A street north of the River Liffey in an impoverished area.

—But is that a fact? asked Mr O'Connor.

—God, yes, said Mr Henchy. Did you never hear that? And the men used to go in on Sunday morning before the houses were open to buy a waistcoat or a trousers—moya![144] But Tricky Dicky's little old father always had a tricky little black bottle up in a corner.[145] Do you mind now? That's that. That's where he first saw the light.

The old man returned with a few lumps of coal which he placed here and there on the fire.

—That's a nice how-do-you-do, said Mr O'Connor. How does he expect us to work for him if he won't stump up?

—I can't help it, said Mr Henchy. I expect to find the bailiffs in the hall when I go home.

Mr Hynes laughed and, shoving himself away from the mantelpiece with the aid of his shoulders, made ready to leave.

—It'll be all right when King Eddie comes, he said. Well, boys, I'm off for the present. See you later. 'Bye, 'bye.

He went out of the room slowly. Neither Mr Henchy nor the old man said anything but, just as the door was closing, Mr O'Connor, who had been staring moodily into the fire, called out suddenly:

—'Bye, Joe.

Mr Henchy waited a few moments and then nodded in the direction of the door.

—Tell me, he said across the fire, what brings our friend in here? What does he want?

—'Usha, poor Joe! said Mr O'Connor, throwing the end of his cigarette into the fire, he's hard up like the rest of us.

Mr Henchy snuffled vigorously and spat so copiously that he nearly put out the fire which uttered a hissing protest.

—To tell you my private and candid opinion, he said, I think he's a man from the other camp. He's a spy of Colgan's if you ask me. *Just go round and try and find out how they're getting on. They won't suspect you.* Do you twig?[146]

—Ah, poor Joe is a decent skin, said Mr O'Connor.

—His father was a decent respectable man, Mr Henchy admitted. Poor old Larry Hynes! Many a good turn he did in his day! But I'm greatly afraid our friend is not nineteen carat. Damn it, I can understand a fellow being hard up but what I can't understand is a fellow sponging. Couldn't he have some spark of manhood about him?

—He doesn't get a warm welcome from me when he comes, said the old man. Let him work for his own side and not come spying around here.

—I don't know, said Mr O'Connor dubiously, as he took out cigarette-papers and tobacco. I think Joe Hynes is a straight man. He's a clever chap, too, with the pen. Do you remember that thing he wrote . . . ?

—Some of these hillsiders and fenians are a bit too clever if you ask me, said Mr Henchy. Do you know what my private and candid opinion is about some of those

144. *Moya* is slang for "as it were."

145. He was selling alcohol illegally when the pubs were closed.

146. Understand.

little jokers? I believe half of them are in the pay of the [Dublin] Castle.

—There's no knowing, said the old man.

—O, but I know it for a fact, said Mr Henchy. They're Castle hacks . . . I don't say Hynes . . . No, damn it, I think he's a stroke above that . . . But there's a certain little nobleman with a cock-eye—you know the patriot I'm alluding to?

Mr O'Connor nodded.

—There's a lineal descendant of Major Sirr[147] for you if you like! O, the heart's blood of a patriot! That's a fellow now that'd sell his country for fourpence—ay—and go down on his bended knees and thank the Almighty Christ he had a country to sell.

There was a knock at the door.

—Come in! said Mr Henchy.

A person resembling a poor clergyman or a poor actor appeared in the doorway. His black clothes were tightly buttoned on his short body and it was impossible to say whether he wore a clergyman's collar or a layman's because the collar of his shabby frock-coat, the uncovered buttons of which reflected the candlelight, was turned up about his neck. He wore a round hat of hard black felt. His face, shining with raindrops, had the appearance of damp yellow cheese save where two rosy spots indicated the cheekbones. He opened his very long mouth suddenly to express disappointment and at the same time opened wide his very bright blue eyes to express pleasure and surprise.

—O, Father Keon! said Mr Henchy, jumping up from his chair. Is that you? Come in!

—O, no, no, no! said Father Keon quickly, pursing his lips as if he were addressing a child.

—Won't you come in and sit down?

—No, no, no! said Father Keon, speaking in a discreet indulgent velvety voice. Don't let me disturb you now! I'm just looking for Mr Fanning. . . .

—He's round at the *Black Eagle*,[148] said Mr Henchy. But won't you come in and sit down a minute?

—No, no, thank you. It was just a little business matter, said Father Keon. Thank you, indeed.

He retreated from the doorway and Mr Henchy, seizing one of the candlesticks, went to the door to light him downstairs.

—O, don't trouble, I beg!

—No, but the stairs is so dark.

—No, no, I can see. . . . Thank you, indeed.

—Are you right now?

—All right, thanks. . . . Thanks.

Mr Henchy returned with the candlestick and put it on the table. He sat down again at the fire. There was silence for a few moments.

---

147. Major Henry Charles Sirr (1764–1841), an Irish-born British army officer, who was the head of the Dublin Police. He relied on paid informers to root out Irish opposition, and in nationalist circles his name was synonymous with treachery. He was instrumental in the arrest of United Irishmen such as Robert Emmet and Lord Edward Fitzgerald (1763–98).

148. Mr. Tierney's pub.

—Tell me, John, said Mr O'Connor, lighting his cigarette with another paste-board card.

—Hm?

—What is he exactly?

—Ask me an easier one, said Mr Henchy.

—Fanning and himself seem to me very thick. They're often in Kavanagh's to-gether. Is he a priest at all?

—'Mmmyes, I believe so. . . . I think he's what you call a black sheep. We haven't many of them, thank God! but we have a few. . . . He's an unfortunate man of some kind. . . .

—And how does he knock it out?[149] asked Mr O'Connor.

—That's another mystery.

—Is he attached to any chapel or church or institution or—

—No, said Mr Henchy. I think he's travelling on his own account. . . . God forgive me, he added, I thought he was the dozen of stout.

—Is there any chance of a drink itself? asked Mr O'Connor.

—I'm dry too, said the old man.

—I asked that little shoeboy three times, said Mr Henchy, would he send up a dozen of stout. I asked him again now but he was leaning on the counter in his shirt-sleeves having a deep goster[150] with Alderman Cowley.

—Why didn't you remind him? said Mr O'Connor.

—Well, I couldn't go over while he was talking to Alderman Cowley. I just waited till I caught his eye, and said: *About that little matter I was speaking to you about. . . . That'll be all right, Mr H.*, he said. Yerra,[151] sure the little hop-o'-my-thumb[152] has forgotten all about it.

—There's some deal on in that quarter, said Mr O'Connor thoughtfully. I saw the three of them hard at it yesterday at Suffolk Street corner.

—I think I know the little game they're at, said Mr Henchy. You must owe the City Fathers money nowadays if you want to be made Lord Mayor. Then they'll make you Lord Mayor. By God! I'm thinking seriously of becoming a City Father myself. What do you think? Would I do for the job?

Mr O'Connor laughed.

—So far as owing money goes. . . .

—Driving out of the Mansion House,[153] said Mr Henchy, in all my vermin,[154] with Jack here standing up behind me in a powdered wig—eh?

—And make me your private secretary, John.

—Yes. And I'll make Father Keon my private chaplain. We'll have a family party.

—Faith, Mr Henchy, said the old man, you'd keep up better style than some of

149. Make a living.

150. Conversation (from Irish).

151. But, now, or really (from Irish).

152. Pejorative slang term for a dwarf.

153. Residence of the Lord Mayor.

154. A play on words on *ermine*, a type of weasel. Its fur is used in the mayor's robes.

them. I was talking one day to old Keegan, the porter. *And how do you like your new master, Pat?* says I to him. *You haven't much entertaining now,* says I. *Entertaining!* says he. *He'd live on the smell of an oil-rag.* And do you know what he told me? Now, I declare to God, I didn't believe him.

—What? said Mr Henchy and Mr O'Connor.

—He told me: *What do you think of a Lord Mayor of Dublin sending out for a pound of chops for his dinner? How's that for high living?* says he. *Wisha!*[155] *wisha,* says I. *A pound of chops,* says he, *coming into the Mansion House. Wisha!* says I, *what kind of people is going at all now?*

At this point there was a knock at the door, and a boy put in his head.

—What is it? said the old man.

—From the *Black Eagle,* said the boy, walking in sideways and depositing a basket on the floor with a noise of shaken bottles.

The old man helped the boy to transfer the bottles from the basket to the table and counted the full tally. After the transfer the boy put his basket on his arm and asked:

—Any bottles?

—What bottles? said the old man.

—Won't you let us drink them first? said Mr Henchy.

—I was told to ask for bottles.

—Come back to-morrow, said the old man.

—Here, boy! said Mr Henchy, will you run over to O'Farrell's and ask him to lend us a corkscrew—for Mr Henchy, say. Tell him we won't keep it a minute. Leave the basket there.

The boy went out and Mr Henchy began to rub his hands cheerfully, saying:

—Ah, well, he's not so bad after all. He's as good as his word, anyhow.

—There's no tumblers, said the old man.

—O, don't let that trouble you, Jack, said Mr Henchy. Many's the good man before now drank out of the bottle.

—Anyway, it's better than nothing, said Mr O'Connor.

—He's not a bad sort, said Mr Henchy, only Fanning has such a loan of him.[156] He means well, you know, in his own tinpot way.[157]

The boy came back with the corkscrew. The old man opened three bottles and was handing back the corkscrew when Mr Henchy said to the boy:

—Would you like a drink, boy?

—If you please, sir, said the boy.

The old man opened another bottle grudgingly, and handed it to the boy.

—What age are you? he asked.

—Seventeen, said the boy.

As the old man said nothing further the boy took the bottle, said: *Here's my best respects, sir* to Mr Henchy, drank the contents, put the bottle back on the table and

155. Variation of *Musha.*

156. "Such a loan of him" is slang for "having so much influence on him."

157. Feeble way.

wiped his mouth with his sleeve. Then he took up the corkscrew and went out of the door sideways, muttering some form of salutation.

—That's the way it begins, said the old man.

—The thin edge of the wedge,[158] said Mr Henchy.

The old man distributed the three bottles which he had opened and the men drank from them simultaneously. After having drank each placed his bottle on the mantelpiece within hand's reach and drew in a long breath of satisfaction.

—Well, I did a good day's work to-day, said Mr Henchy, after a pause.

—That so, John?

—Yes. I got him one or two sure things in Dawson Street,[159] Crofton[160] and myself. Between ourselves, you know, Crofton (he's a decent chap, of course), but he's not worth a damn as a canvasser. He hasn't a word to throw to a dog. He stands and looks at the people while I do the talking.

Here two men entered the room. One of them was a very fat man, whose blue serge clothes seemed to be in danger of falling from his sloping figure. He had a big face which resembled a young ox's face in expression, staring blue eyes and a grizzled moustache. The other man, who was much younger and frailer, had a thin clean-shaven face. He wore a very high double collar and a wide-brimmed bowler hat.

—Hello, Crofton! said Mr Henchy to the fat man. Talk of the devil. . . .

—Where did the boose come from? asked the young man. Did the cow calve?[161]

—O, of course, Lyons spots the drink first thing! said Mr O'Connor, laughing.

—Is that the way you chaps canvass, said Mr Lyons, and Crofton and I out in the cold and rain looking for votes?

—Why, blast your soul, said Mr Henchy, I'd get more votes in five minutes than you two'd get in a week.

—Open two bottles of stout, Jack, said Mr O'Connor.

—How can I? said the old man, when there's no corkscrew?

—Wait now, wait now! said Mr Henchy, getting up quickly. Did you ever see this little trick?

He took two bottles from the table and, carrying them to the fire, put them on the hob.[162] Then he sat down again by the fire and took another drink from his bottle. Mr Lyons sat on the edge of the table, pushed his hat towards the nape of his neck and began to swing his legs.

—Which is my bottle? he asked.

—This lad, said Mr Henchy.

Mr Crofton sat down on a box and looked fixedly at the other bottle on the hob. He was silent for two reasons. The first reason, sufficient in itself, was that he had

158. An expression derived from logging, meaning that once the first step is taken there is no turning back.

159. Street south of the River Liffey consisting of shops and offices.

160. In another story in *Dubliners*, "Grace," Crofton is described as an Orangeman and in *Ulysses* (1922) as a Presbyterian.

161. Is there a reason to celebrate?

162. The part of the casing in a fireplace that has a surface used for cooking.

nothing to say; the second reason was that he considered his companions beneath him. He had been a canvasser for Wilkins, the Conservative, but when the Conservatives had withdrawn their man and, choosing the lesser of two evils, given their support to the Nationalist candidate, he had been engaged to work for Mr Tierney.

In a few minutes an apologetic *Pok!* was heard as the cork flew out of Mr Lyons' bottle. Mr Lyons jumped off the table, went to the fire, took his bottle and carried it back to the table.

—I was just telling them, Crofton, said Mr Henchy, that we got a good few votes to-day.

—Who did you get? asked Mr Lyons.

—Well, I got Parkes for one, and I got Atkinson for two, and I got Ward of Dawson Street. Fine old chap he is, too—regular old toff,[163] old Conservative! *But isn't your candidate a Nationalist?* said he. *He's a respectable man,* said I. *He's in favour of whatever will benefit this country. He's a big rate-payer,*[164] I said. *He has extensive house property in the city and three places of business and isn't it to his own advantage to keep down the rates? He's a prominent and respected citizen,* said I, *and a Poor Law Guardian, and he doesn't belong to any party, good, bad, or indifferent.* That's the way to talk to 'em.

—And what about the address to the King? said Mr Lyons, after drinking and smacking his lips.

—Listen to me, said Mr Henchy. What we want in this country, as I said to old Ward, is capital. The King's coming here will mean an influx of money into this country. The citizens of Dublin will benefit by it. Look at all the factories down by the quays there, idle! Look at all the money there is in the country if we only worked the old industries, the mills, the shipbuilding yards and factories. It's capital we want.

—But look here, John, said Mr O'Connor. Why should we welcome the King of England? Didn't Parnell himself . . .

—Parnell, said Mr Henchy, is dead. Now, here's the way I look at it. Here's this chap come to the throne after his old mother keeping him out of it till the man was grey.[165] He's a man of the world, and he means well by us. He's a jolly fine decent fellow, if you ask me, and no damn nonsense about him. He just says to himself: *The old one never went to see these wild Irish. By Christ, I'll go myself and see what they're like.* And are we going to insult the man when he comes over here on a friendly visit? Eh? Isn't that right, Crofton?

—Mr Crofton nodded his head.

—But after all now, said Mr Lyons argumentatively, King Edward's life, you know, is not the very . . .

—Let bygones be bygones, said Mr Henchy. I admire the man personally. He's

163. A slightly derogative term to describe a person who has an air of superiority or is well dressed.

164. A taxpayer. The *rates* refer to local taxes based on the value of owned or rented property.

165. Queen Victoria died in 1901 at the age of eighty-one. Edward VII was sixty years old when he came to the throne.

just an ordinary knockabout like you and me. He's fond of his glass of grog[166] and he's a bit of a rake,[167] perhaps, and he's a good sportsman. Damn it, can't we Irish play fair?

—That's all very fine, said Mr Lyons. But look at the case of Parnell now.

—In the name of God, said Mr Henchy, where's the analogy between the two cases?

—What I mean, said Mr Lyons, is we have our ideals. Why, now, would we welcome a man like that? Do you think now after what he did Parnell was a fit man to lead us? And why, then, would we do it for Edward the Seventh?

—This is Parnell's anniversary, said Mr O'Connor, and don't let us stir up any bad blood. We all respect him now that he's dead and gone—even the Conservatives, he added, turning to Mr Crofton.

Pok! The tardy cork flew out of Mr Crofton's bottle. Mr Crofton got up from his box and went to the fire. As he returned with his capture he said in a deep voice:

—Our side of the house respects him because he was a gentleman.

—Right you are, Crofton! said Mr Henchy fiercely. He was the only man that could keep that bag of cats in order. *Down, ye dogs! Lie down, ye curs!* That's the way he treated them. Come in, Joe! Come in! he called out, catching sight of Mr Hynes in the doorway.

Mr Hynes came in slowly.

—Open another bottle of stout, Jack, said Mr Henchy. O, I forgot there's no corkscrew! Here, show me one here and I'll put it at the fire.

The old man handed him another bottle and he placed it on the hob.

—Sit down, Joe, said Mr O'Connor, we're just talking about the Chief.

—Ay, ay! said Mr Henchy.

Mr Hynes sat on the side of the table near Mr Lyons but said nothing.

—There's one of them, anyhow, said Mr Henchy, that didn't renege him. By God, I'll say for you, Joe! No, by God, you stuck to him like a man!

—O, Joe, said Mr O'Connor suddenly. Give us that thing you wrote—do you remember? Have you got it on you?

—O, ay! said Mr Henchy. Give us that. Did you ever hear that, Crofton? Listen to this now: splendid thing.

—Go on, said Mr O'Connor. Fire away, Joe.

Mr Hynes did not seem to remember at once the piece to which they were alluding but, after reflecting a while, he said:

—O, that thing is it. . . . Sure, that's old now.

—Out with it, man! said Mr O'Connor.

—'Sh, 'sh, said Mr Henchy. Now, Joe!

Mr Hynes hesitated a little longer. Then amid the silence he took off his hat, laid it on the table and stood up. He seemed to be rehearsing the piece in his mind. After a rather long pause he announced:

166. Rum or, more generally, hard liquor.
167. A stylish yet dissolute man.

THE DEATH OF PARNELL
6th October, 1891

He cleared his throat once or twice and then began to recite:

He is dead. Our Uncrowned King is dead.
O, Erin, mourn with grief and woe
For he lies dead whom the fell gang
Of modern hypocrites laid low.

He lies slain by the coward hounds
He raised to glory from the mire;
And Erin's hopes and Erin's dreams
Perish upon her monarch's pyre.

In palace, cabin or in cot
The Irish heart where'er it be
Is bowed with woe—for he is gone
Who would have wrought her destiny.

He would have had his Erin famed,
The green flag gloriously unfurled,
Her statesmen, bards and warriors raised
Before the nations of the World.

He dreamed (alas, 'twas but a dream!)
Of Liberty: but as he strove
To clutch that idol, treachery
Sundered him from the thing he loved.

Shame on the coward, caitiff[168] hands
That smote their Lord or with a kiss
Betrayed him to the rabble-rout
Of fawning priests—no friends of his.

May everlasting shame consume
The memory of those who tried
To befoul and smear th'exalted name
Of one who spurned them in his pride.

He fell as fall the mighty ones,
Nobly undaunted to the last,
And death has now united him
With Erin's heroes of the past.

---

168. Base, despicable.

No sound of strife disturb his sleep!
Calmly he rests: no human pain
Or high ambition spurs him now
The peaks of glory to attain.

They had their way: they laid him low.
But Erin, list, his spirit may
Rise, like the Phoenix from the flames,
When breaks the dawning of the day,

The day that brings us Freedom's reign.
And on that day may Erin well
Pledge in the cup she lifts to Joy
One grief—the memory of Parnell.

Mr Hynes sat down again on the table. When he had finished his recitation there was a silence and then a burst of clapping: even Mr Lyons clapped. The applause continued for a little time. When it had ceased all the auditors drank from their bottles in silence.

Pok! The cork flew out of Mr Hynes' bottle, but Mr Hynes remained sitting, flushed and bareheaded on the table. He did not seem to have heard the invitation.

—Good man, Joe! said Mr O'Connor, taking out his cigarette papers and pouch the better to hide his emotion.

—What do you think of that, Crofton? cried Mr Henchy. Isn't that fine? What?

Mr Crofton said that it was a very fine piece of writing.

23. Maud Gonne MacBride, Selections from *The Autobiography of Maud Gonne: A Servant of the Queen* (1938)

Maud Gonne MacBride (1866–1953) is among the first women to play a prominent role in the Irish nationalist movement. She was an activist, actress, mystic, and writer. She played a pioneering role in linking women's rights with Irish nationalism, founding Inghinidhe na hÉireann (Daughters of Ireland) in 1900. Gonne was born in England; her father was an officer from a wealthy Irish family originally from Scotland; and her mother died when she was a child. She was educated in a French boarding school and known for her great beauty as a young woman. Gonne grew up as a Protestant but later converted to Catholicism. She had a tempestuous personal life. She had an affair with the politician Lucien Millevoye (1850–1918), with whom she had a daughter Iseult and a son George. She married, had a son with, and eventually divorced John MacBride (1865–1916), who was later executed for his role in the Easter Rising. Only after his death did she adopt his name. Gonne was a close friend of W. B. Yeats and the muse of some of his most memorable poems. Between 1891 and 1901, she turned down no less than four marriage proposals from him.

Maud Gonne as a young woman. (Image from the Library of Congress.)

Gonne made varied contributions to the Irish nationalist movement. She worked on behalf of evicted tenants and Fenian prisoners. She was prominent in protesting Queen Victoria's visit to Ireland in 1900, part of the celebration of the latter's Diamond Jubilee. She opposed the Anglo-Irish Treaty and during the Civil War formed the Women's Prisoners Defence League. As a consequence of her activism, she was imprisoned by the British government in 1918 and by the Irish Free State in 1923. Gonne's recollections of her entry into Irish nationalist politics dramatize the obstacles faced by women in not only political life but also the public sphere more generally. They form part of her memoir, The Autobiography of Maud Gonne: A Servant of the Queen *(1938). The "queen" in the title refers to a vision that Gonne had of the queen of Ireland, Cathleen Ni Houlihan, whom she played in Yeats' nationalist play (no. 21).*

In Oldham's[169] room Ida[170] and I organised a concert in aid of the City of Dublin Hospital, whose matron, Miss Beresford, was teaching me nursing, letting me accompany her round the wards and even take an occasional hand in bandaging and dressings. I had told her how I had tried to become a nurse; she agreed with me that all women should understand nursing and kindly helped me. Ida and I decided the Concert was to be an Irish Concert, with nothing but Irish music and poems by Irish authors; this, we said, precluded naturally the playing of *God Save the Queen*. We replaced it by that grand Irish song, "Let Erin Remember." The Concert was a great success, every seat booked out. All my old Dublin friends were there, to welcome Tommy's[171] daughter, and my new friends, John O'Leary, Willie [William Butler] Yeats and the Contemporary Club,[172] and the general public interested in Irish music. From an artistic point of view the concert was irreproachable, for Ida was a born musician and knew all the good artists. She had a lovely voice trained in Italy, and sang Irish ballads exquisitely. I recited Todhunter's[173] lovely poem, "The Banshee and Dark Rosaleen." To the clamorous encores accorded to Ida and myself, who, because of our novelty, were the great attractions, we gave only rebel songs and rebel poems. The gallery was enthusiastic, but I was amused to see, through a hole in the back cloth, the puzzled looks of many in the expensive seats.

Next day we had great Press notices, but letters, and I think, even a leading article in the *Irish Times*,[174] commented indignantly on the omission of *God Save the Queen*, an unheard of thing at any Dublin concert in those days. I replied, and a regular letter controversy arose. Ida's mother was pained, and after that thought me a dangerous companion for her daughter. Ida, Oldham and I were very proud and thought we had done a little thing for Ireland.

I was inundated with requests to recite at Workmen's clubs and Literary societies. I recited some of [Thomas] Davis's poems to illustrate a lecture of Willie Rooney's[175] at the Celtic Literary Society, and I met there Arthur Griffith for the first time. He was a fair, shy boy one would hardly notice, but I was at once attracted to him, I hardly knew why, for he did not speak, and I got to know him well only in 1899 when he

169. Charles Hubert Oldham (1860–1920), barrister and distinguished economist. He helped found the Contemporary Club in 1885 and the Protestant Home Rule Association in 1886. At the time when Gonne met him, he was a student at Trinity College, Dublin.

170. Ida Jameson, a childhood friend of Gonne's. Their mothers had been close friends when they both lived in Donnybrook.

171. Captain Thomas Gonne (1835–1886), Maud Gonne's father.

172. Founded by Charles Hubert Oldham, the Contemporary Club "acted as a magnet for those self-consciously determined to be raffish and to cross boundaries, against the background of Dublin's intimate and censorious provincialism" (Foster 1997, 39).

173. John Todhunter (1839–1916), Irish poet and playwright.

174. Founded in 1859, and still being published, the *Irish Times* was at the time a Protestant and Unionist newspaper.

175. William Rooney (1873–1901), nationalist journalist and poet. He became the first president of the Celtic Literary Society in 1893.

and Willie Rooney came to me with the first copy of the *United Irishman*.[176] They had collected £30 and hoped it would be enough to start the paper, and found they had not even enough for the second Number.

The Celtic Literary Society produced a Manuscript Journal *An Seanachie*[177] which I found very interesting. I was so delighted with the Club and its activities, that I told the secretary I wanted to become a member. He looked embarrassed. Willie Rooney was called to explain, as politely as he could, that the rules of the Club excluded women from membership.

Laughingly I told the Committee of the Celtic Literary Society that I would have to start a Women's society and I would get all their sisters and sweethearts into it, and they would have to look to their laurels then.

Arthur Griffith and Willie Rooney both disapproved of the exclusion of women and, when I did actually start *Inghinidhe na hEireann* in 1900, gave me all the help they could, and the Celtic Literary Society generously lent us their rooms for our meetings and classes, till we were big enough to have a house of our own, and run lectures on History and Irish, dancing, singing and drilling classes for children in three halls in Dublin. Later the Celtic Literary Society admitted women to membership.

I felt it was hardly fair to kind, hospitable old Mrs. Jameson to go on staying at Airfield, and, much to Ida's disappointment, I took rooms in the Gresham Hotel, until I could get a flat. Almost opposite to the Gresham Hotel were the offices of [Irish] National League. Passing the door, I went in and told the clerk in the outer office I wished to subscribe and to become a member. He ushered me into a large room with a great table down the centre and rows of chairs for meetings; it was rather impressive. From the inner office a secretary appeared, a genial young man called Quinn. He at once congratulated me on my recitations and on my letter in the Press against the playing of the English National Anthem at an Irish Concert and said he was sure his Chief, Mr. Harrington,[178]—who was out,—would like to meet me, and enquired what time I would be in for him to call. I then told him I wanted to join the National League and was ready to do any work suggested. He also looked embarrassed and said:

"There are no ladies in the National League."

"How strange," I replied. "Surely Ireland needs all her children."

Decidedly there was no place for women in the National movement.

Next day, Tim Harrington, weather-beaten and very able, a man to count with, called on me. He was accompanied by two other M.P.s whom he introduced. T. P. Gill,[179] pale and lanky, a typical clerk, and Pat O'Brien,[180] small and companionable. I longed to ask Harrington if he had brought them to chaperone him in an interview with a dangerous lady, but didn't dare.

176. Irish nationalist newspaper founded by William Rooney and Arthur Griffith. It was published from 1899 to 1906.

177. Also *seanachai*. A Gaelic storyteller of old tales (Irish).

178. Timothy Charles Harrington (1851–1910), Irish journalist, nationalist politician, and MP (1883–1910).

179. Thomas Patrick Gill (1858–1931), Irish nationalist MP (1885–92).

180. Pat O'Brien (1847–1917), Irish nationalist politician, MP (1886–92, 1895–1917).

We had hardly sat down when Pat O'Brien got up softly and opened the door; a waiter, who had his ear to the keyhole, rose hurriedly, saying he was coming in to ask if Miss Gonne needed refreshments.

"You got a good look at him, Pat," said Mr. Gill, "just as well to know the appearance of these rascals."

"That is what you are up against, Miss Gonne, when you join the National Movement,—spies watching everywhere. We have our Intelligence Service too," said Mr. Harrington. "This is supposed to be a Nationalist hotel and a good many of our friends stay here. Everyone is watched, and, I need hardly tell you, you are an object of much speculation to both sides. It was reported to me the moment you took rooms here."

I laughed and told him I believed Michael Davitt thought I was a spy in London, and I didn't blame him for it.

"Michael would," said Pat O'Brien.

"And why wouldn't he?" I answered. We all laughed, but I don't think O'Brien and Harrington had any doubts of me. Mr. Gill was effusively amiable and said he would have liked his wife to call on me, but she was in London. He was aiming at great respectability, and I impressed him. Later, when he had attained the giddy heights of Plunket House and the Royal Dublin Society,[181] he looked down on Constance Markievicz and myself as foolish misguided women who had left a world into which with such pains he was climbing.

I told Mr. Harrington that at the National League offices I had been informed no women were admitted to membership. Mr. Harrington's blue eyes twinkled merrily as he said:

"The Constitution of the National League does not allow lady members."

"But there used to be a Ladies' Land League[182] and they did splendid work."

"Indeed they did," said Pat O'Brien; "they were great women and kept things lively while we were all in jail."

"We disbanded the Ladies' Land League when we came out," said Harrington, I thought a little bitterly. "They did too good work, and some of us found they could not be controlled."

"But don't you approve of women in politics, Mr. Harrington?" Again his eyes twinkled and he said, with mock solemnity:

"A woman's place is in the home; but don't be afraid, Miss Gonne, we will find plenty of work for you, if that is what you want."

I was not satisfied, and said so. "I know women can do some things better than men, and men can do some things better than we can; but I don't like this exclusion of women from the National fight, and the fact that they should have to work through back-door influence if they want to get things done."

---

181. The Royal Dublin Society was founded in 1731 for the advancement of arts, agriculture, industry, and science in Ireland.

182. Established in 1881 and disbanded a year later, the Ladies' Land League took on many of the responsibilities of the male leaders of the Irish Land League when the latter were imprisoned in 1881–82. It marked the first formal involvement by women in Irish nationalist politics.

He looked at me questioningly but kindly. Perhaps he was wondering if I was thinking of a woman who had great influence on his leader [Charles Stewart] Parnell, and who was very much in all their thoughts though her name was rarely mentioned; but I was not,—at that time I had never heard of Mrs. [Katharine] O'Shea.[183] . . .

183. Katharine (Wood) O'Shea (1846–1921), English lover, later wife, and mother of three children by Charles Stewart Parnell. When their affair became public knowledge in 1889, it created a scandal that led to Parnell's political downfall. See Glossary.

CHAPTER THREE

New Departures

In October 1878, John Devoy (1842–1928), leader of the republican organization Clan na Gael sent a telegram to Charles Stewart Parnell, an emerging militant leader in the Irish Parliamentary Party. Devoy outlined a new initiative that would unite the nationalist movements on both sides of the Atlantic and bring together constitutional and physical-force nationalists. The movement would simultaneously campaign for political autonomy, or Home Rule, and land reform. The initiative was to be backed by American funding, and Parnell was to be at its head. While Parnell was reluctant to explicitly embrace it, and there were Fenians who opposed it, the New Departure was nonetheless launched and changed the face of Irish nationalist politics. It simultaneously transformed the Anglo-Irish relationship and exacerbated tensions between nationalists and Unionists that eventually brought Ireland to the brink of civil war. This chapter consists of sources loosely organized around the politics either produced or accelerated by the New Departure—notably the Land War and the Home Rule movement. It also includes sources that are concerned with developments in the nationalist and unionist movements, notably Fenianism and Ulster loyalism that are critical to understanding the politics of this period.

Revival of the republican movement took place in the vacuum created by the disintegration of the repeal movement, already in decline when Daniel O'Connell died in 1847. The easily contained Young Ireland rebellion of 1848 ended a period of intense political energy that ultimately resulted in failure and soul searching. Republican renewal was spearheaded by two participants of the 1848 rebellion—James Stephens and John O'Mahony—who escaped the clutches of the authorities, made their way to Paris, and in the subterranean world filled with political revolutionaries that congregated there rethought the basis of Irish nationalist politics. They imagined a highly disciplined revolutionary organization operating on both sides of the Atlantic, an indication of the increasingly important role that the growing Irish immigrant population in the United States would play in nationalist politics. In effect, they laid the foundation for the Irish Republican Brotherhood (IRB) and the Fenian Brotherhood, founded in Ireland and the United States, respectively, in 1858 and 1859. Group participants and sympathizers became known as Fenians, a historical reference to ancient warriors found in Irish mythology.

The Fenians in Ireland were at once a secret oath-bound society and a social club dominated by working-class artisans and middle-class men living in towns. They had their own newspaper—the *Irish People*, begun by Stephens in 1863—and may have had as many as fifty-four thousand members in 1864. Their growth was enough to worry the authorities, who monitored and eventually broke up their activities. The Fenian movement provided an outlet for social and political frustration, and nurtured national pride and a degree of class consciousness. Some Fenians were anticlerical, but most were loyal Catholics and thus befuddled, as John O'Mahony's letter to William Sullivan suggests (no. 27), by Church opposition to them. The pastoral letter of Archbishop William Ullathorne (no. 29) summarizes the dominant feeling among the Church's leaders. He defended the constitutional nationalism of O'Connell and suggested that the Fenian movement could only produce "failure, distress and misery."

James Stephens seized control of the Fenian movement in the early 1860s. In his letter to O'Mahony (no. 28), he sketched out an uprising made up of Irish and Irish-American recruits launched on the back of British involvement in the American Civil War, although he cautioned that Britain's "difficulty" was no guarantee of Ireland's "opportunity." Under pressure to deliver results, Stephens rashly promised a rising, first in 1865, and subsequently in 1866, but was hesitant to launch it. When the Fenian revolt did take place in 1867 (primarily in Dublin and Cork), Stephens had been ousted as the Fenians' leader, and the rebellion was more of a gesture than a serious threat. It attracted little popular enthusiasm. But the standing of the Fenians was enhanced by events that followed. Fenians attempted to liberate two Fenian prisoners—Colonel T. J. Kelly (1833–1908) and Captain Timothy Deasy (1839–80)—on their way from jail to a Manchester courthouse in 1867, resulting in the death of an unarmed British police guard. Twelve Fenians were put on trial. Of these, five were condemned to death. Ultimately three of them—William Philip Allen (1848–67), Michael Larkin (c. 1837–67), and Michael O'Brien (c. 1837–67)—were executed. Not for the first or last time, acts of Irish revolutionaries failed to win popular support; but British reprisals against them produced political martyrs, aroused national resentment and pride, bestowed respectability on the militants, and provided a space for discussion among priests, revolutionaries, and constitutionalists.

A principal beneficiary of this new mood was constitutional nationalism, dormant since O'Connell's time. The repeal movement was refashioned as *Home Rule*, an allusive term that at a minimum meant an Irish legislature with authority over domestic affairs, while the British Parliament would retain control over foreign affairs for the entire UK. Ireland would still send MPs to the British Parliament, but the number would be reduced. The key figure in the early stages of the Home Rule movement was Isaac Butt (1813–79), a brilliant trial lawyer who had defended Young Irelanders and Fenian prisoners. Butt was a professor of political economy, a Tory, and a Unionist. The British government's handling of the Fenian threat—especially its reluctance to consider prisoner amnesties—was critical to Butt's conversion to the principle of legislative autonomy. He founded the Home Government Association in 1870 (renamed the Home Rule League in 1873) and led a loosely-knit group of supporters in Parliament, which after the 1874 elections totaled fifty-nine. Butt always believed that Home Rule would fortify the Union and ensure the continued influence of the Anglo-Irish landowning and professional classes in Ireland. He was thus respectful of, and deferential towards, parliamentary traditions.

This was not the case for Joseph Biggar,[1] a Home Rule MP and a Fenian veteran,

---

1. Joseph Gillis Biggar (1828–90), a nationalist politician and MP in the British Parliament (1874–90). A successful merchant, he was a Presbyterian by birth but converted to Catholicism in 1877. He joined the IRB in 1875 and was a member of its Supreme Council but was expelled for refusing to give up his parliamentary seat. He is best known for developing the political strategy of parliamentary obstruction, which was critical to the emerging leadership of Parnell.

who used parliamentary procedure relentlessly to obstruct the flow of the business of the House of Commons so that Irish issues did not fade from Parliament's agenda. Charles Stewart Parnell, a young Protestant landowner from County Wicklow, soon joined him, becoming the leader of the militant Home Rulers and rather quickly wresting control of the movement from Butt in 1877. Parnell lacked O'Connell's eloquence as a speaker but was a master strategist. He was an aloof yet passionately intense and single-minded leader who simultaneously enraged British opinion and unified a wide swathe of nationalist perspectives, in part because he avoided being too closely connected to any one of them. It was at this juncture that Devoy (and the land reformer Michael Davitt) reached out to Parnell to assume leadership over a new political direction.

The new nationalism coalesced in support of land reform. Throughout the nineteenth century, the roots of Irish poverty were linked to the inequities of the Irish land system. Various observers contrasted the horrendous conditions under which Irish peasants lived with the profligate lives of the remote, often absentee landlord class; although historians have subsequently shown that this representation of landlords was overstated. For English liberal economists, committed to laissez-faire and minimal state intervention (what we might call conservativism today), the answer was a free market in land. They believed that such a market would result in emigration to relieve population pressures and the more productive use of land, as efficient capitalist landowners would supplant inefficient ones.

Radicals, on the other hand, had an alternative perspective. Writing in pre-Famine Ireland, the socialist writer Friedrich Engels (no. 25) attributed Irish poverty to excessive subdivision of the land and to the Irish national character. Writing more than two decades later, his friend and colleague Karl Marx (no. 26) regarded the overthrow of the Irish landlords as a flashpoint for the collapse of British capitalism and the advent of a proletarian revolution. Among the Young Irelanders, James Fintan Lalor (no. 24) was the most prominent advocate of a social revolution. He was not, like Marx and Engels, a socialist or communist. He advocated a system of peasant proprietorships. However, like them, he regarded political independence as meaningless without economic transformation.

In the aftermath of the Famine, land reform became a major cause, stimulated by landlords' efforts at recouping lost revenues and paying for mounting costs. Its premise was that tenants had claims transcending a legal title. Its model was the Ulster practice known as the *Ulster custom*, where tenants under certain circumstances could claim compensation for their improvements upon vacating their holding. The demands were defined by the Irish Tenant League, founded in 1850, as the Three Fs—*fair* rent, *fixity* of tenure, and tenants' *freedom* to be remunerated for improvements. Protestants and Catholics founded the league, a rare occurrence in which class grievances overcame communal divisions; but such cooperation proved impossible to sustain, and land reform was largely appropriated as a nationalist cause. The land question also drew the attention of more intellectually inclined reformers who challenged laissez-faire solutions for Ireland. Influenced by anthropology, evolutionary ideas, and scholarship on the history of legal traditions, they believed that reforms should be based on recognizing Irish and British cultural differences. George Camp-

bell (no. 30), an imperial official with wide experience in India and a scholarly interest in comparative legal traditions pertaining to land, argued that Ireland was more
like India than Britain and that Irish land reform should enshrine the principal of
dual ownership. Campbell's book *The Irish Land* (1869) provoked a lively debate.

Most importantly, the book made a deep impression on William Ewart Gladstone,
the most important British liberal politician of his era, who emerged as the champion
of the Irish cause in Britain. Gladstone was a supporter of the Union. Yet he came to
believe that the best way of preserving it was to address Irish nationalist demands, a
stance that also provided an opportunity of corralling the Irish Catholic vote for the
Liberal Party. In 1869, he pushed through legislation disestablishing the Church of
Ireland. In 1870, he produced land legislation that recognized the principle of dual
ownership and the rudiments of peasant proprietorship. Gladstone was also to learn
how formidable the obstacles to reform in Ireland in fact were. His proposed Irish
University Bill (1873), which would have created a secular Irish university attended
by Catholics and Protestants alike, ended up so full of concessions to the various
interests that it alienated both liberal reformers and the Catholic Church hierarchy
and was defeated by three votes.

By the late 1870s, Ireland was facing an economic crisis unknown since the time
of the Famine. As a result of falling prices, crop failures, and unusually wet weather,
tenants faced insolvency, starvation, and eviction. Yet in contrast to the 1840s, a
popular movement arose that simultaneously fought for tenants' rights and attacked
landlordism. The result was the Irish Land War, which first surfaced with Michael
Davitt's National Land League of Mayo (no. 31), founded in 1879. Later that year
the National Land League, led by Parnell, superseded it. The National Land League
served as a relief agency and as an advocate for threatened and displaced tenants. It
demanded an end to evictions, rent reduction, and land reform and ended up as a
quasi-alternative government, using the boycott to isolate noncompliant landlords
and those willing to rent the land of the evicted.

When Gladstone was elected as prime minister in 1880, he took a two-pronged
approach to solving the Irish crisis. On the one hand, he passed a coercion bill that
gave the government sweeping powers to clamp down on what some perceived to
be an insurrection. On the other hand, he passed the 1881 Land Act, which fully
enacted the Three Fs. It also created a special court to which tenants could appeal
in order to obtain fair rents for a fixed period of fifteen years and a loan program allowing them to borrow up to 75 percent of a land purchase. When Parnell and the
Land League refused to call off the agitation, arguing that peasant proprietorship had
superseded the Three Fs as the goal of the movement, Gladstone's Liberal government responded by arresting several of the leaders, including Parnell, and proscribing
the organization.

Unexpectedly, Parnell's arrest became the occasion not for further confrontation
but for a rapprochement between him and Gladstone that inaugurated an alliance
between British Liberals and Irish nationalists that would have a long-term impact on
the Anglo-Irish relationship. While Parnell was surprised by his arrest, he took it (according to reports) like a gentleman and confessed in his correspondence that he felt
relief (Bew 2007, 329). As a landowner himself, he was concerned at the increasingly

radical turn of the Land War, and his removal from the conflict gave him an opportunity to reclaim the initiative. Gladstone, despite the draconian measures to which
he had resorted, remained committed to Irish reforms. In what became known as the
Kilmainham Treaty of May 1882, Parnell agreed to call off the Land War and support
the government in Parliament in exchange for promises from Gladstone for further
reform. The agreement between the two men was severely tested by the May 6, 1882,
murders of Lord Frederick Cavendish (1836–82), the new chief secretary of Ireland,
and his undersecretary T. H. Burke (1829–82). Yet the agreement survived. In the
1885 election campaign, Gladstone acknowledged that if the vast majority of Irish
MPs were to demand "large local powers in self-government" (quoted in Comerford
1989, 61) then the new parliament must develop a response. This ambiguous remark
was clarified when he became prime minister in 1886 and announced his support for
Home Rule. However sincere Gladstone's support of Home Rule may have been, the
timing of his decision to introduce a Home Rule Bill was informed by the fact that
he did not have enough votes to form a majority. His government was dependent on
Parnell's party, which had been enormously successful in the elections, winning 85
out of 103 Irish seats and an additional seat in Liverpool. This achievement was made
possible both by the stature of Parnell and the nationalist cause as well as the 1884
Reform Act, which more than tripled the size of the Irish electorate. It seemed as if
the aspirations of the New Departure were about to be realized.

The Home Rule Bill, introduced by Gladstone in 1886, was potentially the greatest change to the Anglo-Irish relationship since the Union in 1801: it was the first
time that a British government had accepted the principle of Irish self-determination
however circumscribed. Accordingly, Home Rule was extensively debated. A selection
from a huge literature is included in this chapter. Gladstone's request for public discussion produced responses from the three Irish churches, revealing both Catholic enthusiasm for (no. 36) and Protestant dread of (nos. 37 and 38) a Home Rule future. Other
selections, mostly drawn from *The Times*, the newspaper of the British establishment,
convey a wide diversity of views: Irish nationalist (no. 32), British Liberal (no. 33),
Tory (no. 35), southern Unionist (no. 34), and northern Unionist (nos. 39–41).

Enough has been said about Irish nationalism and British Liberalism so that the selections from Parnell (no. 32) and Gladstone (no. 33), respectively, have a context for
interpretation. But some background for the Unionist response is necessary. Unionist
supporters were diverse, comprising Irish Tories, the Church of Ireland, and Orange
loyalists. Socially, they consisted of much of the landed and professional classes and
the northern Presbyterian bourgeoisie and working classes. Unionism developed as
a political force in relation to internal and external developments. Disputes between
Anglicans and Presbyterians were defused by a shared interest in evangelicalism, while
the disestablishment of the Church of Ireland removed a long-standing bone of contention that fractured Protestant unity. Most important, Unionism was defined at
both the parliamentary and popular levels in relationship to the rapid rise of Irish
nationalism. In a sense they came to be reverse images of each other.

Underneath the Unionist umbrella, there was a diversity of views on the Home
Rule Bill. The historian W. E. H. Lecky (no. 34), a southern Unionist writing in
the liberal patriot tradition, was not opposed in principle to legislative autonomy,

or what he called "local government," but he was also a landowner. Horrified by the violent class forces unleashed by the Land War, he considered Home Rule to be an extension of them. Writing from an English Tory perspective, Randolph Churchill (no. 35) saw the Home Rule movement as being analogous to the Confederacy's secession from the United States. Most important, Churchill's argument was based on his empathy for Ulster Protestants, whose support for the Union he saw in heroic terms. His famous remark—"Ulster will fight; Ulster will be right"—inflamed an already combustible political crisis.

Ulster was indeed a central question. It was the only part of Ireland where Protestants were either a majority or a near majority of the population. Their sense of themselves as being part of a covenant tradition, founded on Protestant liberty and protected by their position in the UK, was embraced by a wide swathe of the population, whether Anglican or Presbyterian. The Orange Order provided a popular loyalist expression, and governments, depending on the time period, embraced it, tolerated it, or suppressed it. The flowering of Ulster Unionism was enhanced by the province's rapid economic growth in textiles and shipping: Ulster's development was more like Britain's than anything taking place in the rest of Ireland, and its growth was widely attributed by Ulster Protestants to the Union. The Ulster Unionist response to Home Rule mixed fear and anxiety, belligerence and solidarity. Reverend T. Ellis' defense of an Orange political strategy (no. 39) was in terms of "The 'Orange and the Blue,' with the good old Union Jack," the basis on which papists and radicals would be driven back. It was not much of a leap from this position to advocating the massing of weapons and the recruitment of volunteers for a coming showdown with the Catholic enemy. Such sentiments were graphically portrayed in *The Belfast News-Letter* on May 15, 1886 (no. 40), less than a month before the House of Commons voted down Home Rule.

Political voices in the province were not univocal. H de F. Montgomery (no. 41), a liberal Unionist, argued in his "Memorandum" that Ireland was being torn apart by radicals on both sides of the religious divide. For Montgomery, when members of the Orange Order committed inflammatory acts toward their Catholic neighbors they were, in fact, replicating those very aspects of Catholic tyranny that they purported to loathe. There were, therefore, nationalists and Unionists that sought to create a middle ground where negotiation, compromise, and dialogue might prevail. However, there were not enough of them. Increasingly, the political process would be driven by extremist positions.

24. James Fintan Lalor, "The Faith of a Felon," *Irish Felon* (July 8, 1848)

The split between Young Ireland and Daniel O'Connell's repeal movement was accompanied by the rise of more radical voices within the Young Ireland movement. Among them was James Fintan Lalor (1807–49), who argued that repeal did not get to the heart of the Irish question. He advocated a moral insurrection that would overthrow the landowners and the British government that supported them and establish popular sovereignty in land, that is, a peasant proprietorship. In his words: "the absolute

(allodial) ownership of the lands of Ireland is vested of right in the people of Ireland"
and "they, and none but they, are the first landowners and lords paramount as well as
the lawmakers of this island" (quoted in English 2006, 151). Lalor did not advocate
collective ownership, and thus was not a socialist per se, but his contention that the
primary injustice suffered in Ireland was the appropriation of its land was echoed in the
socialist republicanism of James Connolly.

Lalor was born in County Laois—the son of a Catholic middle-class farmer who was
an admirer of O'Connell—and he was educated at Carlow College. He injured his spine
as a child and suffered from persistent health problems, yet he still managed an active and
energetic intellectual and political life. He opposed O'Connell's repeal movement (a stance
that would strain his relationship with his father), arguing that it would not transform
the lives of the common people. He even wrote a letter to the British prime minister, Sir
Robert Peel, advocating its suppression. Lalor wrote for the Young Ireland journal The
Nation, *and he sided with the Young Irelanders that split with O'Connell and founded*
the Irish Confederation. The selection from Lalor's writings that follows presents his argu-
ment for taking back the land and his critique of the repeal movement. It is from one of
five essays that he wrote for the Irish Felon, *founded in response to the suppression of John*
Mitchel's United Irishman *and Mitchel's subsequent conviction of treason.*

. . . Here then is the confession and faith of a FELON. Years ago I perceived
that the English conquest consisted of two parts combined into one whole—
the conquest of our liberties, the conquest of our lands.

I saw clearly that the re-conquest of our liberties would be incomplete and
worthless without the re-conquest of our lands—would not necessarily involve
or produce that of our lands and could not, on its own means, be possibly
achieved; while the re-conquest of our lands would involve the other, would at
least be complete in itself and adequate to its own purposes; and could *possibly,*
if not easily, be achieved.

The lands were owned by the conquering race, or by traitors to the conquered race.
They were occupied by the native people or by settlers who had mingled and merged.

I selected as the *mode* of re-conquest, to refuse payment of rent and resist process
of ejectment.

In that mode I determined to effect the re-conquest and staked on it all my hopes
here and hereafter—my hopes of an effective life and an eternal epitaph.

I was biding my time when the potato failure hurried a crisis. The landlords
and English government took instant advantage of the famine, and the small
occupiers began to quit in thousands. I saw that Ireland was to be won at once
or lost for ever. I felt her slipping from under my feet with all her hopes, and
all my own—her lights quenching, her arm withering.

It almost seemed to me as if the Young Ireland party, the quarrel, the secession, the Confederation,[2] had all been specially pre-ordained and produced in

---

2. The Irish Confederation. As a result of Daniel O'Connell's demand that the Repeal Association affirm its opposition to violence to achieve its aims, Young Ireland intellectuals and
activists seceded from the group and formed the Irish Confederation in 1847.

order to aid me. My faith in the men who formed the Council of that body was then unbounded. My faith in them still is as firm as ever, though somewhat more measured. In the paper I published last week, and in a private correspondence that ensued with some of its members, I proposed that they should merge the Repeal question with a mightier project—that of wresting this island from English rule altogether in the only mode in which it could possibly be achieved. I endeavoured to show them they were only keeping up a feeble and ineffectual fire from a foolish distance upon the English government, which stands out of reach and beyond our power; and urged them to wheel their batteries around and bend them on the *English garrison* of landlords who stand here within our hands, scattered, isolated, and helpless, girdled round by the might of a people. Except two or three of them, all refused at the time, and have persisted in refusing until now. They wanted an alliance with the landowners. They chose to consider them as Irishmen, and imagined they could induce them to hoist the green flag. They wished to preserve an Aristocracy. They desired not a *democratic* but a merely *national* revolution. Who imputes blame to them for this? Whoever does so will not have me to join him. I have no feeling but one of respect for the motives that caused reluctance and delay. That delay, however, I consider as a matter of deep regret. Had the Confederation, in the May or June of '47, thrown heart and mind and means and might into the movement I pointed out, they would have made it successful, and settled for once and forever all quarrels and questions between us and England. I repeat my expression of strong regret that they should not have adopted this course, instead of persisting in a protracted and abortive effort, at a most dangerous conjuncture, to form an alliance of *bargain* and *barter* with our hereditary and inveterate enemies, between whom and the people of this island there will never be a peace except the peace of death or of desolation. Regrets, however are useless now.

The opinions I then stated, and which I yet stand firm to, are these: —

1. That in order to save their own lives, the occupying tenants of the soil of Ireland ought, next autumn, to refuse all rent and arrears of rent then due, beyond and except the value of the overplus of harvest produce remaining in their hands after having deducted and reserved a due and full provision for their own subsistence during the ensuing twelve months.

2. That they ought to refuse and resist being made beggars, landless and houseless, under the English law of ejectment.

3. That they ought further, *on principle,* to refuse ALL rent to the present usurping proprietors until the people, the true proprietors (or lords paramount in legal parlance) have in national congress or convention, decided what rents they are to pay, and *to whom* they are to pay them.

4. And that the people on grounds of *policy* and *economy,* ought to decide (as a general rule, admitting of reservations) that those rents shall be paid *to themselves,* the people, for public purposes, and for behoof and benefit of them, the entire general people.

These are the principles, as clearly and fully stated as limit of time will allow, which I advise Ireland to adopt at once, and at once to arm for. Should the people accept and adhere to them, the English government will then have to choose whether to surrender the Irish landlords, or to support them with the armed power of the empire.

If it refuse to incur the odium and expense, and to peril the safety of England in a social war of extermination, then the landlords are nobody, the people are lords of the land, a mighty social revolution is accomplished, and the foundations of a national revolution surely laid. If it should on the other hand determine to come to the rescue and relief of its garrison—elect to force their rents, and enforce their rights by infantry, cavalry, and cannon, and attempt to lift and carry the whole harvest of Ireland—a somewhat *heavy* undertaking which might become a *hot* one too—then I, at least, for one, am prepared to bow with humble resignation to the dispensations of Providence. Welcome be the will of God. We must only try to keep our harvest, to offer a peaceful passive resistance to barricade the island, to break up the roads, to break down the bridges—and should need be, and occasions offer surely we may venture to try the steel. Other approved modes of moral force might gradually be added to these, as we became trained to the system: and all combined, I imagine, and well worked, might possibly task the strength and break the heart of the empire.

Into artistic details, I need not, and do not choose, to enter for the present.

It has been said to me that such a war, on the principles I propose, would be looked on with detestation by Europe. I assert the contrary: I say such a war would propagate itself throughout Europe. Mark the words of this prophecy— The principle I propound goes to the foundations of Europe, and sooner or later will cause Europe to outrise [*sic*]. Mankind will yet be masters of the earth. The right of the people to make the laws—this produced the first great modem earthquake, whose latest shocks even now are heaving the heart of the world. The right of the people to own the land—this will produce the next. Train your hands and your sons' hands, gentlemen of earth, for you and they will yet have to use them. I want to put Ireland foremost, in the van of the world, at the head of the nations, to set her aloft in the blaze of the sun, and to make her for ages the lode star of history. Will she take the path I point out—the path to be free and famed and feared and followed—the path that goes sunward? Or, onward to the end of time will wretched Ireland ever come limping and lagging hindmost? Events must answer that. It is a question I almost fear to look full in the face. The soul of this island seems to sink where that of another country would soar. The people sank and surrendered to the famine instead of growing savage as any other people would have done.

I am reminded that there are few persons now who trouble themselves about the "conquest"; and there may be many, I know there are some—who assent to the two first of the four principles I have stated, and are willing to accept them as the grounds of an armed movement, but who object to the last two of them. I am advised to summon the land-tenants of Ireland to stand up in battle-array for an armed struggle in defence of their rights of life and subsistence, without asserting any greater or more comprehensive right. I distinctly refuse to do so. I refuse to narrow the case and claim of the island into any such petty dimensions, or to found it on the rogue's or the beggar's plea, the plea of necessity. Not as a starving bandit, or desperate beggar who demands, to save life, what does not belong to him, do I wish Ireland to stand up, but as a decrowned Queen who claims back her own with an armed hand. I attest and urge the plea of utter and desperate necessity to fortify her claim, but not to found it. I rest it on no temporary or passing conditions but on principles that are permanent and imperishable, and universal; available to all times and to all countries, as well as to our own—I pierce through the upper stratum of occasional and shifting circumstance, to bottom and base on the rock below. I put the question in its eternal form—the form in which how often soever suppressed for a season, it can never be finally subdued, but will remain and return, outliving and outlasting the corruption and cowardice of generations. I view it as ages will view it—not through the mists of a famine but by the living lights of the firmament. You may possibly be induced to reject it in the form I propose, and accept in the other. If so you will accept the question and use it as a weapon against England, in a shape and under conditions which deprive it of half its strength. You will take and work it fettered and handcuffed not otherwise. To take it in its might, you must take it in its magnitude. I propose you should take Samson[3] into your service. You assent but insist that his locks should be shorn. You moreover diminish and degrade down from a *national* into a mere *class* question. In the form offered it would carry independence, in the form accepted it will not even carry Repeal, in the minimum of meaning. You fling away Repeal, when you fling away the *only* mode of achieving it. For by force of arms alone can it ever be achieved; and never on the Repeal question will you see men stand in array of battle against England. . . .

25 and 26. Marx and Engels on Ireland

Best known for their pivotal role in the history of communism and socialism, Karl Marx (1818–83) and his friend and collaborator Friedrich Engels (1820–95) both grappled with the Irish question. Engels' interest in Ireland was closely connected to his long-term romantic liaison with Mary Burns (died 1863), whose father emigrated from Ireland to Manchester and worked in the textile mill owned by Engels' family. Through Burns, Engels learned about the working class firsthand, and he went with her to Ireland in 1856. In Engels' pioneering work of social history and criticism, The Condition of the Working-Class in England in 1844 *(1844), he analyzed the plight of the Irish peasant from a socioeconomic perspective and in terms of national character.*

Marx did not have the same kind of personal connection to Ireland that Engels did. However, he followed its politics closely and analyzed it through the lens of his

3. Samson, one of the last of the Judges of Israel. His story is told in the Hebrew Bible, Judges 13–16. Known for his enormous strength, Samson was betrayed to the Philistines by Delilah, who seduced him and in turn coaxed out of him that the source of his strength was his uncut hair. Her betrayal of his secret led to the loss of his hair, powers, sight, and life.

materialist theory of history, which viewed the historical process as being grounded in the social relations of production, that is, class relations. The Irish nationalist John Devoy's organ, the Irish Nation, *proclaimed after the death of Marx in 1883: "Whatever Irishmen may think of the general policy of Karl Marx, it must never be forgotten that he was a sincere friend to Ireland. To him as much as any man of the century it is due that the cause of Ireland is now heard on the continent of Europe through other than an English medium" (quoted in Bew 2007, 248–49). Marx did not write about Ireland in a systematic way, but his thoughts can be pieced together from various sources, including his voluminous correspondence. His letter from 1870 views the Anglo-Irish relationship within the context of a broader class struggle, which not only includes the British Isles but extends to the United States as well.*

25. Friedrich Engels, "The Agricultural Proletariat," *The Condition of the Working Class in England in 1844* (1844)

If England illustrates the results of the system of farming on a large scale and Wales on a small one, *Ireland* exhibits the consequences of overdividing the soil. The great mass of the population of Ireland consists of small tenants who occupy a sorry hut without partitions, and a potato patch just large enough to supply them most scantily with potatoes through the winter. In consequence of the great competition which prevails among these small tenants, the rent has reached an unheard-of height, double, treble, and quadruple that paid in England. For every agricultural labourer seeks to become a tenant-farmer, and though the division of land has gone so far, there still remain numbers of labourers in competition for plots. Although in Great Britain 32,000,000 acres of land are cultivated, and in Ireland but 14,000,000; although Great Britain produces agricultural products to the value of £150,000,000, and Ireland of but £36,000,000, there are in Ireland 75,000 agricultural proletarians *more* than in the neighbouring island. How great the competition for land in Ireland must be is evident from this extraordinary disproportion, especially when one reflects that the labourers in Great Britain are living in the utmost distress. The consequence of this competition is that it is impossible for the tenants to live much better than the labourers, by reason of the high rents paid. The Irish people is thus held in crushing poverty, from which it cannot free itself under our present social conditions. These people live in the most wretched clay huts, scarcely good enough for cattle-pens, have scant food all winter long, or, as the report above quoted expresses it,[4] they have potatoes half enough thirty weeks in the year, and the rest of the year nothing. When the time comes in the spring at which this provision reaches its end, or can no longer be used because of its sprouting, wife and children go forth to beg and tramp the country with their kettle in their hands. Meanwhile the husband, after planting potatoes for the next year, goes in search of work either in Ireland or England, and returns at the potato harvest to his family. This is the condition in which nine-tenths of the Irish country

4. *Report of the Poor Law Commission on Ireland* (1837) [Parliamentary Session of 1837]. [Original editor's note.]

folks live. They are poor as church mice, wear the most wretched rags, and stand upon the lowest plane of intelligence possible in a half-civilised country. According to the report quoted, there are, in a population of 8 ½ millions, 585,000 heads of families in a state of total destitution; and according to other authorities, cited by Sheriff Alison,[5] there are in Ireland 2,300,000 persons who could not live without public or private assistance—or 27 per cent of the whole population paupers!

The cause of this poverty lies in the existing social conditions, especially in competition here found in the form of the subdivision of the soil. Much effort has been spent in finding other causes. It has been asserted that the relation of the tenant to the landlord who lets his estate in large lots to tenants, who again have their sub-tenants, and sub-sub-tenants, in turn, so that often ten middlemen come between the landlord and the actual cultivator—it has been asserted that the shameful law which gives the landlord the right of expropriating the cultivator who may have paid his rent duly, if the first tenant fails to pay the landlord, that this law is to blame for all this poverty. But all this determines only the *form* in which the poverty manifests itself. Make the small tenant a landowner himself and what follows? The majority could not live upon their holdings even if they had no rent to pay, and any slight improvement which might take place would be lost again in a few years in consequence of the rapid increase of population. The children would then live to grow up under the improved conditions who now die in consequence of poverty in early childhood. From another side comes the assertion that the shameless oppression inflicted by the English is the cause of the trouble. It is the cause of the somewhat *earlier* appearance of this poverty, but not of the poverty itself. Or the blame is laid on the Protestant Church forced upon a Catholic nation; but divide among the Irish what the Church takes from them, and it does not reach six shillings a head. Besides, tithes are a tax upon *landed property*, not upon the tenant, though he may nominally pay them; now, since the Commutation Bill of 1838,[6] the landlord pays the tithes directly and reckons so much higher rent, so that the tenant is none the better off. And in the same way a hundred other causes of this poverty are brought forward, all proving as little as these. This poverty is the result of our social conditions; apart from these, causes may be found for the manner in which it manifests itself, but not for the fact of its existence. That poverty manifests itself in Ireland thus and not otherwise, is owing to the character of the people, and to their historical development. The Irish are a people related in their whole character to the Latin nations, to the French, and especially to the Italians. The bad features of their character we have already had depicted by [Thomas] Carlyle. Let us now hear an Irishman, who at least comes nearer to the truth than Carlyle, with his prejudice in favour of the Teutonic[7] character:

5. Sir Archibald Alison (1792–1867), English writer, historian, lawyer, and politician. He was appointed as the sheriff of Lanarkshire in 1834. Engels refers to Alison's *The Principles of Population, and Their Connection with Human Happiness*, Vol. II (1840).

6. Prior to the 1838 Tithes Commutation Act, Irish Catholic peasants supported the Church of Ireland through direct taxation. As a result of the 1838 act, the burden was placed on landlords with the expectation that it would be taken out of the rents of the tenants.

7. Pertaining to the characteristics of the ancient Teutons or Germans.

"They are restless, yet indolent, clever and indiscreet, stormy, impatient, and improvident; brave by instinct, generous without much reflection, quick to revenge and forgive insults, to make and to renounce friendships, gifted with genius prodigally, sparingly with judgment."[8]

With the Irish, feeling and passion predominate; reason must bow before them. Their sensuous, excitable nature prevents reflection and quiet, persevering activity from reaching development—such a nation is utterly unfit for manufacture as now conducted. Hence they held fast to agriculture, and remained upon the lowest plane even of that. With the small subdivisions of land, which were not here artificially created, as in France and on the Rhine, by the division of great estates,[9] but have existed from time immemorial, an improvement of the soil by the investment of capital was not to be thought of; and it would, according to Alison, require 120 million pounds sterling to bring the soil up to the not very high state of fertility already attained in England. The English immigration, which might have raised the standard of Irish civilisation, has contented itself with the most brutal plundering of the Irish people; and while the Irish, by their immigration into England, have furnished England a leaven[10] which will produce its own results in the future, they have little for which to be thankful to the English immigration.

The attempts of the Irish to save themselves from their present ruin, on the one hand, take the form of crimes. These are the order of the day in the agricultural districts, and are nearly always directed against the most immediate enemies, the landlords' agents, or their obedient servants, the Protestant intruders, whose large farms are made up of the potato patches of hundreds of ejected families. Such crimes are especially frequent in the South and West. On the other hand, the Irish hope for relief by means of the agitation for the repeal of the Legislative Union with England. From all the foregoing, it is clear that the uneducated Irish must see in the English their worst enemies; and their first hope of improvement in the conquest of national independence. But quite as clear is it, too, that Irish distress cannot be removed by any Act of Repeal. Such an Act would, however, at once lay bare the fact that the cause of Irish misery, which now seems to come from abroad, is really to be found at home. Meanwhile, it is an open question whether the accomplishment of repeal will be necessary to make this clear to the Irish. Hitherto, neither Chartism[11] nor Socialism has had marked success in Ireland. . . .

8. *The State of Ireland*, London, 1807; 2nd ed., 1821. Pamphlet. [Author's footnote.]

9. Mistake. Small-scale agriculture had been the prevailing form of farming ever since the Middle Ages. Thus, the small peasant farm existed even before the Revolution. The only thing the latter changed was its *ownership*; that it took away from the feudal lords and transferred, directly or indirectly, to the peasants. [Author's footnote added in the German edition of 1892.]

10. An influence that results in the modification of the whole.

11. The first nationwide working-class political movement in Britain, which in the 1830s and 1840s demanded that Parliament pass legislation that met the demands of the Charter, most importantly universal manhood suffrage.

26. Karl Marx, Letter to Sigfrid Myer and August Vogt, April 9, 1870

. . . I shall give you here only quite briefly the decisive points. Ireland is the bulwark of the *English landed aristocracy.* The exploitation of that country is not only one of the main sources of this aristocracy's material welfare; it is its greatest *moral* strength. It, in fact, represents the *domination of England over Ireland.* Ireland is therefore the great means by which the English aristocracy maintains *its domination in England herself.*

If, on the other hand, the English army and police were to withdraw from Ireland tomorrow, you would at once have an agrarian revolution there. But the overthrow of the English aristocracy in Ireland involves as a necessary consequence its overthrow in England. And this would fulfil the preliminary condition for the proletarian revolution in England. The destruction of the English landed aristocracy in Ireland is an infinitely easier operation than in England herself, because in Ireland *the land question* has hitherto been the *exclusive form* of the social question, because it is a question of existence, of *life and death,* for the immense majority of the Irish people, and because it is at the same time inseparable from the *national* question. This quite apart from the Irish being more passionate and revolutionary in character than the English.

As for the English *bourgeoisie,* it has in the first place a common interest with the English aristocracy in turning Ireland into mere pasture land which provides the English market with meat and wool at the cheapest possible prices. It is equally interested in reducing, by eviction and forcible emigration, the Irish population to such a small number that *English capital* (capital invested in land leased for farming) can function there with "security". It has the same interest in clearing the estate of Ireland as it had in the clearing of the agricultural districts of England and Scotland. The £6,000–10,000 absentee-landlord and other Irish revenues which at present flow annually to London have also to be taken into account.

But the English bourgeoisie has, besides, much more important interests in Ireland's present-day economy. Owing to the constantly increasing concentration of tenant farming, Ireland steadily supplies her own surplus to the English labour-market, and thus forces down wages and lowers the moral and material condition of the English working class.

And most important of all! Every industrial and commercial centre in England now possesses a working class *divided* into two *hostile* camps, English proletarians and Irish proletarians. The ordinary English worker hates the Irish worker as a competitor who lowers his standard of life. In relation to the Irish worker he feels himself a member of the *ruling nation* and so turns himself into a tool of the aristocrats and capitalists of his country *against Ireland,* thus strengthening their domination *over himself.* He cherishes religious, social, and national prejudices against the Irish worker. His attitude towards him is much the same as that of the "poor whites" to the "niggers" in the former slave states of the U. S. A. The Irishman pays him back with interest in his own money. He sees in the English worker at once the accomplice and the stupid tool of the *English rule in Ireland.*

This antagonism is artificially kept alive and intensified by the press, the pulpit, the comic papers, in short, by all the means at the disposal of the ruling classes. *This antagonism* is the *secret of the impotence of the English working class,* despite its

organisation. It is the secret by which the capitalist class maintains its power. And
that class is fully aware of it.

But the evil does not stop here. It continues across the ocean. The antagonism between English and Irish is the hidden basis of the conflict between the United States
and England. It makes any honest and serious co-operation between the working
classes of the two countries impossible. It enables the governments of both countries,
whenever they think fit, to break the edge off the social conflict by their mutual bul-
lying, and, in case of need, by war with one another.

England, being the metropolis of capital, the power which has hitherto ruled the
world market, is for the present the most important country for the workers' revolution, and moreover the *only* country in which the material conditions for this revolution have developed up to a certain degree of maturity. Therefore to hasten the social
revolution in England is the most important object of the International Working
Men's Association.[12] The sole means of hastening it is to make Ireland independent.
Hence it is the task of the International everywhere to put the conflict between England and Ireland in the foreground, and everywhere to side openly with Ireland. And
it is the special task of the Central Council in London to awaken a consciousness in
the English workers that *for them* the *national emancipation of Ireland* is no question
of abstract justice or humanitarian sentiment, but *the first condition of their own social
emancipation.* . . .

27 and 28. The Fenians

*In the vacuum created by the disintegration of the repeal movement, Irish republicanism
revived in the 1850s, in large part because of the efforts of James Stephens (1824–1901)
and John O'Mahony (1816–77). Before participating in the failed rebellion of 1848,
Stephens was an apprentice railway engineer from Kilkenny. O'Mahony was from Kilbe-
heny, County Limerick. He attended Trinity College, Dublin, where he studied Sanskrit,
Hebrew, and Irish. When the 1848 rebellion collapsed, the two men fled to continental
Europe, and ended up in Paris, where they supported themselves through teaching and
translating. In Paris, Stephens and O'Mahony were part of the revolutionary underground. It was there that they began to commit themselves to building up a network of
secret organizations that would overthrow British rule in Ireland by a joint effort of Irish
and Irish-American militants. The result was the IRB founded in Ireland in 1858 and
the Fenian Brotherhood established in the United States in 1859.*

*Two letters from the early days of the Fenian movement convey the challenges and strug-
gles that it faced. While Stephens was primarily based in Ireland, O'Mahony had immigrated to the United States in 1853 and had the task of building up the American organization.
Stephens' unhappiness with O'Mahony as a leader created tensions between the two men,
but the obstacles that the latter faced in creating an effective organization were formidable.*

12. Also International Workingmen's Association. It is better known as the First International.
It was founded in 1864 as the first transnational working-class political organization. Marx and
Engels played prominent roles in its founding.

Fenian bond for twenty dollars, signed by John O'Mahony (1866). (Michael Kenny,
The Fenians: Photographs and Memorabilia from the National Museum of Ireland
[Dublin: The National Museum of Ireland in association with Country House, 1994].)

*In a letter written to William Sullivan of Ohio, O'Mahony (no. 27) addressed the disap-
proval of the Catholic Church leadership, which condemned the Fenians for being a
secret society. O'Mahony defended the Fenians from these charges, stating that it was an
army.*

*In his letter to O'Mahony, Stephens (no. 28) considered one of the great clichés of the
Irish nationalist movement: England's difficulty is Ireland's opportunity. The letter was
written during the American Civil War, when the tensions between the British government and the United States government under Abraham Lincoln ran high. This tension
was a result of the Union's trade embargo of the Confederacy, which, owing to British
dependence on American cotton, created an economic downturn in Britain sometimes
called the cotton famine.*

27. John O'Mahony, Letter to William Sullivan (1859)

TO WM. SULLIVAN, ESQ:

MY DEAR SIR—I rest satisfied that our organization cannot now go down in
Ohio while under the earnest and influential auspices of yourself and your brothers.
It is but natural that our progress should be slow at first, particularly as our finances
do not yet warrant us in sending round agents to the different centres of the Irish-
American population. Neither have we at our disposal in this country the right kind
of man to send forth as our representative. I could not myself be absent from this

for many days without injury to the movement. We must then wait until the arrival of Mr. O'Leary,[13] who must be now on his way out. As you are most probably already aware, he was to have met Mr. Stephens on his landing, and, having given his report of the progress made by the so-called Phoenixes[14] for the last five months, to have come directly to this, with instructions for our further guidance. After seeing me and staying a few days to rest himself in this city, he will set out on his tour of organization. You will be likely to meet him here when you come in the middle of the month.

We must calculate upon a certain amount of opposition from some of the priests. I do not, however, consider it judicious to come into collision with them openly. Those who denounce us go beyond their duty as clergymen. They are either bad Irishmen, who would not wish to see Ireland a nation, or very stupid and ignorant zealots, who do not understand what they are about. Our association is neither anti-Catholic nor irreligious. We are an Irish army, not a secret society. We make no secret of our objects and designs. We simply bind ourselves to conceal such matters as are needful to be kept from the enemy's knowledge, both for the success of our strategy and for the safety of our friends. I hold that I do not exceed the bounds prescribed by my religion when I swear this, nor shall I ever tax my conscience with it in the confessional. It is ridiculous for men to denounce us for enrolling ourselves under the Irish banner, when they say nothing against those who enroll themselves under the American banner, or even under the banner of such private adventurers as General Walker[15] and others, whose sole apparent aim is most unjustifiable plunder. However, there is no use in arguing with members of the priesthood on such points. It is better to avoid their denunciatory attacks by modifying the form of our pledge so as not to be obnoxious to spiritual censure, even by the most exacting ecclesiastic in America. They cannot deny the goodness, justice and even piety of the object we propose, and, if there be a shade of sin in the words by which we pledge ourselves to effect it, let those words be so altered as to be perfectly innocuous to the soul. This can be done wherever a clergyman insists upon it: but where there are liberal and enlightened priests, there need be no change.

In every case, it will be well to give but as few secrets as possible to individual members. They can do good work without knowing all that is doing, and who are doing it. They should be taught that it is enough for them to know that those in immediate communication with themselves are trustworthy, and that they will truly and faithfully discharge the duties of their position. Men need not be sworn previ-

---

13. John O'Leary (1830–1907).

14. The Phoenix National and Literary Society of Skibbereen. It was founded in Ireland in 1856 as a legal nationalist club with a reading room, but it was a front for a secret society committed to forcing Britain out of Ireland. Inscribed on its wall was "Ireland for the Irish." The IRB subsequently absorbed it.

15. William Walker (1824–60), an American lawyer and physician, who organized private military expeditions in Latin America in order to create English-speaking colonies under his personal control. He was president of the Republic of Nicaragua (1856–57) before he was defeated by a coalition of Central American armies and executed in 1860.

ous to helping us along. They see enough by the newspapers to show them that the time for exertion is come now—that Ireland is thoroughly aroused and that a crisis in England's fate is fast approaching from her external enemies.

A member of the Belfast Arms Club has arrived here within a few days. He was the secretary of the men lately arrested there. The news he brings is highly encouraging. The Ribbonmen,[16] throughout the North, are fully determined to join the Phoenixes, as they call them. In Belfast they have 20,000 stand of arms. Their organization extends through all Ulster and much of Connaught and Meath; it is also widely spread through England and Scotland. This party was not included in my friend's estimate. It is most important that we get into direct communication with it, for by it we could cripple England, by attacking her at home in her large towns. The fear of such a contingency would force her to grant us peace after a short struggle. All these matters must be looked to.

The news from these states has been rather more promising during the past week. The organization is extending rapidly, though as yet but little money has come in since I left. Boston is the best city I have on my roll. In it a full centre is now almost completed. What I like best about its members is that they do their work systematically, each sub-centre sending weekly the regular dues. A list has been also opened there for the contributions of men who will not be initiated. Branches of our society have been also started in Vermont, Maine and Connecticut. From Pennsylvania I have received a most satisfactory communication from the Railroad men. If the plan proposed by them is well carried out, it will bring overwhelming numbers into our ranks. I will speak more about it when I meet you. . . .

Present my compliments to your brother, Mr. Edmund Sullivan. I felt greatly disappointed at not having seen him again at my office previous to his late departure from this city. Tell him that the brothers in New York are beginning to exert themselves more earnestly than of late. On yesterday, I had a very enthusiastic meeting of men who will work, if I mistake not. It is hard to get the mass of the Irish in New York to believe that anyone can be serious who speaks of freeing Ireland. They have had their hopes disappointed, when raised to the highest pitch, twice or three times within the five years I have been here. Then, the majority of them are mere dupes of designing politicians who scoff at the notion that any one could be so green as to hope for Ireland. But this must soon cease. True men are beginning to see that we are really in earnest, and they will not much longer heed the sneers which the venal and corrupt have always at hand for every noble and disinterested action.

> I remain, dear sir,
> Yours very faithfully,
> JOHN O'MAHONY.

16. A loosely used term to describe underground Catholic political groups that used violence to achieve agrarian justice in combatting, for instance, arbitrary evictions. Ribbonmen appeared at various points in the nineteenth century. Their name is derived from the fact that they often wore a green ribbon in a buttonhole.

28. James Stephens, Letter to John O'Mahony (1861)

. . . Crisis or no Crisis?—*that* is the question. Another question, of far more importance to us, is this: If a *real* crisis, what will be its consequences to us? I shall offer
a few observations on these two points. If there be one thing, in connection with
the cause of Ireland, I more cordially detest than any other, it is what scribblers or
spouters call "a Crisis." It has been the chronic bane of Ireland—a more fatal bane
than famine or any other the enemy have had, to perpetuate their rule. A bane—a
scourge—a disease—a devil's scourge it has been to us. Its best known formula has
resolved itself into this: "England's difficulty is Ireland's opportunity." Blind, base
and deplorable motto—rallying-cry—motive of action—what you will. May it be
accursed, it, its aiders and abettors. Owing to it, and them, the work that should
never have stood still, has been taken up in feverish fits and starts, and always out of
time, to fall into collapse when the "opportunity," predestined to escape them, had
slipped through their hands. Ireland's trained and marshalled manhood alone can
ever make—could ever have made—Ireland's opportunity. And this opportunity, the
manhood of Ireland alone, without the aid of any foreign power—without the aid
of even our exiled brothers, could have been *made* any time these thirty years; and,
whether England was at peace or war, with this manhood alone we could have won
our own. But our duped and victimized countrymen, giving ear to the imbecile or
knavish cry of "English difficulty," stood, with mouth agape, and over and over again,
waiting—"biding their time"—till the opportunity came, and left them as before.
Accursed, I say, be the barren, lunatic or knavish clods who raised this dog-souled
cry—a cry to be heard even *now,* in the mouths of the slanderous brood who, as you
say, "first misled and then abandoned a brave and devoted people." They are, I say,
raising the cry once more—the cry of—a crisis—"England's difficulty.". . .

. . . I shall merely say that I augur no good for us from this war,[17] so much desired
by certain Irish patriots. The consummation most devoutly to be wished for by us
is this: An arrangement or compromise of some kind between North and South,
and the consequent disbandment of the army. Then, as well as meantime, our communications would be open with you; money and men might be coming over to
us, and we would choose our own time for the first blow. Indeed, the advantages
to us appear to me so manifest, in this latter case—that of England keeping out of
the struggle—that it would be boresome to you to point them out. Were we in the
field, it would be clearly an advantage to us to have England in a death-struggle with
America; but I am more than doubtful of the advantages to be gained by us should
this struggle begin before we rise. But of course—or is it so?—we can do nothing to
bring about or prevent this war. You say that, should it take place, "your purpose is
to offer your own services and those of your friends to the United States government
to serve against England, in Ireland if possible, but if not, anywhere." I look upon
this as wise, and fully approve of it. You will recollect that, in my letter of the 8th of
June last, I counselled you to make yourself thoroughly aware of the spirit and action of those amongst whom you were living, and then take action yourself, always

---

17. The American Civil War (1861–65).

aiming at the greatest service to Ireland. Now, in case of a war with England, all the Irish race on the American continent will be into it; so that you could not stand aloof without the utter loss of your influence. Clearly you must to the field, and the more prominent your position, the better for Ireland. Granted, then, that you are in the field, and in a foremost position, I would not allow myself, even then, to be too hasty in urging on an expedition. I should keep up my correspondence with home, and be sure that everything was right there, convinced that, without a vast power of trained men at home, armed already, or to be provided with arms by me, the expedition—if not far beyond anything that has ever in that way steered for the Irish shore—could only compromise the last chance like every preceding one. I would not, like so many ignorant or silly men, fancy that 10,000 or 20,000, or even 30,000 Irish-Americans, could if landed on our shores, give freedom to my country, unless, as already said, a vast power of trained men, armed already, or to be armed by me, were ready to fly to my standard. I would not allow myself to be deluded by the lunatic dream, that a mob, however numerous or numberless, could make victory a certain or even a probable thing. I would believe, on the other hand, that a trained power at home—say of 100,000 men—already armed, or for whom I bought arms, could—nay would—be sure to do more with the aid of so small a number as 1,000, than an auxiliary force of even 30,000 could ever effect, if backed by a mere mob, whatever its number. I would therefore and as already said, be sure that there was at home a strong power of trained men to cooperate with the force brought by me, and till I was sure of this, nothing could force me to undertake a descent on the Irish shores, convinced that such descent, so far from serving my country, would only deprive her of the last chance of freedom. These are amongst the many things sure to be suggested to me, should I ever find myself in the position I supposed you in *toute a l'heure*.[18] Let us be provided against all contingencies.

In haste, yours faithfully
J. Kelly, (James Stephens)

29. Archbishop William Bernard Ullathorne, "Pastoral" (1869)

In his letter to William Sullivan, John O'Mahony (no. 27) bemoans the fact that the Catholic hierarchy denounced the Fenians. Indeed, Archbishop (and later Cardinal) Paul Cullen, the dominant Irish Catholic clergyman of his era, excommunicated participants in secret societies and proclaimed that members of such groups were ineligible to receive absolution.

William Ullathorne (1806–89) shared Cullen's point of view. Ullathorne was an English Catholic clergyman, who, as he states in his "Pastoral," was deeply sympathetic to the plight of Irish people. Ullathorne was born in Yorkshire, in the northern part of England. While his father imagined that his son would have a career in accounting, William sought his fortune at sea, and it was during one of his voyages that he had something of a religious conversion. Ordained as a priest in 1831, Ullathorne developed

18. Just now (French).

his sympathies for Irish grievances against the British government in New South Wales, Australia, where he was vicar-general[19] to Bishop William Placid Morris (1794–1872). Ullathorne came into contact with transported Irish political prisoners dating back to the United Irishmen of the late eighteenth century. His "Pastoral" was written when he was the bishop of Birmingham, an English city with a significant Irish population. As a consequence of his opposition to the Fenians, Ullathorne found himself in "hot water." He faced, what he described as a "Fenian conspiracy in this place to alienate the Irish people from me," and his pastoral was intended to warn the poor people against "these wolves" (quoted in Mac Suibhne 1965, 429).

. . . Does it really at this day require to be stated that for nearly forty years I have been the devoted servant of the Irish people? Can it be unknown that from the twenty-fourth to this present sixty-third year of my life, from my vigorous youth to my grey hairs, I have given my energies to the welfare of that people? No sooner did I receive the sacred priesthood than leaving country and friends, sacrificing a life in the religious order to which I was attached and that love of letters which was the one human pleasure left me, I became an exile from free choice in those remote penal colonies[20] which at that time few free men knew anything about, or thought of, or cared for. And why did I thus freely become an exile but for the sake of the most neglected and most suffering portion of the Irish race? I may know something of Ireland from books; I may know something of her people by living a good part of three years upon her very soil and moving much with her bishops and clergy amongst her people; but I have had another way of access to the Irish people opened to me. From 1832 to 1840 I lived amongst the men transported for the affairs of '98,[21] amongst the men who under all sorts of pretexts were transported for O'Connell's famous Clare election[22] and amongst men transported from all parts of Ireland almost as often for political as for criminal causes. I conversed with these men, knew their inmost hearts as well as their histories and they altogether represented some three-quarters of a century of the history of the Irish people. Those men were wont to say that if I looked like an Englishman I felt like an Irishman. It is not for me to say what I did to mitigate their material sufferings as well as to provide for their spiritual wants; what help I brought them from their own country in priests, Sisters of Charity[23] and teachers; what I wrote in their defence; what share I had and at what cost of suffering to myself in bringing the horrible system of transportation itself to an end. Let it be enough to say that my strong constitution was broken down in the service of this Irish people and that I spent the best years of my life in labouring to mitigate the evils, redress the

19. The main deputy of the bishop of a diocese.

20. Australia.

21. The rebellion of the United Irishmen in 1798.

22. Daniel O'Connell's election to Parliament in 1828 as the MP for Clare paved the way in 1829 for Catholics to be members of the British Parliament.

23. A Catholic order of women that was founded in 1815 by Mary Aikenhead of Cork, who was committed to integrating gospel values in daily life and serving and assisting the poor. The order spread to Australia in 1838.

wrongs and so often the sorrows of twenty thousand Irishmen, most of which had been brought about through the misgovernment of their country.

But if it was amongst the most suffering of Irishmen that I learned to fathom the mismanagement of Ireland, it was amongst them also that I learnt to understand the evil results of secret societies and the harm the Irish people have ever done themselves when turning a deaf ear to their bishops and clergy and closing their eyes to the Church's condemnation they have followed the ever-ready tempter and broken themselves in scattered groups against a united and irresistible strength. With the weight which experience amongst the victims of secret societies gives let me ask if they have ever brought other results than failure, distress and misery to those who engage in them?

When Ireland had a great leader, one of those colossal men who appear but rarely, it was neither by breaking the law of the Church nor that of the State that he accomplished his great objects. He was as vigorous in opposing all secret societies as he was in his efforts to redress his country's wrongs. O'Connell never wearied in repeating that he who breaks the law strengthens the enemy; and that nothing is worth having, nothing is blessed, that is gained by bloodshed.

30. George Campbell, Selections from *The Irish Land* (1869)

George Campbell (1824–92) was a colonial administrator from a Scottish landed family. His father had been in the East India Company's Medical Service. His uncle John, 1st Baron Campbell (1779–1861), was a British liberal politician, MP, lawyer, and writer, and in 1834 was appointed attorney general. Owing to family connections, George Campbell secured a career in the East India Company,[24] attended its training establishment at Haileybury in England, and left for India in 1842. Over the course of a long professional career, he held various positions in Indian colonial administration. Due to poor health, Campbell returned to Britain in 1868 and unsuccessfully ran for Parliament as a radical. It was during this period that he was drawn into debates on the Irish land question, which intensified during the 1860s. Campbell made two trips to Ireland, the basis for his widely influential book The Irish Land. *The book made a deep impression on William Gladstone, the British prime minister. It helped shape Gladstone's ideas on Irish land reform, which resulted in the Irish Land Act of 1870.*

The originality of Campbell's contribution to the land question was its comparative perspective, based on firsthand knowledge of land reform in colonial India and a study of it elsewhere. Mainstream economists viewed the land question from a laissez-faire

24. Founded in 1599 to compete with Dutch trading companies in the Spice Islands, the English East Indian Company in the eighteenth century created the foundation of British rule in India. It acquired a territorial empire after the battle of Plassy (1857) and political supremacy in the Indian subcontinent following the defeat of the Maratha empire in 1818. Over time, the company was brought under parliamentary control, beginning with the Regulation Act of 1773. The East India Company was abolished following the Indian mutiny of 1857, and British rule in India was overseen by a secretary of state for India.

perspective, attributing Irish underdevelopment to a stunted free market system in land. For Campbell, this perspective assumed that the foundations of the English and the Irish land system were essentially the same. In his view, the Irish land system was closer to that of India than of England. He argued that in Ireland there was in practice a dual system of land ownership: despite landlords' legal claims to the land, the peasantry had rights as well. This was especially true in Ulster, where it was accepted that tenants had the right to compensation for the improvements they made to their holdings when the land changed hands. This was known as the Ulster custom. *Campbell's prescription for reform was founded on explicitly acknowledging this cultural practice of tenant rights through legislation.*

PART ONE
A VISIT IN THE SPRING

. . . The Irish Land question may, then, be considered the question of the day. I am not an Irishman, and have no personal connexion with Ireland; but I have, I may say, spent my life in intimate relations with the land in different countries, and in various stages of society; and believing that a stranger, possessed of some special knowledge, and free from local entanglements, may sometimes obtain a better bird's-eye view than a native, I have applied myself to try to discover the merits of the question. I have hopes that I may eventually work out in some detail the subject of land-tenure, comparing Ireland with other countries; meantime, on returning from a visit to Ireland, I commit to paper the impressions which the subject has so far made on my mind. I shall only add a word in explanation of my position. I was born and bred amid the agriculture of Scotland; and my present personal interests, experience, and *home* knowledge, are principally derived from that source. I am therefore thoroughly alive to the advantages of the commercial system of farming as carried to its legitimate issue in Scotland. On the other hand, in India it has been my profession to deal with great land questions in many different parts of that country, and in greater variety than falls to the lot of most men; and I have been enabled to watch the rise and growth of property in land from its earliest development to its most advanced stages, and from its form under arbitrary native Governments to that which it acquires after a century of British Law.

I must begin by expressing my belief that no petty measure will in any degree satisfy the Irish. If they are offered anything short of large and substantial concessions, the expectations which have been excited will have led to more harm than good. I do not think that any mere improvement of the law of contract can possibly operate as a great concession—that has already been tried without success. And being one of those people who never can be brought to believe that two and two make five, I set out with much distrust of all schemes for giving to one without taking from another—for satisfying the tenants without trenching on the rights of property, in the sense in which the term is used by landlords—without something of what they call confiscation. There are, in fact, two claimants to the right of occupying the land. You cannot satisfy both: you can only compromise the matter between them. It may be that you may take from one and give to another in such a way as to benefit him to whom is given without really injuring him from whom is taken; just as a man who is oppressed by two coats may feel all the lighter and easier when he has been compelled to give one to him who has none; but from his point of view there is confiscation of property nevertheless. In this view it would only be possible to argue that a moderate measure of confiscation would eventually be beneficial to all parties.

In truth, however, this is not the only, nor as I think, the real view of the case. Those who argue that there is no room for compromise, because the landlords having already everything—that is, absolute and unconditional property in the soil—have no occasion for compromise, and the tenants having no rights, have no basis for compromise, take the very narrowest and the most English-lawyer view of the question. It is hardly possible to approach the subject without first realizing this—viz.,[25] that in Ireland a landlord is not a landlord, and a tenant is not a tenant—in the English sense. In fact, this may be said of most countries. The whole difficulty arises from our applying English ideas and English laws to a country where they are opposed to facts, and to those ἄγραπτοι νομοι,[26] which are written in the hearts, and find expression in the customs of the people.

In Ireland there are two sets of laws—the English laws, and the laws or customs of the country, which, enforced in a different way, are as active and effective. In the clashing of these two systems lies the whole difficulty. In the assumption that the theoretical English law is the only law, and the attempt to put out of sight the customary law of the country, is the fallacy of the argument on behalf of the landlords. In theory the landlords are absolute owners; but in fact are they so? Most assuredly not. The extreme theory of property is everywhere overborne and modified by the custom.[27] In the North that custom has assumed a definite and recognised form, against which it is vain for landlords to contend. There is peace, but peace at the expense of the extreme theory of landlord property. In the South the custom is not so well settled; there is more social and religious discord, the agitated waters have not admitted of the perfect crystallization of that tenant-right element which still exists; and the popular custom in favour of the tenant is supplemented by a custom of "dropping landlords." By an infinitely more disagreeable process, a similar result is arrived at in the South[28] as in the North—viz., that the theoretical landlord cannot do what he likes with what he considers to be his land. Lord Derby[29]—than whom

---

25. Namely.

26. Unwritten laws (Greek).

27. The *custom* refers to the customary practice, predominantly in Ulster, in which tenants accrue an interest in the land when they improve their holdings. If they were to move from their rented land, for instance, they had a right to financial compensation, even though strictly speaking they were not the owners.

28. When I speak of "the South" in the first part of this volume I more especially refer to Tipperary and other counties similarly situated. Perhaps it would have been more correct to have said "the centre of Ireland." I shall subsequently explain how far, on visiting the South-Western counties, I found some variety in the condition of things. [Author's footnote.]

29. Edward George Geoffrey Smith-Stanley, 14th Earl of Derby (1799–1869), statesman, leader of the Conservative Party, was prime minister four times; although each administration was less than two years and combined they were just over four.

no man has had better opportunities of understanding the subject—distinctly tells us that he cannot. The landlord, by the consent of both sides, is entitled to the rent, and he gets the rent without difficulty. But if he tries to take possession of the land as his own, or to give it to whom he chooses, he is at once met by a law stronger than the law; he cannot do it. I say then, again, that there can be no greater fallacy than that the landlord already has everything, and has no occasion to compromise; he has the rent, but he has not the land. The people have, in one sense, the land, but they have not the support of the law administered by the ordinary tribunals. Can we not, then, effect some compromise between these two parties, by which the law of the land and the custom having the force of law may be brought into harmony and made to work together? That is the problem to be solved.

Talk of the sacredness of landlord property as you will, it is quite impossible for any one to hear the common language of, and read the literature regarding, Ireland, without feeling that, law or no law, at this moment the landlords are not the only owners of the soil. All classes talk freely, as a matter of course, of a man as "owning a farm," "selling his farm," "having bought a farm," "having inherited a farm." It is well known that the tenants habitually dispose of their farms by formal will, charge them with fortunes for daughters, and in every respect deal with them as property. . . .

Putting aside extravagant Fenian suggestions, the claim of the people is not to oust the landlords and take their place, but simply to hold according to the custom at a fair rent. Although it is true that some modern landlords have done much in the way of improvement, there can be no question that, as a rule, in Ireland it is the tenant, and not the landlord, who has reclaimed the land, built the homestead, put up the fences, and done most of what has been done. He has done this with-out special contract, in reliance on the custom. The exercise of the extreme legal right of the landlord to turn him out, without full compensation, is a confiscation in the reasonable sense of the word. Yet every attempt to interfere with this right of the landlord to ignore improvements already made, has been met by the cry of confiscation on their side.

It comes then to this, that there can be no settlement of the question without something which would be called confiscation on one side or other; unless, indeed, resort is had to a third plan, to which I for one should strongly object. It is useless to nibble at so serious a question—it must be grappled with by a radical and complete measure. We must either grant something substantial, or firmly refuse it. If it is to be refused, assuredly nothing could be a worse policy than to keep the people in play with the hope of redress by bringing forward a succession of measures which would amount to scarcely more than infinitesimal concessions. If nothing material is to be conceded, the sooner that is made clear the better for all parties. . . .

THE PLAN WHICH I VENTURE TO SUGGEST
. . . It is unnecessary to transfer the whole of the landlord's rights to the tenants, but we might take a middle course between that extreme and the other extreme of refus-ing everything that would afford real satisfaction to the masses.

Considering the question historically, and taking existing facts as facts, an obvious suggestion would be to do what has been done in India and Prussia and Russia—to recognise the occupiers as in some sense co-proprietors of the soil. A law similar to the Indian law might be passed, giving to the classes of tenants who may be supposed to hold rather by status than by contract (to those who have come in without special contract, and have invested their own capital in the soil, or who have paid previous holders for the privilege of occupying) a definite right of occupancy—fixity of tenure in fact. Provision might be made for the right to sell, subject to reasonable veto of the landlord on the new tenant proposed to him, and for inheritance, subject to a veto on excessive subdivision, sub-letting, and so on. The rent would be subject to revaluation from time to time, but provision would be made for enabling the parties to arrange a present increase once for all in lieu of all claims to future enhancements. . . .

It might well be said that all this would only be giving to the people by law what in practice they already have.

It is no conclusive answer to a proposal of this kind that considerable objections may be taken to it. There are few solutions of a difficult question which are not open to objections. It is only a question of preferring lesser to greater evils.

On the whole, however, after turning the matter much over in my mind, with the light of my experience of such systems in India, and an earnest wish to realize the particular circumstances affecting Ireland, I am inclined to think that the objections to the adoption, pure and simple, of the plan which I have suggested preponderate. The plan is one which a strong and impartial foreign Power might perhaps adopt—which we might adopt if Ireland were in India. It might be said, "We must have peace. Peace is only to be got by conceding the popular demand. Why not concede it handsomely at once, have done with the matter, and get a chance of ruling the country quietly and easily?" But still, since we are not altogether foreign rulers, since Ireland is already in some degree a colony, since we have there some landlords who improve, and to whom we must look to lead agricultural improvement (an element altogether wanting in India), I should like to modify the plan. . . .

In my view, the safest course is to keep before our eyes, as the one main object, the maintenance of the present distribution of interests in the land as nearly as possible as they exist, to make as little change as possible, to accept as nearly as may be present facts. I doubt whether any detailed law which could now be drawn would effect this object. What is necessary, is to engraft the custom of the country, and the several customs of the various parts of this country, on the law as now administered by the courts—in short, to enact that custom shall no longer be ignored, but shall have force and effect. To attain this object, the plan which seems to me most likely to succeed, without too much jarring, would be to introduce for a time a sort of despotic power. I would have a commission with power not only to inquire but to act. They should have a general instruction to give effect to the custom, and to restrain landlords from exercising legal rights contrary to the custom, and to restrain landlords from exercising legal rights contrary to the custom. Under them would be local courts of conciliation and arbitration. . . .

31. "Foundation of the National Land League of Mayo," *The Freeman's Journal* (1879)

The land question in Ireland heated up further in the late 1870s, as a decline in prices, crop failures, and extremely wet weather spelled disaster for poor Irish tenants and laborers: they were confronted with bankruptcies, starvation, eviction, and forced emigration. The crisis was reminiscent of the 1840s famine. Yet in contrast to what took place during that earlier calamity, in the late 1870s there arose a movement that confronted simultaneously the immediate crisis and what was seen as its structural underpinnings, the arbitrary power of the landlords. The result was the Irish Land War of the late 1870s and early 1880s, which, the historian T. W. Moody (2001, 238) would later describe as "the greatest mass movement of modern Ireland."

No figure was more important to conceiving and organizing this movement than Michael Davitt (1846–1906). He was in born in Mayo and grew up in England following his family's eviction from their holding in 1850. When he was eleven years old, he lost his arm while working in a textile mill in Lancashire. In 1865, he joined the Fenian movement. His participation in the movement led to his spending seven years in prison for a gun trafficking charge. Davitt emerged from prison no less an opponent of the British connection, but he was also critical of Fenian intransigence, and he imagined a broader nationalist movement that would bring together the drive for political independence and autonomy with the struggle for agrarian justice. He was quick to see the potential of the New Departure, first proposed by the Irish-born but American-based Fenian John Devoy in 1878. The idea was to bring together Irish and Irish-American support, Fenians and constitutionalists, for a movement that would fuse Home Rule and land reform.

The New Departure got off to a rocky start, as both the IRB and Charles Stewart Parnell, the emerging leader of the Home Rule movement, jockeyed for control of it. However, the economic crisis of 1878–79 altered the landscape, and the nationalist movement coalesced in defense of tenant rights. The organization founded by Davitt, the National Land League of Mayo, was the basis for this emerging popular movement. Its inaugural meeting was on August 16, 1879, in Castlebar at the Imperial Hotel (now the Daly Hotel), and delegates from throughout the country were in attendance. This organization provided the foundation for the National Land League founded later that year with Parnell at its head. At the August 16 meeting, Davitt read the following manifesto.

. . . This body shall be known as The National Land League of Mayo, and shall consist of farmers and others, who will agree to labour for the objects here set forth, and subscribe to the conditions of membership, principles, and rules specified below—

Objects: The objects for which this body is organized are—

1. To watch over the interests of the people it represents; and protect the same, as far as may be in its power to do so, from an unjust or capricious exercise of power or privilege on the part of landlords or any other class in the community.

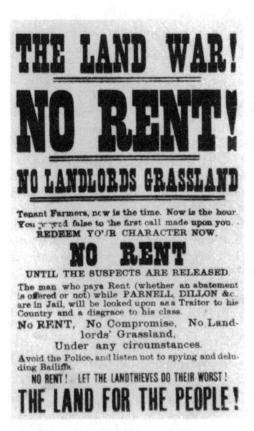

A National Land League poster (1881).

2. To resort to every means compatible with justice, morality, and right reason which shall not clash defiantly with the constitution upheld by the power of the British empire in this country, for the abolition of the present land laws of Ireland, and the substitution in their place of such a system as shall be in accord with the social rights and necessities of our people, the traditions and moral sentiments of our race, and which the contentment and prosperity of our country imperatively demand.

3. Pending a final and satisfactory settlement of the land question, the duty of this body will be to expose the injustice, wrong, or injury which may be inflicted upon any farmer in Mayo, either by rack-renting,[30] eviction, or other arbitrary exercise of power which the existing laws enables the landlords to exercise over their tenantry, by giving all such arbitrary acts the widest possible publicity, and meeting their perpetration with all the opposition which the laws for the

30. Rents at exorbitant rates.

preservation of the peace will permit of. In furtherance of which the following plan will be adopted:—a. Returns to be obtained, printed, and circulated, of the number of landlords in this county; the amount of acreage in possession of same, and the means by which such land was obtained; farms let by each, with the conditions under which they are held by their tenants and excess of rent paid by same over the government valuation. b. To publish by placard, or otherwise, notice of contemplated evictions for non-payment of exorbitant rent, or other unjust cause, and the convening of a public meeting if deemed necessary or expedient, as near the scene of such evictions, as circumstances will allow, and on the day fixed upon for the same. c. The publication of a list of evictions carried out, together with cases of rack-renting, giving full particulars of same, names of landlords, agents, etc., concerned, and number of people evicted by such acts. d. The publication of the names of all persons who shall rent or occupy land or farms, from which others have been dispossessed for non-payment of exorbitant rents, or who shall offer a higher rent for land or farms than that paid by the previous occupier. e. The publication of reductions of rent, and acts of justice or kindness performed by landlords in the county.

4. This body to undertake the defence of such of its members, or those of local clubs affiliated with it, who may be required to resist by law the actions of landlords or their agents, who may purpose doing them injury, wrong, or injustice in connexion with their land or farms.

5. To render assistance when possible to such farmer-members as may be evicted or otherwise wronged by landlords or their agents.

6. To undertake the organizing of local clubs or defence associations in the baronies,[31] towns, and parishes of this county, the holding of public meetings and demonstrations on the land question, and the printing of pamphlets on that and other subjects for the information of the farming classes.

7. And finally to act as a vigilance committee in Mayo, note the conduct of its grand jury, poor law guardians,[32] town commissioners, and members of parliament and pronounce on the manner in which their respective functions are performed wherever the interests, social or political, of the people represented by this club renders it expedient to do so.

Conditions of membership: 1. To be a member of any local club or defence association in the county, and be selected by such club or association to represent the same on the central or county association. 2. A desire to co-operate in the carrying out of the foregoing objects and subscribing to the principles here enunciated with the view of propagating the same and labouring for their successful application in Ireland will qualify non-representative farmers or others for membership of this body, subject to the subscription and rules laid down for same. 3. To pay any sum not under five shillings a year towards the carrying out of the foregoing objects and the end

31. Divisions of a county.
32. Administrators of government-funded poverty relief.

for which this body is created—the obtaining of the soil of Ireland for the people of Ireland who cultivate it.

Declaration of principles. The land of Ireland belongs to the people of Ireland, to be held and cultivated for the sustenance of those whom God decreed to be the inhabitants thereof. Land being created to supply the necessities of existence, those who cultivate it to that end have a higher claim to its absolute possession than those who make it an article of barter to be used or disposed of for purposes of profit or pleasure. The end for which the land of a country is created requires an equitable distribution of the same among the people who are to live upon the fruits of their labour in its cultivation. Any restriction, therefore, upon such a distribution by a feudal land system embodying the laws of primogeniture and entail,[33] the amassing of large estates, the claiming of proprietorship under penal obligations from occupiers, and preventing the same from developing the full resources of the land, must necessarily be opposed to the Divine purpose for which it was created, and to the social rights, security, and happiness of the people.

'Before the conquest the Irish people knew nothing of absolute property in land. The land virtually belonged to the entire sept,[34] the chief was little more than the managing member of the association. The feudal idea, which views all rights as emanating from a head landlord, came in with the conquest,[35] was associated with foreign dominion, and has never to this day been recognized by the moral sentiments of the people. Originally the offspring, not of industry, but of spoilation, the right has not been allowed to purify itself by protracted possession, but has passed from the original spoilators to others by a series of fresh spoilations, so as to be always connected with the latest and most odious oppression of foreign invaders. In the moral feelings of the Irish people, the right to hold the land goes, as it did in the beginning, with the right to till it.' These were the words of John Stuart Mill,[36] the English political economist.

The landlord system which an alien government has imposed upon our country in the place of that which recognized no intermediate ownership between the cultivator of the soil and the state has reduced Ireland to a degree of poverty and social misery incompatible with the natural productiveness of its land and the progressive prosperity of other civilized nations.

The area of Ireland and the natural wealth of its soil is capable of supporting from twelve to twenty millions of inhabitants, if restrictive land laws did not

33. *Primogeniture* refers to the right of the firstborn (usually the son) to be the sole inheritor of an estate. *Entail* refers to the legal arrangements for the inheritance of an estate independent of those who possess it. It ensures that an estate is passed from generation to generation without being divided.

34. Clan (Irish).

35. The Anglo-Norman invasion of Ireland, which began in 1169.

36. John Stuart Mill (1806–73), influential liberal and utilitarian philosopher and writer, political economist, employee of the East India Company, and MP. He is best known perhaps for his defense of individual freedom in *On Liberty* (1859). Mill took a keen interest in the Irish question over an extended period of time, notably in *England and Ireland* (1868). Mill was sympathetic to Irish grievances against Britain, yet he was a staunch supporter of the Union.

operate against the full development of the country's resources and the unfettered cultivation of the land. Yet a population of 8,000,000 previous to the year 1847 was reduced by death, starvation and exile, consequent upon an artificial famine[37] and continued impoverishment to little over 5,000,000 at the present day. Decreased population with its concomitant absorption of small holdings into large estates has produced no beneficial changes in the condition of the existent farming classes who are compelled by the coercion of necessity in the absence of manufacturing industry to the acceptance of a non-alternative bargain in the shape of exorbitant rent in order to obtain the use of the soil. The dread of eviction or rack-renting must necessarily operate against that expenditure of labour and enterprise in the cultivation of the land and improvement of farm dwellings and premises which follow in every country where the fruits of the people's industry is protected by the state; hence the soil of Ireland is worse and less cultivated, and the living and habitations of its agricultural classes more wretched than in any country in the civilized world. Over 6,000,000 acres of Irish land is owned by less than 300 individuals, twelve of whom are in possession of 1,297,888 acres between them, while 5,000,000 of the Irish people own not a solitary acre. For the protection of the proprietorial rights of the few thousand landlords in the country a standing army of semi-military police is maintained which the landless millions have to support, while the conduct of the landocracy in the exercise of its legal privileges occasions almost all the evils under which our people suffer.

Thus the rights of the soil cultivators, their security from arbitrary disturbance and incentives to social advancement, together with the general well-being, peace, and prosperity of the people at large are sacrificed for the benefit of a class insignificant in numbers, and of least account in all that goes towards the maintenance of a country, but which by the aid of existing land laws extracts some twenty million pounds annually from the soil of Ireland without conferring any single benefit in return on the same or the people by whose industry it is produced.

If the land in the possession of 744 landlords in this country were divided into 20-acre farms it would support in ease and comparative independence over two millions and a half of our people.

To substitute for such an unjust and anomalous system as the present land code—one that would show an equal protection and solicitude for the social rights and well-being of the labouring millions as that shown for those of the wealthy but non-operative few—is the principle upon which enlightened statesmanship aims at following in modern times to meet the growing necessities of that popular intelligence and awakening civilization which demands the sweeping away of those feudal laws opposed to the social progress and ideas of the age. Sacrificing the interests of the few to the welfare of the many by the abolition of feudal land codes, has laid the foundation of solid governments and secured the contentment of peoples in most European countries. The interests of the landlords of Ireland are pecuniary and can be compensated, but the interests of the people of Ireland, dependant upon the produce of

---

37. The idea that the Famine was artificial, that is, a natural calamity made much worse by government policies, echoes sentiments famously expressed by John Mitchel (no. 11).

the soil, is their very existence. In denouncing the existing land laws and demanding in their place such a system as will recognize and establish the cultivator of the said soil as its proprietor, we neither purpose[38] nor demand the confiscation of the interest which the landlords now hold in the land, but ask that compensation be given them for loss of said rights when the state, for the peace, benefit and happiness of the people shall decree the abolition of the present system.

We appeal to the farmers of Ireland to be up and doing at once and organize themselves forthwith in order that their full strength may be put forth in behalf of themselves and their country in efforts to obtain what has brought security and comparative plenty to the farming classes of continental countries. Without an evidence of earnestness and practical determination being shown now by the farmers of Ireland and their friends in a demand for a small proprietary which alone can fully satisfy the Irish people or finally settle the great land question of the country, the tribunal of public opinion will neither credit the urgent necessity for such a change nor lend its influence in ameliorating the condition or redressing the social and political wrongs of which we complain. Let us remember, in the words of one of Ireland's greatest sons [John Mitchel], that 'the land is the fund whence we all ultimately draw; and if the terms on which the land is cultivated be unfair—if the agricultural system of a country be unsound, then the entire structure is rotten and will inevitably come down. Let us never forget that mere appeals to the public to encourage native industry in other departments must be utterly futile so long as the great and paramount native industry of the farmer is neglected. In vain shall we try to rouse national spirit if the very men who make the nation sink into paupers before our face. Paupers have no country, no rights, no duties; and, in short, if we permit the small farmers to be reduced to pauperism—if we see them compelled to give up their land and throw themselves on public relief, there is an end of Ireland.'

The manifesto was unanimously adopted.

32. Charles Stewart Parnell, "Mr. Parnell at Cork," *The Times,* January 22, 1885

Charles Stewart Parnell (1846–91) was the "uncrowned king of Ireland," the dominant figure in Irish politics during the 1880s. While John Devoy (in conjunction with Michael Davitt) may have been responsible for conceiving of the New Departure, Parnell's leadership made it a reality. He brought together the two wings of the nationalist movement: the struggles for economic justice and political independence. He was able to create a united coalition of diverse political traditions—from physical-force violence to strict constitutionalism. He was responsible for making Home Rule a serious political cause— not only in Ireland but in Britain as well—culminating in Prime Minister William Gladstone's efforts to make it into law in 1886.

Parnell was an unlikely nationalist leader. He was from an Irish Protestant gentry background in County Wicklow, and in many respects he was a social conservative.

---

38. Propose.

But his mother was American, and his grandfather, William Henry Parnell (1780–
1821), was a liberal patriot MP for Wicklow (1817–20). Following an undistin-
guished spell as a university student at Cambridge University, Parnell inherited his
father's estate, Avondale. In 1875, he was elected as the MP for Meath on a Home
Rule platform, and in just a short time he emerged as the leader of the parliamentary nationalists. He lacked Daniel O'Connell's eloquence as a speaker, but he was a
shrewd organizer and strategist, and he excelled at parliamentary maneuvering. His
mastery of parliamentary obstruction in the late 1870s brought down on him the
enmity of British politicians. It also forced Irish demands onto the legislative agenda
and to the center of the British political world.

Parnell opposed Gladstone's Land Reform Act (1881), which enshrined into law
dual ownership of the land but not peasant proprietorship. As a result, Parnell and other
leaders of the National League were imprisoned in Kilmainham Gaol[39] in 1882. But it
also led to a negotiated peace with Gladstone. The British prime minister made further
concessions to the Irish tenants, and the agreement between Parnell and Gladstone
provided the basis for a political coalition that led to the 1886 Home Rule Bill. Their
working relationship survived the Liberal Party's division over Home Rule, the legislation's failure to gain a majority, and the Conservative's return to power with Liberal
Unionist support following the 1886 election. It was fatally damaged when revelations
of Parnell's longtime romantic relationship with Katharine O'Shea, and his implication
in her divorce, surfaced in 1889. Not only did Gladstone's Liberals spurn Parnell, but he
was also ousted as the leader of the Irish parliamentary nationalists. A minority stayed
loyal to him, creating a rift that remained for years. Parnell's denunciation of the coalition with the Liberals before his early death at the age of forty-five in 1891 enhanced his
status within some quarters of Irish nationalism.

Parnell's 1885 speech at Cork, the constituency he represented in Parliament at the
time, tells us a great deal about his politics. His political optimism about the upcoming
parliamentary elections must be seen in the context of the Reform Act of 1884 (Representation of the People Act) that made it possible for the first time for the majority of Irish
males to vote. Parnell believed that this augmentation of the electorate could only expand
the political clout of Irish nationalism. His speech's focus on a wide compass of economic
and political issues was rooted in New Departure politics. The fact that Parnell refused
to specifically define Irish national aspiration is arguably attributable to the political
challenges that he faced. He had to keep together a diverse coalition of nationalists, and
he was speaking to an audience that contained multiple constituencies. He was better
able to achieve unity by being elusive rather than concrete.

. . . The Mayor has kindly claimed for me your indulgence. Indeed, last night,
when I set out upon the journey which he has described to you, I felt a sinking at
my heart, lest when I reached Dublin I should find myself unable to go any further
or to keep my engagement with you this evening. But when I approached Ireland I
found myself getting better and better (cheers), and when I landed and came near
your beautiful city of Cork the change became increasingly marked (cheers), so that

---

39. British spelling of *jail.*

when I reached your city I felt myself quite restored and strong, as if nothing had ever been the matter with me. (Cheers.) But at the same time I do intend to claim your indulgence this evening, and to make my remarks very much shorter and fewer than they would have been under other circumstances. (Cheers.) It wants a month or two of five years since the constituency of Cork honoured me by making me its representative. (Cheers, and a voice.—"You are worthy of it;" another voice—"And you will kill Whiggery,"[40] and more cheers.) My victory was a very remarkable one. (Hear, hear.) Coming as I did among you and representing the privileges which I did represent,[41] it was extraordinary that in the limited constituency of the city at that time and with the ideas that then prevailed among the constituency you should have selected such a politician as me. (Laughter and cheers.) Your late respected member, Joseph Ronayne[42] (cheers), had often told me that it would be impossible for Cork to return two Nationalists, and my return was the first occasion on which two members of my way of thinking sat for and represented your city. But great as was the advance marked by my return by a very narrow majority, it was as nothing to the change which has since taken place. (Hear, hear.) Altogether, leaving aside the great extension of the constituency which the Franchise Act[43] has made, you have since shown in the election of my able colleague Mr. Deasy[44] (cheers) that it is no trouble for you to elect any number of Nationalists (cheers), and the present constituency of Cork, under the franchise, will leave you in a position free from care, so far as the choice of our representatives goes. I do not suppose that Cork will ever again be contested by the oligarchy in this city. At that election in 1880 I laid certain principles before you and you accepted them. (Cheers, and cries of "We do.") I said, and I pledged myself, that I should form one of an independent Irish party to act in opposition to every English Government which refused to concede just the rights of Ireland (loud cheers), and the time which has gone by since has more than ever convinced me that that is the true policy to pursue so far as Parliamentary policy is concerned, and that it will be impossible for either or both of the English parties to contend for any long time against a determined band of Irishmen acting honestly upon these principles and backed by the Irish people. (Cheers.) But we have not alone had that object in view. We have always been very careful not to fetter or control the people, nor in any way to prevent them from doing anything by their own strength which is possible for them to do. Sometimes, perhaps, in our anxiety in this direction, we have asked them to do what is beyond their strength, but I hold that it is better even to

40. A reference to the Whig Party, the forerunner to, and a component of, the nineteenth-century British Liberal Party. From the 1830s, Whigs were often landowners who advocated moderate reform from above. Many of them ended up as Conservatives, and the term *Whig* disappeared from political discourse.

41. Parnell refers here to the fact that he was born into the Anglo-Irish landowning class.

42. Joseph Philip Ronayne (1822–76), Irish civil engineer, MP (1872–76), and a leading member of the Irish Parliamentary Party.

43. Representation of the People Act (1884).

44. John Deasy (1856–96), Irish nationalist, MP (1884–93).

encourage you to do what is beyond your strength, even should you fail sometimes in the attempt, than to teach you to be subservient and unreliant. (Cheers.) You have been encouraged to organize yourselves, to depend upon the rectitude of your cause for your justification and to depend upon the determination which has helped Irishmen through many centuries to retain the name of Ireland, and to retain the nationhood of Ireland. (Cheers.) Nobody can point to any single action of ours in the House of Commons or out of it which was not based upon the knowledge that behind us existed a strong and brave people, that without the help of the people our exertions would be nothing, and that with their help and with their confidence we should be, as I believe we shall prove to be in the near future, invincible and unconquerable. (Great cheering.) The electors who will be swamped (laughter) in the great mass of Irishmen now admitted to the rights of the constitution, so far as they exist in this country, were on the whole faithful to their trust; indeed it was not until we showed by a good many proofs that we could do without an enlargement of the franchise, and with the old restricted suffrage we could do all that was necessary in the way of Parliamentary operations, that the opposition to the admission of the mass of the Irish people to the franchise disappeared. (Cheers.) But I look forward to the future with a light heart. I am convinced that five or six hundred thousand Irishmen, who within a year must vote for the men of their choice, will be as true to Ireland and even truer to Ireland than those who have gone before them, and that we may safely trust to them the exercise of the great and important privilege, unequalled in its greatness and its magnitude in the history of any nation, which will shortly be placed upon them. I am convinced that when the reckoning up comes, after the general election of 1886, that we in Ireland shall have cause to congratulate ourselves in the possession of a strong party, which will bear down all opposition, and which, aided by the organization of our country behind us, will enable us to gain for our country those rights which were stolen from us. (Cheers.) We shall struggle, as we have been struggling for the great and important interests of the Irish tenant farmer. We shall ask that his industry shall not be fettered by rent. We shall ask also from the farmer in return that he shall do what in him lies to encourage the struggling manufactures of Ireland, and that he shall not think it too great a sacrifice to be called upon when he wants anything, when he has to purchase anything, to consider how he may get it of Irish material and manufacture (hear, hear), even suppose he has to pay a little more for it. (Cheers.) I am sorry if the agricultural population has shown itself somewhat deficient in its sense of duty in this respect up to the present time; but I feel convinced that the matter has only to be put before them to secure the opening up of most important markets in this country for those manufactures which have always existed, and for those which have been re-opened anew as a consequence of the recent exhibitions—the great exhibition in Dublin and the other equally great one in Cork—which have been recently held. (Cheers.) We still also endeavour to secure for the labourer some recognition and some right in the land of his country. (Cheers.) We do not care whether it be the prejudices of the farmer or of the landlord that stand in his way. (Hear, hear.) We consider that whatever class tries to obstruct the labourer in the possession of those fair and just rights to which he is entitled, that class should be put down and coerced, if you will, into doing justice to the labourer. We have shown our desire to benefit the labourer by the passage of the Labourers' Act,[45] which, if maimed and mutilated by many of its provisions, undoubtedly is based upon correct lines and principles, which will undoubtedly do much good for that class, and undoubtedly will secure for the labouring classes a portion of what we have been striving to secure for them. But I go back from the consideration of these questions to the consideration of the great question of national self-government for Ireland. (Cheers.) I do not know how this great question will be eventually settled. I do not know whether England will be wise in time and concede to constitutional arguments and methods the restitution of that which was stolen from us towards the close of the last century.[46] (Cheers.) It is given to none of us to forecast the future; and just as it is impossible for us to say in what way or by what means the national question may be settled, in what way full justice may be done to Ireland, so it is impossible for us to say to what extent that justice shall be done. We cannot ask for less than the restitution of Grattan's Parliament[47] (cheers), with its important privileges and wide and far-reaching constitution. We cannot, under the British Constitution,[48] ask for more than the restitution of Grattan's parliament. (Renewed cheers.) But no man has the right to fix the boundary to the march of a nation (great cheering); no man has a right to say to his country "Thus far shalt thou go and no further," and we have never attempted to fix the *ne plus ultra*[49] to the progress of Ireland's nationhood, and we never shall. (Cheers.) But, while we leave those things to time, circumstances, and the future, we must each one of us resolve in our own hearts that we shall at all times do everything which within us lies to obtain for Ireland the fullest measure of her rights. (Cheers.) In this way we shall avoid difficulties and contentions among each other. In this way we shall not give up anything which the future may put in favour of our country; and while we struggle to-day for that which may seem possible for us with our combination, we must struggle for it with the proud consciousness that we shall not do anything to hinder or prevent better men who may come after us from gaining better things than those for which we now contend. (Prolonged cheers.)

45. The Labourers' Act (1883) was the first of a series of acts that enabled local authorities to tear down inadequate housing and provide cottages and land for agricultural laborers.

46. Parnell refers to the Act of Union passed by both the British and Irish Parliaments in 1800. It was widely believed by Irish nationalists that the Irish Parliament that assented to the Union was neither representative of the nation nor had the authority to dissolve itself. In addition, British authorities in Ireland were seen as having used unscrupulous methods, notably bribery, to pass the act in the Irish Parliament.

47. Grattan's Parliament (1782) takes its name from the Irish Protestant reformer Henry Grattan (1746–1820), who championed legislative autonomy for the Protestant Irish Parliament.

48. The British Constitution is not a written document. It refers to the legal and parliamentary traditions of Britain as manifested in acts of Parliament, judicial decisions, and treaties.

49. The highest point, the limits (French).

33. William Ewart Gladstone, "Mr. Gladstone's Manifesto," *The Times*, May 4, 1886

William Ewart Gladstone (1809–98) was arguably the dominant British politician of his age. His career in public service lasted over sixty years. He was prime minister on four separate occasions. When he resigned as prime minister for the last time in 1894, he was eighty-four. Gladstone was born into a prosperous Liverpool merchant family and attended the University of Oxford. He is best known as the leader of the Liberal Party, but he began his career as a Conservative and as a defender of the established church in Ireland. While the Irish question was one among many issues to which Gladstone devoted himself, in the later part of his life he was deeply committed to resolving it. His interest in Ireland materialized during the 1860s. The reasons were varied, but they certainly involved a blend of moral principle and political calculation. In addition, the surfacing of the Fenians in the 1860s convinced Gladstone that Irish discontent would intensify unless Irish grievances were addressed. He was responsible for the disestablishment of the Church of Ireland and for initiating land reform. He engineered the passage of the Land Act of 1870, which enshrined into law the principle of dual ownership and was responsible for the more wide-reaching Land Act of 1881. The 1881 act enshrined the Three Fs—fixity, fairness, and freedom—fundamental demands made by the land reform movement.

Gladstone was the first powerful British politician to be won over to the cause of Home Rule and to put his considerable political capital behind it. As prime minister, he brought it to a vote on two separate occasions. In 1886, it failed to pass in the House of Commons and split his party. In 1893 it passed in the House of Commons, but it was defeated in the House of Lords. Gladstone defended his advocacy of Home Rule on several occasions. In the text reprinted here, his 1886 written address to his parliamentary constituency in Midlothian, Scotland, he focused on the British rather than the Irish dimension. He considered the arguments of his opponents within the Liberal Party and placed party divisions within a wider history of British Whig and Liberal traditions. Most important, he discussed the implications of Irish Home Rule for Scotland and Wales. Gladstone's critics believed that granting an autonomous Irish parliament would lead to the implosion of the UK. Gladstone imagined that the UK could eventually end up as a federation of its constituent components. His vision was more than a hundred years premature. Today the UK contains a parliament in Scotland and assemblies in Wales and Northern Ireland.

Gentlemen,—I could have wished to take a part in the active operations of the Easter recess, particularly as they have been pushed within the limits of your county. You have given me from your local meetings good reason to believe that I should have found the echoes of those walls, within which I have so often had the honour to address you, much the same as they have been on former occasions. But age grows upon me, and I am obliged to reserve my limited power of voice for any effort which may be required in the House of Commons. I therefore use my pen to revert to the subject which I opened in my address to you of last September. I then said that any concession of local self-government to Ireland which was duly adjusted to the paramount conditions of Imperial unity would, in my view, be a source not of danger, but of increased security and strength to the Empire. Since that time a Bill has been introduced by

Political cartoon satirizing Gladstone's Ireland policy.

the existing Cabinet, on some important provisions of which, as was to be expected, differences of opinion prevail among its friends, but which could not have met, as I conceive that it has met, with such wide and warm approval in the country, unless it had been felt—first, that the principle of local autonomy or Home Rule for Ireland is reasonable; and, secondly, that the demands of Imperial unity have at least been carefully studied in the provisions of the Bill. I have never known an occasion when a Parliamentary event in London so rung throughout the world as the introduction of this Bill under the auspices of a British Government. In extending our view beyond our shores we sometimes obtain valuable aid towards the conduct of our affairs from opinions formed in other countries upon great internal questions of our own, which they often view with a frank good will lifted entirely above the level of any sectional or local prejudice. Naturally we look with the greatest interest to the sentiments of that vast British and Irish public which has already passed beyond one hundred millions, and which spreads with a rapidity unabated from year to year over some of the widest spaces of the globe. From public meetings and from the highest authorities in the colonies and America, from capitals such as Washington, Boston, and Quebec, and from remote districts lying beyond the reach of all ordinary political excitement,

I receive conclusive assurances that the kindred peoples regard with warm and fraternal sympathy our present effort to settle on an adequate scale, and once for all, the
long-vexed and troubled relations between Great Britain and Ireland, which exhibits
to us the one and only conspicuous failure of the political genius of our race to confront and master difficulty, and to obtain in a reasonable degree the main ends of
civilized life.

We must not be discouraged if at home, and particularly in the upper ranks of
society, we hear a variety of discordant notes, notes alike discordant from our policy
and from one another. Gentlemen, you have before you a Cabinet determined in its
purpose and an intelligible plan. I own I see very little else in the political arena that
is determined or that is intelligible. I will now proceed to speak to you on the state
of things in Parliament and beyond its walls, and also upon the nature and import
of the next great step to be taken in the progress of the measure. I speak at present
of the Irish Government Bill,[50] and I leave the Irish Land Purchase Bill[51] to stand on
the declarations we have already made, adding only an expression of the regret with
which I find that, while the sands are running in the hour-glass, the Irish landlords
have as yet given no indication of a desire to accept a proposal framed in a spirit of
the utmost allowable regard to their apprehensions and their interests.

I heartily concur with Lord Hartington[52]—whose absolute integrity and manly
courage in this controversy, like Mr. [John] Bright, I find it a pleasure to acknowledge—in holding that on a question of supreme rank like that of the Irish policy,
party, if need be, must give way, and sound argument at all hazards and all costs must
rule. I do not under-estimate the grave importance of the differences of opinion on
this great subject which have been exhibited within the circle of the Liberal party.
Some are inclined to rule the whole question against us by authority and to say,
"Surely such a number of persons, all of them declared, many of them able and consistent, some of them even extreme Liberals, would not have parted from their friends
except in obedience to the imperative dictates of truth and reason." I will say nothing of the motives which have determined us to confront the risk of such a parting;
but I earnestly recommend, on all the parts and at all the stages of this controversy,
a reference to the lessons which history supplies. It is not the first time in the history
of Liberalism when sections under chiefs of high distinction, character, and ability
have dissented from the general view of the party, to the great joy and, no doubt, at
the moment, to the great advantage of the Tories. In 1793 a great, indeed an illustri-

50. The name of the Irish Home Rule Bill, more precisely the Government of Ireland Bill.

51. Under the terms of the Purchase of Land Act (1885), also known as the Ashbourne Act, a
fund of five million pounds was established in order to lend money to tenants who wanted to
buy the land that they leased from their landlords. The loan would be paid back over a forty-
eight-year period at a fixed rate of 4 percent per year.

52. Spencer Compton Cavendish (1833–1908), Marquess of Hartington and 8th Duke of
Devonshire, MP, and cabinet member in Liberal governments prior to 1886 when he led the
Liberal opposition to Home Rule. Following the 1886 election, which resulted from the defeat
of the Home Rule Bill, Hartington led the Liberal Unionists and supported the Conservative
prime minister Lord Salisbury.

ous, secession of this kind brought on the tremendous war finally closed in 1815.[53] It
left the party thinned and impoverished; but the party lived while the secession died,
and, what is more, we know now that the party was right and the secession wrong.
We have a second instance in 1835, Lord Derby and Sir James Graham seceded from
their party to maintain the Irish Church Establishment.[54] The judgment of the country has again shown that in principle the party were right and the secession wrong.

In comparing the present secession with the examples I have cited (and I am aware
of no examples the other way), it is impossible not to be struck by one great—nay,
vital, difference. Each of the two former secessions was agreed within itself upon
an active and substantial policy. It was war in the first case; it was the sacredness of
Church property and of the principles of a Church establishment in the second. It
is not so with the present secession. Some are for coercion without limit; others for
the moderated doses of it which we have tried without effect (but with a tendency
to increase) during 80 years; a few are against it altogether. On the other side, some
are for giving no local government; some will give it to counties, some to provinces;
some would give an administrative centre to Ireland, but not a legislative; some a
legislative organ, but not an executive; some go beyond the Government and actually
recommend federation. Some agree with themselves no more than with one another,
and their proposals alter in every speech they make—a proof not of weakness in the
men, but of hopelessness in their cause. We, gentlemen, have at least the advantage
as to aim and principle of speaking with one voice; the secession, however respectable
and estimable in other ways, is, as to positive policy for Ireland, a perfect Babel.[55]
It is admitted on all hands that social order is the first of all political aims, and that
its bases are dangerously sapped in Ireland. To meet this state of things the secession
offer us either a hundred conflicting remedies or no remedy at all. I speak of what
is notorious, and I content myself with general statement now; the proof in detail
is for another place. These remarks, gentlemen, are not less applicable to Tory than
to Liberal opponents. In the speeches of both alike I find one remarkable omission.
Whether they suggest or whether they only criticize, one thing they almost uniformly
fail to do—they fail to express confidence in the permanent success of their opposition. To live from hand to mouth appears to be the height of their expectation. They
seem to suspect what we well know, that the strife which they are stirring can only
end one way, can only end in the concession of self-government to Ireland.

53. The Whigs split as a consequence of disagreements regarding the French Revolution, with
those who regarded the Revolution as a development toward constitutional monarchy on one
side and those who opposed the French revolutionary path and were supportive of William
Pitt's declaration of war against France in 1793 on the other. The struggle between France and
Britain lasted a generation, concluding with the defeat of Napoleon in 1815.

54. Lord Derby and Sir James Graham (1792–1861) were conservative Whigs who left the
party in 1834 and joined the Tories in 1837, when the Whig government sought to curb the
privileges of the Church of Ireland.

55. This is a reference to Genesis 11:1–9. The people of Babel seek to build a tower that
reaches heaven. God punishes them by creating a multitude of languages, thereby creating
disorder and incomprehension among the inhabitants.

If this be so, then the real question before us is not the triumph of Irish autonomy, but the length and the character of the struggle by which it is to be preceded. We say, "Let it be short;" they seek to make it long. We say, "Let us give freely;" they say, by their acts if not in words, "Let us only give when we can no longer withhold." We say, "Let us give now, when the position of our country in the affairs of the world is free and strong." They seem to prefer waiting for some period of national difficulty, that we may yield to the Irish demand in terror, as we did to the fear of foreign war in 1778,[56] to the demands of the Volunteers in 1782,[57] to the growing terrors of the conflict with France in 1793, to the alternative of civil war in 1829.[58] We say, "Let us act now, when moderation of thought and language rules in Irish counsels, and when, by willing concurrence on all sides, every arrangement for the reservation of Imperial prerogative can be made complete and absolute." They would postpone the settlement until a day when demands may be larger and means of resistance less. We say "Deal with this matter as a matter between brothers—a matter of justice and of reason." They renew the tale, alas! too often told, which has for its prologue denial with exasperation and resentment, and for its epilogue surrender without conditions and without thanks.

Now, however, a new terror is brought upon the stage, the terror of Home Rule for Scotland, and, some add, for Wales; but this suggestion, gentlemen, brings no alarm to me. Give us a little time only that we may look at each question in its order and on its merits. I am not sorry they are named, for all serious naming of them—all naming of them except in caricature—will serve to help our movement on behalf of Ireland. I can draw no vital distinction of right between the case of Ireland and other cases. There are many distinctions of circumstance. For many years I have hoped that it might be found practicable to apply decentralizing processes, even, perhaps, to portions of England, with a careful consideration of the different conditions of each case, which will naturally require for it differences of treatment. Subject to primary Imperial obligations, I believe that a standard measure of good government for Scotland and for Wales will be eventually determined by the public opinion of Scotland and of Wales, and this without the painful and disparaging circumstances of controversy with which we are now threatened in the case of Ireland, whose woeful history for centuries emboldens some of us to treat her as if she had but a limited share in the great inheritance of human right, and none at all in the ordinary privilege of immunity from gross and wholesale insult—emboldens,

56. As a result of the need to deploy troops to fight the American colonists and because of fears of a French invasion of Ireland, the British government accepted the presence of the Volunteers to defend Ireland by force of arms. However, as the Volunteers were connected with efforts to reform the Irish Parliament, they posed a potential threat to British interests as well.

57. Defeat by American colonists made the British government more vulnerable to the Volunteers' demands for reform. The result was Grattan's Reform Parliament of 1782, which resulted in diminished British control over the Irish Parliament.

58. The potential for civil war loomed large following the election of Daniel O'Connell to Parliament in 1828, as it was not clear whether the British government would allow him to take his seat in 1829.

I say, some of us, but only some of us, and not, I rejoice to think, the nations of Scotland or of England.

Watching from day to day the movement of the currents of opinion during the present conflict, more and more I find it vital to observe the point at which the dividing lines are drawn. On the side adverse to the Government are found, as I sorrowfully admit, in profuse abundance, station, title, wealth, social influence, the professions, or the large majority of them—in a word, the spirit and power of class. These are the main body of the opposing host. Nor is this all. As knights of old had squires, so in the great army of class each enrolled soldier has, as a rule, dependents. The adverse host, then, consists of class and the dependents of class. But this formidable army is in the bulk of its constituent parts the same, though now enriched at our cost with a valuable contingent of recruits, that has fought in every one of the great political battles of the last 60 years, and has been defeated. We have had great controversies before this great controversy—on free trade, free navigation, public education, religious equality in civil matters, extension of the suffrage to its present basis. On these and many other great issues the classes have fought uniformly on the wrong side, and have uniformly been beaten by a power more difficult to marshal, but resistless when marshalled—by the upright sense of the nation. Lord Hartington has reminded us, and I cordially agree with him, that this question, which may be turned over in a thousand ways and placed in a thousand partial lights, can only be settled and set at rest by the nation. From the first I have stated, and I think I may speak for the Government at large, that here is my main and capital reliance—I rely on my colleagues, I rely on an upright and enlightened House of Commons, I rely on the effect of free discussion; but the heart and root, the beginning and ending of my trust is in the wise and generous justice of the nation.

I have still to say a few words on the issue which is more immediately before us at this moment. . . . We have a great aim before us now. It is to restore your Parliament to efficiency by dividing, and by removing obstacles to, its work, to treat the Irish question with a due regard to its specialities, but with the same thoroughness of method by which we have solved colonial problems that 50 years back were hardly, if at all, less formidable; to give heed to the voice of a people speaking in tones of moderation by the mouth of a vast majority of those whom we ourselves have made its constitutional representatives, and thus to strengthen and consolidate the Empire on the basis of mutual benefit and hearty loyalty. Such is the end. For the means we take the establishment in Dublin of a Legislative Body, empowered to make laws for Irish, as contra-distinguished from Imperial, affairs. It is with this that we are now busied, and not with details and particulars. Their time will come. They are now employed with art, before their season, to bewilder unwary souls. So it has been before. You remember well how the campaign against the recent extension of the suffrage was carried on by setting in the front of the battle the pretended difficulties and dangers of the redistribution of seats.[59] We are not now debating the amount of Irish contributions to the Empire, or the composition of the Legislative Body, or the

59. The Representation of the People Act or the third Reform Act (1884).

maintenance of a representative connexion with Westminster. On these questions and many more we may or may not be at odds. But what we are at this moment debating is the still large and far larger question, which includes and, I think, absorbs them all—the question whether you will or will not have regard to the prayer of Ireland for the management by herself of the affairs specifically and exclusively her own. This and no other is the matter which the House of Commons has at once to decide. If on this matter it speaks with a clear and intelligible voice, I feel the strongest assurance that the others, difficult as some of them are, will, nevertheless, with the aid of full discussion, with the aid of a wise and conciliatory spirit, be found capable of a rational and tolerable settlement.

It is little, gentlemen, which I can do in this most grave matter; it is no more than to devote with cheerfulness to the cause the small available residue of my active life. But let me in these closing words extend my view beyond my own honoured constituency, and in one sentence say, You, my countrymen of Scotland and of England, can do much. With you essentially, and not with any person or class or section among you, it rests to deliver the great Aye or No, on your choice between which depend all the best hopes of Ireland, and much that touches in its honour and high interest Great Britain and all the mighty Empire of our Queen.

I remain, Electors of Mid Lothian, your dutiful and grateful servant,
W. E. GLADSTONE.

Hawarden, May 1, 1886

34. W. E. H. Lecky, "Mr. Lecky on Mr. Gladstone's Proposals," *The Times,* May 5, 1886

William Gladstone's efforts on behalf of Home Rule transformed the political debate on the Anglo-Irish relationship. His speech at Midlothian, reprinted in The Times *(no. 33), provoked a spirited discussion in the newspaper. The influential historian W. E. H. Lecky (1838–1903) was among Gladstone's most prominent critics. Lecky was the heir of a small landed property and a graduate of Trinity College, Dublin. His output was prodigious and varied. It included his multivolume work on England and Ireland in the eighteenth century,* The History of Ireland in the Eighteenth Century *(1878–90), part of a larger history of eighteenth-century England. He also wrote about the history of European morals and rationalism. Lecky's critique of Home Rule is noteworthy because his representation of eighteenth-century Ireland found an audience among Irish nationalists. Lecky is a descendant of the liberal patriot tradition. He emphasized the harm done by the penal laws, and he wrote about Grattan's 1782 Irish Parliament in laudatory terms. Yet Lecky, like many nineteenth-century liberals, defended the rule of the propertied classes. It was on the basis of* class *more than* religion *that he rejected Home Rule.*

Unionist poster representing the UK as a whole that is greater than the sum of its parts.

To the Editor of *The Times*

Sir,—Mr. Morley[60] is apparently unable to understand how a writer who in former years dwelt much on the strength of the national sentiment in Ireland, and who even questioned the wisdom of taking the government of Ireland in 1800 out of the hands of the Irish gentry, can object to Mr. Gladstone's present policy. The answer, however, is very simple.

The Nationalist movement has of late passed wholly out of the guidance of the representatives of property in Ireland, whether they be landlords, or leaders of industry, or professional men, and it is in complete and violent opposition to all those classes, who are sincerely loyal to the connexion. The organization which under the different names of the Land League and the National League has during the last few years directed it is subsidized from America by avowed enemies of the British Empire. Its uniform policy since its foundation has been what Mr. Gladstone truly called a "policy of public plunder." Its Press has been steadily stimulating the most savage hatred of England. It has never lost an opportunity of attacking the respect for law and the respect for contracts which are the two main pillars on which the prosperity of society rests, and it has attained its present position partly by unscrupulous appeals to disloyalty and cupidity and partly by the most systematic intimidation and "coercion"—the one form of "coercion" for which politicians of the type of Mr. Morley have no words of blame.

60. John Morley (1838–1923), 1st Viscount Morley of Blackburn, Liberal MP, chief secretary of Ireland (1886, 1892–95), secretary of state for India (1905–1910), writer, and newspaper editor.

I do not think that any one who has carefully followed Irish politics during the last few years can honestly deny that this is a true and unexaggerated description of the organization which has conquered the majority of the Irish representation and would almost certainly dominate in an Irish Parliament. Mr. Gladstone, as Mr. Goschen[61] has just reminded us, once described its leaders as "gentlemen who wish to march through rapine to disintegration and to the dismemberment of the Empire." He is willing to invest an enormous sum of money in the expropriation of Irish landlords, in the well-founded belief that if he did not the Government which he proposes to create would probably begin its career by a series of attacks upon property which is as indisputably entitled to the full protection of the law as any property in the world, and a great part of which is held under a recent Parliamentary title. Another part of his scheme is to pension off Judges who have become obnoxious to the future rulers of Ireland, simply because they have too strenuously enforced the criminal law.

Mr. Morley has done me the honour of quoting some words which I wrote before the agitation of Mr. Parnell or the foundation of the Land League. I confess that in the very different conditions of those days I was more sanguine than I now am about the success of local institutions, and I do not believe that the national sentiment has had the same prominence in the later movement as in preceding ones. The Land League, the no-rent conspiracy, and the constant appeals to the cupidity of tenants have introduced a new and much more formidable element into Irish politics. I still, however, fully acknowledge the strength of the national sentiment, and would gladly see any extension of local government which did not weaken the unity of the Empire, endanger property, or threaten Ireland with anarchy and civil war. It is because Mr. Gladstone's policy seems to me utterly and manifestly incompatible with these essential conditions that I oppose it. A serious politician, who is not governed by mere phrases and formularies, ought surely to ask himself what is likely to be the character of the Home Rule he desires to establish and by what classes and principles it will probably be guided. For my own part, I would as willingly intrust the government of Ireland to its Catholic as to its Protestant gentry, and I know that the law has never been more ably and more uprightly administered than by Catholic Judges. But I do not believe—and I do not think the people of Great Britain will believe—that the government of Ireland can be safely intrusted to the National League—to priests, and Fenians, and professional agitators, supported by the votes of an ignorant peasantry whose passions it has been for many years their main object to inflame. Your obedient servant,

W. E. H. Lecky.
May 3

61. George Joachim Goschen, 1st Viscount Goschen (1831–1907), Liberal MP, who left the party over Home Rule and joined the Conservative government of Lord Salisbury in 1886 as a Liberal Unionist. He served as chancellor of the exchequer (1887–92).

35. Lord Randolph Churchill, "Lord R. Churchill on the Irish Policy of the Tories," *The Times*, May 6, 1886

Lord Randolph Churchill (1849–95) was among the opponents of Home Rule published by The Times *in May 1886. Churchill is perhaps best known today as the father of Winston, the most famous Englishman of the twentieth century. But he was a prominent political figure in his own right, serving briefly as chancellor of the exchequer and leader of the House of Commons in 1886 in the Conservative government of Lord Salisbury.[62] Churchill played a pivotal role in formulating the ideology of Tory democracy, whereby Conservatives welcomed and reframed popular reforms rather than simply opposing them. As his letter to* The Times *suggests, he supported Gladstone's Reform Act of 1884, which greatly augmented the size of the electorate, particularly in Ireland. Yet Churchill held the Union to be sacrosanct, and he equated Irish Home Rule with the secession of the American South, which led to the American Civil War. Most important, Churchill reached out to the Ulster Unionists, who regarded Home Rule with horror and were beginning to organize an armed resistance if it should become law. Churchill himself did not advocate Orange militancy, but his declaration "Ulster will fight; Ulster will be right" was among the most inflammatory utterances ever voiced in the Irish troubles. Not only did it encourage Ulster Unionists to organize for militant action, but, given Churchill's prominence in his party, it also raised questions about what the Conservative leadership might advocate should Home Rule come to pass. Would one of the two largest parties in Britain resist the law of the land? Would British Conservatives support Ulster if it launched an armed resistance and provoked a civil war?*

Lord Randolph Churchill has written the following letter in reply to one from Mr. William Young, a member of the Liberal party in Glasgow:—

2, Connaught-place, May 7.

Sir,—I have read your letter of the 4th of May with great interest, and I am obliged to you for the candour and frankness with which you convey to me your opinions on the state of public affairs as they are affected by Ireland and the Irish policy of the present Government.

You advocate, as a member of the Liberal party, cooperation between the two great parties in the State for the purpose of maintaining the legislative union between Great Britain and Ireland as established by the Act of [Union of] 1800.

You further urge that in order to secure such cooperation it is essential that the Tory party should give some very binding and solemn guarantee to the effect if they were returned to Parliament in strength sufficient to justify them in attempting to conduct the government of the Empire they would (1) "never propose Home Rule for Ireland, or anything beyond local government, (2) resist further special legislation

---

62. Robert Gascoyne-Cecil, 3rd Marquess (also Marquis) of Salisbury (1830–1903). Salisbury became the leader of the Conservative Party in 1881 and served as prime minister on three separate occasions: 1885–86, 1886–92, and 1895–1902.

for Ireland, and (3) insist that all future legislation be Imperial, equally shared by all parts of the realm, the same for England, Scotland, and Wales, as for Ireland."

I cannot admit that any act or incident in the past history of the Tory party or of its leaders can be held to be of such a nature as to call for any guarantee of the kind set forth above.

The effective maintenance of the Act of Union in all its main and essential conditions is a cardinal principle of Tory policy, and to demand from a Tory a pledge that he will never consent to the repeal of the Union, or in other words to Home Rule, is as foolishly supererogatory as to demand from a British Protestant that he will never consent to establish and endow in Great Britain the Church of Rome.

The essence of the legislative union is similarity of institutions and of laws for all three kingdoms as a great general principle.

Scotch habits and customs with regard to comparatively small matters have required in the past, and may require in the future, special treatment. The criminal law of Scotland, the marriage laws of Scotland, are to some extent exceptions to the great principle of similarity.[63] The Crofters Bill[64] now before Parliament is a modern instance of special legislation.

In like manner Irish habits and customs may from time to time call for exceptional legislative treatment.

But these rare and minor incidents do not in any way detract from the sanctity of the great general overpowering principle of one Parliament, one law, for the United Kingdom.

To that principle every member of the Tory party, by the very fact of such membership, must be unalterably attached, and if any such member swerves even in thought from that principle, he instantly loses his right to call himself with truth a member of the Tory party; he becomes false and traitorous to the political principles which he has professed.

Now of this be certain—that Home Rule, as repeal is called at the present day, flagrantly and utterly violates the great principle I have above laid down. No Tory can ever propose it; all Tories must ever resist it, and not only it, in the form of any scheme such as is now before the country, but also all legislative projects which can reasonably be held to contain even the germ of such Home Rule.

My personal opinions on Home Rule are very fully set out in a speech which I made at Edinburgh in 1883 (December). At that time I made three speeches on public affairs on three consecutive nights, and one of those speeches I purposely devoted to Irish matters. For at that time reform was in the air, and it was not difficult to foresee the effects of a large measure of enfranchisement upon the Irish Parliamentary party. Then, and principally on account of Ireland, I was opposed to immediate dealing with reform, but I was all alone in my opposition.

When the Reform Bill [of 1884] was before Parliament I supported its full extension to Ireland, guided entirely by the great principle of similarity of law and institution, in support of which I was not unwilling to face considerable risk.

63. When Scotland became part of Great Britain in 1707, it retained its own legal system.
64. The Crofters Holding Act (1886) granted security of tenure to Scottish crofters, that is, tenant farmers.

But I foresaw very clearly what would be the attitude of the Irish party and the nature and the strength of the demands which they would make, and then I ventured to lay down that if Home Rule was to come within the limits of practical politics the action of the Northern States of America from 1861 to 1865 would have to be the model for the action of the Tory party under closely analogous perils, and that in a close imitation of American action, in spite of every conceivable danger, would be found the only method for the attainment of Imperial safety and for the preservation of Imperial unity.[65] I also well remember that these remarks of mine provoked a copious outburst of ridicule and abuse from many organs of Liberal opinion, with which outburst you yourself as a Liberal very probably sympathized.

Well, in Belfast the other day, as here in Paddington[66] before my constituents, I set forth precisely the same opinions.

The mere numerical action of Mr. Parnell's party in the House of Commons, the action of the Irish vote in English and Scotch constituencies, cannot be considered to have the smallest moral or binding effect upon the loyalists of Ireland, greatly concentrated in Ulster, whose lives and liberties will by such action numerical and mechanical be called in question.

If political parties and political leaders, not only Parliamentary, but local, should be so utterly lost to every feeling and dictate of honour and courage as to hand over coldly, and for the sake of purchasing a short and illusory Parliamentary tranquility, the lives and liberties of the loyalists of Ireland to their hereditary and most bitter foes, make no doubt on this point: Ulster will not be a consenting party; Ulster at the proper moment will resort to the supreme arbitrament[67] of force; Ulster will fight; Ulster will be right; Ulster will emerge from the struggle victorious, because all that Ulster represents to us Britons will command the sympathy and support of an enormous section of our British community, and also, I feel certain, will attract the admiration and the approval of free and civilized nations.

> I have the honour to be your obedient servant,
> Randolph S. Churchill.

William Young, Esq.

36–38. The Churches of Ireland on Home Rule

When William Gladstone introduced his Home Rule Bill in 1886, he triggered a national debate on the Anglo-Irish relationship. In a February 1886 letter to John Robert William Vesey (1844–1903), 4th Viscount de Vesci (an Irish title), he invited "the free

---

65. Churchill argues that Irish nationalists' advocacy of Home Rule is no different than the American South's claim to be an independent state in America. He advocates a British response analogous to Abraham Lincoln's refusal to accept the Confederacy.

66. Metropolitan borough of London, known for Paddington railway station, which opened in 1847.

67. The right or capacity to decide for oneself.

communication of views on Ireland." Among the numerous responses were those by the three major churches—the Church of Ireland, the Presbyterian Church, and the Roman Catholic Church—further demonstrating the deeply intertwined relationship between religion and politics in Ireland. They are noteworthy in so far as they connect Home Rule to other political issues, notably land. For the Catholic Church settling the land issue was a prerequisite for political and social stability, while for the Protestant churches the fusion of Home Rule and land politics represented an assault on law and property that foreshadowed Catholic tyranny and was an attack on freedom and liberty.

36. Irish Catholic Bishops (1886)

COPY OF LETTER addressed to the Prime Minister by the Roman Catholic Archbishop of Dublin, acting on behalf of the Bishops of Ireland (1886)

Dublin, 17 February 1886.

Sir,

YOUR letter to Lord de Vesci, which was published in the Dublin newspapers, has been under the consideration of a large and representative body of Irish Catholic bishops assembled here to-day on important ecclesiastical business. The prelates so assembled substantially represent the whole Irish episcopacy.

At the request of their Lordships I beg to lay before you, in response to your expressed desire, the views they entertain regarding the wants and wishes of the Irish people. There are, as you observe, three great Irish questions demanding the immediate care of the Government, namely, self-government, the settlement of the land question, and social order. First, as regards self-government, or Home Rule, it is our firm and conscientious conviction, based, as we believe, on the fullest, most varied, and, at the same time, most reliable information, that it alone can satisfy the wants, the wishes, as well as the legitimate aspirations of the Irish people. Those wishes and aspirations have been expressed with unmistakable clearness by constituencies of the four provinces of Ireland at the recent elections. We venture to remind you that immediately before those elections you had appealed to the people of this country to speak out their mind on this great question, and that in doing so you clearly laid down the lines within which you believed it to be a question of practical politics. We regard the issue of the elections as the answer given by the Irish people to that appeal. We are fully satisfied that the demand for Home Rule thus put forward in no way transgresses the constitutional limits marked out by you. Its concession cannot trench either on the supremacy of the Crown or on the unity of the Empire, nor can it interfere with the maintenance of all the authority of Parliament necessary for the consolidation of the unity. This being so, we feel convinced, with you, that the granting of Home Rule within those limits will be not a source of danger but a means of averting it, as furnishing a new guarantee for increased cohesion, happiness, and strength. As regards the settlement of the land question, we have no hesitation whatever in stating that in our opinion it now imperatively calls for a final solution, and that this cannot be better effected that by some such measure as that which certain English journalists and statesmen have recently advocated; that is, the purchase up by Government of the landlord interest in the soil, and the reletting of the latter to tenant farmers at a figure very considerably below the present judicial rent.

In addressing one of the foremost financiers,[68] as well as one of the most enlightened statesmen of the age, we do not presume to enter into the details of this weighty, and no doubt complicated, project, but are perfectly satisfied to leave them to your own sense of what is due to the equitable claims of existing landlords on the one hand and of the future tenants of Ireland on the other. We desire, however, to have it perfectly understood that the Irish people do not aim at the confiscation of any species of property, but only ask for fair play as between man and man, or what has been well described as the right to live and thrive in their native land. Third, as regards social order, we shall confine our remarks to two aspects of the case, public outrages, namely, what is called personal intimidation, or, as you otherwise express it, the fulfilment of contracts and personal liberty of action. It is our deliberate opinion that no just cause of complaint on either head will, or indeed can, exist after the settlement of the land question on the basis just indicated, or on any other basis which supposes the utter effacement of that system of landlordism which has so long and so ruinously existed in Ireland. In point of fact, every disturbance of social order that has occurred for years amongst our people, has arisen from the sense of wrong entertained by a large majority of the occupiers of the soil, owing to the remorseless exaction of needy or extravagant landlords. Even now the peace of the country is seriously imperiled by the fact that very many landlords, as if making a final but fruitless effort to collect impossible rents, have entered on an ill-considered course of eviction against their unfortunate tenants.

We would, therefore, earnestly and most respectfully urge that, pending the final settlement of the land question, which we are confident is now near at hand, the power of eviction be suspended in Ireland; at the same time that in the most impoverished districts some provision in the shape of remunerative labour be made out of the public purse to support the starving poor in the present and helping them on to better times.

Wishing you every success in your renewed efforts to restore peace and prosperity to our long-tried and much-loved country,

I have, &c
(signed) *William J. Walsh*,
Archbishop of Dublin,
Chairman of Episcopal Meeting.

37. The Presbyterian Church (1886)

At Belfast, 9th March 1886, which day the GENERAL ASSEMBLY of the PRESBYTERIAN CHURCH in *Ireland* being met and Constituted.

68. William Gladstone was renowned for his financial expertise, having served as chancellor of the exchequer (the cabinet position in control of fiscal matters) on four different occasions and having undertaken extensive budget reforms.

The General Assembly of the Presbyterian Church in Ireland, representing nearly half-a-million of people, having met in Belfast this 9th day of March 1886, to take into consideration the present serious state of the country, and the duty of the General Assembly in relation thereto, after due deliberation, resolved:—

1. That we declare anew our devoted loyalty to the Person and Throne of Her Gracious Majesty Queen Victoria.

2. That we greatly deplore the disturbed and lawless state of many parts of the country, the serious interference with personal freedom of action, and the insecurity which prevails as regards life, liberty, and property, and we pledge ourselves to give our loyal support to the Executive in the efficient maintenance of the authority of the Crown in the administration of the law with impartiality and firmness, and in the suppression of all lawlessness and disorder.

3. That, recognising in the unsatisfactory state of the land question a fruitful source of the unrest and discontent that abound, and sympathising deeply as we do with those classes of our fellow-countrymen who have suffered so much through the prevailing depression, we are strongly of opinion that the permanent settlement of the land question will be best secured by a wise and comprehensive measure which, while dealing equitably with the interest of all parties concerned, shall give material relief to the agricultural classes from their heavy burdens, by the creation of an occupying ownership involving a substantial reduction in their annual payments, or by such other means as Parliament, in its wisdom, may devise.

4. That we would deprecate in the strongest manner, as disastrous to the best interest of the country, a separate Parliament for Ireland, or an elective National Council, or any legislation tending to imperil the Legislative Union between Great Britain and Ireland, or to interfere with the unity and the supremacy of the Imperial Parliament. Legislation in any of these directions would, in our judgment, lead to the ascendancy of one class and creed in matters pertaining to religion, education, and civil administration. We do not believe that any guarantees, moral or material, could be devised which would safeguard the rights and privileges of minorities, scattered throughout Ireland, against the encroachment of a majority vested with legislative or executive functions. As law-abiding and industrious subjects of Her Gracious Majesty, who have, in some degree, contributed to the peace and prosperity of the country, we claim that our present relation to the Imperial Parliament shall be maintained, believing that in this way alone can the liberty of the subject, in the discharge of civil and social duties, be properly secured. We are further of opinion that, under a separate Parliament, the present system of unsectarian national education, which secures equal rights and privileges to all, irrespective of creed, which provides adequate safeguards against proselytism, and which has conferred signal benefits on the country, would, in all probability, be supplanted by a denominational system under which the young of any denomination, residing in districts where they form a small minority of the population, would be deprived of all education, except on terms opposed to conscientious conviction, while a system of concur-

rent endowment, in a most objectionable form, would thus be introduced, in a contravention of the policy that in recent times received the sanction of the Legislature. Whilst acknowledging that large sections of the Irish people have in the past suffered many and grievous wrongs, we believe there are no grievances removable by legislation which cannot be removed by the Imperial Parliament, while the establishment of a separate Parliament for Ireland would most seriously aggravate many existing evils, and would produce other evils greater than any that at present exist.

5. Being persuaded that the religion of Christ is adapted to promote the spirit of brotherhood so much needed in our native land, the Assembly earnestly exhort their ministers to give increased diligence in instructing their people in the principles of the gospel of peace, and they unite in the earnest prayer that the fear of God, the love of righteousness, and mutual forbearance and goodwill, may pervade and govern all classes of the population.

6. That the foregoing resolutions be transmitted by the Moderator and the Clerk, to the Prime Minister, the Lord Lieutenant, the Chief Secretary for Ireland, the Marquis of Salisbury, and the Marquis of Hartington; and that a Committee of Assembly be appointed to watch over this subject, and take such action as the course of events, in their judgment, may require.

Extracted from the records of the General Assembly of the
Presbyterian Church in Ireland by

John H. Orr,
Clerk of Assembly.

38. The Church of Ireland (1886)

RESOLUTIONS of the GENERAL SYNOD.—Special Session,
Tuesday, 23rd March 1886. Tuesday, 23 March 1886

It was unanimously Resolved.

1. THAT we, the bishops, clergy, and laity of the Church of Ireland, assembled in this General Synod from all parts of Ireland, and representing more than 600,000 of the Irish people, consider it a duty at the present crisis to affirm our constant allegiance to the Throne, and our unswerving attachment to the legislative union now subsisting between Great Britain and Ireland. And we make this declaration not as adherents of a party, or on behalf of a class, but as a body of Irishmen holding various political opinions, following different callings, representing many separate interests, and sharing, at the same time, a common desire for the honour and welfare of our native land.

2. That we contemplate with dismay the social disorder, intimidation, and violence which prevail in many parts of Ireland, due to an agitation the promoters of which would, it is evident, have paramount influence in a separate Irish Parliament. We, therefore, protest, in common with large numbers of our fellow-

countrymen who do not belong to our Church, against the establishment of such a Parliament in this land. We are convinced that so revolutionary a change would only aggravate the peril to civil and religious liberty, and the insecurity of property and life which now exist. Nor could any guarantees against such dangers be enforced by the Imperial Government in opposition to the will of an Irish Parliament without a recourse to arms.

3. That we hereby record our devotion to the interests of the great Empire of which this United Kingdom is the centre, a devotion intensified by our attachment to the country of our birth. We recognise the advantage and honour we derive from our present Imperial position, and the conspicuous place which Irishmen have long held among those to whom the Empire owes its prosperity and its fame. We, therefore, protest in the interests both of our country and of the Empire, against any measure that could endanger the legislative union between Great Britain and Ireland, believing that such a step would tend to the complete separation of these countries, and to the consequent dismemberment and humiliation of the Empire as a whole.

4. That believing, for the reasons already stated, that the policy against which we have protested would be injurious to the best interests, social, moral, and religious, of our country, we consider ourselves further bound to resist it as tending to impoverish, if not to expatriate, many of those on whose support the maintenance of our Church, under God, depends, and thereby to disable her in the efforts which she is making to supply the spiritual needs of her people.

> (signed) *Morgan Woodward Joliff*, M. A., LL. D,
> *Henry Alexander Hamilton*, J. P.
> Honorary Secretaries to the General Synod
> of the Church of Ireland.

39–41. Orange Ireland and Home Rule

Home Rule legislation produced an Orange response in Ulster that was as militant as anything conceived within Fenian circles. The following three texts explore the world of Orangeism. Reverend Ellis' reflections (no. 39) on the relationship between the Orange Society and the Conservative Party were undertaken when there was a growing expectation that William Gladstone was prepared to push Home Rule through Parliament. It was written on the eve of the 1885 parliamentary election in North Armagh and indirectly explained the rationale for the Orange Order's support of Major Edward Saunderson (1837–1906), who represented the district from the time of this election until his death and who was a driving force in creating the Ulster Unionist Party. Ellis also conveyed the spirit of Ulster loyalism, its contention that Britishness and Protestantism represented truth and freedom, and that Irishness was tantamount to tyranny and treason. The ultimate logic of this position is found in an 1886 newspaper article published in The Belfast News-Letter *(no. 40). A Home Rule parliament was viewed as an*

*assault on freedom and an attempt to end Protestantism in Ireland. An armed struggle
was seen as necessary if Home Rule were to come to pass. Paradoxically, loyalists swore
their allegiance to the British state, while planning a violent assault against it.*

*Unionism in Ulster was not homogenous, as is clearly seen from the critique of the
Orange Order by Hugh de Fellenberg Montgomery (1844–1924) (no. 41), a landowner
who belonged to the Church of Ireland and at this juncture was a Liberal Unionist.
Montgomery believed that extremists on both sides of the religious divide were driving
Irish politics. He advocated a centrist and moderate position based on support of the
Union.*

39. Reverend T. Ellis, Selections from *The Action of the Grand Orange Lodge of the County of Armagh (And the Reasons Thereof)* (1885)

. . . I never have approved of Orangemen joining the Conservative Association of this
county, for the simple reason that . . . they are already organized under the most perfect system that exists in Ireland; . . . Months before any candidate's name had been
mentioned for either North or Mid-Armagh, the County Grand Lodge declared as
its opinion, that since North Armagh was the most Orange District in Ireland, and
since it had been the cradle of Orangeism, every effort should be made to return, for
that District, a man who was not ashamed to wear the Orange Colours across his
heart, and who, from love of the order and from knowledge of its principles, could
defend the organization against all attacks in the House of Commons; and therefore
it unanimously passed a resolution that it could not, and would not, give its support
to any Candidate for North Armagh who was not an Orangeman. . . .

I cannot conclude these observations better than by quoting the words of one (the
late lamented STEWART BLACKER) whose memory will ever be immortal in the
neighbourhood of Portadown.

"The advantage of the Orange Society is, that on its platform all shades of evangelical Protestantism can meet with fraternal regard and joint reciprocity. It has also
shown itself the only lasting method of action; all the various attempts which exigencies from time to time have called forth, have soon faded away, but the Orange
organization is ever fresh and vigorous, and in spite of the slurs and calumnies cast
against it by foes and pretended friends, it is ever ready and willing to uphold the
cause of truth and loyalty.

Now that the Body is fully united, and that we know the value of our strength and
position, such a continued action must be taken, as will in future ensure our friends
and upholders being respected. The press, the pulpit, and the platform, must be
made to give us fair play, or we, abhorring all shams, no matter with what plausible
titles adorned, of Conservatives or Constitutionalists, will know the reason why. Let
us stand by our colours 'The Orange and the Blue,' with the good old Union Jack,
and let us drive Popery and Radicalism before us, as we have done many a time before, and hope to do many a time again.

Ulster Unionist poster proclaiming Ulster's willingness to fight for its connection to Britain.

'For happy homes, for altars free, we draw the ready sword;
For freedom, truth, and for our God's unmutilated Word;
These, these, the war-cry of our march; our hope the Lord on high;
Then put your trust in God my boys, and keep your powder dry.'"

40. "The Orangemen and Home Rule," *The Belfast News-Letter,* Saturday, May 15, 1886

NEWRY, FRIDAY NIGHT.—The Orangemen and Loyalists of all Protestant persuasions of this district, believing that if Mr. Gladstone's bill for the disruption of the empire passes the second reading and becomes the law of the land, they would be eventually deprived of their political and religious liberties, have determined to throw in their lot with their loyal brethren of the North, and prepare to meet the worst. At all the lodge meetings held last week and this week, the names of all those willing to bear arms were taken, and every member present, without exception, gave his name. Arrangements were also made to drill the volunteers, and a large number of men who have already served in the army and in the navy have offered their services. At a meeting held last night, the arming of the brethren was discussed. The feeling in this district is daily growing more intense. People are now discussing civil war, as if they looked upon it as sure to come. In view of it many old people, and ladies who reside alone, are making the necessary arrangements to go to England and Scotland, and several who have young children are about to sell out and remove to their friends in the colonies, while stalwart young men, who have only their own lives to lose, are anxious for the time when they shall have an opportunity of having a "brush" with the rebels. "Let the Queen withdraw her troops," exclaimed one the other day, "and the men of the North will sweep every rebel off the land, from the Giant's Causeway to the Cove of Cork,[69] in three days." This is the spirit that animates the Loyalists. It is stated here that the Government intend within a very short time to make a search for small arms in every town and district in Ulster, and in view of such a contingency it is said that many of the Nationalists are very uneasy, as it is well known that a large number of them possess revolvers and other arms.

A special meeting of the Orangemen of the Mourne district was held in Bally-martin[70] Orange Hall to-day, for the purpose of taking into consideration what steps they should take should Mr. Gladstone's Home Rule Bill become law. There was a very large attendance of the brethren from every portion of the district. After a good deal of consideration, the following resolution, among others, was adopted:—"That we hereby reaffirm our love and loyalty to our Most Gracious Sovereign Lady Queen Victoria, and unswerving attachment to the Constitution of Great Britain and Ire-land." Other resolutions proclaimed that the body would resist the enforcement of laws enacted by a Parnellite[71] Government. . . .

At a meeting of the members of the Royal Arch-purple Lodge of Orangemen held in the Orange Hall, Newry, last night, the following resolution, relative to the present crisis, was also passed unanimously:—"That we, the members of the Royal Arch-purple Lodge of Newry, in meeting assembled, do hereby enter our loyal, solemn, and earnest protest against the Home Rule Bill at present before Parliament, as we are convinced that this measure would sever the union at present existing, would materi-ally ruin Ireland, bring disgrace upon our country, and ultimately end in the extinc-tion of our Protestant religion, as well as produce civil war. And we assert, moreover, that we are prepared to defend our rights if necessary in another way."

At the close of the meeting every member present handed in his name as willing to be placed on the list of those who were prepared to follow their leaders. . . .

69. From east to west.

70. A village in County Down, Ulster.

71. A reference to the Home Rule politics of Charles Stewart Parnell and his followers.

41. H. de F. Montgomery, Memorandum Criticizing the Orange Order for Its Harmful and Divisive Effect on Irish Protestantism and Society (c. 1873)

It is impossible that a country can be truly free and prosperous unless its inhabitants live and work together as one people and cease to be divided into two tribes by barriers of race or creed. There are two influences at work to keep Irishmen so divided, the one popish bigotry represented by the ultramontane priesthood and the other protestant bigotry as represented by the Orange Institution. It is the interest of the Romish Church to keep her followers as much as possible a people apart as the intellectual contact with protestants in this age of enlightenment would tend to shake their allegiance and destroy the power and influence of that church—this was most clearly illustrated in the opposition they offered this spring to Mr. Gladstone's University bill[72] otherwise so favourably constituted for them. It should manifestly be the policy of protestants, patriots and foes of priestcraft to encourage as much as possible free and equal intercourse between their fellow countrymen of different persuasions and obliterate in all matters unconnected with special religious dogmas and forms of worship all the lines of demarcation between them. In the matter of primary education most protestants appear to perceive this and support the national system of mixed education. The priesthood perceive it too and are now opposing that system. But those protestants who uphold Orangeism appear not to perceive that the very existence of their institution and still more the days they choose for their public, conspicuous and noisy (by which I do not mean disorderly, but refer only to the drumming) gatherings perpetuate the most rigid and bitter line of demarcation possible by recalling the time when the different races and creeds who inhabited and still inhabit Ireland fought against each other in a fierce and bloody civil war. What can be better calculated to keep the descendants of the vanquished party—forming a large numerical majority of the inhabitants of the country—disloyal and disinclined to change or modify their religious and political opinions than to keep them constantly reminded of their defeat and with it of the oppression they subsequently endured and which they are told about in heightened colours by those whose interest it is that they should be more loyal to Rome than to Britain and Ireland's true interests—I maintain then that Orangeism and especially the July celebrations play directly into the hands of the most dangerous and bigoted portion of the priesthood and they are opposed to the true interests of protestantism and patriotism.

In every civilized country heathen or Christian it has been the rule—a rule dictated as much by policy as by Christianity and indeed the simplest morality—not to celebrate the triumphs of civil war. And in no country does the application of this rule seem more called for than in Ireland—for in many countries civil wars have

---

72. William Gladstone's Irish University Bill (1873) sought to create a new University of Dublin, which included the Anglican Trinity College, a Catholic university, and the secular Queen's College. Its goal was to draw students from all religious backgrounds, while excluding controversial subjects, notably religion, philosophy, or modern history. The bill was attacked by several interests, including the Catholic hierarchy, and was defeated by three votes.

been waged between different portions of the same state—the belligerents have been locally divided—as in America, Switzerland and Germany so that local celebrations of victory might be held without immediate offence to the vanquished—but here there is hardly a townland where men of different creeds—descendants of the victors and the vanquished are not found living side by side and yet in Ireland alone are the events of past civil wars publicly commemorated. . . .

Having spoken thus strongly against the principles and practice of Orangemen in general I wish to express as strongly my respect and regard for the large majority of Orangemen as individuals, a more trustworthy well intentioned and gallant body of men are I believe not often to be met with and little or no blame can attach to them individually for observing practises [sic] which they have been brought up to consider not only blameless but meritorious. This is a time of rapid enlightenment and growth and change in public opinion and I confidently hope to live to see the time when the heartiness and energy of this fine race may be turned into channels more calculated to benefit our country. True, noblemen, gentry and clergy have to some number lately joined the institution whose education according to my account ought to have taught them better but I believe that of these some have joined because they were brought up to it and have given as little thought to the matter as the most ignorant farmer, some from the desire of exercising power and influence over so fine a body of men (these forget that the ambition of power and influence is only justifiable when it is desired for the sake of doing good to one's country and mankind), some with the honest belief that by gaining power and influence over Orangemen they could direct their energies into better courses than they would take if left to themselves; these do not consider that they may be doing more harm by the means by which they acquire power and influence than they will be able to do good with this power and influence when acquired and that in these democratic days it is at least as likely that the stream will carry them off their legs as that they will direct the stream. Others again join and encourage Orangeism because they think that by keeping the protestant minority apart from the bulk of their fellow countrymen and giving them their support and countenance and fostering their dread of their Catholic fellow countrymen they will procure support for their class privileges which are threatened by the advance of representative institutions. These men are short sighted themselves—they can only postpone the change for a short time and make it more violent and worse for themselves when it comes—and they seek to degrade protestantism by making it a bulwark of political stagnation and obstructiveness instead of what it naturally is—or should be—a religion of progress, and they enable the Roman clergy to represent themselves as apostles of freedom, and protestantism as a tyrannous and slavish system.

Others less selfish but equally mistaken believe Orangeism to be a bulwark against the agitation for repeal or Home Rule. The more loudly Orange meetings when celebrating extinct civil war and obsolete party spirit pronounce against Home Rule the more inclined will the majority of Irishmen who are taught by the keeping up of these anniversaries to regard themselves as the hereditary enemies of protestantism, be inclined to fall into the arms of the agitators, and even if the minority proves strong enough to hold its own the country must remain in an unsatisfactory and disaffected condition as long as it is ruled in a manner different from what the majority desire.

Let those who oppose Home Rule borrow some wisdom and prudence from the Home Rulers themselves and try to obliterate religious barriers, and a strong party of adherents of all creeds, who have a stake in the country and are growing in prosperity under the present system and know not how it might be under Home Rule, could be formed in defence of the union.

To sum up these observations. While I like and honour the great majority of Orangemen I cannot approve or countenance the institution and celebrations because I consider them opposed to the true interests of Ireland, of protestantism and of civil and religious liberty and to the principles of Christianity, morality, good taste and good policy inasmuch as they tend to divide Irishmen into hostile sects, play into the hands of the bigoted ultramontane party and the Home Rule agitators, violate the golden rule and postpone the development of Ireland's prosperity and freedom civil and religious.

CHAPTER FOUR

IRELAND IN THE NEW CENTURY

By some measures Irish parliamentary nationalism had been a success. Home Rule was successfully passed by the House of Commons in 1912 and set to become law in 1914. Thoroughgoing land reform had also taken place, a result of legislation enacted by both Liberal and Conservative governments. The Wyndham Land Act (1903), passed by the Conservatives, vastly expanded voluntary land purchase and led to a sweeping transfer of land ownership from landlord to tenant. Yet *Ireland in the New Century*, to borrow the title of Horace Plunkett's influential book (no. 43), was in turmoil, and parliamentary nationalism was threatened by an array of forces. Indeed, by 1918 the Irish Parliamentary Party had fallen victim to these forces, and more radical political alternatives prevailed. The readings in this chapter focus on this shifting politics, charting them in the context of major events that shaped twentieth-century Ireland: World War I (1914–18), the Easter Rising (1916), the Anglo-Irish War (1919–21), and the Anglo-Irish Treaty (1921). The 1921 treaty resulted in the partition of Ireland into the Irish Free State and Northern Ireland. The former had dominion status analogous to Canada, while the latter remained in the Union. Northern Ireland had its own parliament and sent representatives to the British Parliament in London. The two Irelands that emerged in the 1920s solved one series of problems, while creating a whole new set.

As a result of the first Home Rule Bill (1886), the British Liberal Party split in two; but the alliance between nationalists and Gladstonian Liberals remained intact. It survived Charles Stewart Parnell's implication in the divorce case involving Katharine and Captain O'Shea in 1889–90. The revelations regarding their long-standing relationship and the scandal that followed divided the Irish Parliamentary Party and led to the downfall and perhaps even played a role in the death of Parnell in 1891. Gladstone had withdrawn his support for Parnell, but he successfully shepherded a second Home Rule Bill through the House of Commons in 1893. The Conservative-dominated House of Lords voted it down, and in 1895 the Liberals were out of power until 1906. When Home Rule was successfully passed in 1912, it was because a rejuvenated British Liberal Party led an assault on the unreformed House of Lords—most importantly its right to veto legislation. Curtailing the power of the Lords could not have taken place without Irish nationalist support. In exchange for those votes, the Liberal government passed a Home Rule Bill in 1912, set to become law in September 1914. Owing to the new constitutional arrangements of the Parliament Act (1912), the Lords could only delay the bill from becoming law for two years.

The process that produced the third Home Rule Bill galvanized Unionist opposition, but it also revealed cracks in its facade. With the decline of landlordism, the increasing prominence of the middle class in politics, and the ongoing process of democratization in the UK, there was a shift in the center of Unionist politics from south to north. Northern Unionists adamantly resisted Home Rule, building on the militancy that had already surfaced in the 1880s (see Chapter 3). Here, the key event was the establishment of the Ulster Unionist Council in 1905, which became a focal point of Unionist resistance to Home Rule. Its leader was Edward Carson, a southern Protestant and Dublin attorney, already known as the prosecutor of the Irish writer and playwright Oscar Wilde, who was convicted for being a homosexual in a famous 1895 trial. Ulster Unionists, mirroring the more militant Irish nationalists who were simultaneously emerging, used the threat of force to dissuade the Liberal government from passing—and then implementing—Home Rule. The group's "Solemn League and Covenant" (no. 44), echoing the Scottish Covenanters of 1643, was signed by 218,000 loyalists committed to using "all means which may be found necessary to defeat the present conspiracy to set up a Home Rule Parliament in Ireland." A second "Declaration" (no. 45) signed by women, simultaneously suggested both women's importance and their secondary status in northern Unionist politics.

With Home Rule set to become law in 1914, northern Unionists intensified their opposition. In 1912 they created the Ulster Volunteers, a paramilitary group that would resist a Dublin parliament if it should be implemented. It became increasingly clear that the Ulster Unionist leadership was willing to jettison Unionism for all of Ireland—and southern Unionists with it—if Ulster was offered exclusion from the new legislation. John Redmond, the leader of the Irish Parliamentary Party, agreed to a six-year delay for Ulster, but northern Unionists refused it. Ironically, the cultural nationalist, republican militant, and future leader of the Easter Rising, Pádraic Pearse, despite detesting Unionism, proclaimed his respect for the militant stance of the Ulster Volunteers (no. 46). They undermined parliamentary politics and provided a model for militant nationalists to emulate. To counter Ulster militancy, nationalists, with IRB support, founded the Irish Volunteers in 1913. The group encompassed a wide spectrum of nationalist opinion, had nearly two hundred thousand supporters by August 1914, and came to be controlled by Redmond. The group split over Redmond's support of World War I. A contingent of the breakaway group eventually was recruited for the Easter Rising of 1916.

Perhaps the most important challenge to the dominance of the Irish Parliamentary Party within Irish nationalism was Sinn Féin, "We Ourselves." Its leading light was Arthur Griffith, who found his inspiration in the inclusive vision of Thomas Davis, the Irish cultural nationalism of the Gaelic League, and Parnell's obstructionism. Griffith was not the first nationalist to argue that the Union was illegitimate. However, the logic of this position, in his view, was that Irish MPs should no longer participate in the British parliamentary process: they should return to Dublin and establish an alternative body to govern the country while maintaining a link with the Crown. Thus, Griffith did not reject the link with Britain outright, as republicans did. In contrast to Home Rulers, he asserted that legislative autonomy was a right to be claimed rather than a privilege to be granted. His model was the dual monarchy of Austria-Hungary.[1]

---

1. The Dual Monarchy, or Austria-Hungary, resulted from a union between the crowns of the Austrian Empire and the Kingdom of Hungary in 1867. The Austrian Habsburgs and a separate Hungarian government shared power based on a division of the Austrian Empire. The arrangement lasted until the end of World War I in 1918.

For Griffith, nationalism came before democracy. This perspective might help explain his opposition to the Irish Parliamentary Party's coalition with British Liberals, his support for an economic boycott against Jews in Limerick, and his admiration for Czarist Russia. Accordingly, a principal plank of Griffith's position was that Ireland should attain economic self-sufficiency. Although Horace Plunkett was a Unionist at this juncture, he also advocated economic independence (no. 43). He argued that Ireland must stop blaming Britain for its troubles and take responsibility for its own future, and he envisioned an economic renaissance grounded in cooperative agriculture.

Other currents of thought were also making their presence felt. Two of these were socialism and feminism. The Irish labor movement was small by British standards and, with the exception of Belfast, lacked a sizeable industrial working class. Yet by the early twentieth century there had been a growth of trade unionism and socialist organizations. Jim Larkin's (1876–1947) Irish Transport and General Workers, founded in 1908, was in the forefront of trade union militancy during these years. To protect workers at labor rallies, Larkin organized the Irish Citizen Army in 1913. James Connolly assumed its leadership when Larkin left for America in 1914, and the organization played a prominent role in the Easter Rising of 1916. Connolly was executed for his role in it. As a figure in Irish politics, he straddled physical-force republicanism, the cultural revival, and Marxism. In "Socialism and Nationalism" (no. 42), Connolly drew from these various strands, arguing that political self-determination and cultural revival did nothing to transform class relations, which were rooted in capitalist imperialism. For Connolly, the logical culmination of nationalism was socialism.

Feminists and supporters of women's right, no less than socialists, were influenced by developments in Britain and continental Europe: their politics developed in a sometimes friendly and sometimes antagonistic dialogue with Irish nationalism. Maud Gonne's Inghinidhe na hÉireann (Daughters of Ireland), founded in 1900, developed from the nationalist opposition to Queen Victoria's visit to Dublin that year. It provided a milieu within the radical nationalist movement for women but was not explicitly feminist. Cumann na mBan (the League of Women) was founded in 1914 to provide female support for the Irish Volunteers. It was criticized by some at the time for its subservience to men, although there were women in the group who were feminists and there were instances in which they challenged masculine norms. A married Quaker couple—Anna and Thomas Haslam[2]—pioneered the Irish women's suffrage movement. Thomas published the first women's suffrage paper in 1874, *The Women's Advocate*. In 1876, Anna was a founding member of the Dublin Women's Suffrage Association—later the Irish Women's Suffrage and Local Government Association in 1901. The Haslams rejected political violence and were Unionists, but they

2. Anna (Fisher) Haslam (1829–1922) and Thomas Haslam (1825–1917), a Quaker couple who were social reformers and pioneers in the suffrage movement. Anna was born into a family of seventeen children. Her parents were social reformers. Her husband Thomas Haslam was interested in the women's question prior to their marriage. In addition to participation in the suffrage movement, they actively campaigned for the reform of girls' education and legal rights for women. A seat in St. Stephen's Green, Dublin, commemorates Anna.

worked in conjunction with a diverse group of nationalists and suffrage supporters. Inspired by the 1903 founding of the British militant suffrage group the Women's Social and Political Union, two Irish couples—Hanna and Francis Sheehy-Skeffington[3] and Margaret and James Cousins[4]—established the Irish Women's Franchise League in 1908.

The Irish suffrage movement, in contrast to its British analogue, was divided over the proper relationship between striving for the vote for women and achieving nationalist goals such as Home Rule. While radicals such as James Connolly were enthusiastic supporters of women's suffrage, many in both the republican movement and the constitutional nationalist movement were either lukewarm or hostile. Hostility intensified when the suffrage movement was seen as interfering with achieving nationalist goals. As the exchange between Mary McSwiney and the editors of the suffragist publication *The Irish Citizen* (nos. 47 and 48) suggests, suffrage supporters were divided as well. Francis Sheehy-Skiffington and James Cousins, the journal's editors, boldly stated: "Suffrage first—before all else." Their nationalist critics replied: "Neither can there be free women in an enslaved nation" (quoted in Curtis 1989, 168).

Ireland, then on the eve of World War I, was plagued by growing polarization between Unionists and nationalists as well as divisions within each of these movements. Volunteers on both sides were arming and training themselves with weapons smuggled from abroad. In what is known as the Curragh Mutiny, a group of British army officers threatened to resign rather than impose Home Rule on Ulster. The Conservative Party leader, Andrew Bonar Law,[5] extending the views once voiced by Randolph

3. Hanna Sheehy (1877–1946) and Francis Skeffington (1878–1916), women's rights activists, nationalists, and supporters of the labor movement. They married in 1903 and combined their names so that their last name became Sheehy-Skeffington. Hanna was among the first women to benefit from educational reforms, receiving an MA from the Royal University of Ireland in 1902. A participant in the militant suffrage movement, she was imprisoned for breaking windows and engaged in a weeklong hunger strike protesting the treatment of two English women suffragettes. Francis was a graduate of University College, Dublin, and as a student was a friend of James Joyce. He was cofounder and coeditor of the suffragist newspaper *The Irish Citizen*. During the Easter Rising, Francis remained true to his pacifist principles and sought to maintain law and order by organizing a citizen's militia to stop the looting of shops. His murder by British troops for no apparent reason caused international outrage.

4. James (1873–1956) and Margaret (Gillespie) Cousins (1878–1954), social reformers and activists in the Irish suffrage movement. They married in 1903. James was a teacher, poet, and writer. Margaret was a founder of the Irish Women's Franchise League in 1908. She attended the Parliament of Women in London in 1910 and was imprisoned in Tullamore Gaol (Jail) for breaking windows in Dublin Castle. She later served prison time for throwing stones at 10 Downing St., London (the British prime minister's residence). In 1915 the Cousins left for India. James became the editor of Annie Besant's *New India*. Margaret founded a girls' school, campaigned for women's rights, and in 1921 was appointed the first female honorary bench magistrate in India.

5. Andrew Bonar Law (1858–1923), Conservative Party leader and prime minister (1922–23). He was described upon his death as the "unknown prime minister," owing to his modesty and melancholic disposition, and because during World War I and its immediate aftermath he seemed content to play second fiddle to the more charismatic David Lloyd George, the Liberal

Churchill, gave his total support to Ulster: "I can imagine no length of resistance to which Ulster will go . . . in which they will not be supported by the overwhelming majority of the British people" (quoted in Lyons 1989, 133). The atmosphere was further poisoned when British soldiers overreacted to a hostile crowd on July 26, 1914, which had gathered following the soldiers' largely unsuccessful attempt to stop Irish Volunteers from gun smuggling and arms distribution. The confrontation in Bachelors Walk, Dublin left three people dead and thirty others wounded. The authorities had ignored similar smuggling efforts by the Ulster Volunteers. It was at this juncture that the British government entered World War I on the side of France and Russia in August 1914, a month before Home Rule was to become law. From the point of view of British policy makers, Home Rule instantly became a marginal priority. Prime Minister Herbert Asquith (1852–1928) allowed Home Rule to enter the statute books but then suspended its implementation until the war's end. He had attempted to satisfy nationalist opinion by making it law and Unionist opinion by suspending it. Of course, he satisfied neither.

For Unionists, support of the war was a given. At a minimum it was an opportunity to demonstrate their loyalty to the UK and solidify their position within it. Accordingly, they enthusiastically entered the government when Asquith established a coalition in 1915. Carson was appointed attorney general. For nationalists, it was more complicated. Support for the war by Irish people outside of Ulster seems to have been qualified: they supported it as long as it did not affect them, but as the war dragged on, and it increasingly impinged on their lives, they became restive and resentful. Still, two hundred thousand Irishmen enlisted in the British army, and casualties were in the range of thirty thousand, a fact often ignored or explained away by nationalists. To what extent was Connolly's contention that the motivation of Dublin enlistees was purely monetary an exercise in rationalization?

A further wedge between Ulster and the rest of Ireland resulted from heavy casualties endured by the 36th (Ulster) Division at the Battle of the Somme (1916). Northern loss of life in the name of king and country stood in stark contrast to militant nationalists in the south negotiating with the German government for the purpose of launching a rebellion. Among moderate nationalists, Redmond supported the war effort on the grounds that Britain was fighting for the rights of small nations. He championed a role for Ireland that prefigured Home Rule and would prove to Unionists that the proposed constitutional change was compatible with imperial obligation. Ireland, he argued, should have its own army unit, and securing the homeland should be the Irish Volunteer's responsibility. The British government accepted neither of these ideas. When Asquith asked Redmond to join the coalition government, Redmond felt that he could not do so until Home Rule was implemented. At least in the early stage of the war, Redmond hung on to his support. Of the 170,000 Volunteers only 17,000 left in protest over Redmond's policies.

---

leader of the wartime coalition. Law was the first Conservative leader to be middle class and unapologetically provincial, but his staunch support of Ulster Unionism was a throwback to an older Victorian Tory cast of mind.

Militant republicans opposed the war and saw it as an opportunity to break free of Britain, but they were divided on the timing of a confrontation. In effect, a political power struggle was going on inside the breakaway Irish Volunteers. For Bulmer Hobson[6] of the IRB and Eoin MacNeill, leader of the National Volunteers, an uprising should come in response to a British miscue in Ireland. Such a miscue was held to be inevitable, would be wildly unpopular, and would form the popular basis of an uprising. A small minority dominant in the IRB Military Council, later joined by Connolly, believed in making a gesture regardless of the timing or the cost. They plotted a rising that was hidden from the Volunteer leadership. The extent to which they imagined the rebellion, in Pearse's terms, as a "blood sacrifice" is unclear, but military triumph does not seem to have been their main concern. The leadership enlisted the Irish-born British diplomat Sir Roger Casement,[7] who in the tradition of Wolfe Tone, went to Germany and entered into negotiations with the German government to procure weapons. By the time that the Easter Rising was launched on Monday, April 24, 1916, the organizers probably knew that it would end in failure. The British navy had intercepted the German ship, the *Aud*, which brought twenty thousand captured Russian weapons; the captain scuttled the ship, and Casement was arrested. When MacNeill discovered that an uprising was scheduled to take place, he seemed to accept it. When he discovered that the insurgency was going to go on even without weapons from Germany, he called off the Volunteers' "special action." The organizers of the Rising were undaunted. MacNeill's last-minute efforts mostly limited the Rising to Dublin.

The Rising was launched by about 1,300 Irish Volunteers and 219 militants from Connolly's Citizen Army. The militants occupied five groups of buildings. As president, Pearse read the "Proclamation of the Irish Republic" (no. 50) on the steps of the General Post Office. The first sentence read: "In the name of God and of the dead generations from which she receives her old tradition of nationhood, Ireland,

6. Bulmer Hobson (1883–1969), leading participant in the Irish Volunteers and the IRB prior to the Easter Rising. He was from a Quaker background. His father was born in Ireland, and his mother was born in England. He joined the IRB in 1904 and was elevated to the Supreme Council in 1911. He was a founder of the Irish Volunteers in 1913 and provided a link between that group and the IRB. When John Redmond moved to take control of the Irish Volunteers, Hobson acquiesced, believing that defying the popular Redmond would lead to the fragmentation of the organization. This led to his resignation from the Supreme Council.

7. Sir Roger Casement (1864–1916), Irish born, British diplomat, and Irish nationalist. Casement joined the British colonial service in 1892 and was known throughout the world for his humanitarianism, particularly his exposure of the oppression of African and South American laborers by European capitalists and imperialists. Knighted in 1911, he retired from the service in 1913 and became active on behalf of Irish nationalism. He was instrumental in procuring German military support for an uprising, but he was disappointed by the German government's level of support and returned to Ireland on the eve of the planned uprising with the aim of stopping it. British authorities arrested him upon his arrival. He was tried, convicted of treason, and subsequently executed. A particularly sordid dimension of his trial was the government's attempt to undermine his character by distribution of his private diaries documenting homosexual activity.

through us, summons her children to her flag and strikes for her freedom." With just thirty-three words, Pearse evoked nationalism, divine sanction, historical continuity, and elitism (Townshend 1999, 76). Those who lived through the Rising experienced it variously: from Constance Markievicz (no. 52), a leader in the Irish Citizen Army, who celebrated the heroic contribution of women to the nationalist cause; to the writer James Stephens (no. 51), whose feelings of confusion as to what was going on probably represented the view of numerous Dubliners. In all, the Rising lasted until Saturday, a mere six days. It left in its wake 450 dead, including 116 soldiers, and 2,600 injured. It was by several accounts unpopular and alienated Dublin middle-class opinion. Historians have described scenes of angry Dublin crowds hurling abuse at the leaders when they were being led out of the post office.[8] That would soon change.

The British authorities unwittingly (but predictably) turned the leaders into patriotic heroes and the Rising into a transformative event. Fighting in a war in which Britain's national existence was seen as being at stake, the British government was initially unprepared, despite knowledge of the conspiracy. Subsequently, it overreacted. Oblivious to the political consequences in Ireland, the British government (and British public opinion) found it impossible to see the Easter Rising (which, it will be recalled, had German support) as anything but treasonous. Executions of fifteen of the leaders along with Sir Roger Casement, and imprisonment of 3,500 militants (although most just briefly), helped transform public opinion in Ireland. W. B. Yeats' poem "Easter, 1916" (no. 53), which despite the poet's ambivalence about the Rising transformed Pearse and company from flesh-and-blood individuals into nationalist heroes, both registered and shaped this shift in perception. George Russell, also known as Æ, sought to immortalize those executed (no. 54), but in an important gesture of national unity grouped them with the fallen Irish soldiers of World War I, who were, in his view, no less heroic and patriotic.

Having inflamed Irish public opinion, the British coalition government sought to balance its actions by rekindling Home Rule. It held an Irish Convention between nationalists and Unionists in 1917–18 but was unable to break the stalemate between the two sides. One genuine casualty of the events following the Easter Rising was the Irish Parliamentary Party, whose support of the war had borne no fruit and which was unable to resist British government plans (ultimately not carried through) to initiate conscription in Ireland in 1918. Conscription had already been implemented in the rest of the UK two years earlier. The undoubted winner during these turbulent years was Sinn Féin. It was originally wrongly blamed for the Rising. It moved to endorse it, opened a dialogue with its surviving leaders (notably Éamon de Valera) and emerging new ones in the Volunteers (Michael Collins, for example), and claimed the political space that the Irish Parliamentary Party had controlled but saw crumbling before its very eyes.

Sinn Féin's displacement of the old party was spectacularly displayed in the first parliamentary election following the end of the war in 1918. Sinn Féin went from having seven to having seventy-three seats. The Irish Parliamentary Party's sixty-eight

---

8. A notable exception is Joseph Lee (1989, 34–35) who takes a more complex view of popular and press sentiment in the aftermath of the Rising.

seats disintegrated into a mere six. In accordance with Griffith's original plan, Sinn Féin MPs refused to take their seats, establishing the parliament of the Irish Republic, Dáil Éireann, better known as the Dáil. De Valera, who combined unbending principles, personal charisma, and political tenacity—and was widely admired for his leadership role in the Rising—was elected president. Given that de Valera was also elected as the head of the Volunteers, the political and military wings of nationalism were brought together. Sinn Féin and the IRB had different origins and different political perspectives, and there was a diversity of opinion within each group. Such differences were temporarily papered over but would resurface in the aftermath of the Anglo-Irish Treaty negotiations.

As a group, the Dáil was dominated by Catholic middle-class, urban professionals—journalists, clerks, and lawyers—steeped in the Gaelic revival. Father Michael O'Flanagan,[9] vice president of Sinn Féin, read a prayer in Irish to inaugurate its opening session. The Dáil never declared war per se, but it passed a resolution declaring that a state of war existed between Ireland and England until the latter "evacuated" its armed forces. The Dáil hoped that other countries would recognize its legitimacy, particularly the United States, whose president, Woodrow Wilson,[10] had advocated that national self-determination be a principle of the postwar settlement. The Dáil sent representatives to the 1919 Paris peace conference to make its case on the world stage, but the Dáil's quest to achieve international recognition never made it onto the agenda. Perhaps the Dáil's greatest achievement was its assertion of governmental authority, circumventing the British controlled system through an array of local initiatives and the establishment of its own judicial system. Despite Irish nationalism's wish to break with the past, the system of parliamentary and cabinet government that it adopted bore a striking resemblance to the British one that it sought to dislodge.

The opening salvo in what became known as the Anglo-Irish War was the murder of two policemen on January 21, 1919, by a group of Volunteers (now being called the Irish Republican Army or the IRA) in County Tipperary. The Dáil did not embrace this turn of events and subsequent acts of violence until April. These acts of violence were obviously aimed at British rule, but they may well have likewise been intended at forcing Sinn Féin politicians, many of whom were formed outside of the republican tradition, to embrace a military campaign. It was during this stage that Michael Collins, minister of finance, came to the forefront. His rise in stature was possible in part because of de Valera's decision to go to the United States to raise money in June 1919, a trip that was supposed to be short but lasted until December

9. Friar Michael O'Flanagan (1876–1942), nationalist priest. Although he was elected vice president of Sinn Féin, he found himself at odds with the leadership of the Dáil, who were committed to settling the Anglo-Irish conflict by violence. His efforts to initiate peace talks with the British government in 1920 were repudiated by the Sinn Féin leadership.

10. Thomas Woodrow Wilson (1856–1924), the twenty-eighth president of the United States. Following the United States' entry into World War I, Wilson produced an influential vision of the postwar era known as the Fourteen Points, which he believed should shape the negotiations between the victorious Allied powers. He saw national self-determination and the League of Nations as ensuring that such a war would never be repeated.

1920. Collins was imaginative, versatile, pragmatic, charismatic, and ruthless. As finance minister he presided over a successful bond campaign that netted £317,848. He is best known for leading the IRA campaign: a guerrilla war whose maximization of its paltry resources, organization into small, independent fighting units adept at quick mobility known as *flying columns*, and successful penetration of security forces produced tangible successes.

The British government, after recovering from the shock of a breakaway parliament, responded with characteristic carrot-and-stick policies. On the one hand, it passed the Government of Ireland Act (1920), creating two Home Rule parliaments, linked by a Council of Ireland, a body that at the time was a political pipedream but eventually (in a different form) found its way into the Good Friday Agreement of 1998. By the time of the Government of Ireland Act, Home Rule was a dead issue for nationalists. In one of the supreme ironies of the conflict, the Ulster Unionists, so ardently opposed to Home Rule, ended up as its chief beneficiary. The Northern Ireland Assembly first met on June 22, 1921. It was dominated, as expected, by the Ulster Unionist Party, which won forty out of fifty-two seats.

On the other hand, the British government met the IRA attacks with ruthlessness equal to its opponents. This stance further isolated it from the Irish population and alienated British liberal and even world opinion. From a military perspective, the government's campaign ended up putting real pressure on the IRA by the time of the treaty negotiations. When it became clear that the regular police, under siege by IRA attacks, were unable to handle the situation on their own, the British side established the Black and Tans and the Auxiliaries. The Black and Tans were non-Irish, often unemployed ex-servicemen, with frequently questionable qualifications and professionalism. The Auxiliaries were an elite group of ex-officers responsible for the counterterrorist operation. Both groups engaged in a campaign of reprisals disastrous for the British government's image.

A few events have often been cited as emblematic of the terrorist and counterterrorist war into which Ireland had been plunged. On November 21, 1920, known as Bloody Sunday, the IRA killed fourteen suspected British intelligence agents. The Auxiliary response came at Croke Park Stadium in Dublin that afternoon, where a large crowd was watching the all-Ireland Gaelic football final between Tipperary and Dublin. An ill-conceived search operation ended up in the massacre of twelve people and the wounding of many more. The actions of the Auxiliaries were widely perceived as revenge for the earlier IRA attacks. A week later, on November 28, a flying column, under the command of Tom Barry[11] destroyed an Auxiliary patrol near Kilmichael, County Cork, shooting all the survivors.

By 1921, the Anglo-Irish War had become a stalemate. In the summer, the British prime minister, David Lloyd George, entered into correspondence with de Valera regarding the grounds of negotiations between the two sides. De Valera agreed that

---

11. Tom Barry (1897–1980), leader of the West Cork Flying Column and a prominent guerrilla leader during the Anglo-Irish War. Before he joined the IRA, he served in the British army during World War I. He subsequently opposed the Anglo-Irish Treaty and fought on the anti-treaty side in the Irish Civil War (1922–23).

the starting point would be "to ascertain how the association of Ireland with the community of nations known as the British Empire might be reconciled with Irish national aspirations" (quoted in Bew 2007, 418). He also accepted that any new Irish entity would never coerce Ulster into accepting a united Ireland. Thus, from the onset of the treaty negotiations, an independent, united Ireland does not seem to have been a real possibility.

The negotiations in London, which took place during the fall, have given rise to numerous controversies. First, de Valera's decision not to go to London, to have Collins go in his place, and to have Griffith lead the Irish negotiating team, have given rise to a long-standing debate regarding de Valera's motives. This debate has included the accusation by his detractors that de Valera did not want to be blamed for the inevitable compromise with which the negotiators would return. Second, there have been disagreements over whether the negotiators had the authority to sign an agreement. Members of the negotiating team believed they had plenipotentiary powers, thus having the authority to sign on their own. De Valera disagreed. Third, the negotiators agreed to the treaty following Lloyd George's purported take-it-or-leave-it offer on December 5. His ultimatum was accompanied by the threat to renew the war if the Irish side did not agree to sign. Given British war exhaustion and Lloyd George's crumbling support among the British electorate, was the threat real? Collins insisted that Lloyd George never made a "threat of immediate and terrible war" (quoted in Bew 2007, 421), so perhaps the Irish negotiators simply believed that this was the best deal they were likely to get. But Collins also believed that the IRA lacked the resources to continue the war. In the end, the negotiators achieved dominion status for Ireland, but at the cost of a loyalty oath to the Crown and putting off the status of Northern Ireland to a later time. They never imagined that an independent six-county entity was anything but temporary.

The Anglo-Irish Treaty (no. 55) signed by Collins, Griffith, and the Irish team of negotiators was approved in the Dáil by the narrow vote of sixty-four to fifty-seven. Popular opinion was more supportive of the treaty, if the subsequent June parliamentary elections are an accurate gauge. The pro-treaty forces won an overwhelming majority of the seats, 78 percent of the vote according to Alvin Jackson (1999, 264). Nonetheless, the signing and approval of the treaty produced a deeply divided and conflicted nationalist movement, ultimately leading to the Irish Civil War of 1922–23. Collins was well aware of the implications of what he had done when he put his name to the treaty, prophetically remarking that he had signed his death warrant. But he (as well as Griffith) ardently believed that Ireland had achieved the *substance* if not the *form* of independence, and that the treaty was a stepping-stone rather than the final act in the long struggle for national liberation. The opponents of the treaty found it hard to swallow that the heroic sacrifices of a generation had achieved something as mundane as dominion status and the retention of the humiliating oath to the British Crown. Indeed, it was the oath, more than any other part of the treaty, which became the focus of the opposition.

Reading the debates on the treaty (no. 56) nearly one hundred years later, it is possible to empathize with those such as Mary McSwiney or de Valera who believed that the treaty had not delivered enough, but, given the subsequent metamorphosis of the Irish Free State into Éire and then finally the independent Republic of Ireland, it is hard to dispute that Collins and Griffith had great foresight. Whatever we might think of the views of the protagonists in the treaty debate, the treaty transformed Irish politics. The roots of the Republic of Ireland's two major parties are not the left and the right as is usually the case in European politics. Their origins are traceable to their stance on the treaty. Fine Gael (Tribe of the Irish) developed out of the pro-treaty forces; and Fianna Fáil (Soldiers of Ireland), founded by de Valera, evolved out of the opposition.

What most of those who debated the treaty shared in common was that they underestimated what turned out to be the most enduring problem of the Anglo-Irish conflict—conflicts emanating from the creation of Northern Ireland. Most importantly, the treaty ended up marginalizing the rights and aspirations of the sizeable Catholic minority that now lived under what James Craig described, in 1934, as "a Protestant Parliament and a Protestant state" (quoted in Barden 2005, 538–39). Craig's remark is often remembered as "a Protestant Parliament for a Protestant state." The system that evolved in Northern Ireland fostered political and economic discrimination against Catholics. When Catholics sought to assert their rights in the civil rights movements of the late 1960s, the troubles erupted once again. Only now the focal point was in the north.

42. James Connolly, "Socialism and Nationalism," *Shan Van Vocht* (1897)

The Home Rule movement dominated mainstream Irish politics, but in the late nineteenth and early twentieth centuries, there were multiple voices vying to be heard, many of them championing ideas that went beyond the confines of parliamentary politics. One of them was James Connolly (1868–1916), a revolutionary activist, writer, and political theorist. He is best known for his role in the pre–World War I Irish radical left and for his participation and his martyrdom in the Easter Rising of 1916. But he is also important for his contributions to political theory. He is arguably the first thinker to fuse Marxism and nationalism, ideologies often thought to be at odds, and his critique of empire is still explored by contemporary critics, most recently by Robert Young (2001, 307) who locates Connolly's thought within the history of resistance to colonialism. Connolly's ideas ultimately had little influence on the shape of twentieth-century Ireland outside of the small communist, socialist, and republican left, but he remains a central figure in the pantheon of Irish nationalism.

Connolly's life was wide-ranging and varied, thus difficult to summarize. Briefly, he was from an Irish Catholic family, and he was born in Edinburgh, Scotland. He left school at eleven to work and later joined, and then deserted, the British army. He subsequently joined the Scottish Socialist League in 1889, helped establish the Irish Socialist Republican Party in 1896, and founded and edited its newspaper, the Workers' Republic. *Disillusioned with the slow growth of Irish socialism and needing to provide for a growing family, Connolly left for the United States in 1903, but he returned to Ireland in 1910 to lead the newly created Socialist Party of Ireland, which developed out of the ashes of the Irish Socialist Republican Party mentioned above. Connolly also acted as the Belfast organizer of the Irish Transport and General Workers' Union (ITGWU) and with the union leader James Larkin founded the Labour Party (of Ireland), whose roots were in the Irish Trade Union Congress. When Larkin left for America, Connolly became the acting secretary of the ITGWU. On the eve of the war, he assumed command of the Irish Citizen Army, one of the groups that participated in the Easter Rising.*

Connolly's ideas were founded on the Marxist contention that societies were rooted in the relations of production, that capitalism would collapse under the weight of its own internal contradictions, and that a revolutionary socialist movement provided leadership for proletarian triumph. But he likewise believed that the distinctive history of Ireland, in which capitalist and imperial oppression were intertwined, called for a struggle on two fronts—nationalist and socialist. These ideas are most extensively developed in perhaps his most influential book, Labour in Irish History *(1910), but they also are found in the short essay "Socialism and Nationalism." Here Connolly argued not only that nationalist triumph without socialism would only bring about superficial change, but he also argued that if nationalists were really serious about restoring the Irish past, their vision of the future must be founded on Gaelic traditions of collective ownership. These traditions had been destroyed by the Anglo-Norman conquest of the twelfth century, paving the way for an unjust system of private property and capitalism.*

In Ireland at the present time there are at work a variety of agencies seeking to preserve the national sentiment in the hearts of the people.

These agencies, whether Irish Language movements, Literary Societies or Commemoration Committees,[12] are undoubtedly doing a work of lasting benefit to this country in helping to save from extinction the precious racial and national history, language and characteristics of our people.

Nevertheless, there is a danger that by too strict an adherence to their present methods of propaganda, and consequent neglect of vital living issues, they may only succeed in stereotyping our historical studies into a worship of the past, or crystallising nationalism into a tradition—glorious and heroic indeed, but still only a tradition.

Now traditions may, and frequently do, provide materials for a glorious martyrdom, but can never be strong enough to ride the storm of a successful revolution.

If the national movement of our day is not merely to re-enact the old sad tragedies of our past history, it must show itself capable of rising to the exigencies of the moment.

It must demonstrate to the people of Ireland that our nationalism is not merely a morbid idealising of the past, but is also capable of formulating a distinct and definite answer to the problems of the present and a political and economic creed capable of adjustment of the wants of the future.

This concrete political and social ideal will best be supplied, I believe, by the frank acceptance on the part of all earnest nationalists of the Republic as their goal.

Not a Republic, as in France, where a capitalist monarchy with an elective head

---

12. Nationalists put on public commemorations of events important to the nationalist cultural imaginary. In 1897, the year when this text was published, plans were in the works for a centenary celebration of the United Irishmen's 1798 uprising.

parodies the constitutional abortions of England,[13] and in open alliance with the Muscovite despotism brazenly flaunts its apostasy to the traditions of the Revolution.[14]

Not a Republic as in the United States, where the power of the purse has established a new tyranny under the forms of freedom; where, one hundred years after the feet of the last British red-coat polluted the streets of Boston, British landlords and financiers impose upon American citizens a servitude compared with which the tax of the pre-Revolution days was a mere trifle.

No! the Republic I would wish our fellow-countrymen to set before them as their ideal should be of such a character that the mere mention of its name would at all times serve as a beacon-light to the oppressed of every land, at all times holding forth promise of freedom and plenteousness as the reward of their efforts on its behalf.

To the tenant farmer, ground between landlordism on the one hand and American competition on the other, as between the upper and the nether millstone; to the wage-workers in the towns, suffering from the exactions of the slave-driving capitalist to the agricultural labourer, toiling away his life for a wage barely sufficient to keep body and soul together; in fact to every one of the toiling millions upon whose misery the outwardly-splendid fabric of our modern civilisation is reared, the Irish Republic might be made a word to conjure with—a rallying point for the disaffected, a haven for the oppressed, a point of departure for the Socialist, enthusiastic in the cause of human freedom.

This linking together of our national aspirations with the hopes of the men and women who have raised the standard of revolt against that system of capitalism and landlordism, of which the British Empire is the most aggressive type and resolute defender, should not, in any sense, import an element of discord into the ranks of earnest nationalists, and would serve to place us in touch with fresh reservoirs of moral and physical strength sufficient to lift the cause of Ireland to a more commanding position than it has occupied since the day of Benburb.[15]

It may be pleaded that the ideal of a Socialist Republic, implying, as it does, a complete political and economic revolution would be sure to alienate all our middle-class and aristocratic supporters, who would dread the loss of their property and privileges.

What does this objection mean? That we must conciliate the privileged classes in Ireland!

But you can only disarm their hostility by assuring them that in a free Ireland their

13. The French Third Republic, founded in 1870, had a parliament consisting of two chambers. Its government, led by a prime minister, was constitutionally answerable to an elected president.

14. To counter the Triple Alliance—the Habsburg Empire, Italy, and Germany—France allied itself with Czarist Russia in 1894. Connolly describes the regime as a "Muscovite despotism," evoking its authoritarianism and equating the Czarist regime with its capital at Moscow. He views the French state's alliance with such a reactionary and oppressive government as a betrayal of French revolutionary principles.

15. The Battle of Benburb (1646) was a major Irish military victory. The forces of Owen Roe O'Neill triumphed over those of the Scottish commander Robert Munroe.

'privileges' will not be interfered with. That is to say, you must guarantee that when Ireland is free of foreign domination, the green-coated Irish soldiers will guard the fraudulent gains of capitalist and landlord from 'the thin hands of the poor' just as remorselessly and just as effectually as the scarlet-coated emissaries of England do today.[16]

On no other basis will the classes unite with you. Do you expect the masses to fight for this ideal?

When you talk of freeing Ireland, do you only mean the chemical elements which compose the soil of Ireland? Or is it the Irish people you mean? If the latter, from what do you propose to free them? From the rule of England?

But all systems of political administration or governmental machinery are but the reflex of the economic forms which underlie them.[17]

English rule in England is but the symbol of the fact that English conquerors in the past forced upon this country a property system founded upon spoliation, fraud and murder: that, as the present-day exercise of the 'rights of property' so originated involves the continual practice of legalised spoliation and fraud, English rule is found to be the most suitable form of government by which spoliation can be protected, and an English army the most pliant tool with which to execute judicial murder when the fears of the propertied classes demand it.

The Socialist who would destroy, root and branch, the whole brutally materialistic system of civilisation, which like the English language we have adopted as our own, is, I hold, a far more deadly foe to English rule and tutelage, than the superficial thinker who imagines it possible to reconcile Irish freedom with those insidious but disastrous forms of economic subjection—landlord tyranny, capitalist fraud and unclean usury; baneful fruits of the Norman Conquest, the unholy trinity, of which Strongbow and Diarmuid MacMurchadha[18]—Norman thief and Irish traitor —were the fitting precursors and apostles.

If you remove the English army to-morrow and hoist the green flag over Dublin Castle, unless you set about the organisation of the Socialist Republic your efforts would be in vain.

England would still rule you. She would rule you through her capitalists, through her landlords, through her financiers, through the whole array of commercial and individualist institutions she has planted in this country and watered with the tears of our mothers and the blood of our martyrs.

---

16. A reference to the color of the uniforms of the British army. While scarlet was traditionally the color of officers, sergeants, and so forth, from the 1870s it was adopted for all ranks.

17. A reference to Karl Marx's historical materialism. For Marx, the economic foundation of society determined the shape of its political forms.

18. After Diarmait Mac Murchada (also Diarmuid MacMurchadha or Dermot MacMurrough) (1110–71), king of Leinster, had been ousted from power, he sought military assistance from Henry II of England, who allowed him to recruit soldiers from the Anglo-Norman nobility to reclaim his kingdom. His most prominent ally became Richard de Clare (c. 1130–76), nicknamed Strongbow.

England would still rule you to your ruin, even while your lips offered hypocritical homage at the shrine of that Freedom whose cause you had betrayed.

Nationalism without Socialism—without a reorganisation of society on the basis of a broader and more developed form of that common property which underlay the social structure of Ancient Erin—is only national recreancy.[19]

It would be tantamount to a public declaration that our oppressors had so far succeeded in inoculating us with their perverted conceptions of justice and morality that we had finally decided to accept those conceptions as our own, and no longer needed an alien army to force them upon us.

As a Socialist I am prepared to do all one man can do to achieve for our motherland her rightful heritage—independence; but if you ask me to abate one jot or title of claims of social justice, in order to conciliate the privileged classes, then I must decline.

Such action would be neither honourable nor feasible. Let us never forget that he never reaches Heaven who marches thither in the company of the Devil. Let us openly proclaim our faith: the logic of events is with us.

43. Sir Horace Plunkett, Selections from *Ireland in the New Century* (1904)

No less than James Connolly, Horace Plunkett (1854–1932) believed that political independence would not solve Ireland's deepest problems. However, where Connolly was a revolutionary socialist and nationalist, Plunkett was a Unionist (until 1912) and a proponent of capitalism. His background was Anglo-Irish, aristocratic, and Protestant. He attended the best English schools—Eton and University College, Oxford. The latter made him an honorary fellow in 1909.

Plunkett worked throughout his life to break down the communal divide. In the aftermath of the Easter Rising, the British government asked Plunkett to chair the Irish Convention, which in 1917–18 sought but failed to create a compromise between nationalist and Unionist groups regarding Home Rule. However, Plunkett's most important contribution to nonsectarian renewal was probably in the economic sphere. He was moved by the plight of impoverished Irish tenant farmers: even though they were gaining control and ownership over their land, they were vulnerable to intensifying international competition, particularly from the United States. He believed that the only solution was cooperative self-help. Plunkett's ideas were based on an extensive knowledge of agriculture that he had learned while ranching in the American West between 1879 and 1889. In Ireland, Plunkett pioneered the cooperative movement. In 1894, he helped found the Irish Agricultural Organization Society, which took the lead in promoting cooperatives. Four years later there were 243 affiliated societies; within a decade, there were 800.

19. Being unfaithful or disloyal to a deeply held principle or belief. Connolly is suggesting that Ireland prior to the Anglo-Norman conquest of Henry II did not have private property, that is, it had a primitive form of socialism. Thus, nationalism without socialism is an abandonment of Irish traditions.

In Ireland in the New Century, *Plunkett set forth his ideas on Irish revitalization, including his plea for agricultural cooperatives. Plunkett did not deny the historical wrongs done to Ireland by Britain, but he believed these had too often justified Irish passivity. His observation that "Anglo-Irish history is for Englishmen to remember, for Irishmen to forget," is often quoted. Yet Plunkett's book produced a backlash among Catholics who were enraged by his contention that Catholicism had played a role in stifling individual drive, initiative, and ultimately economic growth. For them, it seemed yet another instance of the Anglo-Irish condescension and arrogance that Catholics had been subjected to for centuries.*

CHAPTER I
THE ENGLISH MISUNDERSTANDING

. . . For half a century laissez-faire was pedantically applied to Irish agriculture, then suddenly the other extreme was adopted; nothing was left alone, and political economy was sent on its famous planetary excursion.

When Mr. Gladstone was attempting to settle the land question on the basis of dual ownership, the seed of a new kind of single ownership—peasant proprietorship—was sown through the influence of John Bright. The operations of the land purchase clauses in the Church Disestablishment Act of 1869, and the Land Acts of 1870 and 1881, were enormously extended by the Land Purchase Acts introduced by the Conservative Party in 1885 and in 1891, and the success which attended these Acts accentuated the defects and sealed the fate of dual ownership, which all parties recently united to destroy. In other words, Parliament has been undoing a generation's legislative work upon the Irish land question.

This is all I need say about that stage of the Irish agrarian situation at which we have now arrived. What I wish my readers to bear in mind is that the effect of a bad system of land tenure upon the other aspects of the Irish Question reaches much further back than the struggles, agitations, and reforms in connection with Irish land which this generation has witnessed. The same may be said with regard to the other economic grievances. No one can be more anxious than I am to fasten the mind of my countrymen upon the practical things of to-day, and to wean their sad souls from idle regrets over the sorrows of the past. If I revive these dead issues, it is because I have learned that no man can move the Irish mind to action unless he can see its point of view, which is largely retrospective. I cannot ignore the fact that the attitude of mind which causes the Irish people to put too much faith in legislative cures for economic ills is mainly due to the belief that their ancestors were the victims of a long series of laws by which every industry that might have made the country prosperous was jealously repressed or ruthlessly destroyed. Those who are not too much appalled by the quantity to examine into the quality of popular oratory in Ireland are familiar with the subordination of present economic issues to the dreary reiteration of this old tale of woe. Personally I have always held that to foster resentment in respect of these old wrongs is as stupid as was the policy which gave them birth; and, even if it were possible to distribute the blame among our ancestors, I am sure we should do ourselves much harm, and no living soul any good, in the reckoning. In my view, Anglo-Irish history is for Englishmen to remember, for Irishmen to forget. . . .

CHAPTER II
THE IRISH QUESTION IN IRELAND

Whilst attributing the long continued failure of English rule in Ireland largely to a misunderstanding of the Irish mind, I have given England—at least modern England—credit for good intentions towards us. I now come to the case of the misunderstood, and shall from henceforth be concerned with the immeasurably greater responsibility of the Irish people themselves for their own welfare. The most characteristic, and by far the most hopeful feature of the change in the Anglo-Irish situation which took place in the last decade of the nineteenth century, and upon the meaning of which I dwelt in the preceding chapter, is the growing sense amongst us that the English misunderstanding of Ireland is of far less importance, and perhaps less inexcusable, than our own misunderstanding of ourselves.

When I first came into practical touch with the extraordinarily complex problems of Irish life, nothing impressed me so much as the universal belief among my countrymen that Providence had endowed them with capacities of a high order, and their country with resources of unbounded richness, but that both the capacities and the resources remained undeveloped owing to the stupidity—or worse—of British rule. It was asserted, and generally taken for granted, that the exiles of Erin sprang to the front in every walk of life throughout the world, in every country but their own—though I notice that in quite recent times endeavours have been made to cool the emigration fever by painting the fortunes of the Irish in America in the darkest colours. To suggest that there was any use in trying at home to make the best of things as they were was indicative of a leaning towards British rule; and to attempt to give practical effect to such a heresy was to draw a red herring across the path of true Nationalism.

It is not easy to account for the long continuance of this attitude of the Irish mind towards Irish problems, which seems unworthy of the native intelligence of the people. The truth probably is that while we have not allowed our intellectual gifts to decay, they have been of little use to us because we have neglected the second part of the old Scholastic rule of life, and have failed to develop the moral qualities in which we are deficient. Hence we have developed our critical faculties, not, unhappily, along constructive lines. We have been throughout alive to the muddling of our affairs by the English, and have accurately gauged the incapacity of our governors to appreciate our needs and possibilities. But we recognised their incapacity more readily than our own deficiencies, and we estimated the failure of the English far more justly than we apportioned the responsibility between our rulers and ourselves. The sense of the duty and dignity of labour has been lost in the contemplation of circumstances over which it was assumed that we have no control.

It is a peculiarity of destructive criticism that, unlike charity, it generally begins and ends abroad; and those who cultivate the gentle art are seldom given to morbid introspection. Our prodigious ignorance about ourselves has not been blissful. Mistaking self-assertion for self-knowledge, we have presented the pathetic spectacle of a people casting the blame for their shortcomings on another people, yet bearing the consequences themselves. The national habit of living in the past seems to give us a present without achievement, a future without hope. The conclusion was long ago forced upon me that whatever may have been true of the past, the chief responsibility for the remoulding of our national life rests now with ourselves, and that in the last analysis the problem of Irish ineffectiveness at home is in the main a problem of character—and of Irish character. . . .

It is a commonplace that there are two Irelands, differing in race, in creed, in political aspiration, and in what I regard as a more potent factor than all the others put together—economic interest and industrial pursuit. In the mutual misunderstanding of these two Irelands, still more than in the misunderstanding of Ireland by England, is to be found the chief cause of the still unsettled state of the Irish Question. I shall not seek to apportion the blame between the two sections of the population; but as the mists clear away and we can begin to construct a united and contented Ireland, it is not only legitimate, but helpful in the extreme, to assign to the two sections of our wealth-producers their respective parts in repairing the fortunes of their country. In such a discussion of future developments chief prominence must necessarily be given to the problems affecting the life of the majority of the people, who depend directly on the land, and conduct the industry which produces by far the greater portion of the wealth of the country. . . .

Nevertheless, the interest of the manufacturing population of Ulster in the welfare of the Roman Catholic agricultural majority is not merely that of an onlooker, nor even that of the other parts of the United Kingdom, but something more. It is obvious that the internal trade of the country depends mainly upon the demand of the rural population for the output of the manufacturing towns, and that this demand must depend on the volume of agricultural production. I think the importance of developing the home market has not been sufficiently appreciated, even by Belfast. The best contribution the Ulster Protestant population can make to the solution of this question is to do what they can to bring about cordial co-operation between the two great sections of the wealth-producers of Ireland. They should, I would suggest, learn to take a broader and more patriotic view of the problems of the Roman Catholic Church and agricultural majority . . . .

The Irish Question is, then, in that aspect which must be to Irishmen of paramount importance, the problem of a national existence, chiefly an agricultural existence, in Ireland. To outside observers it is the question of rural life, a question which is assuming a social and economic importance and interest of the most intense character, not only for Ireland North and South, but for almost the whole civilised world. It is becoming increasingly difficult in many parts of the world to keep the people on the land, owing to the enormously improved industrial opportunities and enhanced social and intellectual advantages of urban life. The problem can be better examined in Ireland than elsewhere, for with us it can, to a large extent, be isolated, since we have little highly developed town life. Our rural exodus takes our people, for the most part, not into Irish or even into British towns, but into those of the United States. . . .

The solution of all such problems largely depends upon certain developments which, for many reasons, I regard as absolutely essential to the success of the new agrarian order. One of these developments is the spread of agricultural co-operation through voluntary associations. Without this agency of social and economic progress, small landholders in Ireland will be but a body of isolated units, having all the drawbacks of individualism, and none of its virtues, unorganised and singularly ill-equipped for that great international struggle of our time, which we know as ag-ricultural competition. Moreover, there is another equally important, if less obvious, consideration which renders urgent the organisation of our rural communities. From Russia, with its half-communistic Mir to France with its modern village commune,[20] there is no country in Europe except the United Kingdom where the peasant land-holders have not some form of corporate existence. In Ireland the transition from landlordism to a peasant proprietary not only does not create any corporate existence among the occupying peasantry but rather deprives them of the slight social coher-ence which they formerly possessed as tenants of the same landlord. The estate office has its uses as well as its disadvantages, and the landlord or agent is by no means without his value as a business adviser to those from whom he collects the rent.

The organisation of the peasantry by an extension of voluntary associations, which is a condition precedent of social and economic progress, will not, however, suffice to enable them to face and solve the problems with which they are confronted, and whose solution has now become a matter of very serious concern to the British taxpayer. The condition of our agrarian life clearly indicates the necessity for supplementing voluntary effort with a sound system of State aid to agriculture and industry—a necessity fully recognised by the governments of every progressive continental country and of our own colonies. An altogether hopeful beginning of combined self-help and State assistance has been already made. Those who have been studying these problems, and practically preparing the way for the proper care of a peasant proprietary, have overcome the chief obstacles which lay in their path. They have gained popular acceptance for the principle that State aid should not be resorted to until organised voluntary effort has first been set in motion, and that any departure from this principle would be an unwarrantable interference with the business of the people, a fatal blow to private enterprise. . . .

CHAPTER IV
THE INFLUENCE OF RELIGION UPON SECULAR LIFE IN IRELAND
. . . It is, however, with the religion of the majority of the Irish people and with its influence upon the industrial character of its adherents that I am chiefly concerned. Roman Catholicism strikes an outsider as being in some of its tendencies non-eco-nomic, if not actually anti-economic. These tendencies have, of course, much fuller play when they act on a people whose education has (through no fault of their own) been retarded or stunted. The fact is not in dispute, but the difficulty arises when we come to apportion the blame between ignorance on the part of the people and a somewhat one-sided religious zeal on the part of large numbers of their clergy. I do not seek to do so with any precision here. I am simply adverting to what has appeared to me, in the course of my experience in Ireland, to be a defect in the industrial character of Roman Catholics which, however caused, seems to me to have been in-tensified by their religion. The reliance of that religion on authority, its repression of individuality, and its complete shifting of what I may call the moral centre of gravity to a future existence—to mention no other characteristics—appear to me calculated, unless supplemented by other influences, to check the growth of the qualities of

20. Refers to diverse forms of collective ownership and control among peasant communities.

initiative and self-reliance, especially amongst a people whose lack of education unfits them for resisting the influence of what may present itself to such minds as a kind of fatalism with resignation as its paramount virtue. . . .

. . . The real matter in which the direct and personal responsibility of the Roman Catholic clergy seems to me to be involved, is the character and morale of the people of this country. No reader of this book will accuse me of attaching too little weight to the influence of historical causes on the present state, social, economic and political, of Ireland, but even when I have given full consideration to all such influences I still think that, with their unquestioned authority in religion, and their almost equally undisputed influence in education, the Roman Catholic clergy cannot be exonerated from some responsibility in regard to Irish character as we find it to-day. Are they, I would ask, satisfied with that character? I cannot think so. The impartial observer will, I fear, find amongst a majority of our people a striking absence of self-reliance and moral courage; an entire lack of serious thought on public questions; a listlessness and apathy in regard to economic improvement which amount to a form of fatalism; and, in backward districts, a survival of superstition, which saps all strength of will and purpose—and all this, too, amongst a people singularly gifted by nature with good qualities of mind and heart.

Nor can the Roman Catholic clergy altogether console themselves with the thought that religious faith, even when free from superstition, is strong in the breasts of the people. So long, no doubt, as Irish Roman Catholics remain at home, in a country of sharply defined religious classes, and with a social environment and a public opinion so preponderatingly stamped with their creed, open defections from Roman Catholicism are rare. But we have only to look at the extent of the 'leakage' from Roman Catholicism amongst the Irish emigrants in the United States and in Great Britain, to realise how largely emotional and formal must be the religion of those who lapse so quickly in a non-Catholic atmosphere.

It is not, of course, to the causes of the defections from a creed to which I do not subscribe that my criticism is directed. I refer to the matter only in order to emphasise the large share of responsibility which belongs to the Roman Catholic clergy for what I strongly believe to be the chief part in the work of national regeneration, the part compared with which all legislative, administrative, educational or industrial achievements are of minor importance. . . .

44 and 45. Ulster's Solemn League and Covenant (1912)

The determination of Ulster loyalists to resist Home Rule by any means was apparent in 1886, when William Gladstone first proposed it. It was reaffirmed in 1912 when the House of Commons passed the third Home Rule Bill and the House of Lords, as a result of the Parliament Act of 1911, could only delay, rather than stop, Home Rule from becoming law. On and before "Ulster Day," September 28, 1912, nearly five hundred thousand people swore their allegiance to the cause of Ulster in two documents, one for men and another for women. Women, significantly, were destined to play a supporting role. In choosing the name of their declaration, Ulster Unionists dressed themselves in the clothing of the seventeenth-century English Civil War: their model was the Scot-

*tish National Covenant of 1643, a military and religious alliance between the English
Parliament and Scottish Presbyterians. The feeling of betrayal by Britain among Ulster
Loyalists is captured in the opening lines of Rudyard Kipling's poem "Ulster 1912."*

> The dark eleventh hour
> Draws on and sees us sold
> To every evil power
> We fought against of old.
> Rebellion, rapine, hate,
> Oppression, wrong and greed
> Are loosed to rule our fate,
> By England's act and deed.

44. Ulster's Solemn League and Covenant (for Men)

Being convinced in our consciences that Home Rule would be disastrous to the material well-being of Ulster as well as the whole of Ireland, subversive of our civil and
religious freedom, destructive of our citizenship and perilous to the unity of the
Empire, we, whose names are underwritten, men of Ulster, loyal subjects of His Gracious Majesty King George V, humbly relying on the God whom our fathers in days
of stress and trial confidently trusted, do hereby pledge ourselves in solemn Covenant
throughout this our time of threatened calamity to stand by one another in defending for ourselves and our children, our cherished position of equal citizenship in the
United Kingdom and in using all means which may be found necessary to defeat the
present conspiracy to set up a Home Rule Parliament in Ireland. And in the event
of such a Parliament being forced upon us we further solemnly and mutually pledge
ourselves to refuse to recognise its authority. In sure confidence that God will defend
the right we hereto subscribe our names. And further, we individually declare that we
have not already signed this Covenant.
The above was signed by me at _____
"Ulster Day," Saturday, 28th September, 1912.
                    GOD SAVE THE KING

45. The Declaration (for Women)

We, whose names are underwritten, women of Ulster, and loyal subjects of our gracious King, being firmly persuaded that Home Rule would be disastrous to our
Country, desire to associate ourselves with the men of Ulster in their uncompromising opposition to the Home Rule Bill now before Parliament, whereby it is proposed
to drive Ulster out of her cherished place in the Constitution of the United Kingdom,
and to place her under the domination and control of a Parliament in Ireland. Praying that from this calamity God will save Ireland, we here to subscribe our names.
                    GOD SAVE THE KING

46. Pádraic Pearse, "The Coming Revolution" (November 1913), *Political Writings and Speeches* (published 1924)

Like James Connolly, Pádraic Pearse is best known for his role in the Easter Rising of 1916. He served as commander in chief of the revolutionary forces and the president of the provisional government. He read the Easter Proclamation (no. 50) affirming Ireland's independence on the steps of the General Post Office and signed the unconditional surrender that ended the insurgency. He was executed by a firing squad on May 3, 1916. But Pearse's legacy goes beyond his role in these events: he is a leading figure in shaping the cultural politics of Irish nationalism in the early twentieth century.

In addition to being a political revolutionary, Pearse was an essayist, poet, and educator. He was from an Irish Catholic background, born in Dublin, although his father, James Pearse, had been an English stonemason who had immigrated to Ireland and converted to Catholicism in 1860. Pádraic Pearse was educated at the Royal University of Ireland and trained as a lawyer, although he never practiced law. His formation was steeped in the cultural revival. He joined the Gaelic League, edited its journal An Claidheamh Soluis (The Sword of Light) *(1903–9), lectured in Irish at University College, Dublin, and founded St. Enda's School in 1908, a bilingual secondary school that promoted Irishness. Pearse grew impatient with what he perceived as the political passivity of the cultural revival, embodied in Douglas Hyde's efforts at keeping the Gaelic League aloof from politics. He was originally a supporter of Home Rule but came to believe that Unionists would never allow the British government to grant Ireland's legislative independence. He gravitated toward militant politics, helping found the Irish Volunteers, and he joined the IRB, serving on its Supreme Council. Pearse believed that an armed insurrection, even one with little or no chance of success, was a necessary political act. In the mystical Catholic language in which his imagination worked, he described the insurrection as a "blood sacrifice."*

In "The Coming Revolution," Pearse voiced his indebtedness to the Gaelic League as well as his belief that it must be supplanted by a new revolutionary politics. Ironically, Pearse paid his respects to the armed political movement in Ulster, which, of course, was founded on a rejection of the Irish nationalist politics that Pearse embraced. But he applauded the Ulster Volunteers because they were arming themselves based on their beliefs, and he called for an armed movement that mirrored their achievement. While Pearse's call to arms was framed in a specifically Irish context, it was part of a generational sensibility found throughout Europe: it foreshadowed the widespread enthusiasm that seized Europeans in 1914 when World War I broke out.

I have come to the conclusion that the Gaelic League, as the Gaelic League, is a spent force; and I am glad of it. I do not mean that no work remains for the Gaelic League, or that the Gaelic League is no longer equal to work; I mean that the vital work to be done in the new Ireland will be done not so much by the Gaelic League itself as by men and movements that have sprung from the Gaelic League or have received from the Gaelic League a new baptism and a new life of grace. The Gaelic League was no reed shaken by the wind, no mere vox clamantis:[21] it was a prophet and more than a prophet. But it was not the Messiah. I do not know if the Messiah has yet come, and I am not sure that there will be any visible and personal Messiah in this redemption: the people itself will perhaps be its own Messiah, the people labouring, scourged, crowned with thorns, agonising and dying, to rise again immortal and impassible. For peoples are divine and are the only things that can properly be spoken of under figures drawn from the divine epos.[22]

If we do not believe in the divinity of our people we have had no business, or very little, all these years in the Gaelic League. In fact, if we had not believed in the divinity of our people, we should in all probability not have gone into the Gaelic League at all. We should have made our peace with the devil, and perhaps might have found him a very decent sort; for he liberally rewards with attorney-generalships, bank balances, villa residences, and so forth, the great and the little who serve him well. Now, we did not turn our backs upon all these desirable things for the sake of is and tá.[23] We did it for the sake of Ireland. In other words, we had one and all of us (at least, I had, and I hope that all you had) an ulterior motive in joining the Gaelic League. We never meant to be Gaelic Leaguers and nothing more than Gaelic Leaguers. We meant to do something for Ireland, each in his own way. Our Gaelic League time was to be our tutelage: we had first to learn to know Ireland, to read the lineaments of her face, to understand the accents of her voice; to re-possess ourselves, disinherited as we were, of her spirit and mind, re-enter into our mystical birthright. For this we went to school to the Gaelic League. It was a good school, and we love its name and will champion its fame throughout all the days of our later fighting and striving. But we do not propose to remain schoolboys for ever.

I have often said (quoting, I think, Herbert Spencer) that education should be a preparation for complete living;[24] and I say now that our Gaelic League education ought to have been a preparation for our complete living as Irish Nationalists. In proportion as we have been faithful and diligent Gaelic Leaguers, our work as Irish Nationalists (by which term I mean people who accept the ideal of, and work for, the realisation of an Irish Nation, by whatever means) will be earnest and thorough, a valiant and worthy fighting, not the mere carrying out of a ritual. As to what your work as an Irish Nationalist is to be, I cannot conjecture; I know what mine is to be, and would have you know yours and buckle yourself to it. And it may be (nay, it is) that yours and mine will lead us to a common meeting-place, and that on a certain day we shall stand together, with many more beside us, ready for a greater adventure than any of us has yet had, a trial and a triumph to be endured and achieved in common.

21. The voice of one crying out (Latin).

22. Epic poetry or events suitable for being made into epic poetry.

23. *Tá* and *is* in Irish are forms of "to be." Pearse is thus suggesting that there is more at stake in the nationalist struggle than speaking Irish, however important that might be.

24. Herbert Spencer (1820–1903), English philosopher, political theorist, and sociologist. Pearse is correct to attribute the formulation to Spencer, but the actual phrasing is "To prepare us for complete living is the function which education has to discharge" (1910, 12).

This is what I meant when I said that our work henceforward must be done less and less through the Gaelic League and more and more through the groups and the individuals that have arisen, or are arising, out of the Gaelic League. There will be in the Ireland of the next few years a multitudinous activity of Freedom Clubs, Young Republican Parties, Labour Organisations, Socialist Groups, and what not; bewildering enterprises undertaken by sane persons and insane persons, by good men and bad men, many of them seemingly contradictory, some mutually destructive, yet all tending towards a common objective, and that objective: the Irish Revolution.

For if there is one thing that has become plainer than another it is that when the seven men met in O'Connell Street[25] to found the Gaelic League, they were commencing, had there been a Liancourt[26] there to make the epigram, not a revolt, but a revolution. The work of the Gaelic League, its appointed work, was that: and the work is done. To every generation its deed. The deed of the generation that has now reached middle life was the Gaelic League: the beginning of the Irish Revolution. Let our generation not shirk *its* deed, which is to accomplish the revolution.

I believe that the national movement of which the Gaelic League has been the soul has reached the point which O'Connell's movement had reached at the close of the series of monster meetings.[27] Indeed, I believe that our movement reached that point a few years ago—say, at the conclusion of the fight for Essential Irish; and I said so at the time. The moment was ripe then for a new Young Ireland Party, with a forward policy; and we have lost much by our hesitation. I propose in all seriousness that we hesitate no longer—that we push on. I propose that we leave Conciliation Hall behind us and go into the Irish Confederation.[28]

Whenever Dr. [Douglas] Hyde, at a meeting at which I have had a chance of speaking after him, has produced his dove of peace, I have always been careful to produce my sword; and to tantalise him by saying that the Gaelic League has brought into Ireland "Not Peace, but a Sword." But this does not show any fundamental difference of outlook between my leader and me; for while he is thinking of peace between brother-Irishmen, I am thinking of the sword-point between banded Irishmen and the foreign force that occupies Ireland: and his peace is necessary to my war. It is evident that there can be no peace between the body politic

25. The main thoroughfare of Dublin.

26. François Alexandre Frédéric, duc de la Rochefoucauld-Liancourt (1747–1827), French social reformer. Liancourt was elected to the Estates General in 1789, the assembly called by King Louis XVI to solve the French fiscal crisis. He fought for social reform and the cause of the monarchy, while aware of France's revolutionary mood. On July 12, 1789, two days prior to the fall of the Bastille, he warned the king of the state of affairs in Paris. In response to the king's observation that it was a revolt, he replied: "No sire, it's a revolution."

27. The mass rallies presided over by Daniel O'Connell.

28. Conciliation Hall was built for Daniel O'Connell's repeal movement and opened in 1843. The Irish Confederation was the group of Young Irelanders that broke with O'Connell over the use of physical force. Thus, Pearse advocated going from a movement that was peaceful and focused on Parliament to one that was an armed confrontation.

and a foreign substance that has intruded itself into its system: between them war only until the foreign substance is expelled or assimilated.

Whether Home Rule means a loosening or a tightening of England's grip upon Ireland remains yet to be seen. But the coming of Home Rule, if come it does, will make no material difference in the nature of the work that lies before us: it will affect only the means we are to employ, our plan of campaign. There remains, under Home Rule as in its absence, the substantial task of achieving the Irish Nation. I do not think it is going to be achieved without stress and trial, without suffering and blood-shed; at any rate, it is not going to be achieved without work. Our business here and now is to get ourselves into harness for such work as has to be done.

I hold that before we can do any work, any men's work, we must first realise ourselves as men. Whatever comes to Ireland she needs men. And we of this generation are not in any real sense men, for we suffer things that men do not suffer, and we seek to redress grievances by means which men do not employ. We have, for instance, allowed ourselves to be disarmed; and, now that we have the chance of re-arming, we are not seizing it. Professor Eoin MacNeill pointed out last week that we have at this moment an opportunity of rectifying the capital error we made when we allowed ourselves to be disarmed; and such opportunities, he reminds us, do not always come back to nations.

A thing that stands demonstrable is that nationhood is not achieved otherwise than in arms: in one or two instances there may have been no actual bloodshed, but the arms were there and the ability to use them. Ireland unarmed will attain just as much freedom as it is convenient for England to give her; Ireland armed will attain ultimately just as much freedom as she wants. These are matters which may not concern the Gaelic League, as a body; but they concern every member of the Gaelic League, and every man and woman of Ireland. I urged much of this five or six years ago in addresses to the Ard-Chraobh:[29] but the League was too busy with resolutions to think of revolution, and the only resolution that a member of the League could not come to was the resolution to be a man. My fellow-Leaguers had not (and have not) apprehended that the thing which cannot defend itself, even though it may wear trousers, is no man.

I am glad, then, that the North has "begun." I am glad that the Orangemen have armed, for it is a goodly thing to see arms in Irish hands. I should like to see the A. O. H.[30] armed. I should like to see the Transport Workers armed.[31] I should like to see any and every body of Irish citizens armed. We must accustom ourselves to the thought of arms, to the sight of arms, to the use of arms. We may make mistakes in the beginning and shoot the wrong people; but bloodshed is a cleansing and a sanctifying thing, and the nation which regards it as the final horror has lost its manhood. There are many things more horrible than bloodshed; and slavery is one of them.

29. Highest or central branch (Irish); the governing body of the Gaelic League.
30. The Ancient Order of the Hibernians, an Irish-Catholic fraternal organization.
31. The Irish Transport and General Workers Union.

47 and 48. Irish Feminism and the Vote

The Irish suffrage movement was predominantly urban and middle class. It faced many of the same obstacles as its counterpart in Britain. However, its challenges were complicated by the predominance of the nationalist movement in Ireland, to which many of the suffragists belonged. When Irish suffragists worked closely with their English allies or argued that their priority was the vote for women, they left themselves open to nationalist attacks, including that they were closet Unionists. When they argued that the campaign for the vote for women should wait until the establishment of a Home Rule parliament, they risked becoming marginalized within the nationalist movement.

These complexities are explored in two articles published in the newspaper The Irish Citizen, *an organ of the suffragist movement. Mary McSwiney (also MacSwiney and McSwinney) (1872–1942) privileged nationalist over suffragist demands. The newspaper's editorial response argued for the opposite. McSwiney was born in England to an Irish father and English mother, studied at Cambridge University (at the time rarely attended by women), and lived most of her life in Cork, where she ran a school for girls modeled after Pádraic Pearse's St. Enda's School. She helped found Cumann na mBan, the Irish republican organization for women, in 1914, and was imprisoned for her role in the Easter Rising. Following the death of her brother Terence in 1920, the result of a prison hunger strike, she was elected to the Irish Parliament and took her seat the next year. McSwiney was adamantly opposed to the Anglo-Irish Treaty (no. 55).*

47. Mary McSwiney, "A Plea for Common Sense," *The Irish Citizen,* May 23, 1914

To plead with suffragists for a little common sense and political insight may be looked upon nowadays as a request for a dispatch of coals to Newcastle,[32] and yet it seems to be true that many Irish suffragists are rather losing their heads, and by their present tactics injuring their own cause. This does not apply to Militants only, but to all those whose views are expressed in recent "leaders" of the Irish Citizen. In England, convinced suffragists rightly place Votes for Women above and before all other reforms, and this policy expresses itself in consistent and continual opposition to the Government, while the Government, as such, is opposed to Woman Suffrage. No question of Party—no reform of any kind—social, fiscal, agrarian—can in any way compare with the dominant need in England today—the Woman's Voice—backed by the power of the Vote—in all questions of reform. But in Ireland, even those who place suffrage first must take the special circumstances of the country into consideration if they wish to win adherents to their cause. Ireland is struggling to settle not a Party question, but a National one, and opposition to the Government in the present crisis means opposition to Home Rule.

---

32. This is an idiom suggesting a foolish or pointless act. Since the economy of Newcastle was based on the export of coal, importing it was a waste of time.

The fact that many Irish suffragists play the political ostrich and refuse to recognise the essential difference between this and English Party questions, does not minimise that difference; it simply blinds their political intelligence and injures the cause they wish to promote.

Let us take England in an analogous position. Suppose her in thrall to Germany, and that after many fruitless struggles she is at length on the road to receive a measure of freedom. Can you imagine England refusing that measure because it only enfranchised half her people, but left her to enfranchise the other half within a few years? Is it thinkable that English women would try to ruin that measure because for a few years they would have to be governed by English men instead of Germans? Can you fancy Christabel Pankhurst[33] herself hesitating, even if she honestly believed that by clinging to Germany she would get the women's vote sooner? Even if such an unpatriotic course were possible to Englishwomen, it would be none the more acceptable to Irishwomen.

It is idle to pooh-pooh this point of view; it is the actual point of view of the majority of the Irish people, and it has to be reckoned with. If, then, suffragists do not wish to alienate the sympathy of the Irish people—women as well as men—they must not hail with delight the prospect of the destruction of the Home Rule Bill.

Many Nationalist women are of the opinion that Mr Redmond[34] made a big tactical blunder in opposing the Conciliation bill[35] and thus setting the English suffragists so hotly against him. But we must remember that whatever his private opinions, he was helpless here. He could not, even if had wished, risk the Home Rule Bill by opposing the arch-anti Mr Asquith[36] on his pet prejudice. Mr Redmond's one and only business at Westminster is to secure Home Rule.

He received no mandate for Woman Suffrage, and thoughtful and fair-minded Irishwomen of every political belief recognise that.

To maintain that Home Rule is not Home Rule, and should not be accepted unless women are included, is puerile. The point for Irish suffragists to note is this: that no question but the Home Rule one will turn a single vote at an Irish election until Home Rule is finally attained. Therefore it is an absurdity to write that "In Ireland the opposing parties are not yet fully convinced of the importance of the suffrage movement or the need to make terms with it." The suggestion made lately that Irish suffragists should help to "drum Asquith out of Fife"[37] shows so little grasp of the situation in Ireland that one almost asks if we are supposed to be content to be catspaws for English suffragists. In consequence of such deplorable partisan tactics, the suffrage cause is rapidly becoming synonymous with the Unionist cause, and is losing day by day many Nationalist supporters.

33. Christabel Harriette Pankhurst (1880–1958), English militant women's suffrage leader and cofounder of the Women's Social and Political Union (1903).

34. John Redmond, leader of the Irish Parliamentary Party.

35. Legislation that extended the right to vote to women. There were three bills between 1910 and 1912, all defeated.

36. Herbert Asquith, British prime minister.

37. Asquith was the MP for East Fife (1886–1918) on the eastern coast of Scotland.

Englishwomen want the vote for themselves first and foremost. That is natural, and we applaud and sympathise with their efforts. But in order to hasten their political enfranchisement—even by a year—they would not hesitate to wreck the cause of suffrage in Ireland for a generation or more. The sooner Irishwomen open their eyes to that fact, the sooner they will get back to sane methods. What is good for England is not good for Ireland in suffrage tactics any more than in other matters; and as Irishwomen we are concerned with our own country first.

It is no kindness to the cause of suffrage in Ireland that has brought an English society to carry on an active campaign in this country. We cannot logically complain if Englishwomen damage Irish interests in England in order to further their own; but let them confine their campaign to their own side of the Channel. It is not "playing the game" to deliberately injure our movement in our own country in order to advance theirs. The sophistry that answers that in winning the vote for themselves they are winning it for us, does not blind us. The women of Ireland want the vote but they do not want it nor would they take it at the expense of Home Rule—even if we have to wait three years! What are three years in the life of a nation? To those suffragists who are truly sincere in their policy of "suffrage first", I earnestly appeal for wiser methods for the sake of the cause they have at heart. Let them take into account the special conditions of their country—as wise politicians will—and, whatever their private opinions may be, cease to injure that cause by knocking their political heads against the stone-wall of the National Will.

Let us make no mistake. These tactics if persisted in, will not injure Home Rule; they most undoubtedly will injure the suffrage movement, and postpone indefinitely the fulfilment of our hopes.

48. "Editorial: The Slave Women Again," *The Irish Citizen*, May 23, 1914

We publish this week another of those wrong-headed appeals by which Miss McSwiney, the spokeswoman of the Slave Women (Nationalist variety) seeks to justify her placing of a party Nationalism above the cause of her sex. We say a party Nationalism; for in seeking to show that her adherence is not to a party, but to the principle of Nationalism, Miss McSwiney begs the very question at issue. It is not Nationalism as such, but Nationalism as perverted by Mr Redmond, that calls for the uncompromising opposition of Irish suffragists. Miss McSwiney's position shows some advance on that taken up by similar partisans a few years ago. Then Mr Asquith was sacrosanct; now Miss McSwiney admits Mr Asquith's sinister role in wrecking women's hopes, but seeks to exculpate Mr Redmond. The Irish leader, she says, "could not even if he wished" have supported the Conciliation Bill in opposition to Mr Asquith's pet prejudice. Will Miss McSwiney apply herself to this question: Why did Mr Redmond not say so? The excuse she puts forward for him is one he had never dared put forward himself. Had he done so—had he said frankly that his action in deliberately killing the Conciliation Bill was due to the exigencies of the English political situation, and had he accompanied that plea by a promise to take up Votes for Women in a Home Rule Parliament—Miss McSwiney's position would be a logical and tenable one. Nationalist suffragists might then, quite reasonably, have regarded the pledge for the future as a fair recompense for the postponement of their hopes—just as Unionist suffragists were satisfied with Sir Edward Carson's pledge to give them votes under his Provisional Government. But Mr Redmond's course was doubly different. He denied in the face of all the evidence, that he had anything to do with the killing of the Conciliation Bill. He stated categorically that he would always oppose Votes for Women, in a Home Rule Parliament as well as at Westminster.[38] It was this double treachery and hostility that made opposition to him, and to the Party which was the weak instrument of his will, imperative on the part of self-respecting Irish women. Those who do not recognise this categorical imperative are Slave Women, whether they realise it or not.

It is this identification, in Mr Redmond's personality, of official Nationalism with the most virulent anti-feminism that renders irrelevant Miss McSwiney's attempted Anglo-German parallel. To make sure a parallel is at all conceivable, we must imagine Mr Asquith as an English "Nationalist" leader, fighting a German sovereignty. In such a case we hope, and believe, that English women suffragists would have more self-respect than to work for Mr Asquith or facilitate a campaign destined to place them absolutely under his control; they might well think the Kaiser's rule preferable. If they wanted to work for English Nationalism they would form a party of their own for that purpose— a party in which women's right to English citizenship would be explicitly recognised. Here is where the "Irishwomen's Council"[39] might come in. If that body were to declare definitely in favour of the equal citizenship of women, and were to refuse its assistance to any party or leader failing to recognise that principle, it would justify itself, and might do useful work among those Nationalist women who are not yet prepared to put suffrage first. Until it makes such a declaration it is an organisation of Slave Women.

We do not question Miss McSwiney's personal sincerity in the line she takes up. That a woman suffragist should find it possible to take such a line makes it all the more necessary to write plainly on the subject. What Miss McSwiney lacks is political education. It is not at all surprising that many Irish women, both North and South, should suffer under that disability. We are grateful to Miss McSwiney for having put the view of the Southern section of politically uneducated women so forcibly. We are satisfied that the more the question is discussed, the more clearly will Irish women, Nationalist and Unionist, North and South, perceive that an independent suffragist policy, opposing every body of responsible politicians which is hostile to women's citizenship, is the only one consistent with self-respect.

38. The British Parliament is housed in the Palace of Westminster in the London borough of Westminster and thus is often simply referred to as Westminster.

39. Irishwomen's Council, Cumann na mBan, was founded in 1914 to give female support to the Irish Volunteers.

World War I recruiting poster appealing to the Irish
national spirit.

49. John Redmond, "An Irish Brigade: Mr. Redmond's Appeal to His Countrymen, 'War for High Ideals,'" *The Times*, September 17, 1914

Home Rule became law in September 1914, but its implementation was postponed by Britain's entry into World War I. For John Redmond (1856–1918), the leader of the Irish Parliamentary Party, supporting Britain in the war represented an opportunity to demonstrate Ireland's allegiance to the British state, critical to making the case for a Home Rule parliament. But his support was fraught with difficulties: it was potentially viewed among his supporters in Ireland as yet another instance of Irish subservience and capitulation to unfulfilled British promises.

Redmond was from a Catholic background in County Wexford, educated by Jesuits and at Trinity College in Dublin, the eldest son of William Archer Redmond, himself an MP. As a clerk in the House of Commons, John Redmond fell under the influence of Charles Stewart Parnell, was elected to Parliament in 1881, and was an MP until his death in 1918. Redmond remained loyal to Parnell, following the split in the Irish Parliamentary Party in 1890, and he assumed the leadership of the minority pro-Parnell

faction until 1900 when he became the head of the reunited party. He successfully kept
the different factions of his party together through the years that produced the third
Home Rule Bill, but his influence was ultimately undermined by Unionist resistance
to the legislation, a too close association with the British war effort, and the triumph of
Sinn Féin following the 1916 Rising.

Redmond's article, published in The Times, *written in the early stages of the war,*
illustrates his political balancing act. His support for the British war effort was bal-
anced by his insistence that Irish contributions must be kept separate. Most important,
Redmond revealed his hope that the war might bring nationalists and Unionists together
and provide the foundation for a united Ireland after its conclusion. Such hopes were to
be unfulfilled.

Mr. John Redmond, M. P., has issued the following statement:—

The whole-hearted endorsement by the Irish people and the Irish Volunteers of the spirit of my declaration, made on the impulse of the moment and without seeking for any conditions whatever, that the defence of Ireland might safely be left to the sons of Ireland themselves, shows the profound change which has been brought about in the relations of Ireland to the Empire by the events of the past three years.

The Irish people know and appreciate the fact fully that, at long last, after centuries of misunderstanding, the democracy of Great Britain has finally and irrevocably decided to trust them and to give them back their national liberties.

By overwhelming British majorities a charter of liberty for Ireland has been three times passed by the House of Commons, and, in a few hours, will be the law of the land. A new era has opened in the history of the two nations.

During the long discussion on the Irish problem in Parliament and on the platform, we promised the British people that the concession of liberty would have the same effects in Ireland as in every other part of the Empire, and notably in recent years in South Africa;[40] that disaffection would give way to friendship and good will; and that Ireland would become a strength, instead of a weakness, to the Empire.

The democracy of Great Britain listened to our appeal, and have kept faith with Ireland. It is now a duty of honour for Ireland to keep faith with them.

A test to search men's souls has arisen. The Empire is engaged in the most serious war in history. It is a just war, provoked by the intolerable military despotism of Germany. It is a war for the defence of the sacred rights and liberties of small nations, and the respect and enlargement of the great principle of nationality. Involved in it is the fate of France, our kindred country, the chief nation of that powerful Celtic race to which we belong.[41] The fate of Belgium, to whom we are attached by the same great ties of race, and by the

40. Conflicts between Britain and South Africa (the Orange Free State and the South African Republic or Transvaal Republic) led to two Boer Wars, the first being from 1880 to 1881 and the second from 1899 to 1902. In the end, South Africa became an independent dominion within the British Empire as a result of the South Africa Act (1909).

41. Like Ireland, France had a Celtic past; the Celtic people living there (as well as Belgium and Luxembourg) were known as the Gauls.

common desire of a small nation to assert its freedom, and the fate of Poland,[42] whose sufferings and whose struggle bear so marked a resemblance to our own.

It is a war for high ideals of human government and international relations; and Ireland would be false to her history and to every consideration of honour, good faith, and self-interest did she not willingly bear her share in its burdens and its sacrifices.

We have, even when no ties of sympathy bound our country to Great Britain, always given our quota, and more than our quota, to the firing line, and we shall do so now.

We have a right honour to claim that Irish recruits for the Expeditionary Force[43] should be kept together as a unit, officered as far as possible by Irishmen, composed, if possible, of county battalions, to form, in fact, an "Irish Brigade," so that Ireland may gain national credit for their deeds, and feel, like other communities of the Empire, that she, too, has contributed an army bearing her name in this historic struggle.

Simultaneously with the formation of this Irish Brigade for service abroad, our Volunteers must be put in a state of efficiency as speedily as practicable for the defence of the country.

In this way, by the time the war ends Ireland will possess an army of which she may be proud.

I feel certain that the young men of our country will respond to this appeal with the gallantry of their race.

In conclusion, I would appeal to our countrymen of a different creed and of opposite political opinions to accept the friendship we have so consistently offered them; to allow this great war, as to which their opinions and ours are the same, and our action will also be the same, to swallow up all the smaller issues in the domestic government of Ireland which now divide us; that as our soldiers are going to fight, to shed their blood and to die at each other's side in the same Army against the same enemy and for the same high purpose, their union in the field may lead to a union in their home, and that their blood may be the seal that will bring all Ireland together in one nation, and in liberties equal and common to all.

J. E. Redmond

50. Proclamation of the Irish Republic, April 24, 1916

By the day of the Easter Rising, Monday, April 24, 1916, it was clear to the organizers that it would not be a success. The Aud, *a Norwegian cover name for the German ship* Libau, *which had brought weapons to be used in the rebellion, had been intercepted. Eoin MacNeill, chief of staff of the Irish Volunteers, discovered that the insurgents were going to use Volunteer military exercises throughout Ireland on Easter Sunday to launch*

---

42. In roughly the last quarter of the eighteenth century, Poland was partitioned between the Habsburg Empire, Prussia, and Russia, ending the existence of a Polish sovereign state. Hence, Redmond views Polish and Irish nationalists as being engaged in analogous struggles for freedom from foreign rule.

43. The British force sent to the Western Front in France and Belgium during World War I.

POBLACHT NA H EIREANN.

THE PROVISIONAL GOVERNMENT
OF THE
IRISH REPUBLIC
TO THE PEOPLE OF IRELAND.

IRISHMEN AND IRISHWOMEN : In the name of God and of the dead generations from which she receives her old tradition of nationhood, Ireland, through us, summons her children to her flag and strikes for her freedom.

Having organised and trained her manhood through her secret revolutionary organisation, the Irish Republican Brotherhood, and through her open military organisations, the Irish Volunteers and the Irish Citizen Army, having patiently perfected her discipline, having resolutely waited for the right moment to reveal itself, she now seizes that moment, and, supported by her exiled children in America and by gallant allies in Europe, but relying in the first on her own strength, she strikes in full confidence of victory.

We declare the right of the people of Ireland to the ownership of Ireland, and to the unfettered control of Irish destinies, to be sovereign and indefeasible.   The long usurpation of that right by a foreign people and government has not extinguished the right, nor can it ever be extinguished except by the destruction of the Irish people.   In every generation the Irish people have asserted their right to national freedom and sovereignty : six times during the past three hundred years they have asserted it in arms. Standing on that fundamental right and again asserting it in arms in the face of the world, we hereby proclaim the Irish Republic as a Sovereign Independent State, and we pledge our lives and the lives of our comrades-in-arms to the cause of its freedom, of its welfare, and of its exaltation among the nations.

The Irish Republic is entitled to, and hereby claims, the allegiance of every Irishman and Irishwoman.   The Republic guarantees religious and civil liberty, equal rights and equal opportunities to all its citizens, and declares its resolve to pursue the happiness and prosperity of the whole nation and of all its parts, cherishing all the children of the nation equally, and oblivious of the differences carefully fostered by an alien government, which have divided a minority from the majority in the past.

Until our arms have brought the opportune moment for the establishment of a permanent National Government, representative of the whole people of Ireland and elected by the suffrages of all her men and women, the Provisional Government, hereby constituted, will administer the civil and military affairs of the Republic in trust for the people.

We place the cause of the Irish Republic under the protection of the Most High God, Whose blessing we invoke upon our arms, and we pray that no one who serves that cause will dishonour it by cowardice, inhumanity, or rapine.   In this supreme hour the Irish nation must, by its valour and discipline and by the readiness of its children to sacrifice themselves for the common good, prove itself worthy of the august destiny to which it is called.

Signed on Behalf of the Provisional Government,

THOMAS J. CLARKE.

SEAN Mac DIARMADA.   THOMAS MacDONAGH.
P. H. PEARSE.   EAMONN CEANNT,
JAMES CONNOLLY.   JOSEPH PLUNKETT.

The Easter Proclamation, 1916

The Easter Proclamation (April 24, 1916).

the Rising. At first he allowed them to go forward, but then called them off following the British navy's interception of the Libau/Aud. The organizers went ahead anyway, hopeful that their actions would trigger a widespread rebellion but convinced that whatever the outcome, it was essential to alter the political climate.

The establishment of the Irish Republic was initiated by a proclamation in the vein of the American Declaration of Independence. It was to be widely distributed and broadcast to Britain's war enemies and the rest of the world once the organizers seized broadcasting facilities. The Proclamation was drafted by Pádraic Pearse and revised as a result of suggestions made mostly by James Connolly. Connolly's socialist and feminist views are thought to have influenced the inclusion of Irish women as well as men and the insistence that the people were entitled to the "ownership" of Ireland. The

Proclamation was ratified at a meeting of the IRB Military Council on Easter Sunday, the day prior to the Rising.

The Proclamation is an inspirational text that has achieved a canonical status. It establishes the Provisional Government of the Irish Republic, a reference to Robert Emmet's rebellion of 1803, also founded on the basis of a proclamation. In effect, the signatories acknowledge that while the Rising was in the name of the Irish people, they had not consulted them and thus the Republic was "provisional" until a representative body ratified it. This does not settle the issue of whether a small group could speak for the whole, even in exceptional circumstances, but it suggests that the organizers were keenly aware that they were confronted with a problem. Further, while acting on behalf of all of the Irish people, they certainly did not reach across the communal divide, making no mention of the very different historical formation of Ulster. Their reference to the British in Ireland as a "foreign people" responsible for a "long usurpation" of national rights and for the conflicts within Ireland was not likely to win over the Protestant minorities.

The Easter Proclamation is based on a particular view of history. It states that the Rising was a culmination of generations of struggle to achieve national self-determination. Indeed, it asserts that in the last three hundred years, the Irish people had engaged in armed struggle six times. While the writers do not specify what the six times were, they probably had in mind (1) Irish backing of Charles I during the English Civil War (1641–49), and (2) later support of James II, rather than William III (William of Orange), in the aftermath of the English Glorious Revolution (1688–91). They probably also were thinking of the (3) uprisings by the United Irishmen (1798), (4) Robert Emmet (1803), (5) Young Ireland (1848), and (6) the Fenians (1867). This view of history powerfully connects the Easter Rising to the Irish past, but as historical understanding it is not without its problems. First, it would be a stretch to conceive of several of these events—the insurgencies of Emmet, Young Ireland, and the Fenians—as national in scope, although certainly the level of support for them went beyond the actors who participated in them. Second, in the case of Irish support for James II, following the Glorious Revolution in which James was overthrown and William of Orange came to the throne, people from English backgrounds fought on both sides, calling into question whether a national struggle had taken place. The confrontation between the forces of James and William was, in part, a conflict between ruling-class Protestants and Catholics in Ireland that overlapped with but was not identical to the Anglo-Irish antagonism. The war can also be viewed as being deeply entangled in European power politics. William was Dutch and was seeking an alliance with England against the expansionist aspirations of Louis XIV of France. James had the support of Louis.

POBLACHT NA hÉIREANN[44]
THE PROVISIONAL GOVERNMENT OF THE IRISH REPUBLIC
TO THE PEOPLE OF IRELAND

IRISHMEN AND IRISHWOMEN: In the name of God and of the dead generations from which she receives her old tradition of nationhood, Ireland, through us, summons her children to her flag and strikes for her freedom.

---

44. The Republic of Ireland (Irish).

Having organised and trained her manhood through her secret revolutionary organisation, the Irish Republican Brotherhood, and through her open military organisations, the Irish Volunteers and the Irish Citizen Army, having patiently perfected her discipline, having resolutely waited for the right moment to reveal itself, she now seizes that moment, and supported by her exiled children in America and by gallant allies in Europe,[45] but relying in the first on her own strength, she strikes in full confidence of victory.

We declare the right of the people of Ireland to the ownership of Ireland and to the unfettered control of Irish destinies, to be sovereign and indefeasible. The long usurpation of that right by a foreign people and government has not extinguished the right, nor can it ever be extinguished except by the destruction of the Irish people. In every generation the Irish people have asserted their right to national freedom and sovereignty; six times during the past three hundred years they have asserted it in arms. Standing on that fundamental right and again asserting it in arms in the face of the world, we hereby proclaim the Irish Republic as a Sovereign Independent State, and we pledge our lives and the lives of our comrades in arms to the cause of its freedom, of its welfare, and of its exaltation among the nations.

The Irish Republic is entitled to, and hereby claims, the allegiance of every Irishman and Irishwoman. The Republic guarantees religious and civil liberty, equal rights and equal opportunities to all its citizens, and declares its resolve to pursue the happiness and prosperity of the whole nation and of all its parts, cherishing all of the children of the nation equally, and oblivious of the differences carefully fostered by an alien Government, which have divided a minority from the majority in the past.

Until our arms have brought the opportune moment for the establishment of a permanent National Government, representative of the whole people of Ireland and elected by the suffrages of all her men and women, the Provisional Government, hereby constituted, will administer the civil and military affairs of the Republic in trust for the people.

We place the cause of the Irish Republic under the protection of the Most High God, Whose blessing we invoke upon our arms, and we pray that no one who serves that cause will dishonour it by cowardice, inhumanity, or rapine. In this supreme hour the Irish nation must, by its valour and discipline, and by the readiness of its children to sacrifice themselves for the common good, prove itself worthy of the august destiny to which it is called.

Signed on behalf of the Provisional Government:
THOMAS J. CLARKE
SEAN MAC DIARMADA, THOMAS MACDONAGH
P. H. PEARSE, ÉAMONN CEANNT
JAMES CONNOLLY, JOSEPH PLUNKETT[46]

45. Germany.
46. Thomas J. Clarke (1857–1916), Seán Mac Diarmada (John or Sean MacDermott) (1883–1916), Thomas MacDonagh (1878–1916), Éamonn Ceannt (1881–1916), and Joseph Mary Plunkett (1887–1916). For Pearse and Connolly, see Glossary.

Constance Markievicz: revolutionary nationalist (1915).
(Image from the National Museum of Ireland.)

51 and 52. The Easter Rising Up Close

What it would have been like to live through the Easter Rising can be gleaned from two texts: one by the poet and novelist James Stephens (1882–1950) and one by the militant republican, feminist, and labor activist Constance Markievicz (1868–1927). Stephens was a Dubliner, who as a young man was a solicitor's clerk and who later became the registrar of the National Gallery of Ireland. He counted among his literary friends James Joyce, who is reputed to have asked Stephens to finish Finnegan's Wake *(1939) if he (Joyce) should fail to do so. Stephens was living in Dublin at the time of the Rising, and his account of it vividly conveys the mood surrounding the events from the point of view of one who lived through them but who himself was not a participant.*

In contrast, Constance Markievicz's memoir is written from the perspective of a leading figure in the Rising and the woman with the highest military rank. Markievicz, born Constance Gore-Booth, was from an Anglo-Irish landowning family. In her youth, she and her sister Eva were friends of W. B. Yeats, and he certainly had an influence on the development of their thought. It was as an art student in Paris that Constance met Count Casimir Dunin-Markievicz (1874–1932), an artist from a wealthy Polish landowning family. She married him in 1901, following the death of his wife, thus making her a countess.

When Markievicz returned to Ireland, she gravitated toward Irish nationalism, joining the Gaelic League, developing radical views, and becoming a staunch activist. She joined Inghinidhe na hÉireann (Daughters of Ireland), Sinn Féin, and helped found Óglaigh na hÉireann (Warriors of Ireland), a republican youth organization. In 1918, Markievicz became the first woman to be elected to the British Parliament, but in accordance with Sinn Féin strategy she never took her seat. She subsequently became minister of labour for Dáil Éireann; she adamantly opposed the Anglo-Irish Treaty; and she fought on the side of its opponents in the Irish Civil War. During the Easter Rising, Markievicz was part of James Connolly's Irish Citizen Army and would have been executed had she not been a woman. Her account, which stresses women's contribution to the Rising, closes by contrasting the heroism of those who participated in the Rising with those who had sold out republican values in creating the Irish Free State.

51. James Stephens, Chapter V, "Friday," *The Insurrection in Dublin* (1916)

THIS morning there are no newspapers, no bread, no milk, no news. The sun is shining, and the streets are lively but discreet. All people continue to talk to one another without distinction of class, but nobody knows what any person thinks.

It is a little singular the number of people who are smiling. I fancy they were listening to the guns last night, and they are smiling this morning because the darkness is past, and because the sun is shining, and because they can move their limbs in space, and may talk without having to sink their voices to a whisper. Guns do not sound so bad in the day as they do at night, and no person can feel lonely while the sun shines.

The men are smiling, but the women laugh, and their laughter does not displease, for whatever women do in whatever circumstances appears to have a rightness of its own. It seems right that they should scream when danger to themselves is imminent, and it seems right that they should laugh when the danger only threatens others.

It is rumoured this morning that Sackville Street[47] has been burned out and levelled to the ground. It is said that the end is in sight; and, it is said, that matters are, if anything rather worse than better. That the Volunteers have sallied from some of their strongholds and entrenched themselves, and that in one place alone (the South Lotts)[48] they have seven machine guns. That when the houses which they held became untenable they rushed out and seized other houses, and that, pursuing these tactics, there seemed no reason to believe that the Insurrection would ever come to an end. That the streets are filled with Volunteers in plain clothes, but having revolvers in their pockets. That the streets are filled with soldiers equally revolvered and plain clothed, and that the least one says on any subject the less one would have to answer for.

47. The main thoroughfare of Dublin, renamed O'Connell Street in 1924.
48. A Dublin street south of the River Liffey.

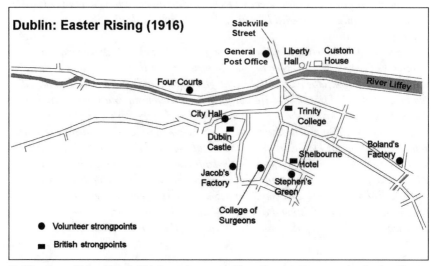

Dublin: Easter Rising (1916). This image is protected by a Creative Commons Attribution-Share Alike 3.0 Unported license (Creative Commons BY-SA 3.0) (http://creativecommons.org/licenses/by-sa/3.0/deed.en). Scolaire http://en.wikipedia.org/wiki/File:Easter_rising_1916.jpg

The feeling that I tapped was definitely Anti-Volunteer, but the number of people who would speak was few, and one regarded the noncommittal folk who were so smiling and polite, and so prepared to talk, with much curiosity, seeking to read in their eyes, in their bearing, even in the cut of their clothes what might be the secret movements and cogitations of their minds.

I received the impression that numbers of them did not care a rap what way it went; and that others had ceased to be mental creatures and were merely machines for registering the sensations of the time.

None of these people were prepared for Insurrection. The thing had been sprung on them so suddenly that they were unable to take sides, and their feeling of detachment was still so complete that they would have betted on the business as if it had been a horse race or a dog fight.

Many English troops have been landed each night, and it is believed that there are more than sixty thousand soldiers in Dublin alone, and that they are supplied with every offensive contrivance which military art has invented.

Merrion Square[49] is strongly held by the soldiers. They are posted along both sides of the road at intervals of about twenty paces, and their guns are continually barking up at the roofs which surround them in the great square. It is said that these roofs are held by the Volunteers from Mount Street Bridge to the Square, and that they hold in like manner wide stretches of the City.

49. A Georgian square in central Dublin laid out after 1762 and mostly finished by the early 1800s.

They appear to have mapped out the roofs with all the thoroughness that had hitherto been expended on the roads, and upon these roofs they are so mobile and crafty and so much at home that the work of the soldiers will be exceedingly difficult as well as dangerous.

Still, and notwithstanding, men can only take to the roofs for a short time. Up there, there can be no means of transport, and their ammunition, as well as their food, will very soon be used up. It is the beginning of the end, and the fact that they have to take to the roofs, even though that be in their programme, means that they are finished.

From the roof there comes the sound of machine guns. Looking towards Sackville Street one picks out easily Nelson's Pillar,[50] which towers slenderly over all the buildings of the neighbourhood. It is wreathed in smoke. Another towering building was the D. B. C. Café.[51] Its Chinese-like pagoda was a landmark easily to be found, but to-day I could not find it. It was not there, and I knew that, even if all Sackville Street was not burned down, as rumour insisted, this great Café had certainly been curtailed by its roof and might, perhaps, have been completely burned.

On the gravel paths I found pieces of charred and burnt paper. These scraps must have been blown remarkably high to have crossed all the roofs that lie between Sackville Street and Merrion Square.

At eleven o'clock there is continuous firing, and snipers firing from the direction of Mount Street,[52] and in every direction of the City these sounds are being duplicated.

In Camden Street[53] the sniping and casualties are said to have been very heavy. One man saw two Volunteers taken from a house by the soldiers. They were placed kneeling in the centre of the road, and within one minute of their capture they were dead. Simultaneously there fell several of the firing party.

An officer in this part had his brains blown into the roadway. A young girl ran into the road picked up his cap and scraped the brains into it. She covered this poor debris with a little straw, and carried the hat piously to the nearest hospital in order that the brains might be buried with their owner.

The continuation of her story was less gloomy although it affected the teller equally.

"There is not," said she, "a cat or a dog left alive in Camden Street. They are lying stiff out in the road and up on the roofs. There's lots of women will be sorry for this war," said she, "and their pets killed on them."

In many parts of the City hunger began to be troublesome. A girl told me that her family, and another that had taken refuge with them, had eaten nothing for three days. On this day her father managed to get two loaves of bread somewhere, and he brought these home.

50. A large granite pillar with a statue of Horatio Nelson (1758–1805), British naval hero in the war against Napoleon, at the top of it. It was destroyed by a republican group in 1966.

51. Refers to the restaurant of the Dublin Bread (or Bakery) Company on Dame Street.

52. Lower Mount Street and Upper Mount Street are parallel and continue through Merrion Square South and Merrion Square North on the eastern side of the square.

53. Street southwest of St. Stephen's Green.

"When," said the girl, "my father came in with the bread the whole fourteen of us ran at him, and in a minute we were all ashamed for the loaves were gone to the last crumb, and we were all as hungry as we had been before he came in. The poor man," said she, "did not even get a bit for himself." She held that the poor people were against the Volunteers.

The Volunteers still hold Jacob's Biscuit Factory.[54] It is rumoured that a priest visited them and counselled surrender, and they replied that they did not go there to surrender but to be killed. They asked him to give them absolution, and the story continues that he refused to do so—but this is not (in its latter part) a story that can easily be credited. The Adelaide Hospital is close to this factory, and it is possible that the proximity of the hospital delays or hinders military operations against the factory.

Rifle volleys are continuous about Merrion Square, and prolonged machine gun firing can be heard also.

During the night the firing was heavy from almost every direction; and in the direction of Sackville Street a red glare told again of fire.

It is hard to get to bed these nights. It is hard even to sit down, for the moment one does sit down one stands immediately up again resuming that ridiculous ship's march from the window to the wall and back. I am foot weary as I have never been before in my life, but I cannot say that I am excited. No person in Dublin is excited, but there exists a state of tension and expectancy which is mentally more exasperating than any excitement could be. The absence of news is largely responsible for this. We do not know what has happened, what is happening, or what is going to happen, and the reversion to barbarism (for barbarism is largely a lack of news) disturbs us.

Each night we have got to bed at last murmuring, "I wonder will it be all over to-morrow," and this night the like question accompanied us.

52. Constance Markievicz, "Some Women in Easter Week" (1926), *Prison Letters of Constance Markievicz* (published 1934)

You ask me to write you an account of my experiences and of the activities of the women of Easter Week. I am afraid that I can only give you a little account of those who were enrolled like me in the Irish Citizen Army, and those who were with me or whom I met during the Week. Some were members of Cumann na mBan, and others, just women who were ready to die for Ireland.

My activities were confined to a very limited area. I was mobilised for Liberty Hall[55] and was sent from there via the City Hall to St. Stephen's Green,[56] where I remained.

On Easter Monday morning there was a great hosting of disciplined and armed men at Liberty Hall.

54. A massive building taking up most of the area between Peter Street and Bishop Street.

55. Originally the headquarters of the Irish Transport and Workers' Union, it became the headquarters of the Irish Citizen Army.

56. A public park in central Dublin, south of the River Liffey, at the south end of Grafton Street.

Pádraic Pearse and James Connolly addressed us and told us that from now the Volunteers and the I. C. A.[57] were not two forces, but the wings of the Irish Republican Army.

There were a considerable number of I. C. A. women. These were absolutely on the same footing as the men. They took part in all marches, and even in the manœuvres that lasted all night. Moreover, Connolly made it quite clear to us that unless we took our share in the drudgery of training and preparing, we should not be allowed to take any share at all in the fight. You may judge how fit we were when I tell you that sixteen miles was the length of our last route march.

Connolly had appointed two staff officers—Commandant Mallin[58] and myself. I held a commission, giving me the rank of Staff Lieutenant. I was accepted by Tom Clarke[59] and the members of the provisional Government as the second of Connolly's 'ghosts.' 'Ghosts' was the name we gave to those who stood secretly behind the leaders and were entrusted with enough of the plans of the Rising to enable them to carry on that Leader's work should anything happen to himself. Commandant Mallin was over me and next in command to Connolly. Dr. Kathleen Lynn[60] was our medical officer, holding the rank of Captain.

We watched the little bodies of men and women march off, Pearse and Connolly to the G. P. O.,[61] Sean Connolly[62] to the City Hall. I went off then with the Doctor in her car. We carried a large store of First Aid necessities and drove off through quiet dusty streets and across the river, reaching the City Hall just at the very moment that Commandant Sean Connolly and his little troop of men and women swung round the corner and he raised his gun and shot the policeman who barred the way. A wild excitement ensued, people running from every side to see what was up. The Doctor got out, and I remember Mrs. Barrett—sister of Sean Connolly—and others helping to carry in the Doctor's bundles. I did not meet Dr. Lynn again until my release, when her car met me and she welcomed me to her house, where she cared for me and fed me up and looked after me till I had recovered from the evil effects of the English prison system.

When I reported with the car to Commandant Mallin in Stephen's Green, he told me that he must keep me. He said that owing to MacNeill's calling off the Volunteers a lot of the men who should have been under him had had to be distributed round other posts, and that few of those left him were trained to shoot, so I must stay and

---

57. Irish Citizen Army.

58. Michael Mallin (1874–1916), second in command in the Irish Citizen Army, commander of the garrison at St. Stephen's Green during the Rising.

59. Thomas J. Clarke, lifelong republican militant, a key participant in the IRB Military Council that organized the Easter Rising, and the first signatory of the Easter Proclamation.

60. Kathleen Florence Lynn (1874–1955), physician, feminist and suffragist, and participant in the Irish Citizen Army from 1913.

61. General Post Office.

62. Sean Connolly (1884–1916), Abbey Theatre actor and captain in the Irish Citizen Army. Connolly led an assault on Dublin Castle during the Rising. He was both the first rebel to kill a British solider and the first rebel to be killed.

be ready to take up the work of a sniper. He took me around the Green and showed me how the barricading of the gates and digging trenches had begun, and he left me in charge of this work while he went to superintend the erection of barricades in the streets and arrange other work. About two hours later he definitely promoted me to be his second in command. This work was very exciting when the fighting began. I continued round and round the Green, reporting back if anything was wanted, or tackling any sniper who was particularly objectionable.

Madeleine ffrench Mullen[63] was in charge of the Red Cross and the commissariat in the Green. Some of the girls had revolvers, and with these they sallied forth and held up bread vans.

This was necessary because the first prisoner we took was a British officer, and Commandant Mallin treated him as such. He took his parole[64] 'as an officer and a gentleman' not to escape, and he left him at large in the Green before the gates were shut. This English gentleman walked around and found out all he could and then 'bunked.'

We had a couple of sick men and prisoners in the Band-stand, the Red Cross flag flying to protect them. The English in the Shelbourne[65] turned a machine-gun on to them. A big group of our girls were attending to the sick, making tea for the prisoners or resting themselves. I never saw anything like their courage. Madeleine ffrench Mullen brought them, with the sick and the prisoners, out and into a safer place.

It was all done slowly and in perfect order. More than one young girl said to me, 'What is there to be afraid of? Won't I go straight to heaven if I die for Ireland'? However it was, they came out unscathed from a shower of shrapnel. On Tuesday we began to be short of food. There were no bread carts on the streets. We retired into the College of Surgeons[66] that evening and were joined by some of our men who had been in other places and by quite a large squad of Volunteers, and with this increase in our numbers the problem of food became very serious.

Nellie Gifford[67] was put in charge of one large classroom with a big grate, but alas, there was nothing to cook. When we were all starving she produced a quantity of oatmeal from somewhere and made pot after pot of the most delicious porridge, which kept us going. But all the same, on Tuesday and Wednesday we absolutely starved. There seemed to be no bread in the town.

63. Madeleine ffrench Mullen (1880–1944), medical officer and hospital administrator. She was a member of the Irish Citizen Army and supervised the medical post at St. Stephen's Green during the Rising.

64. Word of honor.

65. A landmark hotel founded in 1824 overlooking St. Stephen's Green.

66. Medical school founded in 1784, located in St. Stephens Green.

67. Nellie Gifford Donnelly (1880–1971) (born Helen Ruth Gifford), a founder of the Irish Citizen Army and participant in the Rising. She was in charge of feeding the personnel in the College of Surgeons and delivering rations to nearby posts. Following the Rising, she was imprisoned briefly in Kilmainham Gaol.

Later on Mary Hyland[68] was given charge of a little kitchen, somewhere down through the houses, near where the Eithne workroom now is.

We had only one woman casualty—Margaret Skinnader.[69] She, like myself, was in uniform and carried an army rifle. She had enlisted as a private in the I. C. A. She was one of the party who went out to set fire to a house just behind Russell's Hotel. The English opened fire on them from the ground floor of a house just opposite. Poor Freddy Ryan[70] was killed and Margaret was very badly wounded. She owes her life to William Partridge.[71] He carried her away under fire and back to the College. God rest his noble soul. Brilliant orator and Labour leader, comrade and friend of Connolly's, he was content to serve as a private in the I. C. A. He was never strong and the privations he suffered in an English jail left him a dying man.

Margaret's only regret was her bad luck in being disabled so early in the day (Wednesday of Easter Week) though she must have suffered terribly, but the end was nearer than we thought, for it was only a few days later that we carried her over to Vincent's Hospital, so that she would not fall wounded into the hands of the English.

The memory of Easter Week with its heroic dead is sacred to us who survived. Many of us could almost wish that we had died in the moment of ecstasy when, with the tri-colour[72] over our heads we went out and proclaimed the Irish Republic, and with guns in our hands tried to establish it.

We failed, but not until we had seen regiment after regiment run from our few guns. Our effort will inspire the people who come after us, and will give them hope and courage. If we failed to win, so did the English. They slaughtered and imprisoned, only to arouse the nation to a passion of love and loyalty, loyalty to Ireland and hatred of foreign rule. Once they see clearly that the English rule us still, only with a new personnel of traitors and new uniforms, they will finish the work begun by the men and women of Easter Week.

CONSTANCE DE MARKIEVICZ.

68. Mary Hyland (later Mrs. Michael Kelly), actress who worked closely with Countess Markievicz in searching for arms for the College of Surgeons' garrison during the Easter Rising.

69. Margaret Skinnader (also Skinnider) (1893–1971), born in Scotland to Irish parents, joined Cumann na mBan in Scotland. She joined the Irish Citizen Army and was a dispatch rider during the Rising. She was a scout for the St. Stephen's Green garrison. As a result of being wounded, she escaped a prison term.

70. Fred Ryan (1899–1916).

71. William Partridge (1874–1917), trade union activist, one of five vice-chairmen selected by the Irish Citizen Army in 1914, and a Citizen Army liaison with the Irish Volunteers landing German arms. During the Easter Rising, he fought as part of the St. Stephen's Green garrison.

72. The flag of Irish nationalists and now the Republic of Ireland. During the Rising it became the flag of the Irish Republic. It consists of three equal stripes: green for the Gaelic tradition and the nationalist cause, orange for Irish Protestants (followers of William of Orange), and white for the hope of peace and unity between the two groups.

The General Post Office following the Easter Rising.

53. W. B. Yeats, "Easter, 1916" (1916)

W. B. Yeats was ambivalent about the Easter Rising. He had known many of the participants. He had clashed with Pádraic Pearse, whom he described as "a man made dangerous by the Vertigo of Self Sacrifice," but he admired James Connolly whom he thought was an "able man" (quoted in Foster 2003, 46). Yeats' view of the Rising was transformed by the executions of its leaders. In the poem "Easter, 1916," he now viewed them as having become part of the pantheon of fallen Irish heroes. Such sentiments were even extended to a man he despised, John MacBride (the "other man" in the third stanza). MacBride had been violent to his wife Maud Gonne, who was Yeats' close friend and muse, and he possibly sexually abused her daughter Iseult (1894–1954). At the same time, although the poem is often read for its idealization of the participants, it also strikes a cautionary note. Yeats' contrast between the stone and the life forces surrounding it in the third stanza may be viewed as a critique of the hardness and rigidity of dogmatic forms of Irish nationalism, including, according to Yeats' biographer R. F. Foster (2003, 61), views held by Gonne herself. In addition, Yeats wondered whether the Rising would have been worth it if Home Rule became a reality. In his words, "Was it needless death after all?" if England, that is the British government, "keep[s] faith" and delivers on its promises? However Yeats' poem is understood, its importance is indisputable. Given his stature as the leading Irish writer of his time, it was not simply a com-

mentary on political events: the poem was a political act itself, one that helped produce the meaning of the Easter Rising.

I have met them at close of day
Coming with vivid faces
From counter or desk among grey
Eighteenth-century houses.
I have passed with a nod of the head
Or polite meaningless words,
Or have lingered awhile and said
Polite meaningless words,
And thought before I had done
Of a mocking tale or a gibe
To please a companion
Around the fire at the club,
Being certain that they and I
But lived where motley is worn:
All changed, changed utterly:
A terrible beauty is born.

That woman's days[73] were spent
In ignorant good-will,
Her nights in argument
Until her voice grew shrill.
What voice more sweet than hers
When, young and beautiful,
She rode to harriers?[74]
This man[75] had kept a school
And rode our wingèd horse;
This other[76] his helper and friend
Was coming into his force;
He might have won fame in the end,
So sensitive his nature seemed,
So daring and sweet his thought.
This other man[77] I had dreamed
A drunken, vainglorious lout.
He had done most bitter wrong

73. Constance Markievicz.

74. A harrier is a type of hound used for hunting hares. In its plural form it refers to a pack of these hounds, including the people who are part of the chase.

75. Pádraic Pearse.

76. Thomas MacDonagh.

77. John MacBride.

To some[78] who are near my heart,
Yet I number him in the song;
He, too, has resigned his part
In the casual comedy;
He, too, has been changed in his turn,
Transformed utterly:
A terrible beauty is born.

Hearts with one purpose alone
Through summer and winter seem
Enchanted to a stone
To trouble the living stream.
The horse that comes from the road,
The rider, the birds that range
From cloud to tumbling cloud,
Minute by minute they change;
A shadow of cloud on the stream
Changes minute by minute;
A horse-hoof slides on the brim,
And a horse plashes within it;
The long-legged moor-hens dive,
And hens to moor-cocks call;
Minute by minute they live:
The stone's in the midst of all.

Too long a sacrifice
Can make a stone of the heart.
O when may it suffice?
That is Heaven's part, our part
To murmur name upon name,
As a mother names her child
When sleep at last has come
On limbs that had run wild.
What is it but nightfall?
No, no, not night but death;
Was it needless death after all?
For England may keep faith
For all that is done and said.
We know their dream; enough
To know they dreamed and are dead;
And what if excess of love
Bewildered them till they died?
I write it out in a verse—

78. Maud Gonne and Iseult Gonne.

MacDonagh and MacBride
And Connolly and Pearse
Now and in time to be,
Wherever green is worn,
Are changed, changed utterly:
A terrible beauty is born.

54. George Russell (Æ), "The New Nation" (1917), *Imagination and Reveries* (published 1921)

Like W. B. Yeats, George Russell (1867–1935), also known by his pen name Æ, reflects on the meaning of the Easter Rising. Russell was an editor, mystic, painter, poet, writer, and part of the agricultural cooperative movement. He was from an Anglo-Irish family, was born in County Armagh in Ulster, and grew up in Dublin. He was trained as an artist at the Metropolitan School of Art, a leading figure in the Dublin Theosophical Society (1888–1908), vice president of the Irish National Theatre Society (a position that he maintained when it became the Abbey Theatre in 1904), and a participant in the Irish Convention, created by the British government in 1917 to create a compromise between nationalists and Unionists.

In "The New Nation" Russell viewed the Easter Rising in the larger context of Irish history. For Russell, the differences between nationalists and loyalists were less important than the common ground they shared as Irishmen, produced by the intermingling of multiple cultures—Celtic, Danish, English, Norman, and Scottish. He uniquely drew a parallel between those Irish soldiers who died fighting for their country in World War I and the determined nationalists who sacrificed their lives as a consequence of the Easter Rising. In the poem following the essay, "To the Memory of Some I Knew Who Are Dead and Who Loved Ireland," Russell alternated between lamenting the deaths of the participants in the Rising (Pádraic Pearse, James Connolly, and Thomas MacDonagh) and the Irish soldiers who had died fighting in the Great War. He specifically mentioned Alan Anderson (c. 1892–1914), Tom Kettle (1880–1916), and William Redmond (1861–1917), the brother of the leader of the Irish Parliamentary Party.

In that cycle of history which closed in 1914, but which seems now to the imagination as far sunken behind time as Babylon or Samarcand,[79] it was customary at the festival of the Incarnation to forego our enmities for a little and allow freer play to the spiritual in our being. Since 1914 all things in the world and with us, too, in Ireland have existed in a welter of hate, but the rhythm of ancient habit cannot altogether have passed away, and now if at any time, it should be possible to blow the bugles of Heaven and recall men to that old allegiance. I do not think it would help now if I, or another, put forward arguments drawn from Irish history or economics to convince any party that they were wrong and their opponents right. I think absolute

---

79. Important cities in the ancient world.

truth might be stated in respect of these things, and yet it would affect nothing in our present mood. It would not be recognized any more than Heaven, when It walked on earth in the guise of a Carpenter, was hailed by men whose minds were filled by other imaginations of that coming.

I will not argue about the past, but would ask Irishmen to consider how in future they may live together. Do they contemplate the continuance of these bitter hatreds in our own household? The war must have a finale. Many thousands of Irishmen will return to their country who have faced death for other ideals than those which inspire many more thousands now in Ireland and make them also fearless of death. How are these to co-exist in the same island if there is no change of heart? Each will receive passionate support from relatives, friends, and parties who uphold their action. This will be a most unhappy country if we cannot arrive at some moral agreement, as necessary as a political agreement. Partition is no settlement, because there is no geographical limitation of these passions. There is scarce a locality in Ireland where antagonisms do not gather about the thought of Ireland as in the caduceus of Mercury the twin serpents writhe about the sceptre of the god.[80] I ask our national extremists in what mood do they propose to meet those who return, men of temper as stern as their own? Will these endure being termed traitors to Ireland? Will their friends endure it? Will those who mourn their dead endure to hear scornful speech of those they loved? That way is for us a path to Hell. The unimaginative who see only a majority in their own locality, or, perhaps, in the nation, do not realize what a powerful factor in national life are those who differ from them, and how they are upheld by a neighboring nation which, for all its present travail, is more powerful by far than Ireland even if its people were united in purpose as the fingers of one hand. Nor can those who hold to, and are upheld by, the Empire hope to coerce to a uniformity of feeling with themselves the millions clinging to Irish nationality. Seven centuries of repression have left that spirit unshaken, nor can it be destroyed save by the destruction of the Irish people, because it springs from biological necessity. As well might a foolish gardener trust that his apple-tree would bring forth grapes as to dream that there could be uniformity of character and civilization between Irishmen and Englishmen. It would be a crime against life if it could be brought about and diversities of culture and civilization made impossible. We may live at peace with our neighbors when it is agreed that we must be different, and no peace is possible in the world between nations except on this understanding. But I am not now thinking of that, but of the more urgent problem how we are to live at peace with each other. I am convinced Irish enmities are perpetuated because we live by memory more than by hope, and that even now on the facts of character there is no justification for these enmities.

We have been told that there are two nations in Ireland. That may have been so in the past, but it is not true today. The union of Norman and Dane and Saxon and Celt which has been going on through the centuries is now completed, and there is but one powerful Irish character—not Celtic or Norman-Saxon, but a new race. We should recognize our moral identity. It was apparent before the war in the methods

---

80. The scepter or staff of the Greek/Roman God Hermes/Mercury consists of two identical and intertwined serpents that face each other.

by which Ulstermen and Nationalists alike strove to defend or win their political objects. There is scarce an Ulsterman, whether he regards his ancestors as settlers or not, who is not allied through marriage by his forbears to the ancient race. There is in his veins the blood of the people who existed before Patrick, and he can look backward through time to the legends of the Red Branch, the Fianna and the gods as the legends of his people.[81] It would be as difficult to find even on the Western Coast a family which has not lost in the same way its Celtic purity of race.[82] The character of all is fed from many streams which have mingled in them and have given them a new distinctiveness. The invasions of Ireland and the Plantations, however morally unjustifiable, however cruel in method, are justified by biology. The invasion of one race by another was nature's ancient way of reinvigorating a people.

Mr. Flinders Petrie, in his "Revolutions of Civilization,"[83] has demonstrated that civilization comes in waves, that races rise to a pinnacle of power and culture, and decline from that, and fall into decadence, from which they do not emerge until there has been a crossing of races, a fresh intermingling of cultures. He showed in ancient Egypt eight such periods, and after every decline into decadence there was an invasion, the necessary precedent to a fresh ascent with reinvigorated energies. I prefer to dwell upon the final human results of this commingling of races than upon the tyrannies and conflicts which made it possible. The mixture of races has added to the elemental force of the Celtic character a more complex mentality, and has saved us from becoming, as in our island isolation we might easily have become, thin and weedy, like herds where there has been too much in-breeding. The modern Irish are a race built up from many races who have to prove themselves for the future. Their animosities, based on past history, have little justification in racial diversity today, for they are a new people with only superficial cultural and political differences, but with the same fundamental characteristics. It is hopeless, the dream held by some that the ancient Celtic character could absorb the new elements, become dominant once more, and be itself unchanged. It is equally hopeless to dream the Celtic element could be eliminated. We are a new people, and not the past, but the future, is to justify this new nationality.

I believe it was this powerful Irish character which stirred in Ulster before the war, leading it to adopt methods unlike the Anglo-Saxon tradition in politics.[84] I believe

81. Russell is suggesting that all inhabitants of Ireland, even those of Scottish descent, have common pre-Christian ancestors. Thus, they can trace some part of their ancestry before St. Patrick (c. 387–493; credited with converting Ireland to Christianity) to the mythological figures of the Fianna (warriors in the Fenian cycle) and the Red Branch (royal houses of the king of Ulster in the Ulster cycle).

82. The western part of Ireland was the least Anglicized and hence often represented as the most Gaelic and Celtic.

83. William Matthew Flinders Petrie (1853–1942), British archaeologist and Egyptologist. His *The Revolutions of Civilization* (1911) was a comparative history arguing for the cyclical nature of civilizations.

84. Russell is suggesting that when Ulster Unionists armed themselves in opposition to Home Rule, they were acting more *Irish* than *British*, the former signifying a passionate nature prone to action, the latter a spirit of compromise, moderation, and devotion to the parliamentary process.

that new character, far more than the spirit of the ancient race, was the ferment in the blood of those who brought about the astonishing enterprise of Easter Week. Pearse himself, for all his Gaelic culture, was sired by one of the race he fought against.[85] He might stand in that respect as a symbol of the new race which is springing up. We are slowly realizing the vigor of the modern Irish character just becoming self-conscious of itself. I had met many men who were in the enterprise of Easter Week and listened to their speech, but they had to prove to myself and others by more than words. I listened with that half-cynical feeling which is customary with us when men advocate a cause with which we are temperamentally sympathetic, but about whose realization we are hopeless. I could not gauge the strength of the new spirit, for words do not by themselves convey the quality of power in men; and even when the reverberations from Easter Week were echoing everywhere in Ireland, for a time I, and many others, thought and felt about those who died as some pagan concourse in ancient Italy might have felt looking down upon an arena, seeing below a foam of glorious faces turned to them, the noble, undismayed, inflexible faces of martyrs, and, without understanding, have realized that this spirit was stronger than death. I believe that capacity for sacrifice, that devotion to ideals exists equally among the opponents of these men. It would have been proved in Ireland, in Ulster, if the need had arisen. It has been proved on many a battlefield of Europe. Whatever views we may hold about the relative value of national or Imperial ideals, we may recognize that there is moral equality where the sacrifice is equal. No one has more to give than life, and, when that is given, neither Nationalist nor Imperialist in Ireland can claim moral superiority for the dead champions of their causes.

And here I come to the purpose of my letter, which is to deprecate the scornful repudiation by Irishmen of other Irishmen, which is so common at present, and which helps to perpetuate our feuds. We are all one people. We are closer to each other in character than we are to any other race. The necessary preliminary to political adjustment is moral adjustment, forgiveness, and mutual understanding. I have been in council with others of my countrymen for several months, and I noticed what an obstacle it was to agreement how few, how very few, there were who had been on terms of friendly intimacy with men of all parties. There was hardly one who could have given an impartial account of the ideals and principles of his opponents. Our political differences have brought about social isolations, and there can be no understanding where there is no eagerness to meet those who differ from us, and hear the best they have to say for themselves. This letter is an appeal to Irishmen to seek out and understand their political opponents. If they come to know each other, they will come to trust each other, and will realize their kinship, and will set their faces to the future together, to build up a civilization which will justify their nationality.

I myself am Anglo-Irish, with the blood of both races in me, and when the rising of Easter Week took place all that was Irish in me was profoundly stirred, and out of that mood I wrote commemorating the dead. And then later there rose in memory

85. Pearse's father, James Pearse (1839–1900), was an English stonemason who immigrated to Ireland from Birmingham.

the faces of others I knew who loved their country, but had died in other battles. They fought in those because they believed they would serve Ireland, and I felt these were no less my people. I could hold them also in my heart and pay tribute to them. Because it was possible for me to do so, I think it is possible for others; and in the hope that the deeds of all may in the future be a matter of pride to the new nation. I append here these verses I have written:—

TO THE MEMORY OF SOME I KNEW WHO ARE DEAD
AND WHO LOVED IRELAND

Their dream had left me numb and cold,
    But yet my spirit rose in pride,
Refashioning in burnished gold
    The images of those who died,
Or were shut in the penal cell.
    Here's to you, Pearse, your dream not mine,
But yet the thought, for this you fell,
    Has turned life's water into wine.

You[86] who have died on Eastern hills
    Or fields of France as undismayed,
Who lit with interlinked wills
    The long heroic barricade,
You, too, in all the dreams you had,
    Thought of some thing for Ireland done.
Was it not so, Oh, shining lad,
    What lured you, Alan Anderson?

I listened to high talk from you,
    Thomas McDonagh, and it seemed
The words were idle, but they grew
    To nobleness by death redeemed.
Life cannot utter words more great
    Than life may meet by sacrifice,
High words were equaled by high fate,
    You paid the price. You paid the price.

You who have fought on fields afar,
    That other Ireland did you wrong
Who said you shadowed Ireland's star,
    Nor gave you laurel wreath nor song.
You proved by death as true as they,
    In mightier conflicts played your part,

86. Irish soldiers who fought in World War I on the side of the British.

Equal your sacrifice may weigh,
    Dear Kettle, of the generous heart.

The hope lives on age after age,
    Earth with its beauty might be won
For labor as a heritage,
    For this has Ireland lost a son.
This hope unto a flame to fan
    Men have put life by with a smile,
Here's to you Connolly, my man,
    Who cast the last torch on the pile.

You too, had Ireland in your care,
    Who watched o'er pits of blood and mire,
From iron roots leap up in air
    Wild forests, magical, of fire;
Yet while the Nuts of Death were shed
    Your memory would ever stray
To your own isle. Oh, gallant dead—
    This wreath, Will Redmond, on your clay.

Here's to you, men I never met,
    Yet hope to meet behind the veil,
Thronged on some starry parapet,
    That looks down upon Innisfail,[87]
And sees the confluence of dreams
    That clashed together in our night,
One river, born from many streams,
Roll in one blaze of blinding light.

December 1917

55. Anglo-Irish Treaty (1921)

The Anglo-Irish War was prompted by the refusal of Sinn Féin MPs to take their seats in the British Parliament following the 1918 parliamentary elections and their establishment of Dáil Éireann or the Irish Parliament, better known as the Dáil. The military conflict commenced with the murder of two policemen on January 21, 1919, by a group of IRA militants in County Tipperary. By 1921 the Anglo-Irish War had bogged down into a stalemate. In the summer the British prime minister, David Lloyd George, and the president of the Irish Republic, Éamon de Valera, negotiated the grounds for peace talks. De Valera neither insisted on an independent state nor a unified Ireland as a

---

87. Ancient name for Ireland.

precondition for talks. Michael Collins later observed that full-scale independence was no longer a possibility after the Irish side agreed to send a negotiating team to London. De Valera's decision to appoint Arthur Griffith as the head of the negotiating team reinforced this pragmatism, as Griffith had not insisted upon a republic. As discussed in the introduction to this chapter, the decision to send Collins and have de Valera remain behind in Dublin has been controversial ever since. Equally controversial has been de Valera's decision to give the negotiating team full plenipotentiary status while insisting retrospectively that it was to report back to him prior to any final decision. If the negotiating team had reported back to him—which they did not—de Valera would have been in his constituency in Limerick, not Dublin, when the final decision had to be made.

The negotiations took place in London during the autumn of 1921. They hinged not on the status of Northern Ireland, which the negotiators agreed to put off until a later date, but on the position of Ireland within the British Empire and particularly the form of oath that would be required of MPs in an Irish Parliament. De Valera had argued for external association with the British Empire and an oath in which the individual would swear "true faith and allegiance to the constitution of the Irish Free State, to the Treaty of Association and to recognize the King of Great Britain as head of the Associated States" (quoted in Jackson 1999, 261). His proposal, however, was unacceptable to the British negotiators who insisted on an oath that swore personal allegiance to the king, as was the case in other dominions. In the end, the oath agreed upon was intended to satisfy not only Irish nationalists but also British Conservatives who supported continuing the war until Irish insurgents were defeated.

The treaty was signed on December 6, 1921, following Lloyd George's take it or leave it offer. The most important elements were (1) Ireland would achieve dominion status along the lines of Canada, Australia, and New Zealand with a governor-general as the representative of the Crown; and (2) an agreement over Ulster's future status would be delayed, allowing it to be settled by a Boundary Commission of Irish, British, and Ulster representatives.

ANGLO-IRISH TREATY
ARTICLES OF AGREEMENT AS SIGNED
on DECEMBER 6th, 1921

1. Ireland shall have the same constitutional status in the Community of Nations known as the British Empire as the Dominion of Canada, the Commonwealth of Australia, the Dominion of New Zealand and the Union of South Africa, with a Parliament having powers to make laws for the peace, order and good government of Ireland and an Executive responsible to that Parliament, and shall be styled and known as the Irish Free State.

2. Subject to the provisions hereinafter set out the position of the Irish Free State in relation to the Imperial Parliament and Government and otherwise shall be that of the Dominion of Canada, and the law practice and constitutional usage governing the relationship of the Crown or the representative of the Crown and of the Imperial Parliament to the Dominion of Canada shall govern their relationship to the Irish Free State.

3. The representative of the Crown in Ireland shall be appointed in like manner as the Governor-General of Canada and in accordance with the practice observed in the making of such appointments.

4. The oath to be taken by Members of the Parliament of the Irish Free State shall be in the following form:

   I .... do solemnly swear true faith and allegiance to the Constitution of the Irish Free State as by law established and that I will be faithful to H.M. King George V,[88] his heirs and successors by law, in virtue of the common citizenship of Ireland with Great Britain and her adherence to and membership of the group of nations forming the British Commonwealth of Nations.

5. The Irish Free State shall assume liability for the service of the Public Debt of the United Kingdom as existing at the date hereof and towards the payment of war pensions as existing at that date in such proportion as may be fair and equitable, having regard to any just claims on the part of Ireland by way of set-off or counter-claim, the amount of such sums being determined in default of agreement by the arbitration of one or more independent persons being citizens of the British Empire.

6. Until an arrangement has been made between the British and Irish Governments whereby the Irish Free State undertakes her own coastal defence, the defence by sea of Great Britain and Ireland shall be undertaken by His Majesty's Imperial Forces. But this shall not prevent the construction or maintenance by the Government of the Irish Free State of such vessels as are necessary for the protection of the Revenue or the Fisheries. The foregoing provisions of this Article shall be reviewed at a Conference of Representatives of the British and Irish Governments to be held at the expiration of five years from the date hereof with a view to a share in her own coastal defence.

7. The Government of the Irish Free State shall afford to His Majesty's Imperial Forces:

   (a) In time of peace such harbour and other facilities as are indicated in the Annex hereto, or such other facilities as may from time to time be agreed between the British Government and the Government of the Irish Free State; and

   (b) In time of war or of strained relations with a Foreign Power such harbour and other facilities as the British Government may require for the purposes of such defence as aforesaid.

8. With a view to securing the observance of the principle of international limitation of armaments, if the Government of the Irish Free State establishes and maintains a military defence force, the establishments thereof shall not exceed in size such proportion of the military establishments maintained in Great Britain as that which the population of Ireland bears to the population of Great Britain.

---

88. George V (1865–1936), king of the United Kingdom and the British Dominions and the emperor of India between 1910 and his death in 1936.

9. The ports of Great Britain and the Irish Free State shall be freely open to the ships of the other country on payment of the customary port and other dues.

10. The Government of the Irish Free State agrees to pay fair compensation on terms not less favourable than those accorded by the Act of 1920[89] to judges, officials, members of Police Forces and other Public Servants who are discharged by it or who retire in consequence of the change of Government effected in pursuance hereof.

    Provided that this agreement shall not apply to members of the Auxiliary Police Force or to persons recruited in Great Britain for the Royal Irish Constabulary during the two years next preceding the date hereof. The British Government will assume responsibility for such compensation or pensions as may be payable to any of these excepted persons.

11. Until the expiration of one month from the passing of the Act of Parliament for the ratification of this instrument, the powers of the Parliament and the Government of the Irish Free State shall not be exercisable as respects Northern Ireland and the provisions of the Government of Ireland Act, 1920, shall so far as they relate to Northern Ireland remain of full force and effect, and no election shall be held for the return of members to serve in the Parliament of the Irish Free State for constituencies in Northern Ireland, unless a resolution is passed by both Houses of the Parliament of Northern Ireland in favour of the holding of such election before the end of the said month.

12. If before the expiration of the said month, an address is presented to His Majesty by both Houses of the Parliament of Northern Ireland to that effect, the powers of the Parliament and Government of the Irish Free State shall no longer extend to Northern Ireland, and the provisions of the Government of Ireland Act, 1920 (including those relating to the Council of Ireland) shall, so far as they relate to Northern Ireland continue to be of full force and effect, and this instrument shall have effect subject to the necessary modifications.

    Provided that if such an address is so presented a Commission consisting of three Persons, one to be appointed by the Government of the Irish Free State, one to be appointed by the Government of Northern Ireland and one who shall be Chairman to be appointed by the British Government shall determine in accordance with the wishes of the inhabitants, so far as may be compatible with economic and geographic conditions, the boundaries between Northern Ireland and the rest of Ireland, and for the purposes of the Government of Ireland Act, 1920, and of this instrument, the boundary of Northern Ireland shall be such as may be determined by such Commission.

13. For the purpose of the last foregoing article, the powers of the Parliament of Southern Ireland under the Government of Ireland Act, 1920, to elect members of the Council of Ireland shall after the Parliament of the Irish Free State is constituted be exercised by that Parliament.

89. The Government of Ireland Act (1920) provided Home Rule for a partitioned Ireland on British terms.

14. After the expiration of the said month, if no such address as is mentioned in Article 12 hereof is Presented, the Parliament and Government of Northern Ireland shall continue to exercise as respects Northern Ireland the powers conferred on them by the Government of Ireland Act, 1920, but the Parliament and Government of the Irish Free State shall in Northern Ireland have in relation to matters in respect of which the Parliament of Northern Ireland has not power to make laws under that Act (including matters which under the said Act are within the jurisdiction of the Council of Ireland) the same powers as in the rest of Ireland, subject to such other provisions as may be agreed in manner hereinafter appearing.

15. At any time after the date hereof the Government of Northern Ireland and the provisional Government of Southern Ireland hereinafter constituted may meet for the purpose of discussing the provisions subject to which the last foregoing article is to operate in the event of no such address as is therein mentioned being presented and those provisions may include:

    (a) Safeguards with regard to patronage in Northern Ireland:

    (b) Safeguards with regard to the collection of revenue in Northern Ireland:

    (c) Safeguards with regard to import and export duties affecting the trade or industry of Northern Ireland:

    (d) Safeguards for minorities in Northern Ireland:

    (e) The settlement of the financial relations between Northern Ireland and the Irish Free State:

    (f) The establishment and powers of a local militia in Northern Ireland and the relation of the Defence Forces of the Irish Free State and of Northern Ireland respectively:

    and if at any such meeting provisions are agreed to, the same shall have effect as if they were included amongst the provisions subject to which the Powers of the Parliament and Government of the Irish Free State are to be exercisable in Northern Ireland under Article 14 hereof.

16. Neither the Parliament of the Irish Free State nor the Parliament of Northern Ireland shall make any law so as either directly or indirectly to endow any religion or prohibit or restrict the free exercise thereof or give any preference or impose any disability on account of religious belief or religious status or affect prejudicially the right of any child to attend a school receiving public money without attending religious instruction at the school or make any discrimination as respects state aid between schools under the management of different religious denominations or divert from any religious denomination or any educational institution any of its property except for public utility purposes and on payment of compensation.

17. By way of provisional arrangement for the administration of Southern Ireland during the interval which must elapse between the date hereof and the constitution of a Parliament and Government of the Irish Free State in accordance therewith, steps shall be taken forthwith for summoning a meeting of members

of Parliament elected for constituencies in Southern Ireland since the passing of the Government of Ireland Act, 1920, and for constituting a provisional Government, and the British Government shall take the steps necessary to transfer to such provisional Government the powers and machinery requisite for the discharge of its duties, provided that every member of such provisional Government shall have signified in writing his or her acceptance of this instrument. But this arrangement shall not continue in force beyond the expiration of twelve months from the date hereof.

18. This instrument shall be submitted forthwith by His Majesty's Government for the approval of Parliament and by the Irish signatories to a meeting summoned for the purpose of the members elected to sit in the House of Commons of Southern Ireland, and if approved shall be ratified by the necessary legislation.

On behalf of the British Delegation.

Signed

D. LLOYD GEORGE
AUSTEN CHAMBERLAIN
BIRKENHEAD
WINSTON S. CHURCHILL
L. WORTHINGTON-EVANS
HAMAR GREENWOOD
GORDON HEWART

On behalf of the Irish Delegation

Signed

ART GRIOBHTHA (ARTHUR GRIFFITH)
MICHEAL Ó COILÉAIN
RIOBÁRD BARTÚN
EUDHMONN S. Ó DÚGÁIN
SEÓRSA GHABHÁIN UÍ DHUBHTHAIGH[90]

December 6th, 1921

56. Dáil Éireann, Debate on the Anglo-Irish Treaty (1921–22)

The Anglo-Irish Treaty signed by Michael Collins, Arthur Griffith, and the Irish team of negotiators was by any definition contentious. Although it was approved by Dáil Éireann by the narrow vote of sixty-four to fifty-seven, and in the subsequent June parliamentary

---

90. The Anglicized names of the Irish signatories are Arthur Griffith, Michael Collins, Robert Barton, Eamonn Duggan, and George Gavan Duffy.

elections the pro-treaty forces won a substantial majority of the seats, it produced a deeply divided and conflicted nationalist movement, ultimately leading to the Irish Civil War of 1922–23. The opponents of the treaty found it hard to swallow that the heroic sacrifices of a generation had achieved something as paltry as dominion status and the retention of the humiliating oath to the British Crown. Indeed, it was the oath, more than any other part of the treaty, which became the focus of the opposition. For vehement opponents of the treaty such as Mary McSwiney, the negotiators had betrayed the Irish people. But there were more nuanced positions as well. De Valera advocated external association, whereby a self-governing Ireland would voluntarily associate with the British Commonwealth for matters of common concern rather than be a member of it. In de Valera's proposal, Ireland would recognize the Crown as head of that organization.

The excerpts from the treaty debate reproduced here convey the diversity of opinion and argument that took place. They are taken from two of the sessions of the Dáil and comprise only a small sampling of the total discussion, as every member of the assembly was allowed to speak, and the sessions lasted over several days. The second of these sessions includes the vote on the treaty as well as the discussion that followed. I can think of few more poignant moments in politics as Collins' effort to keep a dialogue open with his erstwhile allies, many of whom he had fought with in the armed struggle, or de Valera breaking down in tears when he relinquished the office of president.

December 19, 1921

. . . ARTHUR GRIFFITH: What we have to say is this, that the difference in this Cabinet and in this House is between half-recognising the British King and the British Empire, and between marching in, as one of the speakers said, with our heads up. The gentlemen on the other side are prepared to recognise the King of England as head of the British Commonwealth. They are prepared to go half in the Empire and half out. They are prepared to go into the Empire for war and peace and treaties, and to keep out for other matters, and that is what the Irish people have got to know is the difference. Does all this quibble of words—because it is merely a quibble of words—mean that Ireland is asked to throw away this Treaty and go back to war? So far as my power or voice extends, not one young Irishman's life shall be lost on that quibble. We owe responsibility to the Irish people. I feel my responsibility to the Irish people, and the Irish people must know, and know in every detail, the difference that exists between us, and the Irish people must be our judges. When the plenipotentiaries came back they were sought to be put in the dock. Well, if I am going to be tried, I am going to be tried by the people of Ireland (hear, hear). Now this Treaty has been attacked. It has been examined with a microscope to find its defects, and this little thing and that little thing has been pointed out, and the people are told—one of the gentlemen said it here—that it was less even than the proposals of July.[91] It is the first

91. Proposals made by the British government to serve as a basis for the negotiations between the British and Irish contingents. They called for Ireland to have dominion status within the British Empire subject to a series of constraints regarding defense, trade, war debt payments, and the future of Northern Ireland.

Treaty between the representatives of the Irish Government and the representatives of the English Government since 1172[92] signed on equal footing. It is the first Treaty that admits the equality of Ireland. It is a Treaty of equality, and because of that I am standing by it. We have come back from London with that Treaty—Saorstat na hEireann[93] recognized—the Free State of Ireland. We have brought back the flag; we have brought back the evacuation of Ireland after 700 years by British troops and the formation of an Irish army (applause). We have brought back to Ireland her full rights and powers of fiscal control. We have brought back to Ireland equality with England, equality with all nations which form that Commonwealth, and an equal voice in the direction of foreign affairs in peace and war. Well, we are told that that Treaty is a derogation from our status; that it is a Treaty not to be accepted, that it is a poor thing, and that the Irish people ought to go back and fight for something more, and that something more is what I describe as a quibble of words. . . . At all events, the Irish people are a people of great common sense. They know that a Treaty that gives them their flag and their Free State and their Army (cheers) is not a sham Treaty, and the sophists and the men of words will not mislead them, I tell you. . . .

Now, many criticisms, I know, will be levelled against this Treaty; one in particular, one that is in many instances quite honest, it is the question of the oath. I ask the members to see what the oath is, to read it, not to misunderstand or misrepresent it. It is an oath of allegiance to the Constitution of the Free State of Ireland and of faithfulness to King George V in his capacity as head and in virtue of the common citizenship of Ireland with Great Britain and the other nations comprising the British Commonwealth. That is an oath, I say, that any Irishman could take with honour. He pledges his allegiance to his country and to be faithful to this Treaty, and faithfulness after to the head of the British Commonwealth of Nations. If his country were unjustly used by any of the nations of that Commonwealth, or its head, then his allegiance is to his own country and his allegiance bids him to resist (hear, hear). We took an oath to the Irish Republic, but, as President de Valera himself said, he understood that oath to bind him to do the best he could for Ireland. So do we. We have done the best we could for Ireland. If the Irish people say "We have got everything else but the name Republic, and we will fight for it," I would say to them that they are fools, but I will follow in the ranks. I will take no responsibility. But the Irish people will not do that. Now it has become rather a custom for men to speak of what they did, and did not do, in the past. I am not going to speak of that aspect, except one thing. It is this. The prophet I followed throughout my life, the man whose words and teachings I tried to translate into practice in politics, the man whom I revered above all Irish patriots was Thomas Davis. In the hard way of fitting practical affairs into idealism I have made Thomas Davis my guide. I have never departed in my life one inch from the principles of Thomas Davis, and in signing this Treaty and bringing it here and asking Ireland to ratify it I am following Thomas Davis still. . . . Thomas Davis said: "Peace with England, alliance with England to some extent, and, under

92. In 1171–72, Henry II, king of England, intervened in Ireland and accepted the homage of both native Irish kingdoms and Anglo-Norman barons.
93. The Irish Free State (Irish).

certain circumstances, confederation with England; but an Irish ambition, Irish hopes, strength, virtue, and rewards for the Irish." That is what we have brought back, peace with England, alliance with England, confederation with England, an Ireland developing her own life, carving out her own way of existence, and rebuilding the Gaelic civilisation broken down at the battle of Kinsale.[94] I say we have brought you that. I say we have translated Thomas Davis into the practical politics of the day. I ask then this Dáil to pass this resolution, and I ask the people of Ireland, and the Irish people everywhere, to ratify this Treaty, to end this bitter conflict of centuries, to end it for ever, to take away that poison that has been rankling in the two countries and ruining the relationship of good neighbours. Let us stand as free partners, equal with England, and make after 700 years the greatest revolution that has ever been made in the history of the world—a revolution of seeing the two countries standing not apart as enemies, but standing together as equals and as friends. I ask you, therefore, to pass this resolution (applause). . . .

PRESIDENT DE VALERA: I think it would scarcely be in accordance with Standing Orders of the Dáil if I were to move directly the rejection of this Treaty. I daresay, however, it will be sufficient that I should appeal to this House not to approve of the Treaty. We were elected by the Irish people, and did the Irish people think we were liars when we said that we meant to uphold the Republic, which was ratified by the vote of the people three years ago, and was further ratified—expressly ratified—by the vote of the people at the elections last May?[95] When the proposal for negotiation came from the British Government asking that we should try by negotiation to reconcile Irish national aspirations with the association of nations forming the British Empire, there was no one here as strong as I was to make sure that every human attempt should be made to find whether such reconciliation was possible. I am against this Treaty because it does not reconcile Irish national aspirations with association with the British Government. I am against this Treaty, not because I am a man of war, but a man of peace. I am against this Treaty because it will not end the centuries of conflict between the two nations of Great Britain and Ireland.

We went out to effect such a reconciliation and we have brought back a thing which will not even reconcile our own people much less reconcile Britain and Ireland.

If there was to be reconciliation, it is obvious that the party in Ireland which typifies national aspirations for centuries should be satisfied, and the test of every agreement would be the test of whether the people were satisfied or not. A war-weary people will take things which are not in accordance with their aspirations. You may have a

94. The Battle of Kinsale (1601) was a stunning defeat of the Irish and Spanish forces of Hugh O'Neill and Red Hugh O'Donnell (1572–1602) by the English army of Lord Mountjoy (1563–1606). It was a critical moment in the collapse of the old Gaelic lordships and the solidification of English power in Ireland.

95. In the UK's 1918 parliamentary elections, Sinn Féin won the vast majority of Irish seats and constituted itself as the Irish Parliament or Dáil Éireann, pledging itself to an Irish Republic. In 1921, Dáil Éireann held elections following the Government of Ireland Act in the counties that would later form the Irish Free State. All candidates were unopposed and hence voters did not actually go to the polls. Sinn Féin was victorious in 124 out of 128 constituencies. Independent Unionists representing Trinity College won the other four seats.

snatch election now, and you may get a vote of the people, but I will tell you that Treaty will renew the contest that is going to begin the same history that the Union began, and Lloyd George is going to have the same fruit for his labours as [William] Pitt [the Younger] had. When in Downing Street[96] the proposals to which we could unanimously assent in the Cabinet were practically turned down at the point of the pistol and immediate war was threatened upon our people. It was only then that this document was signed, and that document has been signed by plenipotentiaries, not perhaps individually under duress, but it has been signed, and would only affect this nation as a document signed under duress, and this nation would not respect it.

I wanted, and the Cabinet wanted, to get a document we could stand by, a document that could enable Irishmen to meet Englishmen and shake hands with them as fellow-citizens of the world. That document makes British authority our masters in Ireland. It was said that they had only an oath to the British King in virtue of common citizenship, but you have an oath to the Irish Constitution, and that Constitution will be a Constitution which will have the King of Great Britain as head of Ireland. You will swear allegiance to that Constitution and to that King; and if the representatives of the Republic should ask the people of Ireland to do that which is inconsistent with the Republic, I say they are subverting the Republic. It would be a surrender which was never heard of in Ireland since the days of Henry II; and are we in this generation, which has made Irishmen famous throughout the world, to sign our names to the most ignoble document that could be signed.

When I was in prison in solitary confinement our warders told us that we could go from our cells into the hall, which was about fifty feet by forty. We did go out from the cells to the hall, but we did not give our word to the British jailer that he had the right to detain us in prison because we got that privilege. Again on another occasion we were told that we could get out to a garden party, where we could see the flowers and the hills, but we did not for the privilege of going out to garden parties sign a document handing over our souls and bodies to the jailers. Rather than sign a document which would give Britain authority in Ireland they should be ready to go into slavery until the Almighty had blotted out their tyrants (applause). If the British Government passed a Home Rule Act or something of that kind I would not have said to the Irish people, "Do not take it." I would have said, "Very well; this is a case of the jailer leading you from the cell to the hall," but by getting that we did not sign away our right to whatever form of government we pleased. It was said that an uncompromising stand for a Republic was not made. The stand made by some of them was to try and reconcile a Republic with an association. There was a document presented to this House to try to get unanimity, to see whether the views which I hold could be reconciled to that party which typified the national aspirations of Ireland for centuries. The document was put there for that purpose, and I defy anybody in this House to say otherwise than that I was trying to bring forward before this assembly a document which would bring real peace between Great Britain and Ireland—a sort of document we would have tried to get and would not have agreed if we did not get. It would be a document that would give real peace to the people of Great Britain and Ireland and not the officials. I

96. 10 Downing Street, the residence of the British prime minister.

know it would not be a politicians' peace. I know the politician in England who would
take it would risk his political future, but it would be a peace between peoples, and
would be consistent with the Irish people being full masters of everything within their
own shores. Criticism of this Treaty is scarcely necessary from this point of view, that it
could not be ratified because it would not be legal for this assembly to ratify it, because
it would be inconsistent with our position. We were elected here to be the guardians
of an independent Irish State—a State that had declared its independence—and this
House could no more than the ignominious House that voted away the Colonial
Parliament that was in Ireland in 1800[97] unless we wished to follow the example of
that House and vote away the independence of our people. We could not ratify that
instrument if it were brought before us for ratification. It is, therefore, to be brought
before us not for ratification, because it would be inconsistent, and the very fact that
it is inconsistent shows that it could not be reconciled with Irish aspirations, because
the aspirations of the Irish people have been crystallised into the form of Government
they have at the present time. As far as I was concerned, I am probably the freest man
here to express my opinion. Before I was elected President at the Private Session, I said,
"Remember I do not take, as far as I am concerned, oaths as regards forms of Government. I regard myself here to maintain the independence of Ireland and to do the best
for the Irish people," and it is to do the best for the Irish people that I ask you not to
approve but to reject this Treaty. . . .

MICHAEL COLLINS: . . . The communication of September 29th from Lloyd
George made it clear that they were going into a conference not on the recognition of
the Irish Republic, and I say if we all stood on the recognition of the Irish Republic as
a prelude to any conference we could very easily have said so, and there would be no
conference. What I want to make clear is that it was the acceptance of the invitation
that formed the compromise. I was sent there to form that adaptation, to bear the
brunt of it. Now as one of the signatories of the document I naturally recommend its
acceptance. I do not recommend it for more than it is. Equally I do not recommend
it for less than it is. In my opinion it gives us freedom, not the ultimate freedom that
all nations desire and develop to, but the freedom to achieve it (applause).

A Deputy has stated that the delegation should introduce this Treaty not, he describes, as bagmen for England, but with an apology for its introduction. I cannot
imagine anything more mean, anything more despicable, anything more unmanly
than this dishonouring of one's signature. Rightly or wrongly when you make a bargain you cannot alter it, you cannot go back and get sorry for it and say "I ought to
have made a better bargain." Business cannot be done on those bases. I must make
reference to the signing of the Treaty. This Treaty was not signed under personal
intimidation. If personal intimidation had been attempted no member of the delegation would have signed it.

At a fateful moment I was called upon to make a decision, and if I were called
upon at the present moment for a decision on the same question my decision would

97. De Valera suggests that just as the Irish Parliament's decision to enter into a union with
Britain and create the UK was illegitimate, so was the act of the Irish signatories to the Anglo-
Irish Treaty.

be the same. Let there be no mistake and no misunderstanding about that. I have used the word "intimidation." The whole attitude of Britain towards Ireland in the past was an attitude of intimidation, and we, as negotiators, were not in the position of conquerors dictating terms of peace to a vanquished foe. We had not beaten the enemy out of our country by force of arms.

To return to the Treaty, hardly anyone, even those who support it, really understands it, and it is necessary to explain it, and the immense powers and liberties it secures. This is my justification for having signed it, and for recommending it to the nation. Should the Dáil reject it, I am, as I said, no longer responsible. But I am responsible for making the nation fully understand what it gains by accepting it, and what is involved in its rejection. So long as I have made that clear I am perfectly happy and satisfied. Now we must look facts in the face. For our continued national and spiritual existence two things are necessary—security and freedom. If the Treaty gives us these or helps us to get at these, then I maintain that it satisfies our national aspirations. The history of this nation has not been, as is so often said, the history of a military struggle of 750 years; it has been much more a history of peaceful penetration of 750 years. It has not been a struggle for the ideal of freedom for 750 years symbolised in the name Republic. It has been a story of slow, steady, economic encroach by England. It has been a struggle on our part to prevent that, a struggle against exploitation, a struggle against the cancer that was eating up our lives, and it was only after discovering that, that it was economic penetration, that we discovered that political freedom was necessary in order that that should be stopped. Our aspirations, by whatever term they may be symbolised, had one thing in front all the time, that was to rid the country of the enemy strength. Now it was not by any form of communication except through their military strength that the English held this country. That is simply a plain fact which, I think, nobody will deny. It wasn't by any forms of government, it wasn't by their judiciary or anything of that kind. These people could not operate except for the military strength that was always there. Now, starting from that, I maintain that the disappearance of that military strength gives us the chief proof that our national liberties are established. . . .

Now I have explained something as to what the Treaty is. I also want to explain to you as one of the signatories what I consider rejection of it means. It has been said that the alternative document does not mean war. Perhaps it does, perhaps it does not. That is not the first part of the argument. I say that rejection of the Treaty is a declaration of war until you have beaten the British Empire, apart from any alternative document. Rejection of the Treaty means your national policy is war. If you do this, if you go on that as a national policy, I for one am satisfied. But I want you to go on it as a national policy and understand what it means. I, as an individual, do not now, no more than ever, shirk war. The Treaty was signed by me, not because they held up the alternative of immediate war. I signed it because I would not be one of those to commit the Irish people to war without the Irish people committing themselves to war. If my constituents send me to represent them in war, I will do my best to represent them in war. Now I was not going to refer to anything that had been said by the speakers of the Coalition side to-day. I do want to say this in regard to the President's remark about Pitt, a remark, it will be admitted, which was not very flattering to us. Well, now, what happened at the time of the Union? Grattan's Parliament was thrown away without reference to the people and against their wishes. Is the Parliament which this Treaty offers us to be similarly treated? Is it to be thrown away without reference to the people and against their wishes?

PRESIDENT DE VALERA: What Parliament?

(A VOICE: The Free State)

MARY MACSWINEY: [98] Which Parliament?

MICHAEL COLLINS: I would like you to keep on interrupting, because I was looking at a point here. I am disappointed that I was not interrupted more. In our Private Sessions we have been treated to harangues about principle. Not one Deputy has stated a clear, steadfast, abiding principle on which we can stand. Deputies have talked of principle. At different times I have known different Deputies to hold different principles. How can I say, how can anyone say, that these Deputies may not change their principles again? How can anyone say that anybody—a Deputy or a supporter—who has fought against the Irish Nation on principle may not fight against it again on principle? I am not impeaching anybody, but I do want to talk straight. I am the representative of an Irish stock; I am the representative equally with any other member of the same stock of people who have suffered through the terror in the past. Our grandfathers have suffered from war, and our fathers or some of our ancestors have died of famine. I don't want a lecture from anybody as to what my principles are to be now. I am just a representative of plain Irish stock whose principles have been burned into them, and we don't want any assurance to the people of this country that we are going to betray them. We are one of themselves. I can state for you a principle which everybody will understand, the principle of "government by the consent of the governed." These words have been used by nearly every Deputy at some time or another. Are the Deputies going to be afraid of these words now, supposing the formula happens to go against them? (PRESIDENT DE VALERA: "No, no.") I have heard Deputies remark that their constituents are in favour of this Treaty. The Deputies have got their powers from their constituents and they are responsible to their constituents. I have stated the principle which is the only firm principle in the whole thing. Now I have gone into more or less a general survey of the Treaty, apart from one section of it, the section dealing with North-East Ulster. Again I am as anxious to face facts in that case as I am in any other case. We have stated we would not coerce the North-East. We have stated it officially in our correspondence. I stated it publicly in Armagh[99] and nobody has found fault with it. What did we mean? Did we mean we were going to coerce them or we were not going to coerce them? What was the use of talking big phrases about not agreeing to the partition of our country. Surely we recognise that the North-East corner does exist, and surely our intention was that we should take such steps as would sooner or later lead to mutual understanding. The Treaty has made an effort to deal with it, and has made an effort, in my opinion, to deal with it on lines that will lead very rapidly to goodwill, and

---

98. In Mary McSwiney, "A Plea for Common Sense" (no. 47) the spelling in the original is "McSwiney," but in this text (no. 56) the spelling is "MacSwiney."

99. Both the name of a county and the county town. Both are in Ulster.

the entry of the North-East under the Irish Parliament (applause). I don't say it is an ideal arrangement, but if our policy is, as has been stated, a policy of noncoercion, then let somebody else get a better way out of it. Now, summing up—and nobody can say that I haven't talked plainly—I say that this Treaty gives us, not recognition of the Irish Republic, but it gives us more recognition on the part of Great Britain and the associated States than we have got from any other nation. Again I want to speak plainly. America did not recognise the Irish Republic. As things in London were coming to a close I received cablegrams from America. I understand that my name is pretty well known in America, and what I am going to say now will make me unpopular there for the rest of my life, but I am not going to say anything or hide anything for the sake of American popularity. I received a cablegram from San Francisco, saying, "Stand fast, we will send you a million dollars a month." Well, my reply to that is, "Send us half-a-million and send us a thousand men fully equipped." I received another cablegram from a branch of the American Association for the Recognition of the Irish Republic and they said to me, "Don't weaken now, stand with de Valera." Well, let that branch come over and stand with us both (applause). The question before me was were we going to go on with this fight, without referring it to the Irish people, for the sake of propaganda in America? I was not going to take that responsibility. And as this may be the last opportunity I shall ever have of speaking publicly to the Dáil, I want to say that there was never an Irishman placed in such a position as I was by reason of these negotiations. I had got a certain name, whether I deserved it or not. (Voices: "You did, well"), and I knew when I was going over there that I was being placed in a position that I could not reconcile, and that I could not in the public mind be reconciled with what they thought I stood for, no matter what we brought back,—and if we brought back the recognition of the Republic—but I knew that the English would make a greater effort if I were there than they would if I were not there, and I didn't care if my popularity was sacrificed or not. I should have been unfair to my own country if I did not go there. Members of the Dáil well remember that I protested against being selected. I want to say another thing. . . . I only want to say that I stand for every action as an individual member of the Cabinet, which I suppose I shall be no longer; I stand for every action, no matter how it looked publicly, and I shall always like the men to remember me like that. In coming to the decision I did I tried to weigh what my own responsibility was. Deputies have spoken about whether dead men would approve of it, and they have spoken of whether children yet unborn will approve of it, but few of them have spoken as to whether the living approve of it. In my own small way I tried to have before my mind what the whole lot of them would think of it. And the proper way for us to look at it is in that way. There is no man here who has more regard for the dead men than I have (hear, hear). I don't think it is fair to be quoting them against us. I think the decision ought to be a clear decision on the documents as they are before us—on the Treaty as it is before us. On that we shall be judged, as to whether we have done the right thing in our own conscience or not. Don't let us put the responsibility, the individual responsibility, upon anybody else. Let us take that responsibility ourselves and let us in God's name abide by the decision (applause).

January 7, 1922

. . . THE SPEAKER: The result of the poll is sixty-four for approval and fifty-seven against. That is a majority of seven in favour of approval of the Treaty. . . .

PRESIDENT DE VALERA: It will, of course, be my duty to resign my office as Chief Executive. I do not know that I should do it just now.

MICHAEL COLLINS: No.

PRESIDENT DE VALERA: There is one thing I want to say—I want it to go to the country and to the world, and it is this: the Irish people established a Republic. This is simply approval of a certain resolution. The Republic can only be disestablished by the Irish people. Therefore, until such time as the Irish people in regular manner disestablish it, this Republic goes on. Whatever arrangements are made this is the supreme sovereign body in the nation; this is the body to which the nation looks for its supreme Government, and it must remain that—no matter who is the Executive—it must remain that until the Irish people have disestablished it.

MICHAEL COLLINS: I ask your permission to make a statement. I do not regard the passing of this thing as being any kind of triumph over the other side. I will do my best in the future, as I have done in the past, for the nation. What I have to say now is, whether there is something contentious about the Republic—about the Government in being—or not, that we should unite on this: that we will all do our best to preserve the public safety (hear, hear).

PRESIDENT DE VALERA: Hear, hear.

MICHAEL COLLINS: Now, in all countries in times of change—when countries are passing from peace to war or war to peace—they have had their most trying times on an occasion like this. Whether we are right or whether we are wrong in the view of future generations there is this: that we now are entitled to a chance; all the responsibility will fall upon us of taking over the machinery of government from the enemy. In times of change like that, when countries change from peace to war or war to peace, there are always elements that make for disorder and that make for chaos. That is as true of Ireland as of any other country; for in that respect all countries are the same. Now, what I suggest is that—I suppose we could regard it like this—that we are a kind of a majority party and that the others are a minority party; that is all I regard it as at present; and upon us, I suppose, will be the responsibility of proving our mark, to borrow a term from our President. Well, if we could form some kind of joint Committee to carry on—for carrying through the arrangements one way or another—I think that is what we ought to do. Now, I only want to say this to the people who are against us—and there are good people against us—so far as I am concerned this is not a question of politics, nor never has been. I make the promise publicly to the Irish nation that I will do my best, and though some people here have said hard things of me—I would not stand things like that said about the other side—I have just as high a regard for some of them, and am prepared to do as much for them, now as always. The President knows how I tried to do my best for him.

PRESIDENT DE VALERA: Hear, hear.

MICHAEL COLLINS: Well, he has exactly the same position in my heart now as he always had (applause).

MARY MACSWINEY: I claim my right, before matters go any further, to register my protest, because I look upon this act to-night worse than I look upon the Act of Castlereagh.[100] I, for one, will have neither hand, act, nor part in helping the Irish Free State to carry this nation of ours, this glorious nation that has been betrayed here to-night, into the British Empire—either with or without your hands up. I maintain here now that this is the grossest act of betrayal that Ireland ever endured. I know some of you have done it from good motives; soldiers have done it to get a gun, God help them! Others, because they thought it best in some other way. I do not want to say a word that would prevent them from coming back to their Mother Republic; but I register my protest, and not one bit of help that we can give will we give them. The speech we have heard sounded very beautiful—as the late Minister of Finance [Michael Collins] can do it; he has played up to the gallery in this thing, but I tell you it may sound very beautiful but it will not do. Ireland stands on her Republican Government and that Republican Government cannot touch the pitch of the Free State without being fouled; and here and now I call on all true Republicans; we all want to protect the public safety; it is our side that will do its best to protect the public safety. We want no such terrible troubles in the country as faction fights; we can never descend to the faction fights of former days; we have established a Government, and we will have to protect it. Therefore, let there be no misunderstanding, no soft talk, no ráiméis[101] at this last moment of the betrayal of our country; no soft talk about union; you cannot unite a spiritual Irish Republic and a betrayal worse than Castlereagh's, because it was done for the Irish nation. You may talk about the will of the Irish people, as Arthur Griffith did; you know it is not the will of the Irish people; it is the fear of the Irish people, as the Lord Mayor of Cork says;[102] and to-morrow or another day when they come to their senses, they will talk of those who betrayed them to-day as they talk of Castlereagh. Make no doubt about it. This is a betrayal, a gross betrayal; and the fact is that it is only a small majority, and that majority is not united; half of them look for a gun and the other half are looking for the fleshpots of the Empire. I tell you here there can be no union between the representatives of the Irish Republic and the so-called Free State.

PRESIDENT DE VALERA: All those who have voted on the side of the established Republic, I would like to meet them say at one o'clock to-morrow; the sooner the better; perhaps we could get the use of this building or of the Mansion House,[103] say twelve-thirty to-morrow.

MICHAEL COLLINS: Whatever we may say, whatever we may think, I do believe that some kind of an arrangement could be fixed between the two sides. Even

---

100. Robert Stewart, the Viscount of Castlereagh, was chief secretary of Ireland when the Act of Union was introduced in the Irish Parliament in 1799 and played a major role in getting the legislation passed in 1800.

101. Gibberish (Irish).

102. McSwiney is possibly referring to Terence McSwiney (1879–1920), Lord Mayor of Cork and her brother, a militant nationalist who died from a hunger strike at Brixton Prison in London.

103. Residence of the Lord Mayor of Dublin.

though our physical presence is so distasteful that they will not meet us, I say some kind of understanding ought to be reached to preserve the present order in the country, at any rate over the week-end.

PRESIDENT DE VALERA: I would like my last word here to be this: we have had a glorious record for four years; it has been four years of magnificent discipline in our nation. The world is looking at us now—

(The President here breaks down).

CATHAL BRUGHA:[104] So far as I am concerned I will see, at any rate, that discipline is kept in the army.

The House then adjourned at 8.50 p.m., until 11 o'clock a.m. on Monday, the 9th January.

---

104. Cathal Brugha (1874–1922), a prominent republican in the Anglo-Irish War, he chaired the first meeting of Dáil Éireann and was its first minister of defense. An opponent of the treaty, he died fighting against it in the Irish Civil War.

GLOSSARY

People

Asquith, Herbert Henry (1852–1928), 1st Earl of Oxford and Asquith, prime minister (1908–16). As prime minister, his Liberal government was responsible for major constitutional and social reform prior to World War I. In exchange for Irish nationalist votes for support of House of Lords reform in the form of the Parliament Act (1911), he passed the third Home Rule Bill through the House of Commons in 1912. He was unable to produce a compromise between Unionists and nationalists prior to the act becoming law in September 1914.

Bonaparte, Napoleon (1769–1821), military and political leader during the era of the French Revolution and the French Empire. He staged a coup d'état in 1799, installed himself as first counsel in 1800, and crowned himself emperor in 1804. His military campaigns sparked a European-wide war in which he gained and lost an empire.

Bright, John (1811–89), radical British politician, advocate of free trade, MP (1843–89), and cabinet member in Liberal governments. Bright supported church and land reform in Ireland but opposed the 1886 Home Rule Bill. As part of William Gladstone's first initiative in Irish land reform, the Landlord and Tenant Act (1870), he insisted that clauses be provided for financial assistance to those who wanted to purchase their holdings.

Burke, Edmund (1729–97), Irish-born philosopher, politician, and political writer, best known for his critique of the French Revolution, *Reflections on the French Revolution* (1790), a founding text of modern conservatism. While he was brought up in the Church of Ireland and attended the all-Protestant Trinity College in Dublin, his mother was Catholic, and he had deep sympathies with the plight of Catholics in Ireland. He supported the expansion of Catholic rights, believed that Ireland should have its own parliament, and maintained that Ireland benefited from the British connection. He was greatly influential in framing the political debate in Ireland during the 1790s.

Carlyle, Thomas (1795–1881), Scottish writer, moralist, and historian. Carlyle had a keen interest in Ireland and made multiple visits there, addressing the Irish question on more than one occasion. He felt pity for Irish suffering and contempt for defects in the Irish character, notably drunkenness, superstition, and dishonesty. Most famously, Carlyle discussed his views on the Irish situation in his book *Chartism* (1840), where he wrote: "The time has come when the Irish population must either be improved a little, or else exterminated."

Carson, Edward (1854–1935), Lord Carson of Duncairn, Unionist leader. Elected as a Unionist MP in 1892, Carson became the leader of the Irish Unionist Parliamentary Party in 1910. He blended rhetorical skill, charisma, and able parliamentary leadership during the Home Rule crisis (1912–14). His public intransigence and threats of violence masked a willingness to find a constitutional solution. During World War I, Carson served as attorney general in Herbert Asquith's coalition government (1915), as first lord of the admiralty (1916–17), and as a member of the war cabinet under David Lloyd George's government (1917–19). He opposed the Anglo-Irish Treaty.

Collins, Michael (1890–1922), republican, revolutionary, and statesman. He was a rare figure: a successful revolutionary and a formidable politician. He was from County Cork and immigrated to London when he was fifteen. It was there that he became involved in nationalist and republican politics. He subsequently participated in the Easter Rising and was imprisoned afterward. During the Anglo-Irish War, Collins was minister of finance and played an instrumental role in securing loans for the Dáil in Ireland and the United States. Most important, during the conflict, he was the leader of the Irish Republican Army (IRA) and effective head of military operations, especially when Éamon de Valera departed for America in 1919. Collins was reluctant to be a delegate in the 1921 peace talks in London, but he accepted the role and helped negotiate and sign the Anglo-Irish Treaty as a first step to achieving an independent and united Ireland. He was a key figure in establishing the Irish Free State in 1922 and was the commander in chief of the government's forces when the Civil War began. He was assassinated in his native Cork.

Cromwell, Oliver (1599–1658), English military and political leader, best known for his role in producing the Commonwealth (1649–60), the republic which created the first instance in which England was without a king since arguably the eighth century. He held the position of Lord Protector of England, Scotland, and Ireland (1653–58). In 1649 he and his troops invaded Ireland, putting an end to the rebellion of the native Irish and the old English (English colonists with long roots in Ireland). The invasion was successfully completed in 1653, by which time he had already returned to England.

Cuchullain, Cúchulainn, or Cúchulain, best known of the Irish mythological heroes, his story is told in the Ulster Cycle. He exemplifies the brave and invulnerable warrior who despite having suffered death at a young age was known for his courageous deeds.

Cullen, Paul (1803–78), archbishop and cardinal. Ordained as a priest in Rome in 1829, Cullen subsequently became rector of the Irish College, Rome, in 1832, the archbishop of Armagh in 1849, the archbishop of Dublin in 1852, and a cardinal in 1866. Cullen was a champion of papal authority and a reformer who centralized clerical structures. He supported parliamentary measures to improve conditions in Ireland, while opposing the involvement of the clergy in politics. He was an impassioned opponent of Fenianism and other forms of militant republicanism.

Davis, Thomas (1814–45), poet and essayist, leader of the Young Ireland movement, and one of the founders of *The Nation* in 1842. He advocated an inclusive form of Irish nationalism while having a romantic view of the Gaelic past. He was a supporter of Daniel O'Connell's repeal movement but clashed with O'Connell on the issue of nondenominational education, which Davis supported and O'Connell opposed. Davis died from scarlet fever at the age of thirty-one.

Davitt, Michael (1846–1906), Irish republican and leading figure in the land reform movement. He was among the principal figures to launch and sustain the Land War, establishing the Land League of Mayo and the Irish National Land League in 1879. He was MP for South Mayo from 1895 to 1899, resigning as a consequence of opposition to the Boer War.

de Valera, Éamon (1882–1975), politician, revolutionary, and statesman. He was the major political figure in post-independent Ireland, dominating Irish politics from the 1930s, serving as both *taoiseach* (prime minister) and president, until his final retirement in 1973. He was born in New York and was brought up in Limerick. During the years covered by this book, he commanded the 3rd Battalion at Boland's Mill during the Easter Rising, subsequently emerged as the leader of the Volunteers and Sinn Féin, was elected president of the first Dáil, was an opponent of the Anglo-Irish Treaty, and sided with treaty opponents during the Irish Civil War. Following de Valera's 1919 trip to America, where he raised over five millions dollars for the republic but failed to gain the American government's support, he clashed with Michael Collins over the conduct of the Anglo-Irish War. His decision to send Collins to negotiate with the British government in 1921, rather than himself, has proved controversial. He advocated that the Anglo-Irish relationship should be governed by "external association": Ireland would recognize George V as the head of the Commonwealth but Irish MPs would not be required to swear allegiance to him. This stance, unacceptable to British negotiators, proved to be the basis of his rejection of the treaty, which contained an oath to the Crown.

Devoy, John (1842–1928), nationalist and republican. He was a Dublin clerk who became a Fenian in 1861, subsequently spent time in prison as a result of his activism (1866–71), and immigrated to the United States. He consequently became a tirelessly devoted and skilled organizer of Irish-Americans for Irish nationalist causes. He played a critical role in launching the New Departure (1878) and the National Land League (1879). He was among the early supporters of an act of rebellion during World War I, the embryonic idea from which the Easter Rising in 1916 resulted.

Emmet, Robert (1778–1803), revolutionary nationalist. He was the leader of a failed United Irishmen rebellion in Dublin (1803). However, he is most remembered for his inspiring speech from the dock following his condemnation to death, which made him into a martyr for and a hero of Irish nationalism.

George III (1738–1820), king of Great Britain and of Ireland (1760–1820), elector of Hanover. The first of the Hanoverians to be born in England, he is best known for his madness and for losing the American colonies. Both of these have been shown to be more myth than history. In the context of the Anglo-Irish relationship, he is important for his intervention in the political debate surrounding the creation of the Act of Union (1800). An important component of Prime Minister William Pitt's vision of the United Kingdom was Catholic emancipation. George III viewed this vision as incompatible with his role as the head of the Church of England and was able to stop it. Pitt subsequently resigned.

Gladstone, William Ewart (1809–98), prime minister and Liberal Party leader. Gladstone was arguably the dominant British politician of his age, serving as prime minister on four separate occasions (1868–74, 1880–85, 1886, and 1892–94). He began as a Tory and reinvented himself as a Liberal. Owing to both deeply held principles and political calculation, Gladstone spent the later part of his political life trying to solve the Irish question. He was responsible for major Irish reforms, including the disestablishment of the Church of Ireland (1869) and land reform (1870, 1881). Most important, he was the first powerful British politician to support Home Rule, initiating legislation in Parliament in 1886 (voted down by the House of Commons) and 1893 (passed in the Commons but defeated in the House of Lords).

Gregory, Lady Isabella Augusta, born Persse (1852–1932), playwright, collector of folklore, and translator. A major figure in the Irish literary revival, she was both a collaborator with and a patron of W. B. Yeats. Gregory was a founder of the Irish Literary Theatre. Although not given credit, she was coauthor with Yeats of *Cathleen Ni Houlihan* (1902). She also wrote numerous plays of her own. A student of Irish, she published two collections of Gaelic literature in English translation: *Cuchulain of Muirthemne* (1902) and *Gods and Fighting Men* (1904).

Griffith, Arthur (1872–1922), nationalist writer and politician. Griffith was founder of Sinn Féin (1905), head of the Irish negotiating team that produced the Anglo-Irish peace treaty (1921), and president of the Irish Parliament (1922). Griffith advocated that Irish MPs in the British Parliament withdraw to Dublin and assert their right to legislative autonomy. Originally, he advocated that Ireland's relationship to Britain should be modeled after the dual monarchy of Austria-Hungary, a position that although not advocating an independent Irish republic, was more radical than the stance of the Irish Parliamentary Party.

Hyde, Douglas (1860–1949), literary scholar, writer, and the first president of Ireland (1938–1945). He was among the leaders of the Gaelic revival, arguing against the imitation of English ways and advocating a renewal and extension of the Irish Language. He was the Gaelic League's first president in 1893. He saw the League as promoting cultural nationalism and Irish identity, while staying aloof from politics. He resigned the presidency in 1915, as he believed that his vision of the League was no longer possible.

Lloyd George, David (1863–1945), British prime minister (1916–22). A major political figure in early twentieth-century British history, he played an important role in both domestic and international affairs. As the Liberal chancellor of the exchequer, he helped establish the foundation of the welfare state and progressive taxation. As a result of his tenure as prime minister during World War I, he was viewed as the "man who won the war." He was prime minister during the Anglo-Irish War and led the British side in the subsequent treaty negotiations. He proved to be a wily and flexible negotiator, but his ability to maneuver was limited by his having to placate right-wing Tories whose support he needed to keep his coalition government afloat.

MacDonagh, Thomas (1878–1916), cultural nationalist and Irish Republican Brotherhood (IRB) militant. He joined the Irish Volunteers upon its founding and became its director of training in 1914. He was a member of the IRB Military Council that planned the 1916 Easter Rising, was one of the signatories of the Easter Proclamation, and was executed in the Rising's aftermath. With Pádraic Pearse, he helped found St. Enda's School in 1908 to promote Irish language and Irish culture.

Mac Murchadha, Diarmait (Dermot MacMurrough) (c. 1110–71), king of Leinster. After he was deposed in 1166, he went into exile and sought aid from the king of England, Henry II, to recover his kingship and to gain permission to recruit soldiers among Henry's followers. His most significant ally became Richard de Clare (c. 1130–76), also known as Strongbow, to whom he offered his daughter in marriage. The results were the invasion of Ireland by Anglo-Norman forces (1169), followed by the expedition of Henry II, the first king of England on Irish soil, two years later.

MacNeill, Eoin (1867–1945), historian and activist in the nationalist movement. MacNeill was from a Catholic family in County Antrim, a founder of the Gaelic League, and in 1908 he was appointed a professor of early and medieval Irish history at University College, Dublin. He was important to the formation of the Irish Volunteers and became its commander in chief. He was kept in the dark during the planning of the Easter Rising, subsequently accepted it when he found out, and wrote a last-minute order attempting to stop it following the capture of the German ship, the *Aud*, which contained weapons. He was imprisoned briefly following the Rising, was a minister in the first Dáil, and later was the minister for education in the Irish Free State (1922–25).

Markievicz, Constance, born Gore-Booth (1868–1927), also known as Countess Markievicz, the result of her marriage to Count Casimir Dunin-Markievicz in 1901. From an Anglo-Irish landowning background, she was a nationalist, women's rights supporter, and revolutionary. She played a prominent role in the Easter Rising and would have been executed had she not been a woman. In 1918 she became the first woman to be elected to the British Parliament, but she never took her seat, as the Sinn Féin representatives established Dáil Éireann. She subsequently became the Dáil's minister of labor. She adamantly opposed the Anglo-Irish Treaty and fought on the side of its opponents in the Irish Civil War.

Mitchel, John (1815–75), nationalist and revolutionary. Originally part of the Young Ireland movement, he broke with it, as he found it too moderate. He advocated a peasant-driven revolution against English rule in Ireland, published the revolutionary journal the *United Irishman* in 1848, and was subsequently convicted of treason the same year. He was transported to Tasmania and escaped afterward to the United States, where he continued to be active in Irish radical politics. He returned to Ireland in 1875 and was elected to Parliament, although he was disqualified because of his felony conviction.

O'Connell, Daniel (1775–1847), known as "The Liberator," the dominant Irish politician of his era. He was responsible for the two most important Irish nationalist political campaigns of the first half of the nineteenth century: Catholic emancipation and repeal of the Union. His organization, the Catholic Association founded in 1823, was the basis of nineteenth-century nationalist politics on a national scale, founded, above all, on the support of the Catholic majority.

O'Leary, John (1830–1907), Irish nationalist, militant, and poet. He participated in both Young Ireland and Fenian politics, was sent by James Stephens to the United States in 1859 to help build up the Fenian organization, and spent several years in prison (1865–74). After his release he lived in Paris until 1885 and subsequently returned to Ireland. Upon his return he was influential on the emerging generation of cultural nationalists, including W. B. Yeats.

O'Shea, Katharine, born Wood (1846–1921), English lover, later wife, and mother of three children by Charles Stewart Parnell. Their affair became public knowledge in 1889, when her husband Captain William O'Shea sued her for divorce citing Parnell as co-respondent. As a result, William Gladstone, the British Liberal leader, abandoned Parnell, and the Irish Parliamentary Party was bitterly divided between champions and opponents of Parnell's leadership. The party divided into two.

O'Shea, Captain William (1840–1905), politician and husband of Katharine O'Shea, whom he married in 1867. He knew of his wife's love affair with Charles Stewart Parnell, which he exploited to advance his career. He was willing to accept the affair, in part because he knew that his wife was a beneficiary in her aunt's will. He exposed the affair in 1889 after he was disappointed with what his wife received after her aunt's death.

Ossian The narrator and author of a cycle of poems translated by James Macpherson (1736–96) as *The Works of Ossian* (1765), based on the exploits of the hero Fingal. The authenticity of the texts has long been disputed.

Parnell, Charles Stewart (1846–91), nationalist leader. He was the dominant political figure in Irish politics during the 1880s, bringing together the two great causes of Irish nationalism, parliamentary autonomy and land reform. He created a united coalition of diverse political traditions—from physical-force violence to strict constitutionalism. He was responsible, with William Gladstone, for creating a coalition between Irish nationalists and British Liberals that resulted in the 1886 Home Rule Bill. When he was brought down by scandal in 1889–90, he was at the height of his power.

Peel, Robert (1788–1850), Tory politician, chief secretary of Ireland (1812–18), and prime minister (1834–35, 1841–46). As chief secretary he proposed the

"Peelers" (1813), the basis for the Royal Irish Constabulary. He opposed Catholic emancipation and frequently clashed with Daniel O'Connell, most famously when he outlawed the monster meeting at Clontarf in 1843 and then had O'Connell prosecuted. As prime minister when the Irish Famine began, he was more inclined to use the power of government to compensate for food shortages than his Whig successor, Lord John Russell, who came to power in 1846.

Pitt, William (1759–1806), known as Pitt the Younger (to distinguish him from his father, William Pitt the Elder [1708–78]), prime minister on two separate occasions (1783–1801, 1804–06). In the 1790s, Pitt regarded Irish reform as critical to British security. He sought to alleviate the circumstances of Catholics without antagonizing the Protestant ascendancy. Following the uprising of the United Irishmen, and the unsuccessful invasion of Ireland by its ally, revolutionary France, he proposed a legislative union that would make Ireland less vulnerable to invasion. Substantial concessions to Catholics, including emancipation, would follow the Union. He was able to bring about the legislative union, the Act of Union (1800), but was unable to achieve emancipation, as George III opposed it.

Redmond, John (1856–1918), leader of the Irish Parliamentary Party (1900–18). He succeeded Charles Stewart Parnell as the leader of the Irish nationalist grouping in Parliament, keeping together its factions during the passage of the third Home Rule Bill (1912). However, he was unable to negotiate a compromise with Unionists, his qualified support of the British government during World War I did not produce tangible benefits, and following the Easter Rising his support began to crumble, leading to the triumph of Sinn Féin in the 1918 parliamentary elections.

Tone, Theobald Wolfe (1763–98), radical nationalist. He was among the founders of the United Irishmen, and the group's liaison to the French revolutionary government. He was captured during France's attempted invasion of Ireland in September 1798 and killed himself in his cell rather than be hung. He is often cited as the father of Irish republicanism.

Wellesley, Arthur (1769–1852), 1st Duke of Wellington, military officer, and British prime minister (1828–30, 1834). From a prominent Anglo-Irish family, he is best known for his momentous victory over Napoleon at Waterloo (1815). He subsequently had a career as a diplomat and as a Tory politician. As prime minister, he was opposed to Catholic emancipation, but he capitulated to it rather than risk a confrontation when Daniel O'Connell was elected to Parliament in 1828, and O'Connell sought to claim his seat the following year.

Wentworth-Fitzwilliam, William, 4th Earl Fitzwilliam (1748–1833), lord lieutenant of Ireland (1794–95). An ally of Edmund Burke and Prime Minister William Pitt, his support for Catholic emancipation and liberal appointments produced a confrontation with the leadership of the Protestant ascendancy during his tenure as lord lieutenant. He was recalled after only a brief time in office.

William III (1650–1702), Prince of Orange by birth, stadtholder of Orange (1672–1702), and king of England (1689–1702). His mother was the sister of Charles II and James II of England, and his wife Mary was the daughter of James II and (like William) a Protestant. He invaded England in 1688 in what is known as the "Glorious Revolution," overthrowing James II with the support of parliamentarians who opposed a Catholic succession. He subsequently defeated James in the Battle of the Boyne in Ireland (1690). Because of his role in subduing Irish resistance, he became a symbol of the British connection and a cult figure for Ulster loyalists.

Yeats, William Butler (1865–1939), Irish poet, dramatist, essayist, and leading figure in the Irish literary and cultural revival. He surfaced as a major figure in the 1890s. With Lady Augusta Gregory and others, he founded the Irish Literary Theatre of Dublin in 1899, subsequently renamed the Abbey Theatre in 1904, which sought to create a tradition of Irish drama. His play, written with Lady Gregory and first performed by the Irish Literary Theatre, *Cathleen Ni Houlihan* (1902), was militantly nationalist. Over the course of his career he defended nationalism, artistic freedom, elitism, and aristocracy. He opposed the growing influence of the Catholic Church in the policies of the Irish Free State. In the 1930s he looked favorably on fascism, including its Irish expression, the Blue Shirts.

Terms

Act of Union Legislation passed in 1800 both in the Irish and British Parliaments that created the United Kingdom of Great Britain and Ireland. As a result, the Irish Parliament was dissolved and Ireland received representation in both the British House of Commons and the House of Lords.

Anglo-Irish Treaty Treaty negotiated between the British government and representatives of Dáil Éireann in 1921 creating the Irish Free State and a boundary commission that would meet to discuss the borders of Northern Ireland. The fact that representatives to the parliament of the Free State would have to take a loyalty oath to the British Crown led to an acrimonious debate among the Irish MPs that voted on the treaty. It was ratified in 1922, but divisions over the treaty endured, leading to the Irish Civil War (1922–23).

British constitution The laws, judicial decisions, and treaties under which people in Britain live. Unlike the United States, Britain has no explicit constitutional document, and thus Parliament is able to alter the constitution simply by passing new legislation.

Catholic emancipation The right of Catholics to be members of Parliament. By the 1790s, Catholic men could vote in parliamentary elections—if they met the property qualifications—but they could still not hold parliamentary office. Catholic emancipation was achieved in 1829 following a sustained political campaign led by Daniel O'Connell.

Chancellor of the exchequer The British cabinet member responsible for financial matters and for preparing the government's budget. It is the most prestigious position in the government after the prime minister.

Church of Ireland The Irish branch of the Anglican Church or Church of England. From the time of the sixteenth-century English Reformation until parliamentary legislation was passed in 1869, it was the official or established church of the state, presided over by the English crown and supported through compulsory taxation, despite the fact that the great majority of the country consisted of practicing Catholics. Following disestablishment in 1871, it became a self-governing branch of the worldwide Anglican Communion.

Connacht, Connaught Province in the west and northwest of Ireland.

Conservatism, Conservatives, Conservative Party (British) The ideology and party of the landed classes, which stood for the monarchy, the empire, and the Anglican Church. Conservatives, also known as Tories, were staunchly Unionist, viewing Ireland as integral to the empire. Yet they, no less than Liberals, over time sponsored legislation aimed at pacifying Ireland, notably through land reform.

Cumann na mBan (The League of Women) A women's group established in 1914 in support of the Irish Volunteers. Cumann na mBan consisted predominantly of white-collar and professional women, although it had a contingent of working-class women. It was subservient to the male Volunteers, while containing a cadre of feminists who worked on behalf of women's issues.

Dáil Éireann The Irish Parliament. Its name derived from a council of elders in Gaelic Ireland. It was initially established when the seventy-three Sinn Féin candidates who had been elected to the British Parliament in 1918 refused to take their seats. They declared themselves the Irish Parliament in January 1919 and began to meet in Dublin. Their actions provoked the Anglo-Irish War (1919–21).

The Defenders A militant Catholic agrarian secret society prominent in the 1790s. It originated in Ulster and spread into Leinster. It is perhaps best know for its alliance with the United Irishmen in the rebellion of 1798.

Disestablishment The process by which the state church becomes an independent and self-governing body. Although only representing one-eighth of the population, the Protestant Church of Ireland was the established church. The disestablishment of the Church of Ireland, an important demand made by Irish Catholics, was approved by Parliament in 1869, part of the effort to address the Irish question undertaken by William Gladstone, the British prime minister.

Dublin Castle The site of the British government's authority and administration in Ireland from the thirteenth century until 1922. It is also the official residence of the lord lieutenant, and a metonym for English/British power.

Easter Rising Planned by the Supreme Council of the IRB and carried out with the support of James Connolly's Irish Citizens Army, the Rising paralyzed Dublin for nearly a week beginning on Monday, April 24, 1916. It had little chance of success, but it represented the most sustained manifestation of the Irish revolutionary tradition. It became a symbol of Irish nationalist determination and patriotic pride, in part because of the British government's handling of the situation, which, most importantly, included the execution of the Rising's principal leaders.

Erin (from Éirinn) Ireland.

Fenians, Fenian Brotherhood, Fenianism Revolutionary nationalists. The Fenians were, in the most concrete sense, supporters of the Fenian Brotherhood, the militant nationalist group committed to the overthrow of British rule in Ireland, founded in the United States in 1859. Its sister organization, the Irish Republican Brotherhood (IRB), was founded a year earlier in Ireland. The term more generally was a label for physical-force nationalists.

Flying column A small, independent fighting force adept at quick mobility, deployed by the IRA in its military struggle against British authority in the Anglo-Irish War (1919–21).

Gaelic League Founded in 1893 by Eoin MacNeill and others, with Douglas Hyde as its first president, it brought together activists of many political stripes, nationalist and Unionist, for the purpose of promoting the Irish language in private and public life. The League was based on the premise that its work should be above political ideologies, a position that over time became increasingly difficult to sustain. By 1914 the Gaelic League was dominated by the IRB.

Gauls A Celtic people during the Iron Age and the epoch of Roman rule that lived in what are now Belgium, France, and Luxembourg, most of Switzerland, and parts of Italy, the Netherlands, and Germany.

Good Friday Agreement Peace agreement that began to bring the civil war in Northern Ireland to an end. It was signed on April 10, 1998, by negotiators from Northern Ireland, the Republic of Ireland, and the UK. It was approved by referendum in both Northern Ireland and the Republic of Ireland more than a month later on May 22. The agreement's principal features were the establishment of the Northern Irish Assembly with devolved legislative authority, the release of Catholic and Protestant prisoners, and the decommissioning of weapons.

The Great Famine A period of starvation, disease, and emigration that began in 1845 and lasted approximately five years. It resulted from the failure of the potato crop. There had been famines in Ireland before, but the scale of the Great Famine was unprecedented, resulting in the death of more than one million people, about an eighth of the Irish population. The most controversial dimension of the Famine was whether the British government had done all that it could to limit death and disease, a question that is still debated by historians. Whatever the final verdict, resentments about the Famine became part of the collective memory of Irish nationalists.

Home Rule The movement that mostly dominated Irish nationalist politics from the 1870s to 1914. A term whose meaning shifted over time, place, and according to by whom it was deployed, it stood for two things: (1) Ireland would have its own parliament to govern domestic affairs, and (2) it would send a smaller contingent of representatives to the British Parliament, which was responsible for international affairs.

Inghinidhe na hÉireann (Daughters of Ireland) Women's nationalist organization. Founded by Maud Gonne in 1900, it was dedicated to promoting Irish culture and economic development and opposed recruitment in Ireland for the British army. While its priority was nationalism rather than feminism, participants in the group supported women's suffrage.

Irish Citizen Army Founded in 1913 by the Irish Transport and General Workers' Union (ITGWU) to shield striking workers from police assaults, it is best known for its later trajectory under the leadership of James Connolly, who became the group's commandant in 1914. It was under his direction that the group, consisting of about three hundred members, joined forces with the IRB and militant Volunteers to launch the Easter Rising.

Irish Civil War Armed conflict between a contingent of IRA and Sinn Féin militants who rejected the Anglo-Irish Treaty and the government of the Irish Free State that sought to implement it (1922–23). It resulted in the death of a minimum of one thousand people, nearly eighty being executed by the government. The division, created by the treaty debate and the civil war that followed it, left an enduring divide in Irish politics.

Irish Confederation A group of Young Irelanders that split from Daniel O'Connell's Repeal Association in 1847 over the issue of violence. While the former saw violence as part of the arsenal of resistance, the latter rejected it as an option. Leaders of the confederation figured prominently in the rebellion of 1848.

Irish Free State The state form produced by the Anglo-Irish Treaty for the twenty-six counties outside of Ulster. It had dominion status roughly equivalent to Canada and Australia. Under the 1937 constitution, it was renamed Éire.

Irish Parliamentary Party The group of Irish MPs in the British Parliament that advocated for Irish nationalist causes, notably Home Rule and land reform. It was founded by Charles Stewart Parnell in1882. Although achieving Home Rule legislation in 1912 under John Redmond, it crumbled during World War I, being supplanted by Sinn Féin in the 1918 parliamentary elections.

Irish Republican Army (IRA) A paramilitary group whose origins were in the Irish Volunteers, and more specifically that element of the Volunteers that broke with its leader John Redmond over his support of Britain in World War I. The dissonant Volunteers came under the influence of the IRB, participated in the Easter Rising, and following the establishment of Dáil Éireann in 1919 became increasingly know as the IRA. The IRA's guerrilla warfare in the Anglo-Irish War (1919–21), in tandem with Sinn Féin's political actions, led to negotiations with the British government and the Anglo-Irish Treaty (1921). Divisions within the IRA and Sinn Féin over the treaty led to the Irish Civil War. Following the establishment of the Irish Free State and the defeat of the anti-treaty forces, the IRA played a reduced role in Irish politics. However, it was rejuvenated in 1969 with the establishment of the Provisional IRA in Northern Ireland.

Irish Republican Brotherhood (IRB) See Fenians, Fenian Brotherhood, Fenianism.

Irregulars Opponents of the Anglo-Irish Treaty within the IRA that mounted an armed struggle against the government of the Irish Free State and its supporters (1922–23).

Jacobin, Jacobinism Label given to French revolutionaries in the 1790s. It connotes support for the end of aristocratic rule and church influence in favor of the creation of a secular, centralized government based on universal rights and achieving its ends by authoritarian and violent means if necessary.

Land League, National Land League of Mayo, and Irish National Land League Founded in 1879, the Irish National Land League fought for land reform and against oppressive practices of landowners.

Land War A popular movement that developed beginning in 1879. It simultaneously fought for tenants' rights and attacked landlordism. It was a response to the economic downturn of the late 1870s, which led to a rash of evictions and intensifying economic hardships. The movement began in Mayo, gathering force with the founding of the Irish National Land League. While the first phase of Land War ended in 1882, the agrarian conflicts that it engendered continued into the twentieth century and facilitated sweeping agrarian reform.

Liberals, Liberalism, Liberal Party (British) Grew out of, and was the successor to, the Whig Party in the nineteenth century. Until the 1920s, it was one of the two largest parties in the British Parliament. While in the earlier part of the nineteenth century Liberals stood for laissez-faire and limited government, by the twentieth century they championed a larger role for the state. With regard to Ireland, the Liberals tended to be more sympathetic to Irish grievances than the Tories were. During the Irish Famine, however, their commitment to laissez-faire colored their approach to poverty relief. Liberals split over Home Rule in 1886. Liberal opponents of Home Rule—Liberal Unionists—went into coalition with the Tories.

Loyalists Militant Unionists, usually associated with Protestants in Northern Ireland. They see the Union as sustaining an "orange" culture of liberty and anti-Catholicism descended from the Protestant triumphs of William III. William's victory at the Battle of the Boyne is commemorated in the annual marches of July 12.

Monster meetings A series of mass political gatherings with crowds in the hundreds of thousands organized by Daniel O'Connell's Repeal Association in 1843. When Peel's government banned the October 8 monster meeting at Clontarf, near Dublin, O'Connell called it off for he feared that it would lead to violence.

The Nation A weekly newspaper founded in 1842 to promote the cause of repeal and cultural nationalism. It was the mouthpiece of Young Ireland, and at its height it could claim a readership of 250,000. It was closed down by the government in

1848 for subversion but was allowed to resurface in 1849. It was published until 1900, although it never regained the influence it had commanded in the 1840s.

New Departure The effort in the late 1870s and 1880s to create a broad-based nationalist movement in the United States and Ireland, based on land reform and Home Rule.

Normans Inhabitants of Normandy, a province in northwestern France. The Normans invaded England in 1066, and the descendants of that invasion were among those who subsequently invaded Ireland during the next century.

Northern Ireland Created by the Government of Ireland Act (1920), it is made up of six of the nine counties of historical Ulster. Unlike the Irish Free State created in 1922, which had dominion status, Northern Ireland had a Home Rule parliament, while remaining within the UK. As a result of the long-term discrimination experienced by the Catholic minority, Northern Ireland underwent a prolonged political conflict beginning in the late 1960s. The conflict only began to resolve itself with the signing of the Good Friday Agreement in 1998.

Orange Order A Protestant fraternity mainly associated with Northern Ireland. It was founded in 1795 originally as the Orange Society, following a sectarian confrontation with the Catholic Defenders. The Orange Order militantly defended Protestant interests, embodied in its idealization of King William III, whose victory at the Battle of the Boyne in 1690 represented (for them) the triumph of Protestant liberty over Catholic tyranny.

Patriots, patriot movement Irish political movement that envisioned the Irish nation as predominantly Protestant, while affirming the right to Irish political self-determination free of British control. It might be regarded as a form of colonial nationalism. While it is mostly associated with the parliamentary reforms that were achieved in 1782, which gave increased legislative autonomy to the Protestant parliament, it continued to have adherents in the nineteenth century, an example being Isaac Butt, the founder of the Home Rule movement.

Penal laws A series of laws passed by the Irish Parliament between the 1690s and the 1720s aimed at restricting the practice of Catholicism in Ireland and limiting the landownership and hence political power of Catholics. To a lesser extent the penal laws placed restrictions on Presbyterians. Historians disagree about the extent to which or how long the penal laws were enforced, but their effects were undoubtedly significant. The legislation became part of the collective memory of Irish nationalist resentment.

Poor laws A British term designating legislation for the public relief and support of the poor. The Irish Poor Law Act (1838) created a nationwide system of relief financed by taxes largely paid by landowners. Although it extended poor relief in Ireland, it was modeled after English poor law reforms (1834), and thus critics argued that it did not sufficiently take into account Irish conditions.

Presbyterian, Presbyterianism, Presbyterian Church A Protestant tradition rooted in the teachings of John Calvin (1509–64) as interpreted by John Knox (c. 1505–72), who studied with Calvin and brought his teachings back to his (Knox's) native Scotland. Known for its emphasis on reading and studying the biblical text and the importance of receiving grace through faith in Christ, Presbyterianism reached Ireland primarily as a result of immigration by Scottish Presbyterians to Ulster in the seventeenth century. Presbyterians developed a distinctive governing structure whereby ministers and lay people both participated.

Protestant ascendancy A term designating the political and economic dominance of the Anglo-Irish in the eighteenth century.

Rebellion of 1798 Inspired by the French Revolution, the United Irishmen and the Catholic Defenders launched rebellions in conjunction with an attempted invasion of Ireland by revolutionary France. The result was sectarian violence, the ruthless suppression of the revolts, and the defeat of the French expeditionary force. It was in this context that the government of William Pitt pushed through the Act of Union (1800), which created the UK.

Reform Act of 1884 (the Representation of the People Act) The third great reform of the British electoral system in the nineteenth century (the other two being the reform acts of 1832 and 1867). It greatly extended the size of the male electorate, important for Ireland where the size of the electorate increased more than threefold.

Repeal, repeal movement Irish nationalist demand to end the union with Britain. Daniel O'Connell launched it in the 1830s following the achievement of Catholic emancipation, and it sporadically dominated the nationalist agenda, culminating in the monster meetings in 1843. Home Rule superseded repeal in the 1870s.

Republican, republicanism The demand for a united, independent, and democratic Ireland, free of British interference, by violent means if necessary. In its early stages, republicanism was connected with the United Irishmen who wanted to create an Irish republic modeled after revolutionary France. In the nineteenth century it was a minority current within Irish nationalism. It was closely associated with the IRB.

Ribbonism, Ribbonmen (Ribbon Society) Clandestine and oath-bound groups of rural Irish Catholics who used intimidation and violence to achieve agrarian justice. In Ulster, they clashed with equivalent Protestant groups. The group's name comes from the fact that its members wore green ribbons in their buttonholes. Sporadic outbursts of ribbonism took place throughout the nineteenth century.

Sinn Féin (We Ourselves) A radical nationalist group founded in 1905, committed to economic, political, and cultural independence. Its original political ideology was founded on Arthur Griffith's advocacy of Ireland and England living as partners under a single crown. The party likewise argued that Irish MPs in the British Parliament should refuse to take their seats and establish an Irish Parliament of their own. Following the 1918 parliamentary elections, when the party won seventy-three seats, it established Dáil Éireann, which triggered the Anglo-Irish War.

The Times The newspaper of the British establishment. It was first published in 1785 and continues to this day.

Tithes Taxes imposed for the support of the church. In Ireland, tithes were used to support the minority Church of Ireland, which caused deep resentments among both the majority Roman Catholic population and Protestant dissenters such as Presbyterians. Tithes were reformed in 1836 as a result of the Tithe Commutation Act, which shifted the burden of payment from tenants to landowners. Tithe payment came to an end with the disestablishment of the Church of Ireland (1869).

Tories See Conservatism, Conservatives, Conservative Party (British).

Trinity College, Dublin Ireland's first university. Founded in 1592, its original purpose was to create a Protestant intellectual elite. Catholics could not attend the college until 1793. Ironically, given its origins, Trinity College is known for launching the political careers of numerous Anglo-Irish Irish nationalists, including Thomas Moore, Wolfe Tone, and Robert Emmet.

Ulster The northeastern province of Ireland. Six of its counties make up contemporary Northern Ireland.

Ulster custom The practice in Ulster of giving tenants an interest in their holdings. Thus, when tenants left their land, they could claim compensation for the improvements that they had made while they were in possession of it. The Ulster custom was seen as a restraint on the power of landlords. Generalizing this practice to all of Ireland was a goal of Irish land reformers in the third quarter of the nineteenth century.

Ulster Unionist Party The mainstream Ulster political party that championed the union with Britain. It evolved out of the 1886 Home Rule crisis and became the governing party of Northern Ireland in 1921.

Union, Unionism, Unionist Supporters of the Act of Union (1800), which created the United Kingdom of Great Britain and Ireland.

United Irishmen, Society of United Irishmen Revolutionary group inspired by the French Revolution and committed to the overthrow of British rule in Ireland. Founded in 1791, it is most closely associated with the failed rebellion of 1798 in which it allied itself with the Catholic Defenders and the French revolutionary regime to coordinate a rebellion in Ireland with a French invasion of the island.

University College, Dublin A university founded for Catholics in 1854, it was originally called the Catholic University of Ireland. It was renamed University College, Dublin in 1883. University College was granted a charter and became part of the National University of Ireland in 1908. James Joyce is perhaps its most famous student in the period covered by this book.

Volunteers Nationalist and Unionist paramilitary groups. Founded in 1778 to defend Ireland from invasion and allow British soldiers to fight in the American Revolutionary War, the Irish Volunteers played a prominent role in agitating for the Protestant Irish Parliament to be granted greater autonomy and powers, using the threat of violence to pressure the British government to make concessions. From this very specific origin, the term evolved. In the early twentieth century, armed nationalist and Unionist movements outside of parliamentary politics both regarded themselves as "volunteers." On the eve of World War I, the Ulster Volunteers were formed to resist Home Rule and the Irish Volunteers were created to support it.

West Briton A pejorative term used to describe an Irish person who identified with or who emulated English culture and norms.

Westminster An area of central London north of the Thames River that includes Westminster Abbey and the houses of Parliament. In British political culture "Westminster" is a metonym for Parliament.

Whigs One of the two major political parties in the eighteenth century. It developed in England as the party that supported the Glorious Revolution of 1688 and stood for parliamentary sovereignty, constitutional monarchy, and the rights of dissenters (non-Anglican Protestants). Whigs were absorbed by the Liberal Party in the middle of the nineteenth century but survived as a mostly aristocratic grouping within it that supported moderate reforms.

Young Ireland A movement of Protestant and Catholic nationalist intellectuals inspired by Romanticism and the United Irishmen's emphasis on overcoming religious differences. Their commitment to restoring the prominence of the Irish past prefigured the Irish literary revival of the late nineteenth century. Young Ireland's coalition with Daniel O'Connell's repeal movement was always fragile and fell apart when he demanded that they renounce violence. Even though they had no plans to resort to violence, they refused to rule it out on principle, and a contingent of them established the Irish Confederation in 1847.

CHRONOLOGY OF MAIN EVENTS

1791   The founding of the United Irishmen.

1793   War breaks out between Britain and France.

            The Catholic Relief Act gives Irish Catholics the right to vote if they
            meet the property qualifications.

1795   Following its suppression, the United Irishmen are reinvented as a
            revolutionary group.

            The Battle of the Diamond between the Catholic Defenders and the
            Protestant Peep O' Day Boys (a secret association and predecessor to
            the Orange Order). Consequently, the Orange Order was established.

1796   The French revolutionary regime's attempt to invade Ireland ends in
            failure when its fleet in Bantry Bay is detoured by storms.

1798   The United Irishmen's rebellion is crushed.

            The French fleet, under General Jean Humbert, lands at Killala,
            Mayo, and surrenders at Ballinamuck.

            Wolfe Tone commits suicide in his jail cell rather than face hanging.

1800   The Act of Union passed by both the Irish and the British Parliaments,
            creating the United Kingdom. The legislation takes effect in 1801.

1803   Robert Emmet's rising in Dublin crushed and Emmet executed.

1823   The founding of Daniel O'Connell's Catholic Association to agitate
            for Catholic emancipation.

1828   O'Connell elected to Parliament.

1829   The Catholic Emancipation Act allows Catholics to hold
            parliamentary seats.

1835   The Lichfield House Compact produces an informal alliance between
            Whigs, Radicals, and O'Connell and his followers.

1840   The founding of the Loyal National Repeal Association.

1842   The first issue of Young Ireland's *The Nation* published.

1843   O'Connell presides over several monster meetings resulting in the
            British government's ban on the meeting at Clontarf in October and
            O'Connell's acquiescence to the government's action.

1844   O'Connell convicted of sedition.

1845	The beginning of the Great Irish Famine.
1847	The split between Young Ireland and O'Connell results in the founding of the Irish Confederation.
1850	The founding of the Tenant League to agitate for land reform.
1858	The formation of the Irish Republican Brotherhood in Ireland.
1859	The formation of the Fenian Brotherhood in the United States.
1867	The Fenian rising.
	The execution of Fenians for their role in the death of an English prison guard during a prison break.
1869	The disestablishment of the Church of Ireland through the Irish Church Act of 1869.
1870	William Gladstone's first Land Act gives tenant farmers the right to compensation if they have made improvements to their land.
	The beginning of Isaac Butt's Home Rule movement.
1879	The formation of the Irish National Land League.
1881	Gladstone's second Land Act grants the Three Fs: fair rent, fixity of tenure, and free sale.
	Charles Stewart Parnell imprisoned.
1882	Parnell released as a result of the Kilmainham treaty. It lays the groundwork for an alliance between Parnellites and Gladstonian Liberals.
1884	The Representation of the People's Act (the third great Reform Act) greatly expands the Irish electorate.
	The founding of the Gaelic Athletic Association.
1885	Under the Purchase of Land Act, better known as the Ashbourne Act, loans are given to tenant farmers to buy their land. The loans are to be repaid at low rates of interest.
1886	The first Home Rule Bill is rejected by the British House of Commons. It divides the British Liberal Party between supporters and opponents of Home Rule.
1889	Parnell named as co-respondent in the divorce case of Katharine O'Shea, resulting in the withdrawal of Gladstone's support and a split in the Irish Parliamentary Party.

1891	The death of Charles Stewart Parnell.
1893	The founding of the Gaelic League.
	The second Home Rule Bill is passed by the British House of Commons but rejected by the House of Lords.
1900	The founding of Maud Gonne's Inghinidhe na hÉireann (Daughters of Ireland), a women's organization committed to radical forms of nationalism.
1905	The founding of Sinn Féin.
1912	The passage of the third Home Rule Bill set to become law in September 1914.
	The Solemn League and Covenant (also known as the Ulster Covenant) is signed by thousands of Unionists in Ulster.
1913	The founding of the Ulster Volunteer Force and the Irish Volunteers.
1914	World War I begins and Home Rule legislation is postponed until the war's conclusion.
1916	The Easter Rising is followed by the execution of its leaders.
1919	The Irish Volunteers renamed the IRA.
	Sinn Féin's triumph in British parliamentary elections in December 1918 results in its MPs refusing to take their seats. They instead form their own parliament in Dublin, Dáil Éireann, with Éamon de Valera as president.
1919–21	The Anglo-Irish War.
1920	The Government of Ireland Act creates two Home Rule parliaments in Ireland, one in the north and one in the south. Only the one in Northern Ireland comes into existence.
	The Black and Tans formed to reinforce the Royal Irish Constabulary.
	In what has become known as the first Bloody Sunday (the second being in 1972), the IRA killed fourteen suspected British intelligence agents. In response, the Auxiliaries killed twelve people and wounded many more at the all-Irish Gaelic football final in Croke Park Stadium in Dublin.

1921   The majority Ulster Unionist Party dominated the first meeting of
            the Northern Ireland Assembly.

            A truce between republican forces and the British government leads
            to peace negotiations between the two sides.

            The Anglo-Irish Treaty creates the Irish Free State and establishes
            a Boundary Commission to decide the future of Northern Ireland.
            The treaty's retention of a loyalty oath to the Crown divides Irish
            nationalists.

1922   The Dáil agrees to the Anglo-Irish Treaty, but the result is a civil
            war between pro-treaty and anti-treaty forces within the republican
            movement.

            The murder of Michael Collins.

1923   The end of the Irish Civil War.

WORKS CITED AND SUGGESTIONS
FOR FURTHER READING

Allen, Nicholas. 2003. *George Russell (Æ) and the New Ireland, 1905–30*. Dublin: Four Courts Press.

Anderson, Benedict. 1983. *Imagined Communities: Reflections on the Origin and Spread of Nationalism*. London: Verso.

Augusteijn, Joost. 2010. *Patrick Pearse: The Making of a Revolutionary*. Houndmills, Basingstoke: Palgrave Macmillan.

Barden, Jonathan. 2005. *A History of Ulster*. Belfast: Blackstaff Press.

Bartlett, Thomas. 2004. "Ireland, Empire, and Union, 1690–1801." In *Ireland and the British Empire*, ed. Kevin Kennedy, 61–89. Oxford: Oxford University Press.

———. 2010. *Ireland: A History*. Cambridge: Cambridge University Press.

Beckett, J. C. 1981. *The Making of Modern Ireland, 1603–1923*. London: Faber.

Bew, Paul. 1979. *Land and the National Question in Ireland, 1858–82*. Atlantic Highlands, NJ: Humanities Press.

———. 1987. *Conflict and Conciliation in Ireland, 1898–1910: Parnellites and Radical Agrarians*. Oxford: Clarendon Press.

———. 1994. *Ideology and the Irish Question: Ulster Unionism and Irish Nationalism, 1912–1916*. Oxford: Clarendon Press.

———. 2007. *Ireland: The Politics of Enmity, 1789–2006*. Oxford: Oxford University Press.

Biagini, Eugenio F. 2007. *British Democracy and Irish Nationalism, 1876–1906*. Cambridge: Cambridge University Press.

Biletz, Frank A. 2002. "Women and Irish-Ireland: The Domestic Nationalism of Mary Butler." *New Hibernia Review* 6, no. 1: 59–72.

Blackstock, Allan. 2007. *Loyalism in Ireland, 1789–1829*. Woodbridge: Boydell Press.

Boyce, D. George. 1995. *Nationalism in Ireland*. 3rd ed. London: Routledge.

Boyce, D. George, and Alan O'Day, eds. 1996. *The Making of Modern Irish History: Revisionism and the Revisionist Controversy*. London: Routledge.

———. 2006. *The Ulster Crisis: 1885–1921*. Houndmills, Basingstoke, Hampshire: Palgrave Macmillan.

Buckley, David. 1990. *James Fintan Lalor: Radical*. Cork: Cork University Press.

Buckner, Brenda O'Brien. 2002. *Sydney Owenson and the Idealization of Ireland: Cultural Nationalism in* The Wild Irish Girl *and* The O'Briens *and* The O'Flahertys. Santa Cruz: University of California Press.

Bull, Philip. 1996. *Land, Politics, and Nationalism: A Study of the Irish Land Question.* Dublin: Gill & Macmillan.

Burke, Edmund. 1881. *Letters, Speeches, and Tracts on Irish Affairs Collected and Arranged by Matthew Arnold.* London: Macmillan.

Clarke, Aidan. 2001. "The Colonisation of Ulster and the Rebellion of 1641: 1603–60." In *The Course of Irish History*, eds. T. W. Moody and F. X. Martin, 152–64. Lanham, MD: Roberts Rinehart Publishers.

Comerford, R. V. 1989. "The Parnell Era, 1883–91." In *Ireland Under the Union, 1870–1921*, ed. W. E. Vaughn, 53–80. Vol. 6 of *The New History of Ireland.* Oxford: Oxford University Press.

Comerford, R. V., and Enda Delaney, eds. 2000. *National Questions: Reflections on Daniel O'Connell and Contemporary Ireland.* Dublin: Wolfhound Press.

Coogan, Tim Pat. 1990. *Michael Collins: A Biography.* London: Hutchinson.

———. 1995. *Eamon de Valera: The Man Who Was Ireland.* New York: HarperCollins.

———. 2001. *1916: The Easter Rising.* London: Cassell.

Costello, Francis J. 2003. *The Irish Revolution and Its Aftermath, 1916–1923: Years of Revolt.* Dublin: Irish Academic Press.

Curtis, L. P. 1989. "Ireland in 1914." In *Ireland Under the Union, 1870–1921*, ed. W. E. Vaughn, 145–88. Vol. 6 of *The New History of Ireland.* Oxford: Oxford University Press.

Davis, Richard P. 1988. *The Young Ireland Movement.* Dublin: Gill & Macmillan.

De Paor, Liam. 1997. *On the Easter Proclamation and Other Declarations.* Dublin: Four Courts Press.

Deane, Seamus. 1991. "Edmund Burke." In *The Field Day Anthology of Irish Writing*, ed. Seamus Deane, vol. 1, 807–809. Derry, Northern Ireland: Field Day Publications.

Deane, Seamus, Andrew Carpenter, and Jonathan Williams. eds. 1991. *The Field Day Anthology of Irish Writing.* 3 vols. Lawrence Hill, Derry, Northern Ireland: Field Day Publications.

Dolan, Anne, Patrick M. Geoghegan, and Darryl Jones, eds. 2007. *Reinterpreting Emmet: Essays on the Life and Legacy of Robert Emmet.* Dublin: University College Dublin Press.

Donnelly, James S. 2001. *The Great Irish Potato Famine.* Phoenix Mill, Gloucestershire: Sutton Publishing.

———. 2009. *Captain Rock: The Irish Agrarian Rebellion of 1821–1824*. Cork: Collins Press.

Dunleavy, Janet Egleson, and Gareth W. Dunleavy. 1991. *Douglas Hyde: A Maker of Modern Ireland*. Berkeley: University of California Press.

Dworkin, Dennis. 2007. "Intellectual Adventures in the Isles: Kearney and the Irish Peace Process." In *Traversing the Imaginary: Richard Kearney and the Postmodern Challenge*, eds. Peter Gratton and John Panteleimon Manoussakis, 61–76. Evanston, IL: Northwestern University Press.

Elliott, Marianne. 1982. *Partners in Revolution: The United Irishmen and France*. New Haven: Yale University Press.

———. 1989. *Wolfe Tone: Prophet of Irish Independence*. New Haven: Yale University Press.

———. 2003. *Robert Emmet: The Making of a Legend*. London: Profile.

———. 2009. *When God Took Sides: Religion and Identity in Ireland: Unfinished History*. Oxford: Oxford University Press.

English, Richard. 2006. *Irish Freedom: The History of Nationalism in Ireland*. London: Macmillan.

Fleming, N. C., and Alan O'Day. 2005. *The Longman Handbook of Modern Irish History Since 1800*. New York: Pearson/Longman.

Foster, R. F. 1988. *Modern Ireland, 1600–1972*. London: A. Lane.

———. 1992. "Ascendancy and Union." In *The Oxford History of Ireland*, ed. R. F. Foster, 134–73. Oxford: Oxford University Press.

———. 1997. *The Apprentice Mage, 1865–1914*. Vol. 1 of *W. B. Yeats: A Life*. Oxford: Oxford University Press.

———. 2003. *The Arch–Poet, 1915–39*. Vol. 2 of *W. B. Yeats: A Life*. Oxford: Oxford University Press.

Gellner, Ernest. 1983. *Nations and Nationalism*. Oxford: Blackwell.

Golway, Terry. 1998. *Irish Rebel: John Devoy and America's Fight for Ireland's Freedom*. New York: St. Martin's Press.

Gray, Peter. 1999. *Famine, Land, and Politics: British Government and Irish Society, 1843–1850*. Dublin: Irish Academic Press.

———, ed. 2004. *Victoria's Ireland? Irishness and Britishness, 1837–1901*. Dublin: Four Courts Press.

Hart, Peter. 2003. *The I.R.A. at War, 1916–1923*. Oxford: Oxford University Press.

Higgins, Padhraig. 2010. *A Nation of Politicians: Gender, Patriotism, and Political Culture in Late Eighteenth-Century Ireland. History of Ireland and the Irish Diaspora.* Madison: University of Wisconsin Press.

Jackson, Alvin. 1999. *Ireland 1798–1998: Politics and War.* Oxford: Blackwell Publishers.

———. 2003. *Home Rule: An Irish History, 1800–2000.* London: Weidenfeld & Nicolson.

Joyce, James. 1991. "Ireland, Island of Saints and Sages." In *The Field Day Anthology of Irish Writing,* ed. Seamus Deane, vol. 3, 7–10. Derry, Northern Ireland: Field Day Publications.

Kearney, Richard. 1997. *Postnationalist Ireland: Politics, Culture, Philosophy.* London: Routledge.

Kenny, Kevin, ed. 2004. *Ireland and the British Empire.* The Oxford History of the British Empire Companion Series. Oxford: Oxford University Press.

Kiberd, Declan. 1995. *Inventing Ireland.* London: Jonathan Cape.

———. 2005. *The Irish Writer and the World.* Cambridge: Cambridge University Press.

Kinealy, Christine. 2002. *The Great Irish Famine: Impact, Ideology and Rebellion.* British History in Perspective. Houndmills: Palgrave Macmillan.

———. 2004. *A New History of Ireland.* Stroud, England: Sutton.

Laffan, Michael. 1999. *The Resurrection of Ireland: The Sinn Féin Party, 1916–1923.* Cambridge: Cambridge University Press.

Larkin, Emmet. 1972. "The Devotional Revolution in Ireland." *The American Historical Review* 77, no. 3: 625–652.

Lee, Joseph. 1989. *Ireland, 1912–1985: Politics and Society.* Cambridge: Cambridge University Press.

Lewis, Geoffrey. 2006. *Carson: The Man Who Divided Ireland.* London: Hambledon Continuim.

Loughlin, James. 1995. *Ulster Unionism and British National Identity Since 1885.* London: Pinter Publishers.

Lydon, James. 1998. *The Making of Ireland: From Ancient Times to the Present.* London: Routledge.

Lyons, F. S. L. 1979. *Culture and Anarchy in Ireland, 1890–1939.* Ford Lectures 1978. Oxford: Clarendon Press.

———. 1989. "The Developing Crisis, 1907–14." In *Ireland Under the Union, 1870–1921,* ed. W. E. Vaughn, 123–44. Vol. 6 of *The History of Ireland.* Oxford: Oxford University Press.

MacDonagh, Oliver. 1983. *States of Mind: An Essay on Anglo-Irish Conflict.* London: Allen & Unwin.

———. 2003. *Ireland: The Union and Its Aftermath.* Dublin: University College Dublin Press.

Mac Suibhne, Peadar. 1965. *Paul Cullen and His Contemporaries with Their Letters from 1820–1902,* vol. 3. Naas, Ireland: Leinster Leader Ltd.

Marley, Laurence. 2007. *Michael Davitt: Freelance Radical and Frondeur.* Dublin: Four Courts Press.

Mathews, P. J. 2003. *Revival: The Abbey Theatre, Sinn Féin, the Gaelic League and the Co-operative Movement.* Critical Conditions. Cork: Cork University Press in association with Field Day.

McBride, Ian. 2009. *Eighteenth-Century Ireland: The Isle of Slaves.* Dublin: Gill & Macmillan.

McCartney, Donal. 1994. *W. E. H. Lecky: Historian and Politician, 1838–1903.* Dublin: Lilliput.

McDonough, Terrence, ed. 2005. *Was Ireland a Colony? Economics, Politics, and Culture in Nineteenth-Century Ireland.* Dublin: Irish Academic Press.

McDowell, R. B., ed. 1991. *The Writings and Speeches of Edmund Burke.* Vol. 9, ed. Paul Langford. Oxford: Clarendon Press.

McGarry, Fearghal. 2010. *The Rising: Ireland: Easter 1916.* Oxford: Oxford University Press.

Mitchell, Arthur. 1995. *Revolutionary Government in Ireland: Dáil Éireann, 1919–22.* Dublin: Gill & Macmillan.

Moody, T. W. 2001. "Fenianism, Home Rule and the Land War: 1850–91." In *The Course of Irish History,* eds. T. W. Moody and F. X. Martin, 228–44. Lanham, MD: Roberts Rinehart Publishers.

Moran, Seán Farrell. 1994. *Patrick Pearse and the Politics of Redemption: The Mind of the Easter Rising, 1916.* Washington, DC: Catholic University of America Press.

Mulvey, Helen. 2003. *Thomas Davis and Ireland: A Biographical Study.* Washington, DC: Catholic University of America Press.

Murphy, Cliona. 1989. *The Women's Suffrage Movement and Irish Society in the Early Twentieth Century.* New York: Harvester Wheatsheaf.

Murphy, James H. 2003. *Ireland: A Social, Cultural and Literary History, 1791–1891.* Dublin: Four Courts Press.

Nevin, Donal. 2005. *James Connolly: "A Full Life."* Dublin: Gill & Macmillan.

O'Connell, Daniel. 1833. "To the People of Ireland." *The Times,* January 21.

O'Connell, Maurice R. 1990. *Daniel O'Connell: The Man and His Politics.* Dublin: Irish Academic Press.

O'Grada, Cormac. 1989. *The Great Irish Famine.* Studies in economic and social history. Basingstoke, Hampshire: Macmillan Education.

———. 1999. *Black '47 and Beyond: The Great Irish Famine in History, Economy, and Memory.* The Princeton Economic History of the Western World. Princeton, NJ: Princeton University Press.

Ramón, Marta. 2007. *A Provisional Dictator: James Stephens and the Fenian Movement.* Dublin: University College Dublin Press.

Ryan, Louise, and Margaret Ward, eds. 2004. *Irish Women and Nationalism: Soldiers, New Women, and Wicked Hags.* Dublin: Irish Academic Press.

———. 2007. *Irish Women and the Vote: Becoming Citizens.* Dublin: Irish Academic Press.

Scally, Robert James. 1995. *The End of Hidden Ireland: Rebellion, Famine, and Emigration.* New York: Oxford University Press.

Silvestri, Michael. 2009. *Ireland and India: Nationalism, Empire and Memory.* Basingstoke, England: Palgrave Macmillan.

Simms, J. G. 1976. "The War of the Two Kings, 1685–91." In *Early Modern Ireland,* eds. T. W. Moody, F. X. Martin, and F. J. Byrne, 478–508. Vol. 4 of *The New History of Ireland.* Oxford: London.

Smith, Jeremy. 2000. *The Tories and Ireland: Conservative Party Politics and the Home Rule Crisis, 1910–1914.* Dublin: Irish Academic Press.

Spencer, Herbert. 1910. *Education: Intellectual, Moral, and Physical.* New York: D. Appleton and Company.

Swift, Jonathan. 1991. "Letter to the Earl of Peterborough." In *The Field Day Anthology of Irish Writing,* ed. Seamus Deane, vol. 3, 893–95. Derry, Northern Ireland: Field Day Publications.

Townshend, Charles. 1999. *Ireland: The 20th Century.* London: Arnold.

———. 2005. *Easter 1916: The Irish Rebellion.* London: Allen Lane.

Valiulis, Maryann Gialanella, Mary O'Dowd, and Margaret MacCurtain, eds. 1997. *Women and Irish History: Essays in Honour of Margaret MacCurtain.* Dublin: Wolfhound Press.

Wall, Maureen. 2001. "The Age of the Penal Laws: 1691–1778." In *The Course of Irish History,* eds. T. W. Moody and F. X. Martin, 176–89. Lanham, MD: Roberts Rinehart Publishers.

Wills, Clair. 2009. *Dublin 1916: The Siege of the GPO.* London: Profile.

Young, Robert J. C. 2001. *Postcolonialism: An Historical Introduction.* Oxford: Blackwell Publishers.

INDEX

Volunteers, xxiv, 12–13, 54, 117, 152, 152
    n. 56, n 57, 167, 174–78, 202, 207–12;
    Irish Volunteers, 172–73, 175–76, 176
    n. 6, 192, 199 n. 39, 201–2, 205, 213
    n. 71; Ulster Volunteers, 172, 175, 192;
    volunteer movement, xxiii

Wellesley, Arthur (Duke of Wellington), 4,
    73 n. 64
Wentworth-Fitzwilliam, Lord William, 1,
    16 n. 20
Whig, 4–6, 6 n. 4, 145 n. 40, 148, 151 n.
    54; Whig Club, 9

Whiteboys, xxi–xxii, 36. *See also* secret
    societies
Wilde, Oscar, 172
Women's Prisoners Defence League, 107

Yeats, William Butler, xi, 5, 51–53, 70,
    84–85, 86 n. 114, 89 n. 120, 93, 106–8,
    177, 206, 214, 217
Young Ireland(ers), 5–6, 8, 43, 50–51, 53,
    55–56, 59, 77, 77 n. 92, 79, 112,
    113–14, 117–18, 119 n. 2, 194, 194 n.
    28, 204; Young Irelandism, 72